366 DAILY DEVOTIONS CELEBRATING COMMUNION

J. VANNEVEL

A YEAR AT THE TABLE: 366 DAILY DEVOTIONALS CELEBRATING COMMUNION
Copyright © 2025 by J. Vannevel

All rights reserved. Neither this publication nor any part of this publication may be reproduced or transmitted in any form or by any means, electronic or mechanical, including photocopying, recording or any information storage and retrieval system, without permission in writing from the author.

Scripture taken from the New King James Version®. Copyright © 1982 by Thomas Nelson. Used by permission. All rights reserved.

ISBN: 978-1-4866-2542-0
eBook ISBN: 978-1-4866-2543-7

Word Alive Press
119 De Baets Street Winnipeg, MB R2J 3R9
www.wordalivepress.ca

Cataloguing in Publication information can be obtained from Library and Archives Canada.

To Pastors Bob and Amber: Thank you so much for your teachings, your support, and for giving me the opportunity to lead the congregation in the practice of communion.

Welcome to the Table

THERE'S SOMETHING VERY special about taking time to spend a few moments at the Lord's table, reflecting on the amazing work Jesus has done for us at the cross. Some time ago, I started on a journey of pausing most mornings at the very start of my day to partake of communion. It wasn't complicated. I didn't get special elements, but rather used that first morning cup of tea and either a cracker or small piece of a homemade communion bread (recipe to follow).

I can't provide an exhaustive list of Scriptures that deal with this special ordinance. In fact, one day I had a dream that I was leading the church in communion and using an Old Testament reference. When I awoke, I said to the Lord, "But that isn't a communion Scripture." I immediately felt His reply that the entire Bible is about communion. They are all communion Scriptures. As I thought about this, I saw the wisdom of it. After all, the act of partaking in communion is a reminder of the very essence of Christianity—loving the Lord our God with all our heart, soul, mind, and strength, and loving our neighbor as ourselves. The entire Bible is based on these commandments.

Without an understanding of Jesus's death on the cross for our sins, the words of the Bible lack life. Without His death, they become words of rules and judgment, but with the cross, they become words of love and sacrifice. It's through the atoning work of the cross that the Bible shines forth grace. Communion is pausing to remember the price Jesus paid and the change it has brought in our hearts and lives. It inspires us to love others and do good works. It inspires us to walk in forgiveness for ourselves and others. It inspires us to a deeper relationship with the Trinity.

This book is a set of 366 daily devotions meant to be used in a time of communion, whether with a group of people at church or in your personal daily devotional time. There's one for each day of the year, including a leap year devotion. The daily topics are inspired by both the Old and New Testament, by secular news events, and even by other books or movies, and they all come back to our relationship with the Lord and with each other. They all tie into Scripture, and if you wish to delve deeper, I've included related Scriptures in the footnotes for further study. I pray this leads you into a deeper relationship with Christ and with others, just as these devotions have inspired me.

Although the book has been written as a daily, year-long devotional, you don't need to follow it day-by-day if that's not your style. Use this book in whatever way the Lord inspires you. There is no guilt in skipping days or jumping to different topics as you see fit. Each day's topic can stand on its own. If you're not one to do a daily devotional–type book, you're under no pressure here! Not everyone likes being told what to do on a given day. Some topics might reflect things happening at that season, but we need those same lessons every day of the year, so feel free to jump around if that's your preference. I hope you come to love spending time in communion, as I have, and that you'll be excited to spend a few moments every day communing with our Savior.

Will you come with me on a special journey into the marvelous grace of the body and blood of the Lord?

This is a simple communion bread recipe. I score the dough before baking so it breaks nicely into small pieces that keep for many weeks in an airtight container in the fridge.

Communion Bread

1 cup flour
Pinch salt
1/3 cup oil
1/3 cup water

Mix all into a dough and roll on a cookie sheet. Stoneware works well for this, but any baking tray will do. Score as desired. If you want to make it look like a Passover Matzah bread, poke with a fork in rows. Bake at 350°F for 20 minutes or until desired crispiness.

As mentioned, I use a cup of tea instead of wine, although juice, water, or any other drink would be fine to use. Pre-filled and packaged communion cups and wafers can also be purchased from many online and brick-and-mortar Christian bookstores. The important part of the Lord's Supper is what the elements remind us of, not what the elements themselves are made of. In the Bible, Jesus and the disciples were actually eating the Passover meal, and of course had both bread and wine on hand. There are many reasons for Jesus to choose those particular elements at that time and in that context. What you choose for the elements and the time you choose to celebrate this ordinance is up to you. Do whatever you feel Jesus would have you do to bring it home to your heart.

JANUARY 1
Relationships, Not Resolutions

Therefore let all the house of Israel know assuredly that God has made this Jesus, whom you crucified, both Lord and Christ. (Acts 2:36)

IT'S COMMON AT the beginning of a new year for people to make New Year's resolutions, but it's a rare person who follows through on them. Most people quickly fail and give up. I think Peter would understand.

On the night Jesus was betrayed, He sat at the table with His disciples and told them that He was going to be crucified and they all would abandon Him. Peter was adamant that this wouldn't happen. Even when Jesus said that before a rooster crowed twice, Peter would deny Him three times, Peter resolved to stay with Jesus. A few hours later, Peter discovered that resolving to do something wasn't good enough to follow through on his ideals. Soon he was swearing and saying that he "never knew the man" while the rooster crowed and Jesus looked on.

Haven't we found ourselves in similar situations? We resolve to love our fellow man. We resolve to forgive someone who hurt us deeply, to be more Christ-like with our family, to tell people about Jesus. The truth is, resolving to follow Jesus will never be enough. In ourselves we're not able to be the kind of person we want to be. Only through a deep relationship with the Savior of our souls can we be more like Him. When we realize the depth of His love, the incredible price He paid, and His constant presence with us, then we can become something more than we otherwise would be.

Peter discovered this truth. After Jesus rose from the dead, He appeared to Peter. The Bible doesn't record the exact words Jesus said to Peter, but I suspect it was something like, "I forgive you. This was why I had to die. You thought I was going to defeat the Romans, when all along the plan was to defeat something much more deadly and sinister—the sin within all humanity, the sin within you."

By the time Pentecost rolled around, Peter knew that God loved him. He understood the significance of Jesus's sacrifice on the cross. Peter wasn't running away now but standing up in front of a large crowd, proclaiming why Jesus died. He was no longer resolving to follow Jesus but had entered into a deeper relationship with Jesus, and as a result, was following Him. In the intimacy of that relationship, we are empowered to forgive others as we ourselves have been forgiven. We are enabled to love others as we ourselves have been loved by Him. We are given the strength to stand up and try again when we fall, knowing Jesus stands beside us, reaching His hand down to help us up. Taking part in communion is pausing to remember just what He did for us and who He is in us.

> *Jesus, we pause today to partake of this piece of bread signifying Your body broken and bruised. We sip this drink remembering Your blood that dripped from the cross to buy our salvation. We tried to be good people on our own, but we failed. We still fail at times. Only with You can we be all You are calling us to be. Amen.*

For further study: Matthew 26:26–35, 69–75; Luke 22:54–62, 24:33–35; Acts 2:14–42.

JANUARY 2
Symbols

> And He took the bread, gave thanks and broke it, and gave it to them, saying, "This is My body which is given for you; do this in remembrance of Me." Likewise He also took the cup after supper, saying, "This cup is the new covenant in My blood, which is shed for you." (Luke 22:19–20)

A SYMBOL CAN be a powerful tool. A country's flag, for example, represents the ideals the people of that country stand for. The people are united under the flag and call themselves fellow countrymen. The flag is not the country, yet it's treated with great respect by all who call that country their homeland. A solidarity arises among those who unite under that symbol.

Likewise, the elements of communion are not Christ Himself, but they serve to remind us of Jesus and what He represents. The bread reminds us that His body was broken so that ours could be whole. The wine reminds us that His blood was shed so that we could be saved. The practice of Holy Communion unites us together as followers of Jesus Christ. This symbolism of the Lord's Supper is a reminder that we collectively are His body. We stand together in solidarity, all saved by the same blood that flowed in Jesus's veins, all sinners saved by His grace. We are united with the first-century apostles and all the Christians who have gone before us, and with those yet to become Christians. The symbols of Christianity—the cross first and foremost, but also the bread and wine of communion—remind us that we are united together in one faith, born again into one true, eternal homeland.

The traditional elements of the Lord's Supper are an unleavened wafer and wine. At the Last Supper, when Jesus instituted the practice of Holy Communion, the bread on the table was unleavened. Leaven is sometimes used to represent sin, so the unleavened bread is symbolic of Christ's sinless life. The red wine they drank represented His blood, which would soon flow from His body as He died on the cross. Just as a flag can be made of many different types of material, yet it still represents its country, so it is with the elements of communion. The elements symbolically remind us of Jesus's death for us. They call us to walk in harmony with one another, dependent on one another as fellow members of the same body. The specific symbol we use isn't critical. What we do with Jesus, and how we treat His body—now that is critical.

As we partake of the communion elements, let's take a moment to examine our hearts. How strong is our relationship with Jesus? Do we remember that His body was broken so that ours could be whole? Do we acknowledge that His blood was shed to save us from our sins? How close is our relationship with His body, our fellow Christians, united with us in communion with Christ? Have we wronged someone? If so, now is the time to repent and set things right.

> Lord Jesus, we come to You in Your Holy Name, thanking You that Your body was broken and Your blood was shed for us. Forgive us for striving against one another, and unite us as members of one body—Your body. Help us to walk together in unity and gratitude. Amen.

For further study: Matthew 26:17–29; 1 Corinthians 11:17–34; Colossians 2:1–7; 1 John 1:8–9.

JANUARY 3
Where the Grass is Greenest

Not that I have already attained, or am already perfected; but I press on, that I may lay hold of that for which Christ Jesus has also laid hold of me. (Philippians 3:12)

YOU'VE LIKELY HEARD the saying "The grass is always greener on the other side of the fence." This proverb speaks to how we tend to think others have a better life than we have. Especially in these days of social media, it always looks like everyone else is in a better relationship, took a better vacation, is raising nicer kids, lives in a more beautiful home, and leads a better life.

Appearances can be deceiving. The truth is, the grass is always greenest where you water it. If you want a beautiful garden, you have to work at it. You need to move rocks, pull weeds, water the ground, add fertilizer. It's work. If you want a good relationship, you need to work at it. God has done all He can to develop a relationship with us. He watered the soil of our relationship with His sweat dripping as big drops of blood as He agonized in prayer in the Garden of Gethsemane. He watered it as His blood flowed from the stripes on His back after being whipped, and from the wounds in His hands and feet as He was nailed to the cross to pay for our sins. He also watered it from a heart that burst in pain, allowing blood and water to flow out, when a soldier drove a spear into His side. He waters our relationship by calling to us and whispering in our hearts. He waters it with His Word given to us. He waters it by putting people around us to encourage us, correct us, and pray for us.

We can water our relationship with Him by being in fellowship with other believers, by reading His Word, by spending time in prayer and worship, and by taking a moment of our day to think of what He has done for us as we partake of communion. If we never water the garden of our faith, it can become dry and wilted. If we tend it, however, clearing away the weeds and nourishing the seeds of faith that have been planted, our relationship with God can really blossom.

Let's pause and take a moment to water our relationship with the Lord of all creation. He is the one true God, the one who made a way for us to be forgiven and have a place always at His table.

> *Jesus, we recognize the sacrifice You made for us. Your body was broken to give us life, and Your blood shed to enable us to be forgiven for all shortcomings—past, present, and future. Your blood established us in a relationship with You, and we are eternally grateful. Amen.*

For further study: Mark 4:1–20; Luke 22:39–46; John 19:1–37; 1 Corinthians 3:6; Ephesians 5:25–27; Philippians 3:10–16.

JANUARY 4
Examine Yourself

> But let a man examine himself, and so let him eat of that bread and drink of the cup. For he who eats and drinks in an unworthy manner eats and drinks judgment to himself, not discerning the Lord's body. (1 Corinthians 11:28–29)

IN PAUL'S LETTER to the Corinthians, he addresses a problem they're having in the church: people are walking in discord and being self-serving. In Chapter 11, Paul rebukes them for pushing ahead of others to eat, for leaving some hungry, and for being drunk. He then reminds them that the purpose of the Lord's Supper is to remember what Jesus has done for us.

Paul ends this passage with a warning to examine ourselves. He explains that some are sick, or even die prematurely, because they take the Lord's Supper in an unworthy manner. It's therefore important to know just what an "unworthy manner" is. Paul gives us the answer in verse 29. An unworthy manner means not discerning the Lord's body. As we look at the entire passage, it becomes clear that Paul is referring to the Church as the Lord's body. He has commanded us to examine ourselves and see if we are treating the Lord's body—each other—with respect. Are we honoring one another and preferring one another, or do we seek our own glory and satisfaction?

If we are self-serving and treat others with disrespect, we can be guilty of eating and drinking judgment on ourselves, but we can avoid this by examining ourselves. The Holy Spirit is our helper here. If we ask Him to reveal where we are self-serving, disrespectful, or walking in discord with our fellow humans, He will be sure to show us. We must then repent of our sins before partaking of Holy Communion. In 1 John 1:9, John writes that *"if we confess our sins, He is faithful and just to forgive us our sins and to cleanse us from all unrighteousness."* It only takes a single heartfelt, honest moment, and once again we are clean and free to partake of communion with Christ.

We are all sinners saved by His grace. We all continue to live in this fallen world. Everyone makes mistakes in their dealings with others. Communion is an opportunity for us to be restored in close fellowship with Jesus and with His body.

> *Lord Jesus, we come to You with our hearts bare and exposed before You. Holy Spirit, reveal to us our selfish desires and acts. We repent of our sins and ask for Your forgiveness for all those times when we failed to correctly discern Your body. Help us to love and prefer one another, recognizing we are all united in You. Amen.*

For further study: 1 Corinthians 11:17–34; 1 John 1:5–10, 2:1–2, 28–29, 3:16–24.

JANUARY 5

Love Trumps Power

Let this mind be in you which was also in Christ Jesus, who, being in the form of God, did not consider it robbery to be equal with God, but made Himself of no reputation, taking the form of a bondservant, and coming in the likeness of men. And being found in appearance as a man, He humbled Himself and became obedient to the point of death, even the death of the cross. (Philippians 2:5–8)

SOME TIME AGO, I heard a person on the radio talking about all people in power becoming corrupted. I was thinking that this couldn't be right, because God has absolute power, yet He isn't corrupt, manipulative, or selfish. The speaker mentioned that the only common exception was motherhood; something prevents mothers from generally wielding power over their children in a harmful or corrupted manner. As I listened, I could only think, *Duh*. Of course mothers don't become corrupted by power. Love trumps power. This is also why God doesn't wield His power in an evil or self-serving manner. He may have ultimate power, but He is also ultimate love. Jesus Himself said that there is no greater love than this, that a man would lay down his life for his friends (John 15:13).

As we partake of communion, we are remembering that Jesus chose to put aside His Godhead and come as a man, to lay His life down for us. He chose to let His body be broken so we could be healed, to let His blood be shed so we could be forgiven and have eternal life. He tells us to love each other as He has loved us—to prefer one another, to lay down our selfish ambitions in order to serve one another. Let this time of communion serve to remind us that the one with ultimate power didn't lord it over us, or use us, but instead laid down His life for us in demonstration of His love.

Let's take a moment and think about our relationships. Where do we have power over another as a boss, parent, or spouse? Have we ever used another to further our own desires? Have we forgotten God's great love for us and become corrupted by power? If we have, the answer is to let Jesus call us back to a walk of love. We remember His great love for us so that we might walk in the same great love for one another.

Lord Jesus, we thank You that You were obedient to lay Your life down out of love for us. Your love is so deep and strong! We remember right now Your great love for us and ask You to forgive us for all the ways we've fallen short of that love in our relationships with others. Help us to walk in love one for another that we might truly be a reflection of You. Amen.

For further study: John 10:7–18, 15:12–13; Philippians 2:1–11; 1 John 4:7–21.

JANUARY 6
The Chastisement for Our Peace

> But He was wounded for our transgressions, He was bruised for our iniquities; the chastisement for our peace was upon Him, and by His stripes we are healed. (Isaiah 53:5)

ISAIAH PROPHESIED ABOUT the suffering and death of Jesus Christ. In Chapter 53, he states that Jesus would be rejected and despised, oppressed and afflicted. He would say nothing in His defense, and He would be killed. Isaiah also explains why this would happen. The Messiah would be offered as a sacrifice for our sins, paving the way for us to be justified before God and eternally forgiven. His wounding would not be because He had sinned, but because we have.

Isaiah's prophecy doesn't stop at the forgiveness of sins, though that would be more than enough. He also prophesies that the perfect sacrifice of the sinless Christ would bring us healing and peace. This peace means so much more than peace in our souls. The Hebrew word for peace is *shalom*. It implies a wellness in our entire life: happiness, health, and prosperity. Paul in his letter to the Ephesians reminds us that this sacrifice was for everyone, not just the Jews of Israel. We were once far from God, but by the blood of Christ, we can now come into the very presence of God.

We're all together, fellow citizens of the household of God. And God's house is a great and good house. We can walk in all the blessings of God because of the sacrifice of Christ. When Jesus instituted the practice of Holy Communion, it was to remind us that we are united together in peace: peace in our mind, in our rest, in happiness, in health, and in prosperity. He gave His all for us and to us. He has blessed us with a peace that non-Christians struggle to grasp, not having experienced it. It truly is a peace that passes all understanding.

Even the angels that announced the birth of Christ proclaimed that He came to bring peace and good will to men. When Christ was born, it had already been ordained for Him to die and offer His blood on the altar of heaven so that we could be forgiven of our sins. Jesus came to be our Savior—the perfect, sinless sacrifice, wounded for our transgressions. The chastisement for our peace was upon Him. God desires that we receive Christ in our hearts, and so dwell with Him in peace.

> *Father, we recognize and remember the sacrifice of Your Son for us. You planned it from the very beginning in order to bring us back into fellowship with You and to provide for us Your wonderful peace, with all the blessings that implies. You have blessed us, and we give You our praise and thanks. Amen.*

For further study: Song of Solomon 2:4; Isaiah 53:1–12; Luke 2:8–11; Galatians 3:26–29; Ephesians 2:12–22; Philippians 4:4–7.

JANUARY 7
Manna from Heaven

Then Jesus said to them, "Most assuredly, I say to you, Moses did not give you the bread from heaven, but My Father gives you the true bread from heaven. For the bread of God is He who comes down from heaven and gives life to the world." (John 6:32–33)

WHEN THE ISRAELITES were delayed in getting to the Promised Land, God fed them with manna—a type of wafer they could make into cakes. It appeared every morning with the dew, and they'd go out each day to collect it. Whatever they gathered was enough for the day. They couldn't store it, and it would become wormy and start to stink if they tried to hoard it. Every day they had to trust that God would give them what was needed for the day.

When Jesus was on the earth, He multiplied five small loaves of bread and some fish to feed thousands of people. Afterward, He left and went to the other side of the lake. When the people He had fed noticed He was gone, they followed after Him. They asked to be shown a miracle, just like the one their ancestors knew of manna appearing in the wilderness. Jesus pointed out that the main reason the multitude came after Him was because He'd met their physical need of hunger by feeding them bread. He also told them that they were focused on the wrong thing. There He was before them—the bread of life, who had come to meet their spiritual hunger. He explained that He would give His life to save them from their sins. Anyone who believes in Him and comes to Him will be saved and have eternal life.

He spoke of the sacrament of communion and explained that they would need to eat His flesh and drink His blood. Many didn't understand and were offended. They still thought He was speaking of physically eating and drinking and failed to understand that He was speaking of their spiritual hunger. Many chose that day to leave Him and follow Him no more. The disciples who stayed, however, recognized Him as their source of eternal life. He was there to meet their needs, spiritual and physical. He was more than enough for each day. His mercies would be new every morning and sufficient for whatever the day would hold.

There is an element of trust involved in following Jesus. We need to rely on His grace daily. Every day, we need to remember His sacrifice for us. Communion helps us remember. As we eat of the bread and drink the wine even this day, let us remember the true bread that came down from heaven to satisfy our spiritual hunger.

> *Father, we thank You for sending us the true bread from heaven, Jesus Christ. He is the one who came and died on the cross for our sins. His body was broken for us, His blood spilled for us, that we might have eternal life and life more abundantly. We recognize that we need Him daily, and that daily He is more than enough to meet our spiritual needs. We choose to remember Him. Amen.*

For further study: Exodus 16:1–6, 14–25; Numbers 11:7–9; Lamentations 3:22–24; John 6:1–14, 22–35.

JANUARY 8
Whatever Things Are True

> Finally, brethren, whatever things are true, whatever things are noble, whatever things are just, whatever things are pure, whatever things are lovely, whatever things are of good report, if there is any virtue and if there is anything praiseworthy—meditate on these things. (Philippians 4:8)

IN PAUL'S LETTER to the Philippians, he instructs them on what they should do if they are anxious or troubled. He counsels them to pray and give thanks and to think on things that are true, noble, just, pure, lovely, of good report, virtuous, and praiseworthy—encouraging them to stay focused on those things rather than on their trial or trouble. Interestingly, if we think of those things, we realize that they all describe Jesus Christ. Let's look at the list more closely.

True: God is the ultimate truth. It's impossible for Him to lie. Jesus is the Way, the Truth, and the Life.

Noble: This means being regal, of excellent character, magnanimous. Jesus, the King of kings, showing His excellence even at His crucifixion, never reviled in return. He gave His life for us. Could there be anyone more noble than Him?

Just: This means to be morally right. Jesus never sinned—ever. Even Pilate and his wife knew that Jesus was a just man and that the chief priests had delivered Him out of envy, not because He'd done anything evil.

Pure: Jesus is our spotless Passover lamb, with no impureness of any kind in Him. He was untainted by sin.

Lovely: The Bible says that He was not lovely to look at, but to those of us who have found grace in His sight, He is the loveliest thing we've ever laid eyes on.

Of good report: Jesus went about doing good to all.

Virtuous: This means having moral excellence and goodness, or being upright. That definitely defines our Lord.

Praiseworthy: To praise is to show our approval and admiration and to glorify God with our words. There is no one more worthy of praise than our Lord and Savior, Jesus Christ.

As we partake of communion today, let's remember Him who is all these things and more.

> *Jesus, we thank You that You are true, noble, just, pure, lovely, and of good report. If there is anything in this world that is virtuous and praiseworthy, it's You. We are so grateful for You and all You have done for us, and for who You are. Blessed be Your name forever and ever. Amen.*

For further study: Isaiah 53:1–12; Matthew 27:19; Mark 15:9–10; John 14:6; Acts 10:38; 1 Peter 1:18–19, 2:21–24; Revelation 19:1–10.

JANUARY 9
Our Kinsman Redeemer

Then Naomi said to her daughter-in-law, "Blessed be he of the Lord, who has not forsaken His kindness to the living and the dead!" And Naomi said to her, "This man is a relation of ours, one of our close relatives." (Ruth 2:20)

DID YOU EVER wonder why the God of the universe, the Holy One, the all-powerful Creator, would choose to come to earth and be a man in order to redeem us from our sins? It's incredible, isn't it? The book of Ruth explains it when it lays out the picture of a kinsman redeemer.

Naomi, her husband, and their two sons leave Israel because of famine and poverty and go to Moab. While there, both her sons marry women of that land. Tragedy strikes the family, and Naomi's husband and both sons die. She decides to return to her hometown in Israel, but her daughter-in-law Ruth refuses to leave her. She loves Naomi and Naomi's God, the God of Israel. She won't return to her prior life or her old ways and lifeless gods.

The two women go to Israel, but things aren't much better for them there. They're still living in abject poverty. There's no food for them, so Ruth sets out to pick up the bits of grain left behind when the men are reaping their crops. She comes to the field of a man named Boaz, who blesses her for choosing to find refuge under the wings of the Lord God Almighty. He provides for her protection and makes sure the men leave her lots of grain. At lunch time, he prepares a place for her at his table and serves her bread and wine.

When Ruth recounts all this to her mother-in-law, Naomi explains that Boaz is a near kinsman. He has the right as a relative to buy back the land Naomi and her husband had sold years before, restoring their property and wealth, and he has the right to marry Ruth to raise descendants for them. Because he is rich, he also has the means to do it.

Under the principle of a kinsman redeemer, only a blood relative could buy back what was lost. Jesus came as a man to be our blood relative. Eve was created from the rib taken from Adam's side, signifying that all humanity was created from the same blood. We all inherited the curse of sin and death. It would take someone related by blood to buy us back from death to eternal life. Jesus is that blood relative—the Son of Man.

It would also take someone with the wealth or the ability to pay the price. The cost to redeem us was the death of the sinless, perfect, spotless lamb. Jesus, the Son of God, had the ability to pay that price. He is the Son of Man—our near kinsman—*and* the Son of God, our redeemer. Jesus asks us to be His bride. He prepares a place for us at His table, where He offers us bread and wine. He restores to us all that we lost to sin and gives us the wealth of His righteousness. He is our Kinsman Redeemer.

Lord Jesus, thank You for choosing to come to earth as a man, to suffer and die at the hand of sinners and to redeem us by Your blood. Amen.

For further study: The book of Ruth; John 3:29; Romans 3:23–25; Ephesians 1:7.

JANUARY 10
Jesus Is the Door

I am the door. If anyone enters by Me, he will be saved, and will go in and out and find pasture. (John 10:9)

JESUS TAUGHT HIS disciples that there is only one way to salvation. There is only one doorway. Jesus is that door. His blood flowed from His body when He was sacrificed on the cross, and His blood paid the penalty of sin so that we could be redeemed.

This very thing was symbolized at the first Passover supper, long before anyone ever thought of killing someone on a cross. The Israelites were slaves to harsh masters in Egypt, where they longed to be free. God sent Moses to call forth plagues in the land so that Pharaoh would let the people of Israel go. The final plague was the Angel of Death coming to take the firstborn child of every family. God told Moses to tell the Israelites to kill a spotless, perfect lamb, take some of the blood of that lamb and dip a hyssop branch in it and strike the two doorposts and the lintel of their house. In doing this, the Angel of Death would pass over that house so all would live.

Take a moment to picture this: If Jesus (our spotless lamb) was in the doorway, arms outstretched as He was dying on the cross, the blood from the wounds on His hands would be on the doorposts. The blood on the lintel, or top of the door, would be where His head, covered with the crown of thorns, would bleed. The blood that dripped down to the floor would represent the blood where His feet were pierced. The blood on the doorway was in the image of a cross. The Israelites were slaves in Egypt, but in our present-day world, we are slaves to the harsh taskmaster of sin. The place of protection from the Angel of Death is on the other side of the cross of blood for us today, just as it was for the Israelites those thousands of years ago.

Our belief in the sacrifice of Jesus places us behind the protection and covering of His blood. Death no longer has a hold on us, and we now inherit eternal life. God's firstborn from the dead, Jesus Christ, took the penalty, and death now passes over us.

When Jesus instituted communion, it was during the feast of the Passover, when the Israelites remembered their deliverance from slavery in Egypt to new life in the Promised Land. At that supper, Jesus handed out the bread and wine to His disciples, declaring Himself to be the Passover Lamb. The wine represented His blood being shed, like the lamb's blood was sprinkled on the door. The way of salvation is through the doorway of His blood. The bread and the wine remind us that we have been delivered from sin and death to righteousness and a new life through His death on the cross.

Jesus, we remember Your death on the cross. You are the doorway that leads to salvation. There is no other way. We thank You that You paid the price of death so we could be free from being slaves to sin. You made the way for us to have new life in You, and we are forever grateful. Amen.

For further study: Exodus 12:1–51; Matthew 26:17–29; John 10:7–9; 1 Corinthians 5:7; 1 Peter 1:18–21.

JANUARY 11
All of You

> Then He took the cup, and gave thanks, and gave it to them, saying, "Drink from it, all of you. For this is My blood of the new covenant, which is shed for many for the remission of sins."
> (Matthew 26:27–28)

WHEN JESUS SHARED communion with His disciples, He gave the cup to all of them. His disciples were fishermen, tax collectors, and even the one who would betray Him. Likewise, the blood of Jesus that flowed for the remission of sins is offered to all. The forgiveness of sins is offered to everyone. Paul tells the Galatians that there is neither Jew nor Greek, slave nor free, male nor female. We could paraphrase this and say that the blood of Christ was shed for blue-collar and white-collar workers, men and women, adults and children, rich or poor, and North Americans, Africans, Asians, Europeans—even those currently making their home in Antarctica! If you're a human being, His blood was shed for you. If you accepted His sacrifice and call Jesus Lord, then you are a brother or sister to all others who call Jesus Lord and Savior. We are all part of His one body. We are all covered by the one blood.

The Lord's Supper serves to remind us that we are individuals but also part of a much bigger whole. How we relate to and deal with the other individuals in the body is a critical aspect of our walk with God. When we partake of communion with Christ, we also partake of communion with all Christians everywhere—past, present, and future. The second thing we can note from the passage above is that Judas also took the cup and drank from it. Judas already had it in his heart to betray the Lord.

Jesus offers His blood to all, but not all will truly receive it. It's possible to go to church, partake of communion, and even mingle and fellowship with other believers yet not be a true believer. It's possible to do all the right things and not have His blood truly cover your sins. The blood of the new covenant is offered to all, but salvation doesn't come to all.

Paul admonishes us to examine ourselves before partaking of the Lord's Supper, particularly regarding our walk as it relates to other believers, but it can equally be an admonishment to ask ourselves if we've come to the cross as a true disciple. Have we laid our sins at the foot of the cross? The sacrifice of Christ on the cross is the only perfect work sufficient to pay the price of sin and death. If we haven't accepted Him, or if we've sinned against our brothers and sisters, even today that blood is offered to us to bring us forgiveness for all our sins and make us new. The cup is offered to all. Will we drink it with the thankful heart of a true disciple?

> *Lord Jesus, we thank You that You shed Your blood and established the new covenant of the forgiveness of our sins. We come humbly and thankfully, recognizing You as our Lord. Amen.*

For further study: Matthew 26:20–29; Acts 17:26–28; 1 Corinthians 11:17–34; Galatians 3:26–28.

JANUARY 12
The New Covenant

> How much more shall the blood of Christ, who through the eternal Spirit offered Himself without spot to God, cleanse your conscience from dead works to serve the living God? And for this reason He is the Mediator of the new covenant, by means of death, for the redemption of the transgressions under the first covenant, that those who are called may receive the promise of the eternal inheritance. (Hebrews 9:14–15)

WHEN THE ISRAELITES came out of a life of slavery in Egypt, God made Moses a mediator of a covenant between Him and the people. Moses made an earthly copy of a heavenly tabernacle, and every year the high priest would take the blood of animals and sprinkle it in the Holy of Holies. This was the place behind a veil, where there was a chest containing the Ten Commandments written on stone by the finger of God. The blood was used to temporarily cover the sins of the people. This ceremony, repeated year after year, couldn't take away those sins but rather served to remind all of us that we fall short of keeping the law of God.

Jesus came as a mediator of a new and better covenant. He wasn't a high priest who would kill a bull or a lamb and sprinkle its blood on an earthly, physical place. He was a high priest who would live a perfect life, fulfilling all the law, and then in His death present His blood in the true Holy of Holies in heaven. The earthly tabernacle Moses made was a mere copy of the true thing. Jesus was the true sacrifice, whose blood was taken through the veil made of His own flesh and was sprinkled in the true holy place in heaven. His blood enabled the complete remission of sins.

In the earthly tabernacle, the law was written on stone to show us that our good works would never fulfill the law. Those works would be dead like that stone. In the New Covenant, Jesus's sacrifice enabled the law to be written now in our hearts of flesh. We no longer strive to do good works; instead, now those good works naturally flow out of our living hearts. It's like the law was a muzzle preventing a vicious dog from biting. Jesus comes along, and by His sacrifice the muzzle can be removed, because the dog no longer wants to bite anyone. The law is now willingly fulfilled without the need for restraints and punishments.

Does that mean we never make mistakes? Do the teeth of the dog never accidentally wound someone? No! As long as we live in the world, we're subject to error and imperfection. Holy Communion is a chance for us to remember where our heart truly lies. It's a time to remember that Jesus has made the way for us to enter into God's presence with our conscience clear and our sins forgiven.

> Holy Spirit, reveal any area where we have fallen short in our relationship with God and others. Jesus, we remember that Your blood has cleansed us from all sin and made us new. Thank You. Amen.

For further study: Hebrews 7:11–10:24.

JANUARY 13
The Show Bread

> Then Aaron and his sons shall eat the flesh of the ram, and the bread that is in the basket, by the door of the tabernacle of meeting. (Exodus 29:32)

THE TABERNACLE OF Moses housed a table that had bread continuously shown upon it. This was called the showbread. Once a week, the priests would come and eat the bread, but immediately it would be replaced with fresh, warm bread. There was never a lack or a time when the bread wasn't present and visible. The bread was made of fine flour, grain that was crushed and had no coarseness or impurities in it. It was then mixed with oil. It was baked in fire and pierced through with holes. Twelve loaves were placed on the table. Frankincense was also poured over the bread. On this table were also cups containing wine that was poured out as a drink offering.

In the New Testament, Jesus clearly shows Himself to be the true showbread, the bread of life. He was crushed and bruised for our transgressions, yet there was no impurity in Him. He was filled with the Holy Spirit like the flour was mixed with the oil. His sufferings on the cross were represented by the bread baked in fire. He was pierced for our iniquities when His hands, feet, and side were pierced, yet His life and death gave a sweet aroma, like the frankincense poured on the bread.

Jesus brought His twelve apostles together at the table. As they ate and communed together, He showed them that He was the living bread. His body was the bread broken for us. His blood was poured out as the drink offering of wine poured out in sacrifice. He would be with us always, and we would now be priests in His kingdom.

The priest is the one who offers sacrifices to and serves his God. Likewise, we are called to offer ourselves as a living sacrifice, no longer serving the lusts of the flesh but serving the one true God. We minister to one another in the grace of God. We're able to prove the good, acceptable, and perfect will of God by renewing our minds to His Word. Jesus is the very Word of God, and by communing with Him at His table, we pause to remember His sacrifice, and that we are cleansed from our old worldly ways. We recall that we are called to a new life as His representative and servant.

> *Jesus, we recognize the symbolism that was present in the table of the showbread in the tabernacle of Moses. We see how God was foreshadowing Your perfect sacrifice. You would be crushed and bruised for our iniquities, and Your blood poured out for our sins. You would be the sweet-smelling sacrifice that would once and for all pay the penalty for our sins and enable us to become priests in Your kingdom. Help us to remember You that we might live for You and show forth Your good and perfect and acceptable will. Amen.*

For further study: Leviticus 24:5–9; John 6:48; Romans 12:1–2; 1 Corinthians 10:16–17; Hebrews 9:1–5.

JANUARY 14
A Lamb for a House

> Speak to all the congregation of Israel, saying: "On the tenth day of this month every man shall take for himself a lamb, according to the house of his father, a lamb for a household." (Exodus 12:3)

JESUS INSTITUTED THE Lord's Supper during the Jewish celebration of Passover, specifically on the very day they slaughtered the Passover lamb. It was also the day before He would be sacrificed on the cross. It's significant that He chose this day to take the bread and wine and compare it to His body and blood—His body that would undergo suffering, and His blood that would be shed for the remission of sins. He was about to be sacrificed as the true Passover lamb.

The Passover lamb was a male lamb from the flock. It had to be perfect and without blemish. It was the picture of innocence that would be sacrificed for others. At the very first Passover, the blood of the lamb was put on the lintel and doorposts so that the Angel of Death would pass over that house and not destroy anyone in it. The Israelites were given specific instruction that none of the bones of the lamb should be broken, and the lamb was to be roasted in fire and eaten in haste with unleavened bread and bitter herbs. The Israelites had to be ready to depart from slavery at any moment.

This Passover lamb was a shadow of the true Lamb to come. Jesus was the perfect man, innocent of all sin, whose blood was shed so we could have eternal life. He willingly gave up His life. The two thieves crucified with Him had their legs broken to speed their death, but this wasn't done to Jesus, as He had already laid His life down for us. He took the fire of hell for us and was bruised in His body for our transgressions. His blood that ran down the cross paid the price of sin so our spirit could be made new and saved from destruction. The bitter herbs, which represented the bitter life of slavery, remind us now that without the sacrifice of the Lamb, we are in a bitter life of slavery to sin. There is also a haste, an urgency. Today is the day of salvation. We shouldn't wait another day before recognizing the true Lamb of God, our Savior. We can't afford to put it off for another time. Who knows when the destroyer will come and claim our very life.

Finally, as one small innocent lamb was enough for an entire house, how much more is the blood of the Lamb of God sufficient for the entire world? His sacrifice is more than enough to save us all, if only we receive Him.

> *Jesus, we remember and acknowledge that You are our Passover Lamb. Your blood has been put on the doorposts of our heart and saves us from the destruction due us by sin. You were perfect and without sin, yet You bore the penalty of sin, which is death, so that we can live with You forever in eternity. We receive You and accept You into our hearts as our Lord and Savior. Thank You for all You have done for us and for who You are. Amen.*

For further study: Exodus 12:1–51; Isaiah 53:4–7; John 1:29; Romans 6:17–18; 2 Corinthians 6:2; 1 Peter 1:18–21.

JANUARY 15
"For-giveness"

In Him we have redemption through His blood, the forgiveness of sins, according to the riches of His grace. (Ephesians 1:7)

THE WORD "FORGIVE" is an interesting one. It means a releasing, a letting go of offense, a canceling of a debt that is owed, but in a literal translation, it means "to give before." Let's explore this thought a little more deeply.

Jesus Christ, as God Himself, knew the debt we would owe because of sin. Even those of us who weren't yet born when He died on the cross would be born under the shadow of sin. God has known from the beginning the mistakes we would make and the sins we'd commit. When Jesus was dying on the cross, He already knew that future generations would do evil. He knew how much we'd mess up, how much we'd hurt each other and Him. Nevertheless, He felt that His sacrifice was worth it. Even knowing how much evil was in the world and what would come, He still willingly walked the Via Dolorosa—the way of pain. He still chose to stretch out His hands on the cross and let His blood flow for us. As the Scriptures say: *"For scarcely for a righteous man will one die; yet perhaps for a good man someone would even dare to die. But God demonstrates His own love toward us, in that while we were still sinners, Christ died for us"* (Romans 5:7–8).

Now let's go one step further. Think of someone who has betrayed or hurt you. Maybe a spouse said they didn't love you anymore and walked away. Maybe your marriage was full of hurt and pain. Now picture yourself back at your wedding day, on the day you were so full of hope for the future of that relationship. What if you could see all the things that would occur? Imagine yourself standing at the altar, turning to your spouse, and saying, "I can see all the hurt and pain you'll cause me. I can see you giving up on us and abandoning me; nevertheless, I choose right now to forgive it all, and I will still marry you."

What if a close friend stole something from you? Let's go back to the start of the relationship and say, "I see that things will go wrong and you will betray my trust and steal from me; nevertheless, I'm choosing to have a relationship with you. I choose to forgive you now, even before you betray my trust."

That's what Jesus did for us. He saw all the evil we would do, yet He said, "I will still go to the cross for you." He asks us to forgive others as He has forgiven us. Communion with Christ is as much about our communion with each other as it's about communion with Him. Let's take a moment to mentally walk through our pain and trials and forgive those who have hurt us as we remember how He has forgiven us.

Jesus, thank You for being willing to go to the cross, even though You knew how much wrong we would do and that we wouldn't deserve Your sacrifice. Help us also to forgive those who have harmed us, just as You have forgiven us. Amen.

For further study: Matthew 18:21–35; Ephesians 4:32.

JANUARY 16
You Did It to Me

> And the King will answer and say to them, "Assuredly, I say to you, inasmuch as you did it to one of the least of these My brethren, you did it to Me." (Matthew 25:40)

JESUS TOLD A parable about judgment that was coming to those who thought they were Christians but didn't care at all for others. He told how a King would separate the sheep from the goats. He would tell the sheep that they would enter into everlasting joy because when He was hungry, they fed Him; when He was thirsty, they gave Him drink; when He was sick, they visited Him; when He was naked, they clothed Him; and when He was in prison, they visited Him. Those righteous people would be confused, saying they had never done those things for the King. However, the King would explain that how they treated others was how they treated Him.

To the people represented by the goats, the King would say that they would go to everlasting judgment because they didn't give Him food or drink or clothes, or visit Him. Those unrighteous people would be confused too, saying that wasn't right. If they had seen the King, they wouldn't have ignored Him. The King, however, again would explain that because they didn't do those good things to others, they didn't do it for Him either. It was one and the same thing.

Think now of someone who has done you wrong. Maybe they cut you off when driving and almost wrecked your car. Maybe they did wreck your car. Maybe you needed someone and they let you down. Perhaps someone abandoned you. Possibly someone took something from you. No matter what, it's just the same as if they did it to the Lord of Glory, the perfect One, the Holy God, the King of the universe. When I recall this, I want to fall on my knees and say "Father, forgive them. They didn't know what they were doing. They thought their selfish acts were just to help themselves—or maybe they even knew they were hurting me—but they didn't realize they were hurting You."

Now think about all the times you let others down and weren't there for them when they needed it. You turned a blind eye to people's needs. Maybe you chose not to do good, even when it was in your power to do it. Maybe you also messed up and hurt someone by your actions or inaction. Perhaps you shrugged it off, thinking they would understand, or that they'd think it wasn't important. The King would say that as much as we did it to others, we did it to Him. When I think of this, it makes me want to fall on my knees and say, "Father, forgive me. I really didn't know what I was doing. I failed to see You in others."

In 1 Corinthians 11, Paul writes that communion is about discerning the Lord's body. We are the Lord's body, His hands and feet. How we treat each other is how we treat Him. Let us remember that today.

Father, we come in Jesus's name. Please forgive those who have sinned against us, and also forgive us our trespasses. Help us to see Jesus in the people around us. Amen.

For further study: Matthew 25:31–46; 1 Corinthians 11:17–31.

JANUARY 17
He Understands

For we do not have a High Priest who cannot sympathize with our weaknesses, but was in all points tempted as we are, yet without sin. (Hebrews 4:15)

SOMETIMES PEOPLE JUSTIFY their bad attitudes by citing their trauma or pain, believing they have a right to be unforgiving, angry, or self-righteous. They don't think that others can possibly understand what they've been through. To some degree, they're right. Other people may not be able to understand someone's pain or trouble. Jesus, however, can understand and sympathize with us.

Has someone close to you betrayed you or stolen from you? Judas, a follower and friend of Jesus—even a leader and the treasurer—stole money from the money box. He sold out the Lord of Glory for thirty pieces of silver, betraying Him with a kiss! A sign of love!

Have your friends let you down? Peter denied Jesus three times in one night, even after saying he would die with Jesus before he would let that happen.

Have people lied about you? People lied about Jesus and bore false witness against Him.

Have you been falsely accused? Jesus was. He was accused of blasphemy and sentenced to death.

Have you been beaten or abused? Mocked or made fun of? Jesus was. They blindfolded Him and struck Him and said, "Prophesy! Who hit you?" They mocked His kingship. They beat Him so badly you could barely recognize Him as a man, and they murdered Him on the cross.

Have you ever been shamed and had your nakedness exposed? Our images of Christ show a piece of material around His waist to protect our sensitivities, but He was stripped of His clothes and hung naked on the cross. The soldiers even gambled over His clothing like it was a trophy to their ability to abuse this man.

Have those who have suffered in the same boat as you picked on you too—the very people who should have some compassion and understanding, but who choose instead to gang up on you? The thieves crucified with Jesus also reviled Him.

Jesus endured all this, and He even wore a crown of thorns. Thorns symbolize the curse on the earth from sin. Yet He did not sin. He did not revile in return. He forgave. He loved. He gets it. He knows how hard it is, but He's willing to live through us and help us forgive as He did.

Jesus, we come to You, recognizing that You know and understand how hard it can be to choose to walk in love and forgiveness. Help us remember You and be more like You. Amen.

For further study: Genesis 3:17–18; Matthew 26:47–56, 69–75, 27:35–44; Mark 14:53–65, 15:15–26; John 12:6.

JANUARY 18
Melchizedek

> The Lord has sworn and will not relent, "You are a priest forever according to the order of Melchizedek." (Psalm 110:4)

MELCHIZEDEK APPEARS IN Scripture for the first time in the book of Genesis. His name means "king of righteousness," and it's recorded that he was the King of Salem (King of Peace). He appears suddenly, having neither beginning nor end, father nor mother, nor genealogy. We understand Melchizedek, the King of Righteousness, to be a pre-incarnate image of Christ—that is, an appearance of Jesus in the Old Testament before He was born on the earth.

Melchizedek met Abraham returning from battle. Abraham blessed Melchizedek by giving Him a tithe of all the spoils of the battle, and Melchizedek blessed Abraham, bringing Abraham bread and wine. It's interesting that the pre-incarnate Christ shows up preparing a table and bringing the same elements we traditionally associate with communion. These are the very symbols He will later use to represent His body, broken for us, and His blood that was shed for us.

God had made a covenant with Abraham to bless him, but He'd also made a promise to Abraham that through his seed, meaning his offspring, all the nations of the world would be blessed. Jesus was born in the lineage of Abraham. He was the Seed through which all the nations would be blessed. Jesus is the King of Righteousness and Peace. Although He appeared as a man, born of a woman, He is also without beginning or end. He was present at the creation of the world and is eternal. He is our true high priest, according to the order of Melchizedek. The earthly priests before Jesus would once a year place the blood of an animal in the Holy of Holies to cover the people's sins for another year, but the sinless Jesus came once, with His own blood, into the true Holy of Holies in heaven to wipe away our sins forever. Through His sacrifice, we have salvation for all eternity.

When He appeared to Abraham, He brought bread and wine to foreshadow the day He would present His body and blood as the sacrifice for our sins. Jesus would pay the price so that we could now walk in righteousness and peace with Him for all eternity. He has blessed us and delivered us from the true enemy of our souls. The bread and wine serve to remind us that He is our true high priest who takes away our sins once and for all.

> *Jesus, we see that You were calling to us through all the ages, to all people, showing us who You are. You are our high priest, the only one able to deliver us from sin and death. We take this moment to remember You and what You've done for us. Your body was broken so that ours could be whole; Your blood shed so we could live always with You in righteousness and peace. Amen.*

For further study: Genesis 3:14–15, 14:14–20, 22:15–18; Psalm 110:3–4; Galatians 3:15–18; Hebrews 5:5–10.

JANUARY 19
They Broke Bread Together

And they continued steadfastly in the apostles' doctrine and fellowship, in the breaking of bread, and in prayers. (Acts 2:42)

BREAKING OF BREAD is symbolic of being in fellowship with one another. When the Church began after the resurrection of Jesus, they were in unity. They held everything in common, and the Bible says they were steadfast in this. They were faithfully learning from the apostles, fellowshipping with each other, sharing meals daily, praying for one another, and loving and looking out for one another. Because of this unity, the way was paved for great signs and wonders to occur, and people were joining the Church daily.

A short time before Jesus was crucified, He prayed for them, and for us today, that we would be in unity with each other and with Him, just as He is in unity with God the Father. He also says that very unity will show the world that He was sent to save us all and that God loves us. Given that the early church was in unity, it's not surprising to read that people were being saved daily.

Before He died, Jesus instituted communion so that the bread and wine would serve as a reminder that we are in Him, and He is in us, but also that we are to be united to one another in His body. All the individuals in the church now make up the body of Christ. As we walk in fellowship and unity—praying for one another, caring for one another—the world can't help but sit up and take notice. The love of God for humanity is manifested by His love flowing through us to one another.

Jesus knew we would at times be distracted and stressed in this world and that we'd forget His sacrifice. We'd get caught up in petty disagreements. We'd potentially be waylaid by false doctrine. We'd find reason to fight with one another. Our selfish nature could raise its ugly head and give us a "me first" attitude. For this reason, He gave us bread and wine, the communion table, and told us to remember Him. He gave us simple, readily available tools so that every time we'd partake of communion, we'd remember that we are united in Him and through Him to each other. As we do this, His love is manifested to all around us. Our friends and family will see what serving God is all about, and maybe those around us who don't yet know Him will be daily added to the church as they accept Jesus's saving grace.

> *Father, we come to You in Jesus's name, thankful for His prayers for us, His sacrifice for us, His communion, and His reminder that we are all one in Him, united in His body. We are so grateful for the life we have in Him, and we want our friends and family to share in this life. Help us to walk in unity and fellowship with one another to be a true witness of Your love for all, so that they too will come to know You and be part of Your body. Amen.*

For further study: John 17:20–23; Acts 2:42–47.

JANUARY 20
By His Stripes

> Who Himself bore our sins in His own body on the tree, that we, having died to sins, might live for righteousness—by whose stripes you were healed. (1 Peter 2:24)

THE PRACTICE OF communion reminds us that Jesus came to heal us completely. Peter tells us that by His stripes (the wounds on Jesus's back from the whipping) we are healed. This healing may be physical, but it's also a healing of our spirits, as our soul is sick from sin.

As we partake of communion, we are reminded that He bore our physical sickness as well as our spiritual sickness. When Jesus was sitting at the table in the house of Simon, a few days before the crucifixion, Mary of Bethany brought an alabaster flask of costly oil and poured it on Jesus. This story is repeated in all four Gospels, each bringing out different aspects of the event. In Luke, we find out that Simon was a Pharisee, and Mary a sinner. We also discover that Mary showed her love for Jesus more than Simon did, and Jesus says she loved more because she'd been forgiven more. But in Matthew and Mark, we learn that Simon was also a leper. Since leprosy was contagious, lepers were outcasts and not allowed around people. In the story, Simon was having a party and entertaining guests, so I think it's safe to say that Jesus had healed him physically. That physical healing would have been incredible and changed his whole life, yet Mary, who understood her spiritual healing, loved Jesus more.

So what can we take from this? First, God loves us and desires our complete healing. He wants us physically well, and there is provision in His sacrifice for that. Second, and more importantly, God wants us spiritually well. This is the critical aspect—an awareness of what He has done for us spiritually that makes us fall at His feet and pour out our love to Him. The physical is temporal; the spiritual, eternal. Certainly believe for healing, and when you partake of the bread, thank Him for that, but it's even more critical to examine yourself to see if you have a spiritual need to be met. Recognize that He took the punishment due us so that He could forever heal us from the power of sin and death.

> *Lord Jesus, we come to You recognizing we are all sinners in need of a Savior. Our spiritual need is great. We thank You for pouring out Your blood so that we could have eternal life with You. We also are grateful for Your broken body that brings us physical health. We thank You for redeeming us from all aspects of the curse that sin brought into the world. Amen.*

For further study: Genesis 3:17–19; Matthew 26:6–13; Mark 14:3–9; Luke 7:36–50; John 12:2–8; Romans 8:18–23.

JANUARY 21
The Bread of Life

And Jesus said to them, "I am the bread of life. He who comes to Me shall never hunger, and he who believes in Me shall never thirst." (John 6:35)

IN JOHN 6, the people come to Jesus because He satisfied their physical hunger. They are thinking of how God fed their ancestors when they wandered in the wilderness, and they wonder if Jesus will provide bread for them day after day. Jesus explains to them that He didn't come to just satisfy their physical hunger but to satisfy their spiritual hunger. He makes an amazing claim here. If anyone receives Him—the very bread of life sent from heaven—they will never hunger or thirst again. Jesus is trying to explain their spiritual need, but the people are stuck on physical needs.

Bread is symbolic of provision for the necessities of life. The life Jesus mentions here is *zoe* in the Greek. *Zoe* means so much more than existence. This is the life God has in the Father and the Son and the Holy Spirit. It's an eternal life of the spirit that will at some point extend also to our bodies when He raises us up in the last day. It implies a holiness and righteousness. It speaks of our very communion with God Himself and our fellowship with Him. This is the life we lost when sin entered the world, and it's the life Jesus bought back for us.

His Word tells us that the life is in the blood. Jesus, who had no sin, voluntarily poured out His blood in an offering, paying with His life, so that we might have eternal life with Him. It's no surprise that when Jesus instituted the practice of communion, He chose bread and wine to symbolize His body and blood. He had already told them that He was the bread of life. He was the provision for all our spiritual needs. We would have a sharing of the life He had with the Father because of His lifeblood being poured out on the cross.

So often we get stuck on the cares of this world, focused on our physical needs. Jesus is calling to us, reminding us. He can meet physical needs, but He longs to meet our true spiritual needs—our need for the life God provides. He will provide for us His holiness and righteousness so that we can commune and fellowship with God. Our life is so much more than this earthly existence or just food and drink. It is so much more than the stuff we possess. Our life is connected for eternity with the holy, righteous, glorious, and perfect Savior. That thought inspires me to be so much more than I am; it enables me to walk with more grace as I focus on the life we have for all eternity with Him.

> *Jesus, thank You that You are the bread of life. You made provision for us to have eternal life with You and the Father and the Holy Spirit. Help us to keep our thoughts fixed on You and the life we have in You. Teach us so that we're not distracted by temporary worries or cares, because You have given us all we need for life and godliness. Amen.*

For further study: Leviticus 17:11; Matthew 6:19–34; John 6:22–59; 2 Peter 1:3.

JANUARY 22
He Was Lifted Up

And as Moses lifted up the serpent in the wilderness, even so must the Son of Man be lifted up, that whoever believes in Him should not perish but have eternal life. (John 3:14–15)

AS THE CHILDREN of Israel wandered in the wilderness, the way started to seem long. They became discouraged and then started to murmur and complain. They said there was no food or water, even though God made manna appear to feed them and provided water from a rock. They went so far as to say that as far as the manna was concerned, they loathed this worthless bread! This resulted in fiery serpents coming into the camp, biting people and killing them. As people started dying, God told Moses to make an image of the serpent and put it on a pole. If anyone was bitten, they only had to look at the serpent and they would live.

We might like to think that if we were in their shoes, we wouldn't complain. After all, we're talking about manna, that miraculous bread from heaven. The Bible calls it food for angels! How could they look on such a blessing, a daily miracle and provision, and consider it more like a worthless curse? We would never do that. Or would we? How many of us have prayed for a job and then gotten the job of our dreams, but now the way seems long. It's the same old thing day after day. Even though this is our very bread, we're discouraged and frustrated, and we start to loathe it. How many of us were blessed with a spouse but now the trials and boring routine of life seem loathsome. We start to complain about the very blessing of God. How many of us have murmured against our pastor or government leaders? We criticize them and say they are leading us in circles in the wilderness!

Humanity's disobedience gave that old serpent, the devil, the ability to sting us, and it brought death into the world. God, however, had a plan to save us. Jesus was raised on the cross to pay the penalty for our sins. Just as when the Israelites could look to the bronze serpent on the pole and be healed from the serpent's sting and live, so we also, when we look to Jesus on the cross, will be saved from the serpent's sting that caused spiritual death. We must keep our eyes on God's blessing and provision for our salvation.

Communion is about remembering what He has done for us. This has two aspects: reminding us what He did for us when we first asked Him to be our Lord and He wiped our sins away, and also the day-to-day reminder that although the way seems long, He has provided blessings and provision for us. It's a reminder to be grateful and thankful for all He has done.

> *God, forgive us for speaking against You and our leaders, for murmuring and complaining and seeing Your blessings as a curse. Jesus, You are the bread of life who came from heaven, and you meet all our needs. Help us to keep our eyes fixed on You and be thankful. Amen.*

For further study: Exodus 16:1–5; Numbers 20:2–13, 21:4–9; Psalm 78:17–25; John 3:14–17.

JANUARY 23
Man Shall Not Live by Bread Alone

But He answered and said, "It is written, 'Man shall not live by bread alone, but by every word that proceeds from the mouth of God.'" (Matthew 4:4)

AFTER JESUS WAS baptized, He was led by the Spirit to the desert to be tested. He had fasted for forty days and was physically very hungry. That was when the devil came to Him to tempt Him. The devil said to Him, "If you are the Son of God, command these stones to become bread." With this, the devil was mocking Jesus, like a child on a playground telling another child to prove just how tough he is. The devil was also trying to get Jesus to doubt Himself and God. If the Father really loved Jesus, why was He experiencing physical need? Hasn't God promised to take care of those who love Him?

Jesus answers with a quotation from Deuteronomy, spoken to the children of Israel as they wandered in the wilderness. In Deuteronomy 8:3, the Israelites are reminded that God humbled them and allowed them to hunger, and then He fed them with manna so they would know that man should not live only by bread alone but by every word that proceeds from the mouth of God. In other words, we shouldn't be focused only on our physical needs but rather on our spiritual needs. When we focus on our spiritual needs, God will make sure He meets our physical needs. After all, the world with all its fruit, grain, animals, and fish was created by God's spoken word. He is well able to meet our physical hunger. What's really important is that we let Him meet our spiritual hunger. Jesus called to mind this verse when He answered the devil's taunts.

Adam and Eve had failed the test. The devil had done the same thing in the Garden of Eden when he came to Eve first with a question: "Has God really said …?" The devil was making Eve question the goodness and provision of God. He made her hunger after the fruit of the tree of knowledge of good and evil. Adam and Eve gave in to their hunger and let sin into the world. Jesus, however, came to reverse the effects of sin. When He was tempted to give in to hunger and to doubt God the Father, He stood strong.

He succeeded where humanity failed. He wasn't swayed by questions about His relationship to the Father or about God's love and provision. He wasn't moved by any dare to prove Himself. He knew He was the bread of life who had come down from heaven. Mere physical hunger wouldn't keep Him from completing His mission. He would bring salvation to humanity by being the perfect, sinless sacrifice.

> *Jesus, we thank You that You came to destroy the effects of sin. You are the bread of heaven, able to meet our spiritual hunger and restore us to a right relationship with God. You gave us the act of communion to remind us that we need not be driven by our physical needs. Our physical needs will be met as we seek You and let You meet our spiritual hunger. Amen.*

For further study: Genesis 1:1–25, 3:1–7; Deuteronomy 8:1–3; Matthew 4:1–4, 6:19–34.

JANUARY 24
The Road to Emmaus

Now it came to pass, as He sat at the table with them, that He took bread, blessed and broke it, and gave it to them. Then their eyes were opened and they knew Him ... (Luke 24:30–31a)

THREE DAYS AFTER Jesus was crucified, on the very day He had risen from the dead, two of His disciples traveled on a journey to the town of Emmaus. Jesus came along and joined them, but they didn't recognize Him because He appeared in another form. They talked of how their hopes had been dashed when they saw Jesus crucified, and shared that some of the women had come to them, claiming that Jesus was alive. They were confused. They thought Jesus was the Messiah, but with His death, they weren't sure.

Jesus explained all the Scriptures to them, which they must have heard countless times growing up. Their hearts burned within them as He talked, and when they reached Emmaus, Jesus looked as if He was going to continue walking, but the disciples constrained Him to stay with them. As they sat to eat, Jesus took the bread, blessed it, broke it, and gave it to them. In that same act He had done when He established communion, they recognized and knew Him.

From the Scriptures, we know that we are now the body of Christ on earth. Also, whatever we do to others, Jesus considers that we have done it to Him. He appears to us today in another form. Like the disciples on their way to Emmaus, it's possible to grow up in church and not know or recognize Jesus. It's possible to hear and read the Scriptures and not realize how they point to Jesus. It's possible to follow Him and witness miracles yet not know Him. It's possible to hear the testimony of others and still not know Him. It's possible to even be in His very presence and not recognize Him as Jesus, the Lord and Savior, the Messiah. However, if we take the time to commune with Him, there's a good chance we will start to know Him.

Just as the disciples had to ask Him to stay, we also have to ask Him to come into our lives to truly understand what it means to take part in fellowship with Him and other believers. Our heart burns within us when we hear the Word of God as the Holy Spirit calls out to us to receive Jesus, to recognize who He is and what He has done for us. As we spend time in communion with Him, we're more likely to recognize Him and what He's doing with those around us.

As we look at other believers, we look at Jesus choosing to appear to us in another form. How will we treat Him? Will we recognize Him? Will we spend time in fellowship with Him? Or will we just walk away?

Jesus, as we break the bread and drink the wine, help us to know You and to recognize the body of Christ—Your presence among us. Amen.

For further study: Matthew 25:31–46; Mark 16:9–13; Luke 24:13–32; 1 Corinthians 11:17–29.

JANUARY 25
The Rich Young Ruler

For God so loved the world that He gave His only begotten Son, that whoever believes in Him should not perish but have everlasting life. (John 3:16)

WHEN MOSES CAME down from the mountain, he carried two tablets of stone written with the finger of God. The writing contained the Ten Commandments. The first four relate to our relationship with God, and the second group of six concern our relationship with each other. In Luke 18, a certain rich young ruler comes to Jesus and asks Him, "What must I do to inherit eternal life?" Jesus tells him to keep the commandments, and He lists those that relate to our relationship to each other—you shall not murder, you shall not commit adultery, honor your father and mother, etc. The rich ruler says he has kept those from his youth, but inside he knows that he's still missing something, as does Jesus.

Jesus turns the young man's attention to his relationship with God. He tells the ruler to sell what he has and give to the poor and to follow Him. With this instruction, He points out that the rich young ruler has neglected the first commandments relating to our relationship with God. He hasn't put God first, nor is he prepared to honor the Lord. Money is his idol, and he's not willing to give it up, even if God Himself asks him to.

The Ten Commandments were written on two tablets of stone to reflect how they would be summarized in the New Testament by two commandments: to love the Lord our God with all our heart and soul and mind and strength, and to love our neighbor as ourselves. Both aspects are important in the life of the Christian. First and foremost comes our relationship with God, but the second is also important to remember—our relationship with each other.

Both of these aspects of the Christian walk are brought to our remembrance through the elements of Holy Communion. The blood, represented by the wine, symbolizes our relationship with God and is summed up in John 3:16: *"For God so loved the world that He gave His only begotten Son, that whoever believes in Him should not perish but have everlasting life."* The bread, symbolizing the body of Christ, points us to our relationship with each other. This is summed up in 1 John 3:16: *"By this we know love, because He laid down His life for us. And we also ought to lay down our lives for the brethren."* Because we are forgiven and loved by God, we can forgive and love others. The fulfillment of the second group of commandments flows naturally from the fulfillment of the first part, by loving God and recognizing His love for us.

> *Father, as we partake of communion today, we're reminded that You gave Your only Son to die in our place so that we could be forgiven of our sins and have everlasting life. We also remember that His body was broken so that we could be united as His body, serving and loving one another just as He has loved us. Amen.*

For further study: Exodus 20:1–17, 31:18; Mark 12:28–34; Luke 18:18–27.

JANUARY 26
The Marriage Supper

So those servants went out into the highways and gathered together all whom they found, both bad and good. And the wedding hall was filled with guests. (Matthew 22:10)

JESUS TOLD A parable to describe the kingdom of heaven. He said it was like a marriage feast a king had arranged for his son. He sent the servants out to invite the guests, but one by one the guests made excuses. Some were too busy with their business or farm; one said he'd just gotten married and couldn't come, and some beat the servants and treated them shamefully or even murdered them. The king was angry and said that those who'd been invited first were not worthy, so he sent his servants out to the lame and blind, the beggars, the homeless, both good people and bad people. The servants were to compel all they could find to come to the wedding feast. In Matthew's version of this parable, one who accepts the invitation to the feast is found without a wedding garment and is cast out into the darkness.

The parallel to Christianity is very clear, for indeed God has prepared a marriage feast for His Son. All is ready. All are invited. Some, however, refuse the invitation. Some are too busy right now making money and can't be bothered to listen to the servants of the Lord calling them. Some are busy with their own homes and lives. Some have married, and their spouse doesn't agree with this faith, so they choose to follow their spouse and refuse the invitation. Others treat the servants of God shamefully by mocking them, teasing them, or even beating and murdering them. But to anyone who will accept the invitation, the table is set, the bread and the wine are prepared, the feast is ready. Today is the day of salvation. The invitations have been sent out.

Whether people are good or bad, rich or poor, healthy or lame, upper class or lower class, all will fall into one of only two groups—those who accept the invitation and enter into the feast, and those who refuse it. However, all who would come must come properly clothed. No one has enough money to buy a wedding garment for this celebration, nor can anyone make one. The garment is the robe of righteousness God has paid for with Jesus's precious blood, and we receive it by accepting Jesus as Lord of our lives. There is no other way to enter into the wedding feast of the Lamb of God. We can do no deed good enough to earn the righteousness of God, nor can any sin keep us from being clothed with righteousness should we come to Jesus. Without this clothing of His righteousness, there will be no place at the table.

As Christians, we are servants of the King and are sent to call all to come to the feast, to compel them even. Some may refuse the invitation, making excuses, but others will accept. Will we tell others of the feast prepared for them? Will we explain how God will clothe them with righteousness, enabling even the worst sinner to be able to attend the heavenly celebration?

Jesus, we receive You and Your righteousness. We acknowledge what You have done, and we come to the feast thankful that we were invited and accepted. Help us invite others. Amen.

For further study: Matthew 22:1–14; Revelation 19:7–9.

JANUARY 27
Treasure in Earthen Vessels

> But we have this treasure in earthen vessels, that the excellence of the power may be of God and not of us. (2 Corinthians 4:7)

IMAGINE YOU HAVE a great treasure, a priceless gem, but instead of putting it in a safety deposit box or some other secure place, you put it in a simple clay pot on the kitchen counter. It seems ridiculous, but that's what God does. When we ask Jesus to come into our hearts, He comes and makes His home with us. We are filled with the Holy Spirit. God lives in us, simple beings made of clay, for our ancestor Adam was formed from the dust of the ground. We aren't even special fancy porcelain tea cups; we're more like well-used mugs that are chipped and cracked. I have a small ceramic turtle that sits by my kitchen sink. I use it to hold pot scrubbers. It's been with me for decades and has seen many moves. It's a little beat up and sometimes even has mold growing in it, but I love it. Imagine if I put a precious jewel inside this ordinary little object.

We are God's creation. We are so ordinary yet so special because of the relationship He has with us. He puts the priceless treasure of Himself in us. He doesn't then put us somewhere aside for safekeeping but lets us interact with the world. Some of us have been ill used or dropped. We're chipped or broken and maybe even a little contaminated by the world's mold. God isn't offended by those chips and cracks. He recognizes that if you put light in a broken pot, it will shine brightest through the cracks.

He makes our body the temple of the Holy Spirit. In 1 Corinthians 6:20, Paul adds that we are not our own but were bought at a price, so we should glorify God in our bodies. Instead of walking willingly into sin, we should recognize that our salvation was costly. It cost more than all the riches and treasures of the world. It cost the very body and blood of Christ—a priceless treasure indeed. Now He can live in us, and His glory can shine through us. As we recognize the precious treasure in us because of the sacrifice Jesus made, we're humbled that He would love us, and we're thankful that He has chosen to live in us. We can walk among the rich and famous with our head held high because we have bowed our heads in humble acceptance of His grace. We are ordinary clay, filled with treasure beyond price. We can rejoice in the wounds the world has given us, as His glory can shine even brighter through them.

> *Lord, we come to You and recognize that because of the sacrifice of Your body and blood, we are special. You chose us to carry Your glory in these ordinary lives and to let Your light shine out to the world around us. Thank You for making your home in us. Amen.*

For further study: Genesis 2:7; 2 Corinthians 4:5–7; 1 Peter 1:13–21.

JANUARY 28
The Good Shepherd

I am the good shepherd. The good shepherd gives His life for the sheep. (John 10:11)

IMAGINE YOU'RE A shepherd watching over a little flock of sheep near Bethlehem. This flock includes lambs being prepared for slaughter at Passover. Now imagine that the owner of the flock, the chief shepherd, comes and says, "I love all these little lambs so much. I don't want any of them to die. I will go in their place and give my life. I'll let my blood be poured out on the altar."

Doesn't that seem shocking? Would you try to talk Him out of it? Peter did just that. But the chief shepherd was so determined to lay His life down for our salvation—His little lambs—that He rebuked Peter harshly. Maybe you'd think those lambs weren't worth the sacrifice of the chief shepherd. Maybe some of those lambs were a little wayward and tended to run off, or were always getting into trouble. Jesus, the chief shepherd, still felt we were worth it. He still chose to lay His life down for any lamb willing to come to Him. He wants all to be saved, even if some refuse to come into His fold. Nevertheless, He receives all who come to Him, and lays His life down for them.

The Bible says David was a man after God's own heart. Many qualities in David could account for that, like his heartfelt worship, or his ability to forgive; however, what comes to my mind is that David was willing to put his life on the line for the smallest lamb of the flock. When a lion and a bear came and snatched a lamb, David didn't run away like a hireling. He ran straight to the attacking beast, grabbed it by its beard, and delivered the little lamb right out of the beast's mouth. Jesus also has snatched us right out of the jaws of death, and He has defeated the enemy of our souls. I am convinced that even if only one person in the whole world were to receive Jesus into his heart and life, Jesus would still have gone to the cross. Thankfully, many have come to Jesus from all walks and races of life. We all become one flock under the one Shepherd. This Shepherd is not a hireling who lets the beast destroy the flock, but He is the Good Shepherd who gives His life so that we might live. He had the ability to lay down His life in our place as the perfect, sinless, spotless Passover lamb, and He had the ability to take it up again, rising from the dead on the third day.

When Jesus established communion, He showed us that He was the Shepherd but also the Passover lamb. He gave us the bread and wine to remind us that we are all part of His one flock, united in Him. We, like sheep, had gone astray, but we are now returned to the Shepherd and overseer of our souls because He laid His life down like a sacrificial lamb, paying the price for our redemption.

Jesus, we recognize You, the Good Shepherd, who gave His life for the sheep. Though we were wayward lambs, You still came and died for us so that we might live. You bore our sins in Your body, and by the stripes on Your back You have brought us healing. We are eternally grateful! Amen.

For further study: 1 Samuel 17:32–37; Isaiah 53:6; Matthew 16:22–23; John 1:12, 10:11–18; Acts 13:22; 1 Peter 2:21–25, 5:1–4.

JANUARY 29
Barabbas

For you did not receive the spirit of bondage again to fear, but you received the Spirit of adoption by whom we cry out, "Abba, Father." (Romans 8:15)

WHEREVER YOU SEE the prefix "Bar" on a name in the Bible, it means "son of." You likely remember that Barabbas was the man the crowd cried out for to be released by Pilate instead of Jesus. Barabbas was on death row for committing murder. His name means "son of father." He was indeed showing forth the deeds of his father, the devil. The devil is a liar and a murderer. Barabbas was born in a world of sin and lived in sin, yet Jesus's death on the cross gave him a chance to walk away from the effects of sin. Jesus took Barabbas's place, and Barabbas was set free.

I also am my father's daughter. I often talk like him; I walk like him. I like a lot of the things he likes. I see a lot of those same traits in my brother and sisters. Some of those traits are good, some less so, and some not good at all. Sometimes I feel powerless to keep from doing the less welcome behaviors, and I remain my father's child. Born into this sinful world, those sinful traits come through and, as it says in James, sin, when it is full-grown, brings forth death. In other words, since the penalty of sin is death, before Christ takes our place, we too are living on death row. We are the children of the father of this world—the devil.

Jesus, however, came to take our place so that we could be set free. He provided the means for us to be fully pardoned. We are made just as if we had never sinned—free and alive. He not only takes away the chains of the fear of death that held us, but He also makes it possible for us to be adopted by our heavenly Father. We are members now of a new family.

As we spend time with the Father, we start to talk like Him, to walk like Him, to like the things He likes. We cry out "Abba Father," with a capital A on Abba! He is the Father with no bad traits for us to pick up on. We're no longer conformed to the world but transformed by the renewing of our minds through His Word. We have a new family resemblance. The world will look at us and say like it was said of the apostles—it is obvious we have been with Jesus. Jesus was the perfect representation of God the Father. He said, *"I and my Father are one"* (John 10:30). Because of Jesus, we can now be sons and daughters of our Father in heaven, growing more like Him every day.

> *Jesus, as we partake of the bread and the wine, we recognize that we were once the children of the world, lost in our sins and in chains of the fear of death. With Your broken body and shed blood, You have made a way for us to be adopted into Your family. We are now sons and daughters of God. Holy Spirit, help us to be more like our heavenly Father—to walk like Him, talk like Him, forgive like Him, love like Him. Amen.*

For further study: Luke 23:13–25; Romans 5:1, 12:1–2; Ephesians 1:3–6; James 1:15; 1 John 2:1–2.

JANUARY 30
Am I My Brother's Keeper?

And just as you want men to do to you, you also do to them likewise. (Luke 6:31)

THE BOOK OF Genesis includes the account of the first murder. Cain brought an offering to the Lord, but he didn't bring his best. His heart motive wasn't really love and honor of the Lord. His brother Abel, however, brought the best he had and gave it to God. God accepted Abel's offering but not Cain's. Cain was jealous and angry. The Lord came and asked Cain why he was upset. After all, if he did what was right, he had just as much opportunity to have his offering accepted as Abel's. Cain still let it bother him, and he ended up killing Abel.

God came to Cain and asked him where Abel was, and Cain lied. He said, *"I do not know. Am I my brother's keeper?"* (Genesis 4:9b). God then said that Abel's blood cried out to Him from the ground. He told Cain that he was now cursed. He would have trouble and always be on the run. He'd brought this on himself by not dealing appropriately with his offense.

Jesus tells us to not only put away jealousy and offense, but to love our enemies. After all, if we only love those who love us, how are we different from sinners who live in the world? We're told to bless those who curse us and pray for those who use us. Where other religions may say things like "Don't do to others what you don't want done to you," Jesus calls us to a higher calling. He tells us to do to others what we want others to do to us. This is so much more than just not doing bad things. It's more than not being jealous or offended with others. It means doing good even to those who do us evil. It means being the first to extend grace and forgiveness. It entails being our brother's keeper, even if our brother doesn't like us or treat us well.

In 1 Corinthians 11, Paul is angry with the Christians of Corinth because they have forgotten this very calling and nature of being a Christian. He says that they're coming to the Lord's communion table thinking only of themselves and not their brothers and sisters. Some are drunk and some are greedy, helping themselves without regard to others. There are divisions among them and infighting. Paul goes on to say that because they don't recognize each other as members of the Lord's body, some are weak, sick, or even have died prematurely. Paul admonishes them and instructs that when they come together, they should take a moment to examine their own hearts and judge themselves. We should be different from others in the world, concerned more with others than we are with our own selves. Even today as we partake of communion, we must examine ourselves and see if we are doing unto others as we want them to do to us.

> *Lord, we thank You that You are our example. You died for us while we were yet sinners. You gave Your all for us. Forgive us our sins and remind us to be our brother's keeper. Amen.*

For further study: Genesis 4:1–15; Matthew 5:43–48, 7:12; Luke 6:27–38; 1 Corinthians 11:17–28.

JANUARY 31
God Is Love

And we have known and believed the love that God has for us. God is love, and he who abides in love abides in God, and God in him. (1 John 4:16)

MANY OF US have heard the "love chapter," often read at weddings. First Corinthians 13 begins by instructing us to do everything in the context of love. Let's modernize it a bit for a North American living in modern times:

"Though I have five thousand friends on Facebook, and ten thousand followers on X and Instagram, if I don't have love, I'm not posting anything worthwhile. Although I am super smart and have my master's and a PhD, and my talents can accomplish miracles, if I don't have love, I am nothing—a real nobody. Although I've been generous to others and have taken a righteous stand so that my family and co-workers mock me and give me a hard time about being a Christian, if I have no love, I gain no brownie points with God or others."

Having love as the motivator for all we are and do is pretty important! Without it, we're spiritually broke. Paul goes on in that chapter to describe what love is. One who loves sacrifices themselves for the beloved. That, of course, describes God. We can substitute God's name for the word "love" in this chapter and gain a clear description of the God of all creation, Lord of heaven and earth. God suffers long and is kind. God does not envy; He does not parade Himself. He is not puffed up. God does not behave rudely; He is not self-seeking. He is not provoked. God thinks no evil. He does not rejoice in iniquity but rejoices in the truth; God bears all things, believes all things, hopes all things, endures all things. God never fails! A truer picture of God the Father, Jesus Christ, and the Holy Spirit could not be given.

Can we put our names in this list, just like we did with God's name? We're told by Paul to examine ourselves when we partake of communion. We can look at that list in 1 Corinthians 13 and ask ourselves: "Have I been longsuffering? Kind? Proud? Envious? Provoked? Truthful? Hopeful? Have I given up or failed in my love for others?" If some failure comes to light, now is the time to repent, so that you might once again receive His cleansing grace.

When Jesus established communion, He was telling us, "Here I am, your example, giving my life in love for you." Not only was He giving us an easy way to remember that He is sacrificial and perfect love, but He was also saying that we are now one body and should follow His example in love one for another. For truly, as it says in 1 John 4:16, if we abide in love, we are abiding in God, and He in us.

Jesus, we want to be Your true disciples, learning to be like You and to walk in love, as You are love. Reveal to us our short-comings in our love and forgive us. Let Your love nature flow through us to others, affecting all we are and do. In Your Holy Name we pray. Amen.

For further study: Matthew 20:25–28; 1 Corinthians 13:1–8, 11:28; 1 Peter 2:21; 1 John 4:7–20.

FEBRUARY 1
"I Am the Vine"

> I am the vine, you are the branches. He who abides in Me, and I in him, bears much fruit; for without Me you can do nothing. (John 15:5)

IT'S UNDERSTANDABLE THAT Jesus would use a cup of wine to symbolize His blood being poured out for us so that we could have new life in Him. He had earlier used the vine and the fruit of the vine to symbolize our relationship with Him.

It's easy to picture a branch connected to the life-giving sap of the vine, versus one that has been cut off from the source of life. The branch still on the vine is vibrant, tender, bringing forth fruit in its season. The cut-off branch at first looks like it's okay, but within a short time it becomes hard and rigid. It dies and can bring forth no fruit. It's good only to be thrown on the fire.

When we're connected to Jesus, the source of all life, we're strong, vibrant, and full of abundant life. Our hearts are tender and bend readily without breaking from the winds of life's storms. And just as the branch doesn't strive to produce fruit, which comes naturally from the sap that flows through the branch from the vine, so we also naturally manifest the fruits of the Spirit. In Galatians, Paul reveals that this fruit is love, and that love is manifested in joy, peace, longsuffering, kindness, goodness, faithfulness, gentleness, and self-control. Just as the fruit is not produced to nourish the branches but to carry the seed of the vine and to nourish those who eat of the fruit, so our loving nature carries the seed of the gospel of Christ to others and nourishes them with the blessings of God.

Like the cut-off branch, if we depart from the faith, at first we won't look any different. Within a short time, however, our hearts start to die and become dry and rigid. We're no longer able to bend in the stormy winds but will break under pressure. Instead of manifesting the fruit of the Spirit, we'll once again manifest the works of the flesh, such as adultery, fornication, uncleanness, idolatry, and so much more. We become conceited and provoke one another. We no longer nourish others or carry the seed of the gospel. We become good only for the fire.

Communion reminds us to abide in Him, to let His life flow through us. In examining ourselves, we look to see if we are manifesting the fruit of the Spirit or the works of the flesh. If it's the latter, now is the time to repent and receive again His cleansing blood that delivers us from the power of sin.

> *Jesus, we remember today that You shed Your blood on the cross so that Your lifeblood now can flow through our veins. We remember that we can abide in You, and the Holy Spirit can produce the fruit of love in us. Thank You for the work You are doing in each one of us. Amen.*

For further study: John 15:1–11; Galatians 5:16–26; 1 John 4:14–16.

FEBRUARY 2
From Water to Wine

John answered, saying to all, "I indeed baptize you with water; but One mightier than I is coming, whose sandal strap I am not worthy to loose. He will baptize you with the Holy Spirit and fire." (Luke 3:16)

JESUS PERFORMED HIS first miracle while attending a wedding in Cana. The bridegroom ran out of wine, but he had six large stone waterpots used in ceremonial washing for purification. Jesus had the servants fill them to the brim with water and then draw water out, which had now been turned to wine, and take it to the master of the feast. Only the servants knew where the wine had truly come from. When the master tasted it, he called the bridegroom and said that most people put out the best wine first, but the bridegroom's prior wine was inferior to what he had just tasted.

The Pharisees would do ceremonial washing to try to obtain purification, but no deed or act, no amount of washing, no good works can purify us from our sins. John came baptizing with water, but it wasn't to save people. It was an opportunity for the people to demonstrate that they were repenting from sin. When the Pharisees came to be baptized, John saw it as just a show for them. They weren't truly interested in repentance and submission to God. They didn't see that they needed God to wash away their sins, since they already felt righteous by their deeds. Jesus came because there is no good deed that will wash away our sins. Only His blood has the power to not only wash away our sins but to give us new life in the Spirit—like going from water to wine. We take the first step of truly repenting of our sins as we turn to recognize His sacrifice on the cross to save us. He then cleanses us and fills us with the Holy Spirit.

The men at the wedding in Cana had put out their very best wine, but compared to the wine that Jesus gives, it wasn't very good. The very best we can do in the world is nothing compared to what He does for us, in us, and through us. He came not only to give us life, but life more abundantly.

Nicodemus, a Pharisee, came to Jesus by night, asking how to be saved. Jesus said that he must be born again, meaning he must be born of water (of the flesh) and of the Spirit in order to enter the kingdom of heaven. Again, this is like the symbol of water turned to wine. Our fleshly, earthly life (being born of water) turned to a spiritual life in Him (born again into the body of Christ). Communion reminds us that we are born again and made new because of what He has done.

Jesus, thank You for giving us the Holy Spirit and calling us to be Your bride. We recognize that You paid the price with Your body and blood to cleanse us from our sins and give us new life. Amen.

For further study: Matthew 3:1–12, 23:25–26; John 2:1–11, 3:1–36, 10:10.

FEBRUARY 3

For the Joy Set Before Him

> Looking unto Jesus, the author and finisher of our faith, who for the joy that was set before Him endured the cross, despising the shame, and has sat down at the right hand of the throne of God. (Hebrews 12:2)

JESUS ENDURED THE physical and mental abuse and the shame of the cross because He looked ahead to a greater joy. The shame of the cross meant nothing to Him compared to the greatness to come. So what was that joy? Was it His reuniting with the Father and Holy Spirit in heaven? No! If His greatest joy was to be in heaven with the other members of the Trinity, He never would have left it in the first place.

The purpose of the cross was to pay the price to redeem us from our sins; therefore, the joy that Jesus kept before His eyes in His time of trial was our salvation. It was for the other thief on the cross. You know the one—the thief who said, *"Lord, remember me when You come into Your kingdom"* (Luke 23:42). It was for Peter, who returned to Jesus despite denying Him three times. It was for Mary Magdalene. It was for Saul, who would become Paul, the great apostle. It was for the Jews and the Greeks who would come to believe on Him. His joy was for all who would believe because of the testimony of His disciples, both near and far off. It was for you, and it was for me.

The Bible says there is great joy in the presence of the angels when even one sinner repents and turns to Him. Who is in the presence of the angels? The redeemed already in heaven, certainly, but also the Father, the Son, and the Holy Spirit. God rejoices and sings over us.

The neat thing about joy is that it's not dependent on circumstances. Jesus had great joy in the midst of His greatest trial. The disciples also endured great trials but had great joy in seeing others coming to know Christ. In 1 John, John tells us that if we fellowship with each other and with God, it will bring joy to all. Jesus said that if we keep His commands, we will abide in His love. His joy will be in us, and our joy will be full. He loved us enough to endure the cross and lay down His life for us. I don't find it surprising that the Greek word in the New Testament for giving thanks has its roots in the word for rejoicing. We rejoice in His sacrifice for us and we give thanks, as He also looked to the joy of our salvation and gave thanks as He broke the bread and poured the wine.

> *Jesus, You are indeed our example. You showed us that it is possible to endure all kinds of circumstances when we keep the perspective of eternity in mind. You were able to endure the cross by thinking of us. We recognize that You paid the price for our salvation, and we rejoice. Amen.*

For further study: Zephaniah 3:17; Luke 15:10, 23:39–43; John 15:10–12; Philippians 2:1–4; 1 John 1:1–4.

FEBRUARY 4
Giving Our All

So He called His disciples to Himself and said to them, "Assuredly, I say to you that this poor widow has put in more than all those who have given to the treasury; for they all put in out of their abundance, but she out of her poverty put in all that she had, her whole livelihood." (Mark 12:43–44)

ONE DAY, JESUS sat by the temple and watched what people put into the treasury. In North America, we like our offerings to be a private matter, but in that time and culture, it was very public. Anyone could see and hear what people were giving. The rich could make a show of the great sums they gave. This poor widow comes along with her two mites—mere pennies. Her head is cast down and she walks furtively, almost embarrassed that she has such a small offering. Others might look on her with scorn. I'm sure she sees Jesus sitting there, watching. She's probably hoping He gets distracted and doesn't see what she puts in. But Jesus does see. In fact, He takes special notice and singles her out for special praise. The others gave what they didn't need, as a show to others, to pad their ego. She gave everything she had out of love for God. She kept nothing back.

Likewise, Jesus gave His all out of love for us. He held nothing back. He gave up His place in heaven to be born in a stable, in the lowest place on the earth. He gave His body to be broken for us so we could be healed. He gave His blood, pouring it all out, so we could be saved and have eternal life. He gave up His life so we could live and be filled with the Spirit of God. He held nothing back, and because He gave it all, God has exalted Him and given Him a name that is above every name.

As His followers, we should also give our all out of love for Him. So we must ask ourselves: Do we? Do we pray to Him only out of our abundance to show off to others, or do we cry out to Him from our poverty and need? Do we worship only when we have energy and feel like it, or do we worship at all times? Do we give Him our tithe and pat ourselves on the back for our generosity, or do we recognize that all we have received comes from Him? Do we give Him our speech and words when we're around Christians, but curse or complain when no one sees? Do we do service for others out of our abundance of time, energy, and finances, or do we do all things as unto the Lord, even when we feel impoverished in time, energy, and finances? Jesus sits up and takes notice when we give out of our poverty. This is when we give our all, not when we give out of our abundance.

> *Lord Jesus, we recognize that all we have has come from You. You also said that freely we have received, so freely we should give. Forgive us for not giving to You at all times—in abundance and in poverty. Help us to follow Your example in our love for one another. Amen.*

For further study: Matthew 10:8; Mark 12:41–44; Luke 2:8–14; Philippians 2:5–16.

FEBRUARY 5
Walking on Water

> But when he saw that the wind was boisterous, he was afraid; and beginning to sink he cried out, saying, "Lord, save me!" And immediately Jesus stretched out His hand and caught him, and said to him, "O you of little faith, why did you doubt?" (Matthew 14:30–31)

JESUS SENT HIS disciples away in a boat while He went off by Himself to pray. In the dark of the night, He saw them in the middle of the lake, struggling to row against a contrary wind. He went to them, walking on the water.

When the disciples saw Him, they were afraid and thought they were seeing a ghost. Jesus identified Himself, and Peter said, "Lord, if it's You, command me to come to You on the water." Of course, Jesus can't say, "It's not Me; don't come." He could only say one thing in response to Peter's statement: "Come."

Peter starts out okay. He walks on water toward Jesus! But when he takes his eyes off Jesus and starts looking at the waves, he starts to sink. Peter cries out for help, and instantly Jesus reaches out and saves him. Together they get in the boat, and all kneel and worship Him. The storm stops, and they reach their destination.

Don't you just love Peter? His audacity! And his humanity! Would you or I have walked on water, or would we have stayed in the relative safety of the boat? We've been on stormy seas. How many times have we been swamped by life's trials, or had experiences that are contrary to the direction we want to go? We can be overpowered by waves of shame, sickness, depression, or pain. Jesus says, "I see what you're going through, and I am here." We cry out in our heart, "Jesus, are You really here in my trial? Is it really You? Can I come to You in this storm?" And Jesus says, "Come."

If we keep our eyes on Him, we rise above, but take our eyes off Him and put them on the stormy sea and we begin to sink under the waves. Now here's the great news—even if we start to sink, we cry to Him and immediately He reaches out and catches us. He doesn't let us down, even though it may be our own doing that we're out of the boat. He could calm the storm, but He would rather see us grow in faith by walking on the water. He can always calm the storm later. We need not fear sinking, or not reaching our destination, when Jesus holds our hand and keeps our head above the water.

When we were sinking in the depth of our sin, Jesus came. Immediately when we called to Him, He stretched out His arms and saved us. We remember with the symbols of the bread and the wine that He gave His body and blood for us so that we could be saved from our sins. When storms of shame come our way, He still enables us to walk on the water of His grace!

> *Jesus, thank You for saving us from ourselves. You stretched out Your arms on the cross and shed Your blood so that we would be forgiven of our sins and free from the law of sin and death. Remind us always to keep our eyes fixed on You and not on the waves. Amen.*

For further study: Matthew 14:22–33; Mark 6:45–52; John 6:15–21.

FEBRUARY 6
A Certain Man Fell Among Thieves

And he said, "He who showed mercy on him." Then Jesus said to him, "Go and do likewise."
(Luke 10:37)

A LAWYER WHO knew he needed to love God with all his heart, and love his neighbor as himself, wanted to justify his unloving acts. Loving your neighbor surely couldn't mean loving everyone, so he asked Jesus to tell him just who was his neighbor. Jesus responded with the parable of the good Samaritan.

A man walking along the road falls among thieves. They strip him of his clothing, rob him, beat him, and leave him for dead. The religious people come by and see the wounded man but cross to the other side of the road. They don't want to get involved; after all, it's none of their business. A man from Samaria comes by and has compassion on the injured man. He helps the man, takes him to shelter, and pays the debts incurred. The Samaritans were enemies of the Jews. Jesus was telling the lawyer that everyone is your neighbor and has a claim on your love, even your enemies.

Religion without the love of Christ causes us to relate to others like the priest and the Levite in the story. We want to be separate and uncontaminated by the world, so we shun others and cross to the other side of the road of life. Even though those people have been broken and wounded, we feel it's none of our business. Jesus is like that good Samaritan. He came to us to heal us even while we were yet sinners and enemies of the gospel. He paid our debts, poured the oil of the Spirit on our wounds, carried us to shelter, and brought us life.

Jesus is like the good Samaritan, but He's also like the man who fell among thieves. He gave His body to be beaten. He was robbed of His dignity and the honor due Him. He was crucified among thieves. Our sins were the tool that broke Him, so we are the thieves that beat Him. Yet when He was reviled, He didn't revile in return. He was falsely accused yet did not insist on His rights. He was crucified, yet He prayed for His torturers. Jesus was our example of how to behave when we feel like we're the wounded man who was abused by thieves, because once we were the thieves who wounded Jesus, but He still reached out to us with love.

Let's take it even one step further. What if we were the good Samaritan who saw Jesus beaten and abused by the thieves of sin. How could we go to Him and bind His wounds? He walked on the earth as a man two thousand years ago. We can't reach out to Him to care for His wounds. Or can we? Jesus said that whenever we feed the hungry, clothe the naked, take in a stranger, visit the sick, or go to those in prison, that we do it to Him. Let's do just that—serve the wounded among us as if they were Jesus.

Jesus, thank You for paying our sin debt. Help us to be merciful just as You are merciful. Amen.

For further study: Matthew 25:40–45, 26:48–50; Mark 14:53–61; Luke 10:25–37, 23:34; 1 Peter 2:23–24.

FEBRUARY 7
His Banner over Us Is Love

He brought me to the banqueting house, and his banner over me was love. (Song of Solomon 2:4)

THE BOOK OF the Song of Solomon is a beautiful love story between a Shulamite woman and her beloved, and it's an analogy of Jesus and His bride, the Church. In chapter two, the Shulamite says that her beloved brought her to the banqueting table. Literally, this translates as "house of wine." This indicates more than a feast that meets your physical hunger but rather being intoxicated with His love. She is so overcome by love that it's evident to all around her, like a banner flying high. The whole world has changed for her because of his love.

Do you remember when you first gave your heart to Jesus? Maybe you couldn't stop singing praises to Him. People were easier to love. The whole world changed in your eyes because you were overcome and intoxicated with His love.

Jesus commended the Church at Ephesus for their works and service. They had studied the Scriptures, persevered in the faith, and labored in His name without giving up or becoming weary. They had taken a stand for moral righteousness. They sounded like a pretty healthy church and a good group of Christians. Then Jesus dropped the bombshell! He said that they had left their first love. Where once they were intoxicated with love for Christ, now they were just doing the work out of habit, or duty. Jesus said that unless they repented, the Spirit would no longer shine in their lives. He would remove their lampstand, and they would no longer have an effect or be important in the kingdom. All their good works and deeds, unless they were done out of a heart of love for Him, wouldn't count for much.

Are we walking the walk and talking the talk just because it's what we do, or because we love God with all our heart, soul, mind, and strength? Do we sing praise to Him out of love, or because everyone else is singing? Are we doing good deeds because we love Jesus and want to do what would please Him, or for some sort of recognition or self-satisfaction? Do we study the Word just to prepare the next lesson, or because we love His Word and how Jesus is expressed in it? Have we left our first love? Are we no longer intoxicated by the wine of His love? If we have left our first love, we will find it again at the foot of the cross, recognizing in the sacrifice of His body and blood how much He loves us.

Jesus, we remember what You did at the cross, and we come to You with heartfelt remembrance of the day we fell in love with You. Forgive us for any deed we have done that was not out of love for You. Intoxicate us again with Your love and fill us anew with Your Spirit, that we might shine in Your kingdom and not walk in darkness. Amen.

For further study: Deuteronomy 6:5; Revelation 2:1–7.

FEBRUARY 8
Spiritual Leprosy

Therefore strengthen the hands which hang down, and the feeble knees, and make straight paths for your feet, so that what is lame may not be dislocated, but rather be healed. (Hebrews 12:12–13)

BIBLICALLY, "LEPER" REFERS to persons afflicted with various diseases, including the specific disease of leprosy. Leprosy is a chronic and disfiguring bacterial infection caused by a type of bacteria called *Mycobacterium*. These bacteria can cause lumps or granulomas in any tissue, but they have a predilection for the nervous system. When they affect the nerves, people lose feeling to the part of the body served by that nerve. Because they lack feeling, they don't feel pain. This means that they won't notice when that part of the body is injured or diseased. The end result is the loss of that part of the body due to infection and injury that is left unattended to. The original disease isn't found in the part that was lost but in the part of the body that remains.

Let's give some thought to what I call spiritual leprosy. As life speeds up and gets busy, and we're pressured on every side, we risk becoming infected in a manner that we no longer feel the pain or injury in other members of the body. As a result, we don't tend to them or try to bring healing or restoration. Eventually, the wounded person might even lose faith, but the primary disease remains in the body of Christ collectively.

This isn't to say that we don't need people in the body with a high pain tolerance. They may seem cold or heartless, but they can push others who are in pain to overcome difficulties and get the job done. In some cases, pushing through the pain is the path to healing. At other times, we need those in the body who are more sensitive to pain. They may appear to others to be whiners or complainers, but they can see where the hurting people are so that the body of Christ can reach out to them and bring healing. Being part of a healthy body is all about recognizing each other, our strengths *and* our weaknesses. It's about caring for one another and trying to bring healing to those parts that are injured and hurting.

In 1 Corinthians 11, Paul tells the Corinthians that many of them are weak, sick, or have even died prematurely because they're concerned only about themselves instead of looking to the needs of the body as a whole. He exhorts them to examine themselves. If we judge ourselves, we won't be judged. Paul says that to take communion in an unworthy manner is to be guilty of the body and blood of the Lord; however, to eat and drink worthily is to proclaim the Lord's death and all He did for us. There is provision for healing in partaking of communion—for ourselves individually and for the body of Christ as a whole. So let's examine ourselves. Have we deadened the feelings in our soul to the needs of the body?

> *Holy Spirit, reveal to us where we've failed to recognize the needs of others. Forgive us for being self-centered and unfeeling. Heal us, Lord, individually and corporately. Amen.*

For further study: 1 Corinthians 11:28, 12:12–31; Philippians 2:4.

FEBRUARY 9
The Five Love Languages— Spending Time Together

As the Father loved Me, I also have loved you; abide in My love. (John 15:9)

GARY CHAPMAN WROTE a book called *The 5 Love Languages*. His premise is that different things say "I love you" to different people. If you're not speaking their language, then they don't understand what you're saying. The five languages are: spending time with one another, words of affirmation, acts of service, giving of gifts, and touch. It makes sense to think that Jesus would speak all five languages fluently as the Creator and God of the universe. Let's look at these one at a time.

Jesus spent a lot of time with His disciples. For three and a half years, while He walked physically on the earth, He poured out His life and teachings to them. They walked together, ate together, and communed with one another as He taught them the Word of God. Just before His final supper with them, He spoke of how He desired to spend time with them and impart His final teachings to them.

Their final supper together was an intimate time, with John resting his head on Jesus's chest, and Jesus taking time to serve them by washing their feet. During His physical life on earth, He demonstrated His willingness to spend time with those who were His own. But what about after His death and resurrection?

Jesus told His disciples that it was expedient that He die, because then God would come and make His home in us. In the Great Commission, He said *"lo, I am with you always, even to the end of the age"* (Matthew 28:20b). In several places in the Bible, God says that He will never leave us or forsake us. This is quite the promise—a holy God choosing to live in sinful people.

When Jesus was physically present on the earth, He spent time with those He loved, but after His death, His desire and ability to spend time with us didn't end. It just changed from a physical presence to a spiritual one. His few short years incarnate on the earth foreshadowed the spiritual truth that He would be with us always. Likewise, the physical action of eating bread and drinking wine as we celebrate communion points toward His spiritual presence with us.

On the shores of the Sea of Galilee at Capernaum, Jesus tried to explain this. He spoke of eating His flesh and drinking His blood, meaning we would spiritually abide with Him and He with us, but the people could only think of physically eating His flesh and drinking His blood, and they were offended. Many left Him after that and followed Him no longer. This time of communion, when we partake of the bread and wine, is to remind us of the spiritual truth: He has made His home in and with us, and by His sacrifice imparts to us His righteousness.

Jesus, thank You for loving us, making Your home with us, and being with us always. Amen.

For further study: Deuteronomy 31:6–8; Joshua 1:9; Matthew 28:18–20; Luke 22:15–20; John 6:56, 13:1–30, 14:16–18, 16:7.

FEBRUARY 10
Five Love Languages—Words of Affirmation

And the Word became flesh and dwelt among us, and we beheld His glory, the glory as the only begotten of the Father, full of grace and truth. (John 1:14)

DR. GARY CHAPMAN, in his book *The 5 Love Languages*, reminds us that showing our love with words of affirmation means much more than just saying "I love you." Words are powerful. They can encourage or discourage, build up or tear down, bring healing or cause deep wounds. The Bible says that death and life are in the power of the tongue. A good word, spoken in the right time, can inspire, even stimulate people to greatness, and can cause others to be all they can be.

Dr. Chapman speaks of affirming words being ones that think of the other person, that are kind, that are requests made with humility rather than demands. They communicate that the other is loved and appreciated. They are words that don't hold the past against people but instead extend forgiveness. They are spoken truthfully, with no intent to deceive or coerce.

The world was created by God's spoken word. Jesus Himself is the Word of God made flesh, as it says in the first chapter of John. Likewise, Jesus's words show that it's His kindness that leads us to repentance. Jesus, the Word of God, humbled Himself, and He stands at the door, requesting to come in. He doesn't force Himself on us. His words tell of His love and His willingness to sacrifice Himself for us. They tell us that He forgives us, and He has chosen to forget our past sins. His words are truth, with no deception in them, and we know they are true because they were backed up with the actions of love. He inspires us to want to hear Him say at the end of the age, "Well done, thou good and faithful servant." The Word of God has inspired millions of people to greatness. People have laid down their lives for others based on His Word. We are changed when His Word enters our hearts.

As we look today at the bread and the wine, we recognize that without the words that Jesus taught as He broke the bread and passed the cup, communion wouldn't have the same meaning. Imagine if He just gave them the bread and said nothing. The disciples would think it was nice of Him to pass the food along, but Jesus took it further. He explained that the bread and wine would be a memory cue for us to remember that He loves us, that He allowed His body to be broken to provide for our healing. He was going to shed His blood as the perfect sacrifice so we could be forgiven and have eternal life. Then He backed up these words with His actions. It wasn't just empty talk but true words of love.

> *We bless You, Jesus, for giving us Your Word and the sacrament of communion as a reminder of Your deep and sacrificial love for us. You laid down Your life so we can live. Thank You. Amen.*

For further study: Genesis 1:1–31; Psalm 103:12–13; Proverbs 4:20–22, 18:21; Matthew 25:20–21; Luke 22:19–20; John 1:1–4; Romans 2:4, 10:8–10; Hebrews 6:17–19; Revelation 3:20.

FEBRUARY 11
The Five Love Languages—Giving Gifts

For the wages of sin is death, but the gift of God is eternal life in Christ Jesus our Lord. (Romans 6:23)

A GIFT IS the act of freely and willingly transferring ownership of something to another person or entity. Jesus is the ultimate gift-giver.

What can we say of a God—the God of the universe, creator of all—who would humble Himself, giving up His rights as God, to become a man? And not just any man, but one who would lay down His life to give sinners the gift of eternal life. He took what He possessed—holiness and a relationship with God the Father and the Holy Spirit—and freely made the way to give this to us.

His gift enabled us to be sanctified—His holiness was imparted to us.

His gift enabled us to be reconciled—He gave us the ability to have a relationship and communion with God Himself.

He gave us His righteousness—He gave us the gift to be in right standing with God.

He gave us justification—He was without sin, and His gift enables us to be justified with God, as if we also were without sin.

God demonstrated His great love for us in that while we were yet sinners, Christ died for us.

If all Jesus gave us was the gift of salvation and reconciliation with God, that would have been more than enough, but He gave even more. He gives us physical and emotional healing. He provides for us. He sets the captive free. He gives us the Holy Spirit. He gives us wisdom. He gives peace. He gives us talents and abilities to help and teach others. He gives us His Word. He meets all our needs. Jesus told His followers that even they knew how to give good gifts to their children. If a child asked a father for bread, the father wouldn't give him a stone, so how much more does the heavenly Father know how to give good gifts to His children.

As He sat at the table with His disciples, Jesus gave them bread and wine to serve as a reminder that He is the greatest gift-giver of all. He paid the price by His sacrifice—the gift of His very life—to give us the gift of eternal life.

> *Jesus, we thank You for all the great gifts You have given to demonstrate Your great love for us. We remember that You have made us Your righteousness so that we can be reconciled to God the Father. We remember all You have given, and we are forever grateful. Amen.*

For further study: Psalm 84:11; Isaiah 61:1–3; Jeremiah 33:6; Matthew 6:33; Luke 11:11–13; John 1:14, 3:16, 14:25–27; Romans 5:9–21; 2 Thessalonians 2:13; James 1:5, 17; 1 Peter 4:10–11.

FEBRUARY 12
The Five Love Languages—Acts of Service

You call Me Teacher and Lord, and you say well, for so I am. If I then, your Lord and Teacher, have washed your feet, you also ought to wash one another's feet. For I have given you an example, that you should do as I have done to you. (John 13:13–15)

ONE OF THE five love languages mentioned by Gary Chapman is acts of service. In other words, doing things for other people to show you love them. Jesus demonstrated His love in many ways. The entire book of Mark shows Jesus as a servant. There is one very notable demonstration Jesus gave of this principle.

On the same night Jesus was betrayed, when He knew this was His last chance to impart instruction to His disciples, He chose to give them an example of acts of service. In the Middle East in the first century, people wore sandals and gathered dust and dirt from the road on their feet. It was customary to give people a basin of water and towel to wash the dust from their feet, or better yet, a servant would come and do this menial labor. It wouldn't be the important servant who would do this job, but the least of all the servants. I can imagine it was not a welcome task. Jesus, however, took off His robes of a rabbi, put the towel of a servant on His waist, and humbled Himself to wash the feet of His disciples. He explained to them that He was setting the example. Love is demonstrated by the things we do for one another. He was about to perform the ultimate act of service in laying down His life, yet He took a moment to demonstrate to His followers that they could do acts of service for one another in even small and menial jobs.

When we look around at the Christian community, sometimes we see an interesting phenomenon. Someone will bake special cakes and tarts for a ladies meeting, but woe to the family member who dares to try one. Someone will usher and lovingly guide a stranger to their seat, but they'll tell a spouse to hurry up as they keep the car running, and they won't bother to help them get into the car. We'll serve at the soup kitchen and fight at home over who does the dishes. We seem to be able to do all kinds of acts of service for people we barely know, but we expect our family to wait on us as we put our feet up to watch TV. It was significant that Jesus gave this demonstration to His friends. I think He was definitely saying that we need to serve strangers, but He was also telling us not to forget our friends and family. This Scripture comes to mind: *"These you ought to have done, without leaving the others undone"* (Matthew 23:23).

Jesus is indeed our example. He laid down His life for us while we were still His enemies, but He also called us His friends. He laid down His life for His friends. Let us remember Him and do likewise.

Jesus, we remember that You laid down Your life for us in the ultimate act of service, demonstrating Your great love for us. Help us to lay down our lives for one another. Amen.

For further study: John 13:1–17.

FEBRUARY 13
The Five Love Languages—Touch

Then He put out His hand and touched him, saying, "I am willing; be cleansed." Immediately the leprosy left him. (Luke 5:13)

THE FIFTH LOVE language discussed in Gary Chapman's book is touch. Jesus was remarkable in how He touched people when He walked the earth. When the disciples tried to stop children from coming to Jesus, He rebuked them and instead let the children approach. He then touched them and blessed them. He touched Peter's mother-in-law and healed her. He touched blind eyes. He grabbed Peter by the hand when Peter sank below the waves, and He let John lean upon His breast as they sat at the table and ate. But the most amazing account of touch in the Bible is the story of the leper who came and fell at His feet and said, *"Lord, if you are willing, You can make me clean"* (Luke 5:12).

Leprosy is a contagious disease. Someone with leprosy was a social pariah, an outcast. Even today we use the word "leper" to refer to someone who is shunned socially for whatever reason. A leper in Bible days wasn't allowed to touch people. They had to keep their distance from others and walk around crying out, "Unclean, unclean," lest anyone inadvertently bump into them. They were sick with a horrible disease but also plagued by a lack of love and human touch. Yet when a leper cries to Jesus, Christ's first move is to reach out and touch him. Before the leper was cleansed, Jesus touched him. Before Jesus even spoke a word, His touch reached out and said "I love you."

Jesus no longer walks physically on the earth, so how are we to feel His loving touch now? Many people overcome with emotion will say "He touched me," because although Jesus hasn't touched us physically, He has touched us emotionally in our very soul and spirit. This is accurate and good, but when Jesus sat with His disciples at the Last Supper, He took it a step further. He took the bread and blessed it and broke it, and said "This is my body; do this in remembrance of Me." We are to remember the body of Christ.

Paul reminds us in his teaching on communion in 1 Corinthians 10–12 that we collectively are the body of Christ. Communion is about recognizing Jesus's sacrifice of His body and blood for our salvation, but it's also about remembering that we are all now part of the same body. We can show love to one another in many different ways: a gentle touch on the arm, a hug, the shaking of hands in greeting, and always being sensitive to the other person. The key here is putting the needs of others ahead of our own, and appropriate touch can bless people and let them know they are part of the body and loved. Take some time this week to speak the love language of others, letting them know they are not outcasts and are welcome in the fellowship.

Jesus, we recognize Your great love for us. You touched us in the very center of our being. You gave Your life for us. Help us to put others' needs above our own and to love them like You love us. Amen.

For further study: Matthew 8:14–15, 14:22–32, 19:13–15, 20:32–34; Mark 1:40–42; John 13:23.

FEBRUARY 14
Be My Valentine

The Lord has appeared of old to me, saying: "Yes, I have loved you with an everlasting love; therefore with lovingkindness I have drawn you." (Jeremiah 31:3)

SAINT VALENTINE WAS a priest who was martyred for aiding persecuted Christians. It's said he also married Christian couples who were in love, which at the time was illegal. There are also stories that he prayed for a blind girl to receive her sight. God answered that prayer, and when the girl was healed, her family all became Christians. He was killed for his faith on February 14, AD 269 by Claudius Gothicus. It's believed that just before he was martyred, he wrote a letter to the girl, signing it "from your Valentine."

Just over two hundred years later, in AD 496, Pope Gelasius I declared February 14 a feast day for Saint Valentine. This is observed by the Catholic, Anglican, and Lutheran traditions. Because of that history, February 14 is often celebrated as a day of love and devotion. People write cards, hoping to develop a romantic relationship by asking the receiver to "be their valentine." There are pictures everywhere of hearts with an arrow through them, as if they'd been struck by Cupid's arrow. Restaurants are sold out as couples honor their "valentine" with a special meal. Flowers are purchased, candies and chocolates given, and some people even get on their knees in a proposal of marriage to their beloved.

Everywhere you turn, there are reminders of romantic love. For those without a partner, these reminders can be heartbreaking, making them feel unworthy of love. We need to remember that there is more than one kind of love. Romantic love is all about desire and getting those desires satisfied. In some ways, it's more about the lover than the beloved. True love is all about sacrifice, about wanting to see the beloved become all they can be. It's about wanting to see eyes blinded by the world beholding the love of God. True love is more about the beloved than the lover. Saint Valentine understood this love.

True love is about the spear that pierced the heart of Jesus, causing His blood to flow down the cross. He laid down His life so we could be saved. He calls us His beloved and wants us healed in body, soul, and spirit, able to spend all eternity with Him in the wonder and beauty of heaven. Everywhere we turn we see the gifts He gives us. As His body was broken and bleeding, His Spirit cried out, "Be My Valentine. Give Me your heart. Love Me like I love you." His Spirit still cries out today, calling all to come to salvation.

> *Jesus, we are so amazed by Your love. You demonstrated Your great love for us when You willingly laid down Your life so we might live. We choose to respond to Your love and accept it. Fill us completely with Your love. Amen.*

For further study: Hosea 2:23; John 3:16, 10:10, 15:12–17, 19:32–34; Romans 9:25; 1 Timothy 2:4; 1 John 3:16, 4:7–21.

FEBRUARY 15
God's Vineyard

> Now at vintage-time he sent a servant to the vinedressers, that they might give him some of the fruit of the vineyard. But the vinedressers beat him and sent him away empty-handed. (Luke 20:10)

JESUS SPOKE A parable about a man who planted a vineyard. He prepared everything that was needed and put it in the charge of others while he went to a far country. When the time came for there to be fruit, the owner of the vineyard sent servants to receive part of the harvest. Those in charge of the vineyard didn't give the requested fruit; instead, they beat some of the servants, threw stones at some, wounded some in the head, treated some shamefully, and sent them away empty-handed. Last of all, the owner of the vineyard sent his only son to the tenants. The vinedressers beat and killed the son and cast him out of the vineyard. Jesus said that the owner would come and destroy those tenants and give the vineyard to others.

Jesus spoke this parable against the Pharisees of that day. They'd been given charge of God's vineyard—the presence and gifts of the Holy Spirit. They were to bring the harvest to God by bringing the gospel to the Gentiles, but they did not. Instead, they abused God's servants and even killed the very Son of God. The vineyard and its fruit have now been put into the hands of others—that is, all of us who call ourselves Christians.

Because of Christ's sacrifice, we are now the vinedressers, but we're also the branches on the vine. As His life flows through us, the fruit of the Holy Spirit should be produced in us. The question then becomes: When God sends people to us to receive the fruit of His vineyard, do we do a better job than the first-century Pharisees did? Have we abused any of His servants? Cheated them? Have we wounded them in the head by the things we've said or done? Have we shamed others? Have we killed anyone? Do we let others taste of the fruit God develops in us, or do we send them away empty-handed?

Partaking of communion reminds us that this vineyard and the fruit of the vine have been freely given to us. Do we give to others as freely as we have been given to? By God's grace, the fruits of love, joy, peace, longsuffering, kindness, goodness, faithfulness, gentleness, and self-control can abound to all we meet. Remembering what He has done for us and where we have come from enables us to tend the vineyard with humility and grace.

> *Jesus, You broke the bread and shared it with others, reminding us that Your body was broken to bring healing to many. You passed the cup of wine to all at the table, reminding us that Your blood was shed for the salvation of many, and that the fruit of the Spirit would abound. Forgive us for any time we have been selfish and sent others away empty. Let Your fruit abound in us. Amen.*

For further study: Matthew 5:20–26, 10:7–8; Luke 20:9–18; John 15:1–17; Galatians 5:22–26.

FEBRUARY 16
Rituals

The Pharisee stood and prayed thus with himself, "God, I thank You that I am not like other men—extortioners, unjust, adulterers, or even as this tax collector. I fast twice a week; I give tithes of all that I possess." And the tax collector, standing afar off, would not so much as raise his eyes to heaven, but beat his breast, saying, "God, be merciful to me a sinner!" I tell you, this man went down to his house justified rather than the other; for everyone who exalts himself will be humbled, and he who humbles himself will be exalted. (Luke 18:11–14)

IN THE BOOK of Mark, Pilate makes the observation that the Pharisees had delivered Jesus to him out of envy. It might have been that they were envious that Jesus had so many followers, but I suspect it was more than that. Here they were tithing, fasting, praying, and strictly observing the Sabbath, yet no one was getting healed from their touch! Then along comes this man—the illegitimate son of a carpenter, who regularly broke the Sabbath law, who didn't wash His hands the prescribed way, who partied with sinners! Yet when He spoke, demons fled. The touch of His garment brought healing, and the touch of His hand raised people from the dead! How dare God honor this man over them after all they had done for Him!

The Pharisees failed to see that the ritual was only important as far as it pointed to and reflected the love of God to humanity and humanity to God. They were trying to reach God by good works, as if their good deeds were like climbing a stepladder toward God. They saw themselves towering over their fellow men, and they looked down on the rest of humanity. What they didn't notice was that the first rung on the ladder to heaven was a million miles high. If they had looked up instead of down, they would have seen that there was absolutely no way they could reach God, unless God reached down and lifted them up. Jesus came to show that was exactly what God was doing by Christ's death and resurrection—God reaching down to humans. The rituals had to flow out of that relationship, and they couldn't create the relationship.

Catholics have an interesting ritual of crossing themselves. They touch their head and then their chest, and then move their hand from one side to the other in the form of a cross. To do that just because that's what they do doesn't have much value. But if every time someone touched their head and then heart they remembered it was God coming down to us to live in our heart, and then by touching across they remembered that we are now to reach to others with the love of God, what a powerful reminder of the glory of the cross!

Likewise with Holy Communion—to just go through the motions because it's what we do doesn't have much value. But if we bless and break the bread as Jesus did, remembering God came to give His life for humanity, and then pick up the cup and drink, gratefully remembering His blood shed for our sins, it's a powerful reminder of grace and love.

Jesus, thank You for the cross and for bridging the gap so that we can be lifted to heaven. It's only through You that we are justified. We could not do it on our own. We are forever grateful. Amen.

For further study: Matthew 9:20–22, 15:1–6; Mark 15:9–10; Luke 7:11–17, 13:10–16, 14:1–6; John 6:42.

FEBRUARY 17
Flour and Oil

> But as many as received Him, to them He gave the right to become children of God, to those who believe in His name. (John 1:12)

WHEN JESUS ATE the Passover meal with His disciples, they were eating unleavened bread. There aren't many ingredients in unleavened bread. It's made up mainly of flour and oil. This was all the widow of Zarephath had when Elijah the prophet was sent to her. There was a severe drought and famine in the land, and God told Elijah that He'd commanded a widow to provide for him. When Elijah entered the city, he saw her gathering sticks to make a fire. He asked her for some water and a small cake of bread. She told him that all she had was a small jar of flour and a jug of oil. She was about to make the last supper she could for her and her son, and then they would die of hunger.

Elijah told her to bring him a cake first and then make some for her family, and God would make sure the flour and oil would last to the end of the drought. Every day, this is what she did, and the flour and oil fed all three of them for many days. Every day she must have wondered if she'd scrape her hand around the bottom of the jar and find no flour. Would she tip the jug and no oil would come out? Would this be the day it all stopped? Yet every day, there was enough for another day. She had received the man of God and took him at His word, and she and her family were saved from death.

Jesus Himself is the seed that was beaten and crushed, just like the wheat is beaten and crushed to make flour. The night of the Last Supper, He was in the Garden of Gethsemane—the Oil Press—where the pressure was so intense He sweat drops of blood. He was later pierced and took the fire of Hell for us. He was the unleavened bread that was broken for our sins.

Just like the widow of Zarephath, those who receive Jesus and take Him at His word find there is enough grace for the day and to stretch back to cover our brokenness from our very conception to the day we leave this earth. His supply never runs dry. Maybe some days we feel like we're scraping the bottom of the barrel, or maybe we feel like today His grace will run out and it will all end, yet we find there is grace enough for another day. We're saved from our sins and the death sin brings. And we have life, and life more abundantly.

Jesus says in Luke that there were many widows in Elijah's day, but not all were saved. So also there are many today who suffer spiritual drought and famine, but only those who receive Jesus into their hearts find life and all their heart desires. If you've never received Jesus, don't wait until there's nothing left in your soul. If you have received Him, remember that He is enough. He provides enough grace for today, no matter how intense the spiritual famine is around us.

Thank You, Lord, for Your grace that is more than enough and never runs dry. Amen.

For further study: 1 Kings 17:1–16; Luke 4:25–26, 22:39–46; John 10:10; 2 Corinthians 12:7–10; Ephesians 2:4–7.

FEBRUARY 18
Crumbs from the Feast

For as often as you eat this bread and drink this cup, you proclaim the Lord's death till He comes. (1 Corinthians 11:26)

IN MATTHEW 15, we learn about a Gentile woman seeking healing for her daughter. She cried out after Jesus, pleading with Him to help her. Jesus said not a word. He knew that the gospel is for all, and His disciples will be charged with taking the gospel to all nations, but He didn't say a thing. Given that He was such a good teacher, I can only imagine that He was waiting to see if His disciples would understand the higher call to the whole world. Was He waiting for them to say "Jesus, can't You help her?" If so, He must have sighed when instead they came and said to Him, "Jesus, send her away. She's bothering us."

Jesus turned to her and said, "It's not right to take the children's bread and throw it to the little dogs." This sounds like He wasn't going to help her, but I can imagine Him smiling as He saw that she understood. He is indeed the bread of life for all nations. He knew it, and she knew it, but it wasn't quite the right time. The disciples needed to know it. They needed to take Him, the bread of life, and give it out to the rest of the world, but they didn't yet understand.

She got it, though, and replied that even the dogs eat the crumbs that fall from the children's table. She knew her biggest need was a mere crumb of the bread within Him. Even if the children weren't ready to hand out the bread to the nations, the miracles couldn't help but happen all around them as mere crumbs falling from the table of the Lord.

Just like this woman received her miracle because of her faith, we also can bring our biggest need to the Savior and know the answer is a mere crumb falling from the table. He will not run out of ability or concern for us. He is more than enough.

The crumbs that fall from the Lord's table are amazing, but they have a bigger significance. The evidence of the crumbs points to the fact that there is a feast! And so it is for us. Healing and miracles are only small things to point to the greater miracle of God becoming man and dying for us. His shed blood paid the price for the sins of the world. He is the bread that was broken to bring life to the world. His blood was the wine poured out for our salvation. As we partake of communion, we remind ourselves of His sacrifice. We can welcome and rejoice in the crumbs, but even more so, we rejoice because we're invited to sit at the table and partake of the feast. Let us rejoice and give thanks as we remember all He has done for us.

Lord Jesus, today, we remember all You have done. You have provided for us healing, health, provision, and help, and we bring those needs before You. Even more than that, we remember and thank You for preparing Your table and providing for us the feast of salvation. Your blood has paid the price for our sins so that we can live with You in eternity. We worship You. Amen.

For further study: Isaiah 25:6–9; Matthew 15:21–28, 26:26–29; Luke 10:17–20; John 6:35; Revelation 19:9.

FEBRUARY 19
Immanuel

"Behold, the virgin shall be with child, and bear a Son, and they shall call His name Immanuel," which is translated, "God with us." (Matthew 1:23)

LET'S TAKE OUR imagination on a little tour and pretend that we're entrepreneurs. We make a little creature, give it a home, and provide food and everything it needs, but something goes wrong with our creation. These little beings start destroying the home we gave them and also eating each other. What would you do? What if the only way you could get these little creatures to understand what you really wanted for them was to give up everything you are and become one of them. And you'll not only become one of them, but you'll let some of them attack and kill you! I can't imagine doing that. I suspect most of us would just destroy the whole mess. But not God.

It's a testament to how loved we are by God that Jesus would give up His privilege as God the Son and become a man. He would be born in the lowest place on the earth, where parts of the land are even below sea level. He would humble Himself and be born a helpless infant, born of an ordinary young girl, in an ordinary family. He would be born under a shadow of a reputation of sin. How tongues must have wagged: "Mary was pregnant before they were married! Joseph didn't denounce her. He must be the father and a sinner too! How shameful!"

Jesus, the Son of God, was born in a stable and laid in a manger. He was in submission to His parents, even though He was the creator of all. He lived as a boy, having to grow physically and spiritually. He grew to a man, and even though He was equal with God, He became a servant, and not just any servant but a bond servant. This is a slave who chooses to be a slave because of love. He was obedient to that call and purpose even unto a brutal death on the cross. It's incredible that God would become a man to lift humans out of our pit of sin and raise us up with Him. God with us. Immanuel. Son of God, yet Son of Man, and so able to pay the price for sin with His perfect blood.

Philippians 2:5–11 reminds us that He is our example of humble submission. We also are to serve one another in love. Today as we partake of communion, let's remember that God humbled Himself to become a servant of humanity, and we also should serve one another out of love for God.

Jesus, we overflow in gratitude for all You have done. It's incredible that God would become a man, yet that's what You did, humbling Yourself to save us. Help us to be humble one to another, serving one another in love for You and all You have done for us. Amen.

For further study: Matthew 1:18; Luke 2:51–52; John 6:42; Galatians 5:13–14; Philippians 2:1–11.

FEBRUARY 20
He Makes All Things New

> Therefore, if anyone is in Christ, he is a new creation; old things have passed away; behold, all things have become new. (2 Corinthians 5:17)

TO CREATE IS to cause something that did not exist before to come into existence. God tells us in the book of Genesis that in the beginning, He spoke His Word and the world was created. His very Word caused that which did not exist before to come into existence. The Gospel of John tells us that Jesus Christ is the Word of God become flesh who dwelt among us. All those who receive Him become the children of God. He has spoken into our darkness and created light in us. By the Word of God, we become a new creation. We have become something new that never existed before.

This is analogous to the metamorphosis of a caterpillar. Cartoons may depict a caterpillar just sprouting wings to become a butterfly, but that's not what happens in the cocoon. A butterfly has an entirely different structure and body shape from a caterpillar. It has done much more than just grow wings. The entire caterpillar must be broken down and destroyed and then remodeled into its true form. It must be hard for the caterpillar to see what it's becoming when wrapped in the cocoon. Would it even recognize itself if it looked in the mirror after it emerges a beautiful butterfly?

Here we are, wrapped in this cocoon of flesh. We're no longer the lowly worms we once were, but we sometimes have trouble seeing the new creation we have become. Do we see who we are in Christ? When we look into the mirror of God's Word, do we see the righteousness of God? Do we see ourselves holy and without blame? Do we see the treasure and beauty He has placed in us? Do we see ourselves truly forgiven, or do we still beat ourselves up for the sins of our past? Do we see how we were dead in trespasses and sins, but now we are made alive in newness of life, flying on wings of the Spirit and raised up in heavenly places with Him? Do we see ourselves clothed in the glory of God? Do we see the beautiful bride walking down the aisle to her beloved?

We are now so much more than the lowly sinners we once were. We are now children of God because of His love and sacrifice for us.

> *Jesus, as we partake of the bread and the wine, we remember that You redeemed us from our old life and made us a new creation, by faith in Your name. We are dead to sin and alive with You. Help us to be a witness to others, and to do the works befitting who we are in You. Amen.*

For further study: Isaiah 61:10; John 1:1–13; Romans 12:5; 2 Corinthians 5:21; Ephesians 2:4–10, 5:25–27; Hebrews 11:3.

FEBRUARY 21
On the Night He Was Betrayed

> For I received from the Lord that which I also delivered to you: that the Lord Jesus on the same night in which He was betrayed took bread; and when He had given thanks, He broke it and said, "Take, eat; this is My body which is broken for you; do this in remembrance of Me." (1 Corinthians 11:23–24)

JESUS KNEW THAT the cross, torture, and death lay before Him, and that all would forsake Him; however, He paused to give thanks. He wasn't bitter or angry. He remained thankful in spite of the trial ahead. In fact, when Judas came to betray Him, Jesus still called him friend. He didn't curse Judas, or rant and rave. He didn't resent His disciples for abandoning Him in His hour of greatest need.

How many times have we been betrayed? How many times have people let us down? When that happened, were you bitter or angry? Maybe you were frustrated or confused. You likely felt rejected. Maybe someone even abused you and betrayed you with a kiss. This sign that should show love was used to betray Jesus into a situation of abuse and torture. What worse sign of betrayal could there be, especially coming from a friend? Indeed, only someone close to us can truly betray us and let us down. We don't have the same expectations of love or support from a stranger or enemy. The wounds from an enemy are painful but don't cut as deeply as those from a friend.

When we are betrayed or disappointed by those close to us, we tend to hold on to the hurt and pain. It's hard to let go of the bitterness. The wounds on our soul are a constant reminder of the harm done to us. Yet Jesus calls us to forgive others as He has forgiven us. He calls us to let go of the bitterness and allow Him to heal the wounds as only He can, since He also bears the scars of the ultimate betrayal. He knew the pain and the wounds that awaited Him, yet He chose to treat Judas with respect and call him friend.

Let's pause to examine ourselves. Has anyone hurt us by betrayal, disappointment, abuse, or abandonment? If so, choose now to take a moment to thank God that Jesus bears the scars of those wounds, and we don't have to carry them any longer. We also must ask ourselves if we have let others down or betrayed them. If so, now is the time to repent. He chose to take the wounds so that we could be free from the effects of sin, both those sins committed against us and those we've committed against others.

> *Jesus, we take this time to thank You for taking the wounds of sin, for paying the price for our redemption. We ask, Father God, that You forgive us for all the times we've let others down, and also that You heal us from all the times people have let us down. We choose to remember now that You, Jesus, bear the scars so that we can be truly free. Amen.*

For further study: Psalm 41:9, 55:12–14; Matthew 26:20–35, 47–50; Ephesians 4:32; 1 John 2:1–2.

FEBRUARY 22
Eucharist

> Then He took the cup, and when He had given thanks He gave it to them, and they all drank from it. And He said to them, "This is My blood of the new covenant, which is shed for many."
> (Mark 14:23–24)

THE WORD "EUCHARIST" is the traditional name given to represent the Lord's Supper as well as the elements of the bread and wine. It's from the Greek word *eukharistia*, which is translated "thanksgiving." It's rather amazing that the word representing giving thanks was used to indicate a remembrance of Jesus's death. At first glance, it can seem somehow inappropriate.

When Jesus instituted the Lord's Supper, He blessed the bread and wine and gave thanks. We also use the bread and wine to give thanks as we remember what He did. There's nothing greater or more worthy of our gratitude than the death and resurrection of Jesus. With His death on the cross, He paid the price of sin for us all. His sinless life, substituted for ours in death, paves the way for us to live with and for Him. We're grateful for the life He now gives us and the eternal life yet to come. We're grateful that God so loved the world that He gave His only begotten Son, that whosoever should believe on Him should not perish but have eternal life. We are grateful that He bore our sickness and healed our diseases.

If we only had His gift of eternal life in heaven with Him, that would be reason enough to extend our gratitude, yet He gives us so much more. First and foremost, He gives us freedom from guilt and shame. He frees us from the fear of death. He gives us abundant life. He gives us peace that passes all understanding, and He makes us kings and priests. He heals all our diseases and daily loads us with benefits. He takes the lonely and places them in families. He is the father to the fatherless. He clothes us and meets all our needs. He crowns us with lovingkindness and righteousness. There's no end to the love He manifests to us, and He demonstrated and confirmed His love by His willing sacrifice on the cross. He was thankful through the trial.

Sometimes when we have tests and trials, we forget to remember Him and be thankful. We can get caught up in our frustrations and pains. Today, let's remember what He has done for us, whether our current situation is favorable or not, and let's give Him our heartfelt gratitude.

> *We remember today all that You have done for us, Jesus. Your body was broken for ours to be whole; Your blood was shed so we could be forgiven, and You have given us life, and life more abundantly. We take this moment today to remember and to give You thanks. We thank You for the forgiveness of our sins, for eternal life, and most of all for You and who You are. We thank You for Your great love manifest to us. We can't earn it, yet You freely give it. For this we are indeed eternally grateful. Amen.*

For further study: Psalm 68:5–6, 19; Matthew 6:30–33; John 3:16, 10:10; Acts 17:28; Philippians 4:7; 2 Timothy 4:8; Hebrews 2:14–15, 10:19–23; 1 Peter 2:9, 23–24.

FEBRUARY 23
Love Songs

> You are our epistle written in our hearts, known and read by all men; clearly you are an epistle of Christ ministered by us, written not with ink but by the Spirit of the living God, not on tablets of stone but on tablets of flesh, that is, of the heart. (2 Corinthians 3:2–3)

I ASKED JESUS into my heart at a church service many years ago. When I got home from church, I walked into the kitchen and heard Kenny Rogers' song "You Decorated My Life" playing on the radio. This song perfectly expressed how I felt.

It was like my life was meaningless before I met Jesus. He brought the color and song into my life and heart. The world was suddenly a brighter place. The green of the grass was somehow greener; the blue of the sky was bluer. Now many decades later, I'm still in love with Jesus, but as I've grown in my faith, I have a glimpse of just how much He loves me.

I could sing this song to Jesus, and it would express my love for Him, but I see now that He also sings this song to me and to you. Our lives are like the words being written on His white page. As the body of Christ, we bring color and music to His life, and without people coming to Him and receiving His love, His life on earth would have been meaningless. Just as He painted His love on our hearts, we now paint our love on His. This song is from me to Jesus, but I feel now it's also from Jesus to me and to you.

Pausing to take communion is to pause and remember just how much He loves us, and why we love Him. There's something about remembering the depth of His love that makes the world a bright place. It renews hope and love in our own hearts. It brings out the song He has written on our hearts. It reminds us that when others look at our lives, they just may see Jesus reflected in our eyes.

> *Jesus, You did indeed decorate our lives. Your body is beautiful and full of color, song, and harmony as You write Your love on our hearts. May You be always reflected in our eyes and in our lives. Amen.*

For further study: Psalm 40:3; Matthew 5:14–16; Romans 5:5; Galatians 2:21.

FEBRUARY 24
We're All on the Same Level

Where there is neither Greek nor Jew, circumcised nor uncircumcised, barbarian, Scythian, slave nor free, but Christ is all and in all. Therefore, as the elect of God, holy and beloved, put on tender mercies, kindness, humility, meekness, longsuffering; bearing with one another, and forgiving one another, if anyone has a complaint against another; even as Christ forgave you, so you also must do. (Colossians 3:11–13)

GOD IS HIGH above us in holiness, and we cannot reach Him on our own. If we climb the highest mountain on earth, we're no closer to heaven than if we were brought down to the deepest mine in the bowels of the earth. Picture it as if we were all standing on one side of a great gulf, with an impossibly high mountain on the other side. There is no human way to cross the gap to reach God. We can't do a deed or make anything that will bridge it. But God, in His great mercy, lays the cross across the gap to reach us. Even then, the best we can do is come to the foot of the cross. We can't walk up the cross; Jesus must carry us.

Sometimes we think that we've climbed a bit of the mountain toward God. We picture ourselves a little higher and better than the really bad sinners of our town. We're thankful that we're not like that murderer, child molester, or thief we hear about on the news. After all, we walk with Jesus. He knows our name, and we speak to each other in prayer and hymns. It's easy to forget that without Christ, the holiness of God is unattainable. We're all on the same ground level when it comes to having sinned and fallen short of the glory of God. The sinner doesn't reside deeper in the earth, and the saint is no higher on the mountain.

Until we leave this earth, we walk the same ground with co-workers, family, friends, strangers, enemies, saints, and sinners. Jesus commands us to walk this earth humbly before our God, recognizing that the sinner across from us could easily be us. Without the cross and Christ, all we can say is, "There but for the grace of God go I."

When I think of us all on one side of this great chasm, milling around and bumping elbows with those around us, it's easy to remember that we're all on the same level—sinners who must be saved by grace. There's no other way to come into the holy presence of God but by Jesus Christ and Him crucified. How much easier is it to walk with coworkers and friends, knowing we stand on the same ground physically and spiritually.

Jesus, have mercy on us. We are sinners in need of grace. Help us to walk humbly with those around us, forgiving them as You forgave us. We're all equal in Your sight, and there is nothing we can do to earn our way to You. Thank You for the cross that made the way for us to be with You. Amen.

For further study: 1 Samuel 2:2; Isaiah 53:6; Micah 6:8; Luke 18:9–14; Acts 4:12; Romans 3:10–12.

FEBRUARY 25
Aaron's Rod

> I have been crucified with Christ; it is no longer I who live, but Christ lives in me; and the life which I now live in the flesh I live by faith in the Son of God, who loved me and gave Himself for me. (Galatians 2:20)

WHEN ISRAEL WAS wandering in the desert, they were discouraged and started to murmur against Moses and Aaron. God then gave them a sign to show that He had indeed called Aaron to be the priest. He asked every tribe to bring a rod—essentially a walking stick. They were to write the name of the leader of the tribe on the rod. Aaron's name was put on the rod for the tribe of Levi. All the rods were put before the tabernacle, where God met with Moses. The next day when Moses retrieved the rods, Aaron's had become alive. It had leaves, blossoms, and ripe almonds growing from it.

A walking stick is a pretty dead stick. If you bend it, it will break, and it won't mend itself. There's no sap or life in it because it's not connected to the source of sap and life. The bark is peeled away, the cells of the wood are dead and empty, and there's no way to carry sap to the wood should it be replanted. God took this dead thing and made it alive—and not just alive but blossoming and bearing fruit!

A cross—a symbol of death made of dead wood—becomes for the Christian the representation of life. Jesus was nailed to that cross. His lifeblood poured out from the wounds on His body as He died for us. But this death brought life to His body. We are the body of Christ. We were dead in our sins, but Jesus's sacrifice and atonement on the cross made it possible for His life to flow in and through us. He made it possible for us to not only live but to blossom and bear fruit. Like Aaron's walking stick, we couldn't have been more dead, but because of Jesus, we now have abundant and flourishing life. Truly in Him we live and move and have our very being. Now we are dead to sin and alive to righteousness.

A symbol of death becomes a symbol of life. The actual death of the Son of God brings spiritual life to we who are the children of God. As we partake of communion, we are reminded that He died to make atonement for us so that we could be alive with Him, not only eternally in heaven but also abundantly with grace, truth, and righteousness, bearing fruit to His glory.

> *Jesus, we remember that You died for us, paying the penalty for sin so that we would be alive to righteousness. We are able to bear fruit of righteousness because of Your life flowing through us. We couldn't do it on our own. It took a miracle—the miracle of You. Thank You. Amen.*

For further study: Numbers 16:42–17:8; John 10:10; Acts 17:28; Colossians 1:10–14, 2:13; 1 Peter 2:24.

FEBRUARY 26
Our Priest Makes Atonement for Us

But now He has obtained a more excellent ministry, inasmuch as He is also Mediator of a better covenant, which was established on better promises. (Hebrews 8:6)

THERE WAS A time in Israel's wandering in the desert that they spoke ill of their leaders and brought accusations against them. God was displeased, and a plague broke out among the people. Moses commanded Aaron, the high priest, to fill a censer with incense and make atonement for the people. Aaron stood between the dying and the living, and the plague was stopped.

Can you imagine yourself in that crowd? A wave of dying people falls toward you. You try to flee but look over your shoulder in terror and see that the plague has reached the very ground upon which you stand. Suddenly, your high priest stands between you and death. The incense rises up to heaven and surrounds you, along with his prayers. The plague is stopped, and you are saved. What would you do? Would you still run in terror? Do you consider yourself just lucky, feeling it was all mere chance that you were spared? Do you continue to rage at God, accusing Him of sending the plague? Or do you fall at the feet of your high priest in gratitude and praise?

We also have a high priest who came between us and death. The plague of sin had overtaken us, and we were helpless to save ourselves. Sin had reached the very ground on which we stood and filled us with its sickness. But our high priest stretched out His hands and lifted His voice to say, "Father, forgive them." His prayers rose as a sweet incense to heaven. He became the priest to mediate a better covenant, not just life and freedom from sickness and disease, but eternal life and freedom from sin and spiritual death.

So what is our response to our high priest? Do we scoff and disbelieve it, saying that all that happens is mere chance? Do we run from Jesus, thinking He can't save us? Do we rage at God for every bad thing in the world, accusing Him of it all? Or do we fall at His feet, recognizing we have a high priest, one without sin, whose precious blood has paid the price to redeem us from evil? Most of us can point to a day when we realized the plague of sin was at our feet, but we turned to Jesus and our life was forever changed. We now live by faith in Him who gave Himself for us. We fell at His feet in gratitude on that day, so today let's remember Him and speak our praise and gratitude again.

Jesus, we praise and thank You for standing in the gap for us. You bore our sin in Your body on the cross that we might be alive to righteousness. We remember the day we first acknowledged You, and we once again speak forth our praise and gratitude. You are our high priest. There is none like You. Thank You for loving us, even while we were yet plagued by sin. Amen.

For further study: Numbers 16:42–50; Mark 8:36; Luke 23:34; Galatians 2:20; Hebrews 4:14–16.

FEBRUARY 27
Our King Sacrifices for Us

Blessed is the King who comes in the name of the Lord! Peace in heaven and glory in the highest! (Luke 19:38)

IN THE OLD Testament, David sinned by counting the people under him. He chose to trust not in God but in the strength of his army. As punishment for his sin, a destroying angel would take three days to kill the very people David was counting on.

The destroying angel made it to the threshing floor of Ornan the Jebusite, whose ancestors had been slaves of Israel. He had somehow overcome his heritage and had land, a threshing floor, oxen, and sons. When he and his four sons looked up and saw the destroying angel, his sons fled in terror, but Ornan just kept on working. He didn't fear death nor hide himself from it.

David came to the place to offer sacrifices, and when Ornan saw his king coming to him, he went and knelt at his feet. David explained his purpose in that place, and Ornan freely offered all he had—his threshing floor for the place of the sacrifice, his oxen for the sacrifice, and the yoke for the wood for the fire. He freely offered his very livelihood and future. David, however, insisted that he pay for it all, at full price. The price was paid, the sacrifice was made, and the destroying angel put his sword back in its sheath.

Here we are today. There is sin in the land. Sin affects us, whether sins we have committed or the sins of another. The angel of death comes to all. Our King, however, came to make a sacrifice and atone for sin. Unlike David, our King is without sin—spotless and pure. And unlike David, our King didn't come to offer the blood of a beast. He paid the price of His own sinless blood to atone for sin so that we would have life and not perish.

Like Ornan, we see our King and the sacrifice He is making, and we run to Him and kneel at His feet. We offer Him all we have, but it can't be the atoning sacrifice. Only the King has the ability to pay the price with His precious blood. We don't fear death, knowing God has given us eternal life. We fear no lack because the bread of life gives us our daily bread. He is the King of kings and the Lord of lords. The destroying angel cannot touch us. The destroyer's sword is powerless against us because of the sacrifice of our King and Lord.

> *Jesus, we thank You for coming to us where we were. We had no means to come to You, but You came to us. You sacrificed Yourself for us so that we would be free from sin and death and have life forevermore. We remember all You have done for us today and we give You praise, kneeling at Your feet, the feet of our King. Amen.*

For further study: 1 Chronicles 21:1–27; Matthew 6:11–13; 2 Corinthians 5:21; Hebrews 9:12; Revelation 19:16.

FEBRUARY 28
My House Is Your House

Therefore let that abide in you which you heard from the beginning. If what you heard from the beginning abides in you, you also will abide in the Son and in the Father. (1 John 2:24)

I ONCE HAD a close friendship with someone, and we would do everything together. We loved to be in each other's company, and it didn't matter what we were doing. We knew where everything was in each other's houses and could comfortably raid the fridge or fetch our own tea or coffee. We'd laugh together, cry together, and share important moments.

Then the relationship slowly began to change. It became more one-sided. I would call her to chat, but she was often busy or unavailable. When she called me, it was only when she wanted something or needed money. Instead of looking forward to her calls, I started to dread them. When I stopped answering her requests the way she wanted, she stopped calling altogether. The sad part is, I still long for the relationship we once had. I haven't stopped loving her.

When we ask Jesus into our hearts and are born again, we have a wonderful relationship with Him. We feel His presence, and we love spending time with Him and His people. Sunshine or rain, laughter or pain, we share all with Him. Sometimes, however, we let time and happenstance change the relationship. We start only talking to Jesus when we want or need something. Jesus, can't you see I am out of money this month? Jesus, can't you hear my pleas? Jesus, I need … If He doesn't answer our prayers the way we want, we slowly stop praying at all. Why ask if the answer isn't going to be the one we want to hear? Yet Jesus longs for the relationship we once had, when we shared everything. He has never stopped loving or caring for us. He longs to be with us, to spend our days together, to commune together.

Here we are about to partake of communion. It's a reminder of the relationship we have, or had, with Jesus Christ. He poured out His blood to save us from our sins so we could be with Him for eternity. He gave His body for us to make us whole. Today, ask yourself if you have let your relationship with Jesus slip from one of communion with God to a demand to have your needs met. Has it become one-sided? Do we only go to Him with "gimme gimme" requests, or have we stopped going to Him at all? Do we remember what it was like when we first believed? Do we love to break bread with Him, eat with Him, drink with Him, be with Him? To share our laughter and our pain? Is He the rich uncle who lives out of town, whom we only call when we're in need, or is He the friend who sticks closer than a brother, the one who abides in us and has an open door to our heart and lives?

> *Jesus, we come to You today with the taking of communion as a reminder to us that we need You in our lives, abiding with us. You gave Your life so that You could give us life and live in us, sharing all with us. Forgive us for coming only with our needs instead of just abiding in Your glorious presence. Thank you for being with us, staying with us, knowing us, yet always loving us. Amen.*

For further study: Proverbs 18:24; Matthew 6:25–33; John 8:31, 17:20–26.

FEBRUARY 29
Pirates of Penzance

> Knowing that you were not redeemed with corruptible things, like silver or gold, from your aimless conduct received by tradition from your fathers, but with the precious blood of Christ, as a lamb without blemish and without spot. (1 Peter 1:18–19)

I GREW UP in a quiet neighborhood across the river from an outdoor theater. Every summer night, I'd fall asleep listening to the singing of the musicals being performed. Whenever possible, I'd also go to see the show in person so that I had the images to go with the music as I drifted off to the land of dreams.

One of these musicals was Gilbert and Sullivan's *Pirates of Penzance*. This is the story of a young man who's indentured to a pirate ship instead of a pilot ship, due to a mistake his deaf nurse makes in receiving instructions from the boy's father. Young Frederic longs to be a policeman instead of a pirate and can't wait until he turns twenty-one years old so he can put the pirate life behind him. Unfortunately, just when he thinks he's free, he finds out that he was indentured until his twenty-first birthday, and he was sadly born on February 29. It would be many decades yet before his twenty-first birthday came about. Because Frederic is an honorable man, he returns to life as a pirate!

We're born into a fallen world, indentured to sin. The conduct of our ancestors has affected our lives. We're bound by the contract that states that sin results in death and separation from God. There is no way we can be free from the contract unless its terms are fulfilled. The situation would be hopeless, since no amount of money is sufficient to tear up the contract. God, however, made a way. Jesus was able to pay with His precious blood, redeeming us from the effects of sin. He sets us free and calls us to a higher calling. We can align ourselves with what is good and pure and righteous. Only by Christ paying the price for us are we set free, and we don't have to wait decades or for any arbitrary date. We can be free today. Today is the day of salvation.

> *Jesus, thank You for freeing us from sin and its effects. You were willing to pay the price to set us free. We have been redeemed by Your precious blood, and we are forever grateful. Amen.*

For further study: Acts 4:12; Romans 5:12–21; 2 Corinthians 6:2.

MARCH 1
We Are His Temple

> ... For you are the temple of the living God. As God has said: "I will dwell in them and walk among them. I will be their God, and they shall be My people." (2 Corinthians 6:16b)

IN THE OLD Testament, God's presence dwelt in the Holy of Holies. In this place was also the Ark of the Covenant. The Ark contained the Ten Commandments, written on stone by the finger of God. In front of the Ark were Aaron's budded rod and a pot of manna. There was a great holiness associated with the Ark and the presence of God. The Philistines' statue idol of Dagon fell down before the Ark. Sinful men died for looking in the Ark. When Solomon made a temple and home for the Ark of the Covenant, the presence of God was so strong that the priests couldn't stand on their feet because of the incredible glory of the Lord filling that place.

In the New Testament, God doesn't abide in a temple of wood and stone, but He makes His dwelling with us. We are His temple. His presence is with us and in us. His laws are no longer written on blocks of stone, but He has written His laws in our hearts. We once were dead like Aaron's rod, but He has now made us alive. Like the pot of manna, He Himself is the bread of life, given to us. The act of communion, as we break the bread and drink of the wine, reminds us that His presence is now with humanity. We are in communion with Him. We are the temple of the living God, who dwells in us.

As we ponder this thought, it's humbling. The Holy God, whose presence caused men and idols to fall to the ground, dwells now in our hearts. When I take the time to remember that the Holy Presence dwells in me, I have no desire to curse, mistreat others, or walk in a sinful manner. I am humbled by the presence of the Most High God. I recognize that it's not possible to walk a holy life on my own, but the work of the Holy Spirit in me allows the presence of God to live through me. We can be thankful for His mercy, for we will now live eternally instead of die in our sins. Jesus paid that price.

As we partake of communion today, let's remember the sacrifice of Christ that made the way for us to be the temple of God. His holiness can dwell with us and in us because of His broken body and His blood that was shed on the cross for us.

> *Jesus, we are humbled by the thought of such a Holy God choosing to make His home in sinful man. Without Your sacrifice paying for our sins, it would never be, but You paid the price to bring us life and to sanctify us and make us holy. Help us, Holy Spirit, to allow that glory of the Most High God to shine through us and out into this dark world. Amen.*

For further study: Exodus 25:10–22; 1 Samuel 4–6; 1 Corinthians 6:19–20; 2 Corinthians 3:3; Ephesians 2:1; Hebrews 9:1–5.

MARCH 2
The Real Symbol of Love

This is My commandment, that you love one another as I have loved you. Greater love has no one than this, than to lay down one's life for his friends. (John 15:12–13)

THE WORLD HAS a popular symbol for love—that of a heart with an arrow through it. The arrow is supposed to symbolize a love arrow, shot by Cupid into one's heart and making them fall in love with someone. It's an interesting symbol—a heart being wounded signifying something special and treasured. The image may not be so far from the truth, but I think it's backwards. The love comes before the wounds.

What if we replaced Cupid with a Roman soldier? In that soldier's hand is a spear instead of an arrow strung on a bow. The soldier thrusts his spear and drives it into the heart of Jesus, who has just died on the cross. The love doesn't follow the wounding; rather, the wounding occurs because of the great love He has for us. Simeon, a devout man in the temple at the time Jesus was circumcised, told Mary that a sword would pierce her heart when she would see the pain and struggle her beloved Son would go through.

With great love, there is opportunity for great wounding and sorrow. The greater the love, the greater the chance for pain. We've all experienced wounds in our hearts inflicted by those close to us. Whether the wounding was intentional or not, it still hurts. Should we choose to avoid love in order to avoid pain? As tempting as that may be at times, it's not the example Christ gave us. He is love in bodily form, and He has laid down His life for us. He called us His friends when we were lost in sin and treating Him as the enemy. He willingly submitted to the wounds so that we might be set free from sin and death. He also asks us to do the same for others. He asks us to love others as He loves us, sacrificially laying our lives down for them even if they're acting more like an enemy than a friend.

I think we often forget that if we love someone, it's easier to be wounded. We receive the wounds, and instead of laying our lives down, we fight back, we hold grudges, we complain to others, and we generally carry on about how unjust it was that this person we love wounded us. We rip the spear out of our heart and turn it around and brandish it against others.

As we partake of communion we do two things: we remember how much He loves us and sacrificed Himself for us, and we look at our own lives to see where we've fallen short of loving others as He loves us. If the Spirit reveals to your heart where you have taken the spear to brandish against another, now is the time to repent.

Jesus, You laid down Your life for us. You took the wounds out of love for us. Often when we're wounded, we try to destroy those who hurt us. Help us to continue to love them and to recognize that with great love comes a chance for great wounds, but You have shown us that love is well worth the pain. Amen.

For further study: Zechariah 12:10; Luke 2:35; John 13:34–35, 19:34; Romans 5:8; 1 John 1:9, 3:16, 4:16.

MARCH 3
He Calls Us by Name

> But he who enters by the door is the shepherd of the sheep. To him the doorkeeper opens, and the sheep hear his voice; and he calls his own sheep by name and leads them out. (John 10:2–3)

EACH OF US has many names. People who don't know us well might call us Mr. or Mrs. so-and-so. To the government, we're known by our full name, often including our middle name(s) or initials. Parents may have used our full names when we were in trouble. A friend or sibling will almost always call us by our first name. A close friend might have the right to use a special nickname, showing that they're closer to us than some of our other friends. To some of our closest family members, we may be known by an intimate expression, like honey, sweetie, dear, or darling. We talk about being on a first-name basis with someone if there's a close relationship between us. As you can imagine, only a close family member would have the right to walk up to a king and call him by his first name.

Jesus knows us all and calls us all by name. I don't think He calls us by our full names, or by our title. I can't see Him saying to Peter, "Mr. Bar-Jonah, may I please borrow your boat?" He calls us by our first names. He's our friend. He's our family member—our brother. He's our intimate spouse. He calls us by our first names or maybe even our pet names, and He allows us to call out to Him on a first-name basis. We're on a first-name basis with Jesus, the King of all kings.

On the day Jesus rose from the dead, Mary Magdalene was at the tomb. Jesus appeared to her, but Mary didn't recognize Him until He spoke her name. There was something in the way He said "Mary" that caused her to recognize her Savior at once. A close friend need only speak our name and we're reminded of the intimacy of the relationship, and our hearts are drawn to them.

There was another time when Jesus's friends didn't recognize Him right away. They had walked with Jesus to Emmaus and talked with Him. When they sat down together at the table, Jesus took bread, gave thanks, and broke it. In the intimacy of that moment, they recognized Jesus. He was gently reminding them of that Last Supper, when He'd taken time to wash their feet, when He'd broken bread with them, and John was so close that his head had rested on Jesus's breast. Our communion with Christ reminds us of our intimate relationship with Him, that He knows our name. He is our intimate friend, our brother, our beloved.

> *Jesus, we remember today that You are our intimate friend. You call us by name. When You speak our name, we know You, and we know that You know us. We take the time to remember that Your body was broken to make ours whole, and Your blood was shed to pay the price for our sins. You made the way for us to be in close relationship with You, and we love You. Amen.*

For further study: Luke 5:1–11, 24:13–35; John 3:29, 13:1–26, 15:15, 20:11–16; Hebrews 2:11; Revelation 19:7–9.

MARCH 4
We Are All His Children

With it [the tongue] we bless our God and Father, and with it we curse men, who have been made in the similitude of God. Out of the same mouth proceed blessing and cursing. My brethren, these things ought not to be so. (James 3:9–10)

ONE DAY, I was passing by storefronts promoting things that were undesirable and would lead people to sin. The images and posters in the window contained demons and dragons and were repulsive to me. As I started talking to God about the store owners and patrons, I wondered if Christians should curse these places, hoping for them to close down.

Immediately, the Holy Spirit reminded me that these people were made in the image of God. They are His creation, and He loves them. I felt as if the people in the stores were sons and daughters of a very close friend whom I love dearly. I felt the anguish and pain in His heart for the brokenness of His children. Instead of cursing, blessing poured out of my mouth, for that is what God chooses to do. He is kind to the just and the unjust. He blesses us all, and we are all His children. He calls us to bless those who would curse us, to be kind as He is kind, and to love as He loves.

A few days later at work, it occurred to me that it's much harder to bless those I work with closely and whom I count as family or friends. These people can get on my nerves in ways a stranger never could. They know how to push my buttons, and I know how to push theirs. It's easy to forget that they are the sons and daughters of my very close friend who loves them dearly. I forget that they're broken in this broken world, and the Lord's heart aches for them. He longs to soothe their pain and see them come to Him so that He can set them free. We have higher expectations for those who know us well, so we're more easily offended by their failure. Only those close to us can cause us the pain of betrayal. One of the twelve of Jesus's closest followers would betray Him with a kiss. Yet Jesus didn't curse Judas; in fact, He called him "friend" at the very moment of the treasonous act.

On the same night Jesus was betrayed, He took the bread and gave thanks. He spoke blessing over that broken bread. He didn't speak curses or complain. He continued to love the broken people who would abandon Him in His time of anguish and need. Let's take a moment and look at ourselves. Have we spoken curses or blessing over the lost and broken of the world? What about over our friends and family? If we have cursed instead of blessed, let us now repent and allow the blood of Jesus to cleanse us from all sin.

Jesus, we remember that on the same night You were betrayed, You gave thanks. You spoke blessings. You continue to love even those who did You harm. Help us to be more like You. Thank You for Your body that was broken for us, and Your blood that was shed for the remission of our sin. Amen.

For further study: Genesis 1:26–27; Matthew 5:43–48, 26:50; Luke 6:27–28; John 13:34–35; 1 Corinthians 11:23–26; 1 John 1:9.

MARCH 5
The Life of the Beloved

And as they were eating, Jesus took bread, blessed it and broke it, and gave it to the disciples and said, "Take, eat; this is My body." (Matthew 26:26)

HENRI J.M. NOUWEN wrote a wonderful little book called *Life of the Beloved*. It consists of a series of letters he wrote to a Jewish friend, trying to explain Christianity. Interestingly, it's based on the simple act of communion and the four things Jesus did when He established this ritual.

First, He took bread, and we too are taken by Jesus. Before the foundation of the world, He chose us. He knew us when we were still in our mother's womb, and He loved us enough to lay down His life for us. We are taken. We are accepted. We are loved.

Secondly, He blessed the bread. We are certainly blessed. We are blessed by His sacrifice that paid the price for our sins that we might live in eternity with Him. God also blessed us when we were still sinners. He makes the sun to rise on the just and unjust. He set the world in order to provide our food and livelihood. He causes the rain to fall to grow the crops. He makes the beautiful flowers grow. He provides for all and gives Himself to all.

Third, He broke the bread. You don't have to look far to recognize that the world is broken. Ever since Adam and Eve ate of the forbidden tree, sin has reigned in the world. People do evil things, and bad things happen. The earth produces thorns as well as flowers.

Finally, the bread was given. Oddly enough, it's in the areas we've been the most touched and broken by sin that we're able to give the most to others. We understand the pain of others in the same areas where we've had pain. As Christians, we can comfort others with the same comfort we ourselves have received from God.

There we have the whole of the gospel, and the whole of our Christian walk. Jesus Himself was beloved of the Father (taken). He was the blessed one, yet He allowed His body to be broken and crucified. He sacrificed Himself and gave Himself for us so that we might have an eternal relationship with a holy God. Now we also recognize that we are loved and accepted (taken), and we have also been given to each other. Somewhere between the taken and the given, there is brokenness but also blessing. In taking communion, we recognize Jesus taken, blessed, broken, and given, but we also recognize that we are now His body taken, blessed, broken, and given.

> *Jesus, we are so grateful to You. You gave Yourself willingly out of love for us. You allowed Yourself to be broken, even though You are the Holy One. We remember today all You have done and given to us. We also thank You that we are loved and blessed, and in our brokenness, we are given to one another. Help us to be a little more like You and to walk more deeply in Your love. Amen.*

For further study: Genesis 3:17–19; Psalm 139:13; Jeremiah 1:5; Matthew 5:44–45, 6:25–34; 2 Corinthians 1:3–7; Ephesians 1:4–6.

MARCH 6
Zacchaeus

> Jesus answered and said to him, "If anyone loves Me, he will keep My word; and My Father will love him, and We will come to him and make Our home with him." (John 14:23)

ZACCHAEUS WAS A tax collector from the town of Jericho. He'd heard about Jesus and really wanted to see Him. Maybe he'd heard how Jesus had just healed old blind Bartimaeus, who had sat begging for alms just outside of town.

Zacchaeus was a short man, and Jesus was surrounded by large crowds, so he was worried he wouldn't get to see Jesus. Knowing Jesus would be passing by a certain area, Zacchaeus ran ahead of the crowd and climbed up a sycamore tree so he could look down and see Jesus when He passed by. All Zacchaeus wanted was just a glimpse of the Master. Jesus, though, had a surprise for him. When Jesus passed by, He looked up and called Zacchaeus by name. Jesus told him to make haste and come down, because He was going to spend time with Zacchaeus at his house. He was going to eat with him; they would sit at the same table and share a meal. Zacchaeus's life was totally changed after he joyfully received the Lord and Savior.

Sometimes I think we run ahead and strive to see Jesus. We want to see Him do the miraculous in our lives and in the lives of our friends or family. Maybe we want to see Him open the eyes of our spiritually blind family member. Maybe we want to see someone healed. We just want a glimpse of Him. But Jesus wants to give us so much more. He wants to come and make His home with us. He wants to dwell with us. We are to share His table and break bread together.

The Master calls us by name. When we receive Him joyfully, our whole life is changed. We strive for the glimpse, but Jesus calls us to the table. We strive to try to see Him, when all the while He's looking at us and calling us by name, telling us to hasten and come down to receive Him into our lives.

Communion is about remembering that He has come down to dwell in the hearts of people. If you don't yet have a personal relationship with this Man, He is calling you by name to hasten to receive Him. When you do, your whole life will change. For those of us who have already asked Jesus into our hearts, communion is about taking the time to remember that He gave His life for us. He has gone to prepare a table for us in eternity. He lives in us, and we in Him. It's a reminder that we once were sinners but now are saved by His grace. We were lost, but now we're found. We were blind, but now we see.

> *Jesus, we remember You this day. You called us by name and have come to live with us and in us. You bore the wounds so that we could be made whole. Your blood has saved us. We forget sometimes and revert back to some of our old life patterns. Forgive us for that, and lead us in the truth of who You have made us to be. Amen.*

For further study: Isaiah 43:1; Mark 10:46–52; Luke 19:1–10; 2 Corinthians 3:3.

MARCH 7
The Thief Came to Steal

The thief does not come except to steal, and to kill, and to destroy. I have come that they may have life, and that they may have it more abundantly. (John 10:10)

IN VICTOR HUGO'S novel *Les Miserables*, Jean Valjean is released from prison and placed on parole. He takes shelter one night in a monastery. In the middle of the night, he takes some of the cups and silverware and runs away. The police, knowing him to be a thief, come across him and rightly assume he has stolen the precious goods he's carrying. Jean tells them that the priest gave them to him. The police take him back to the priest to find out the truth. The priest, however, doesn't denounce Jean but instead adds to the goods he has taken, saying, "Brother, you left so quickly you forgot to take the candlesticks also." The policeman can't charge Jean with stealing, since you can't steal that which is freely given.

Jesus, while teaching His disciples, told them that the thief—that is, the devil—comes to steal, kill, and destroy. Satan tempts Judas into betraying the Son of God. The devil was trying to steal Jesus away, to deliver Jesus to be murdered, and to destroy Him and His ministry on earth. But Jesus willingly submits to His betrayer and lays His life down before rising again and taking His place in heaven. His life couldn't be stolen, as it was freely given. He couldn't be murdered, since He'd laid down His life. He can't be destroyed on earth because He has taken His rightful place in heaven.

Abraham took Isaac to Mount Moriah to sacrifice him to the Lord, believing the promise of God that in Isaac his seed would be established. He entrusted his son to God because he knew God had given him his son. As Abraham raised his knife over Isaac, he heard God say, "Stop." The Lord provided a lamb for the sacrifice to die in place of Isaac.

Now we, like Isaac, come to the altar at the foot of the cross. We lie upon the altar, and the knife that would slay us is raised high. Then we hear God say, "Stop." We see He has provided the Lamb for the sacrifice, and Jesus takes our place. As we accept the knife plunging into Jesus's heart in our place, something happens in us too. The spiritual wound goes deep into our soul and pulls out our wicked human heart, blackened by sin and hardened by the world. In its place, He puts a tender heart of flesh that reaches out in love. We now can lay our lives down as we put others' needs ahead of our selfish desires. What is freely given can't be stolen. The life willingly laid down can't be taken. The treasure stored in heaven can't be destroyed on the earth.

When Jesus took the bread, He broke it and told His disciples that this represented His body being broken and given to them. He took the cup and said it was His blood shed for them in the gift freely given of His life laid down for us. This simple act reminds us of all He is and has done, and who we now are in Him.

Jesus, we are so grateful You freely gave Your life, laying it down for us at Calvary. You came that we might have life, and have it more abundantly. You are our treasure, our strength, and our hope. Amen.

For further study: Genesis 22:1–19; Ezekiel 36:26–27; Matthew 6:19–21; John 10:17–18; Romans 4:13–22; 1 John 3:16.

MARCH 8
He Prepares the Table—Part One

You prepare a table before me in the presence of my enemies; You anoint my head with oil; My cup runs over. (Psalm 23:5)

DAVID WROTE IN Psalm 23 that our great and chief Shepherd, the Lord of Hosts, prepares a table for us in the presence of our enemies. Like God, we are three-part beings, because we're made in His image. We are body, soul, and spirit, and we have enemies in all those areas. Let's start by looking at our spiritual enemy, Satan.

Peter writes that Satan is an adversary who walks around roaring like a lion, looking for someone to devour. In Genesis, Satan is present in the Garden of Eden. In Chronicles, we find Satan enticing David to sin by putting his trust in his army and not in God. In the book of Job, Satan presents himself before God, requesting permission to attack Job. In the Gospels he is with Jesus in the wilderness, trying to tempt Him to sin. At the Last Supper, before Jesus's betrayal, there's Satan asking to sift Peter as wheat. He was also entering the heart of Judas, impelling him to betray the Lord of Glory. In the book of Acts, Satan inspires Ananias and Sapphira to lie to the Holy Spirit and to God's people. Satan sends a messenger to buffet Paul. He hinders the work and travels of the apostles. He transforms himself so that he appears as an angel of light. In Revelation, we learn that there are cities where Satan has strongholds.

We can come to the table God has prepared, and our spiritual enemy is there also. Despite his presence, Satan is unable to block God's spiritual provision. He may have been present in the midst of the bounty of the Garden of Eden, causing Adam and Eve to fall, but God had already put in place the ultimate provision of His son, the sacrificial Lamb of God who would come from the seed of a woman to pay the price for our sin. Satan was present to tempt Christ, but he couldn't make Him sin. Satan was present at the Last Supper, but the bread was still broken and given.

God provided for us a perfect, sinless sacrifice to be our Savior, even in the very presence of our spiritual enemy, who wants to see us fall. The next part of Psalm 23 says that He anoints us with oil, and our cup runs over. To be anointed is to be set apart for a special purpose—sanctified. Jesus our priest was a willing, sinless sacrifice who made the way for us to be sanctified. He also has ordained a purpose and ministry for us. The presence and attacks of the enemy may hinder us, but they cannot stop the purposes of God from coming to pass. He gives to us the Holy Spirit abundantly—like a cup overflowing—to help us. Our enemy may roar in our ears, but he has no teeth or claws. He comes to the table, but he can't stop us from partaking of the feast.

Jesus, thank You for calling us to the table. We thank You, Holy Spirit, for Your help. God, You have sanctified us and provided for all our needs, especially our need for a spiritual Savior. We are so very grateful that You have saved us. Thank You. Amen.

For further study: Genesis 1:26–27, 3:1–5; Exodus 30:30; 1 Chronicles 21:1; Job 1:6–11; Matthew 4:1–11; Luke 22:31; John 13:27, 20:22; Acts 5:1–5; 2 Corinthians 5:21, 11:14, 12:7–11; 1 Thessalonians 2:17–18; Hebrews 13:12; 1 Peter 5:8, Revelation 2:13, 12:10.

MARCH 9
He Prepares the Table—Part Two

Bless the Lord, O my soul, and forget not all His benefits: Who forgives all your iniquities, who heals all your diseases. (Psalm 103:2–3)

IN PART ONE, we looked at the enemy of our spirit, but now let's consider the enemies of our body. As long as we live on this earth, in this fallen world, enemies will attack our body. Before Adam and Eve ate of the tree of the knowledge of good and evil, the earth was perfect. There were no thorns, just the beautiful flowers. Animals didn't kill for food but were vegetarian. The earth naturally grew all that was good for food and pleasant to the eyes. People didn't deteriorate with age. After the fall, things changed. Now there are thorns. We have to work hard to grow or earn our food. Some animals kill others for food. Our bodies deteriorate and break down. Sickness and death affect us.

God has provided for our healing through the sacrifice of Christ, but sadly, for some reason not all are healed. Some Christians judge those who are ill, saying they must not have faith. During the First World War, some soldiers were down in a foxhole during a gas attack. They had put on their gas masks and were safe, but they noticed some other soldiers out of the foxhole who had taken off their masks, so they thought the danger had passed. Unfortunately, the poison gas had settled in the low areas. When they took off their masks, they breathed the toxic fumes in the hole and died. Maybe a Christian who's ill is lacking faith, or maybe they saw you sitting higher in the air and thought they could take off their gas mask. Their faith was misplaced in you! In any war, some battles may be won easily, some are only won with difficulty, and some are lost. Would you judge the soldiers who die in the battle as having failed, even though the war itself is won? Or would you be grateful for their fight and sacrifice?

This is a fallen world. Our enemies share our life and come to our table. Some soldiers make it through without injury, but some are wounded, and some fall. The good news is that God has ensured that, ultimately, we win the war. He has prepared the table for us at the victory celebration. He has healed all our diseases and forgiven all our iniquities. Psalm 103 reminds us to bless the Lord, who forgives all our iniquities, heals all our diseases, redeems our life from destruction, and crowns us with lovingkindness and tender mercies. In the end, all our enemies will be defeated, and in the meantime, He still prepares the table for us. Communion serves to remind us that the Lord of Hosts has made the way for us to win the war.

Jesus, thank You for giving Your body and blood to provide for our salvation and healing. We thank You for defeating all our enemies and providing for us even today, in this fallen world. Forgive us if we have judged others, and help us to lay down our lives for each other. Amen.

For further study: Genesis 1:1–3:24; Psalm 103:1–5; John 14:1–3; 1 Timothy 6:12; 2 Timothy 2:3–4; 1 Peter 2:24; Revelation 22:1–2.

MARCH 10
He Prepares the Table—Part Three

For the weapons of our warfare are not carnal but mighty in God for pulling down strongholds, casting down arguments and every high thing that exalts itself against the knowledge of God, bringing every thought into captivity to the obedience of Christ. (2 Corinthians 10:4–5)

EARLIER WE TALKED about how God prepares a table in the presence of our enemies. We have enemies of our spirit, enemies of our body, and enemies of our soul. Our soul is our mind, our will, and our emotions. Our biggest enemy is often the thoughts in our own head and intents of our own heart. Our feelings can betray us just as easily as another person can. Thoughts can rise up to tempt us astray. Those thoughts that are acted on can lead us to sin, and those actions can become habits that take us far away from Christ.

Jesus explained that we're not defiled by things that we eat but by our words and actions coming from sin still in our hearts. Mark records Jesus saying *"For from within, out of the heart of men, proceed evil thoughts, adulteries, fornications, murders, thefts, covetousness, wickedness, deceit, lewdness, an evil eye, blasphemy, pride, foolishness. All these evil things come from within and defile a man"* (Mark 7:21–23). All these evil deeds began with a thought. Paul admonishes us to take those thoughts into captivity. This is an enemy that we must always cast down and bring into obedience to Christ and the Christian life.

When we're born again, we are instantly made new and placed in right standing with God, cleansed from our sins. At that moment, we are promised eternal life with Him. That's all true. However, those evil thoughts are not all done away with, and there's a process of working out our salvation. We have the seed of righteousness growing in us, and that seed must be tended and watered and allowed to grow for us to truly become all that we have the potential to become.

When we come to the Lord's table, we're called to remind ourselves of what Jesus did for us at the cross, and who we are now. We have to be reminded because we forget. We let those evil thoughts take root from time to time, but we come to the table, the table He prepared, to break bread and drink wine in order to remember.

We have to proclaim the cross often. Daily would not be too often, given the enemy within our own head!

> *Jesus, we take a moment today to break the bread to remember Your body broken for us. We take the cup to remember Your blood shed on the cross. Help us to daily grow more like You. Amen.*

For further study: Psalm 23:5; Mark 7:14–23; 1 Corinthians 3:6–8, 11:23–26; 2 Corinthians 10:3–5; Philippians 2:12–13; James 1:13–15.

MARCH 11
He Remains Faithful

If we are faithless, He remains faithful; He cannot deny Himself. (2 Timothy 2:13)

MANY OF US have heard the common marriage vows: "Do you take this woman/man, for better or for worse, for richer or for poorer, in sickness and in health, as long as you both shall live?" The person being asked says "I do." Yet many of us have seen things go wrong with the fulfillment of those vows. One partner suddenly decides that they didn't really sign on for the worse, or the poorer, or the sickness, or whatever has arisen. Where once there had been the faith-filled "I do," now there's only brokenness, pain, and betrayal. The "I do" is forgotten, and in its place "I do not" remains.

This world is broken and fallen, and we're so often unfaithful to each other. God comes to us seeking His bride. He meets us at the altar, and when the Father asks, "Do you take this bride for better or worse, for richer or poorer, in sickness and in health?" Jesus answers "I do." The cool thing here is that He really means it. We struggle to lay down our lives for each other, but He's already laid His down for us. He carried His cross up the hill and took the nails for us. He's already proven that He's in this relationship faithfully. We may be faithless, but He remains faithful. He will not change His mind. His "I do" remains "I do," and He means it for as long as we both shall live!

In John 3:16, Jesus says that God so loved us that He gave His only Son so that whosoever believes in Him will never perish but have eternal life. He has called us to eternity with Him. We shall live forever, always loved, always wanted, never rejected or betrayed by Him. He doesn't leave us for another. He doesn't walk out slamming the door behind Him. He never leaves us. He never forsakes us. He never abandons us. He'd already seen the wickedness in our hearts before He laid His life down, yet still He was willing to say "I do." When we partake of communion, we remind ourselves that He loves us that much, despite our failures. At times we are faithless, but as we spend time with Him, we become a little more like Him. His faithfulness starts to manifest in our lives, and He enables us to start laying down our lives for others, even if they're faithless themselves.

As we receive the bread and wine, take a moment to remember that He was able to break the bread and explain His sacrifice before He was crucified because He had already decided at the foundation of the world to lay His life down for us. He loves us that much.

Jesus, we thank You for loving us and being faithful for better or worse, for richer or poorer, in sickness and in health, for as long as we both shall live. Thank You for paying the price for us and giving us eternal life in You and with You. Help us to lay down our lives, and forgive us for our faithlessness. Amen.

For further study: Psalm 139:1–18; Isaiah 49:15–18; Malachi 3:6; Matthew 26:36–46; 2 Corinthians 11:2; Hebrews 13:5–8; 1 John 3:16; Revelation 19:7–9.

MARCH 12
Bitter-Sweet

> And I will put enmity between you and the woman, and between your seed and her Seed; He shall bruise your head, and you shall bruise His heel. (Genesis 3:15)

MY MOM IS an excellent baker. One of our favorite things to make is chocolate cake. The first step involves a lot of sugar mixed with butter. We used to love to lick the beaters when she did that part. It was so sweet. One day my sister made a whole batch of just that so that she could sit and eat it. She found out after a spoonful or two that it wasn't quite so good. Licking beaters was great, but eating a whole bowl? Not so much.

A later step in the process involves mixing some cocoa powder with hot water. The dark chocolate looks so appetizing. All of us kids, at one time or another, snuck a spoon into it and tried it. It was disgusting! It was so bitter. Individually, the cake's ingredients weren't very tasty, but once the bitter and the sweet were mixed together, the most delicious chocolate was achieved.

God understands the mix of bitter and sweet. Before the foundation of the world, He had already planned what He'd do if humans handed the world over to Satan by eating from the tree of the knowledge of good and evil. He prepared for the Seed of a woman to come and pay the price for our sins. Jesus would lay down His life, and in doing so would buy us back from a life of sin and death. Our redemption carries more value and is all the sweeter because of the bitterness in this fallen world. If humanity had never sinned and all was sweet life in the Garden of Eden, I suspect we wouldn't have come to appreciate the great depth of His love, or just how precious our salvation is. God mixed the sweet with the bitter to make something truly marvelous.

Jesus Himself went through bitter pain and distress at His crucifixion, but He fixed His mind on the joy and sweetness of giving us eternal life. For that joy, He endured the cross. He mixed the sweet with the bitter, and something wonderful came out.

Life can deal us bitter blows, but mixed with those bitter blows are simple and sweet joys. God adds His sweet justification and peace to the bitter trials of our life, creating something glorious. Sometimes we forget about all the good things He does for us, and our minds stay stuck on the bitter. We even talk about people being bitter or embittered. These are those who have forgotten what Christ has done for us. We need to stop and take a moment to remember the sweetness of His sacrifice. Communion is our reminder that He has paid the price. There's nothing so bitter that it can't be made precious by the sweet blood of Christ.

> *Jesus, we recognize that You endured the cross for us. You took the bitterness and sin of a fallen world on Your shoulders and mixed it with the joy of our salvation. Forgive us for when we've forgotten and allowed ourselves to become embittered. Restore to us the joy of our salvation, and make those sad things in our life something more precious because of Your comfort and peace. Amen.*

For further study: Genesis 3:14–15; John 16:33; Romans 6:20–23; Ephesians 5:1–2; Hebrews 12:2.

MARCH 13
We Are a Breath Away from Eternity

Whereas you do not know what will happen tomorrow. For what is your life? It is even a vapor that appears for a little time and then vanishes away. (James 4:14)

HAVE YOU WALKED outside on a cold winter day and noticed your breath? It appears as a wisp of vapor, disappearing before you even draw your next breath. In the light of eternity, our entire life on earth can be compared to a mere breath. Breathe in and out. That's it. It's such a brief time. We tend to feel like we'll always have another tomorrow, but that's not always the case. We could walk out the door in the morning but not make it home in the evening. We could pass from this life to the next at any moment. When the disciple Stephen was brought before the council for speaking about Christ, he probably didn't know that very hour he would close his eyes in death and be received into heaven.

In the book of James, we read a caution from James to remember that life can be uncertain. Our lives are short, a vapor, and we don't know what tomorrow holds for us. He warns us against boasting about our plans for future success without acknowledging God as sovereign. We need to take opportunities to do good today, as tomorrow we may not have the chance.

Jesus was one of the few who knew the exact time of His death. He was laying down His life for us. He took time at His last supper with His disciples to teach them the most important things they would need to know. One of those lessons was to serve one another, which He demonstrated by washing their feet. The other thing He taught them was to always remember the sacrifice He was about to make for them. His body was to be broken and His blood poured out for us so that we could be forgiven of our sin and live with Him for eternity. He knew we would tend to forget and start living our lives as though we had a lot of time left to do His will.

His last message was to remember His sacrifice, to remember there is an eternity, and to remember that during our short time on earth, we can serve and do good for one another. If this was our last breath, would we be proud of the way we treated people around us today? It does us good to remember that we're always only a breath away from our last breath on this earth. The cross reminds us that we're forgiven of our sins, but it also inspires us to make the most of the day. One day we'll leave this earth and stand before our Lord, rejoicing in His very real presence.

If you've never asked Jesus to forgive your sins and come into your heart, you also are only one breath away from calling on His name. You're only one breath away from being welcomed into His family for all eternity. It only takes one breath to call on Him to save you, and He will answer you.

> *Jesus, we take a moment to remember Your sacrifice. You paid the price for us to live in eternity with You. You made the way so we could be justified and forgiven for all our failings. Remind us always, with every breath we breathe, that we're only a breath away from You. Amen.*

For further study: Jeremiah 33:3; Luke 22:14–20; John 13:1–20, 31–35; Acts 6:9–7:60; 2 Corinthians 5:10, 6:2; James 4:13–17.

MARCH 14
Traditions

> Knowing that you were not redeemed with corruptible things, like silver or gold, from your aimless conduct received by tradition from your fathers, but with the precious blood of Christ, as of a lamb without blemish and without spot. (1 Peter 1:18–19)

TRADITIONS CAN BE a great thing. They can unite us with others and remind us of love and friendship. Some traditions are long established, while others are relatively new, emerging almost by accident. With some traditions, we aren't even aware that we have them.

One day, a good friend and I stopped on the way home from church at a little tea shop for dessert. We had such a special time enjoying our conversation and friendship that we stopped there every Sunday thereafter. It was the relationship that established the tradition, and the tradition that enhanced the relationship.

Some established traditions aren't necessarily good ones. Maybe our parents yelled too much or were abusive. Maybe they were critical, and we felt we would never measure up. We grow up saying we'll never be like that. We'll be different with our kids! Unfortunately, we sometimes find out that we inherited a tradition we never wanted. We also discover that this tradition doesn't enhance relationships; it destroys them.

Christ came to redeem us from the aimless conduct passed down by tradition from our forefathers. Some traditions are hard to break. We often find ourselves falling back into our old ways and manner of living. Christ, however, gave us a tradition to remind ourselves that we're no longer that old person stuck in our old ways.

On the night He was betrayed, He picked up the bread, broke it, and gave it to His disciples. He said, "Take this and eat it; this is My body broken for you." After that He took the cup, and as He passed it to them, He said, "Take this and drink, all of you; this is My blood shed for you." He was explaining that He was going to take the punishment to redeem us from our sins with His blood. He would make us a new creation. The old would pass away, and all would become new. From the moment of our salvation, we are a new creation. But there's also a process of working out our salvation, because those old traditional ways of acting that we learned growing up keep resurfacing.

The tradition of communion speaks of Christ's body and blood that made us new, but it also speaks of the body of Christ represented by all of us together. We're called to serve one another, to wait for one another, to love one another. These are the traditions we follow now. This tradition of communion arises out of our relationship with Christ, and our relationship with each other is enhanced by this tradition. The old habits, or traditions, of our sinful ways can be put aside. Behold, all has become new.

> *Dear Lord, we recognize that we need to be reminded that we're not the people we once were. At one time we were lost in our sins, behaving by default in the ways of sinful men, but now we have been redeemed by Your precious blood from that aimless conduct. You have made us new, and we are thankful. Amen.*

For further study: Romans 12:1–2; 1 Corinthians 11:17–34, 2 Corinthians 5:17; Philippians 2:12–13.

MARCH 15
Cleansing Our Hearts and Hands

Who may ascend into the hill of the Lord? Or who may stand in His holy place? He who has clean hands and a pure heart, who has not lifted up his soul to an idol, nor sworn deceitfully. He shall receive blessing from the Lord, and righteousness from the God of his salvation. (Psalm 24:3–5)

THE BIBLE TELLS us that the Pharisees were offended that Jesus's disciples didn't wash their hands before eating. Jesus explained that we aren't defiled by eating with unwashed hands but rather by the evil in our hearts, which manifests as sin in our lives. In a way, it's not the dirt of the world on our hands that really needs washing but the sin on our hands flowing from a sinful heart. It reminds me of Lady Macbeth. In *Macbeth,* Shakespeare imagined Lady Macbeth struggling to wash the stain of blood off her hands, but she was unable to do so. No matter how thoroughly she washed, she still saw the stain of blood, the stain of her sin. Only the sacrificial blood of Christ can wash away our sins. His sacrifice on the cross is the only thing that truly cleanses our hearts.

The Pharisees were trying to earn salvation and righteousness by their observance of the laws. They didn't recognize that no amount of ceremonial washing can wash away the sin in our lives. Like Lady Macbeth, their hands were still stained, because their heart was uncleansed.

In Psalm 24, David asks who is able to go to the holy place—the place where God resides. God is the creator of the universe. He is holy and just. He is the King of Glory. How could anyone presume to come into the presence of a holy God? David answers his question with *"he who has clean hands and a pure heart."* This is the person who doesn't serve an idol but recognizes Christ's sacrifice for us. When we come to the cross, Jesus purifies our hearts and cleanses our lives of sin. We no longer wish to sin, and our hands are clean. We become righteous in His sight. What a great blessing and a wonderful mystery.

Today as we reach for the bread and wine, we recognize that Jesus has made the way to save us from our sins. He purified our hearts and washed away our sins. Because our hearts are cleansed, our actions now should follow. Communion is about taking a moment to remember what He has done for us and to ask ourselves where we have fallen short. Where have our actions still carried the stain of sin? Take a moment to examine your heart and ask the Holy Spirit to reveal any faults. Then repent of any failures. He will make the way for us to once again be clean and holy, and free to come gladly into His presence without reservation or fear.

> *Jesus, we remember how You came as a man that You might die in our place on the cross. You made a way to redeem us from our sinful nature and to cleanse us. You have purified our hearts and our hands. You have made us new. Forgive us for the deeds that haven't reflected our pure heart, and cleanse us again. Amen.*

For further study: Psalm 24:1–10; Mark 7:5–23; 2 Corinthians 5:17; James 4:7–8; 1 Peter 1:15, 22–23; 1 John 1:9.

MARCH 16
The Covenant

> I, the Lord, have called You in righteousness, and will hold Your hand; I will keep You and give You as a covenant to the people, as a light to the Gentiles, to open blind eyes, to bring out prisoners from the prison, those who sit in darkness from the prison house. (Isaiah 42:6–7)

A COVENANT IS an agreement, a contract between two or more people. In the Hebrew language, it comes from the root word for "cutting." The rite of circumcision, with the cutting of the flesh, was witness or confirmation of the covenant God made with Abraham that he would be the father of many nations, and that through Abraham's seed all the people of the earth would be blessed. David and Jonathan made a covenant with each other because they loved each other. Jonathan took off his robe, signifying him as a king's son, and put it on David. He also gave David his armor and weapons. David also promised Jonathan that he'd be good to all Jonathan's offspring and take care of them, even after Jonathan was dead. It would be an everlasting covenant.

The English word "covenant" has its root in the French language, literally meaning to come together. God and man come together through Jesus Christ and His sacrifice on the cross. Jesus is the mediator of the new and better covenant. As mediator, He stands between God and man, and through Him we can come into agreement with God. He's also the executor of the will and testament of God. Through Christ the terms of the will are carried out. Jesus is the mediator of the covenant between God and man, but He is also the Covenant itself.

Through Jesus—the seed of Abraham—all people in all nations are blessed. He places the robe of righteousness on us and calls us His sons and daughters. We become children of the King of kings. He gives us His armor and His sword, which is the Word of God, so we can fight the enemy of our souls. He took on our humanity so that we could take on His divinity. He took on our brokenness so that we could take on His wholeness. He took on our death so that we could be joined with Him in His life. He is the one who breaks the bread with us, and He is the bread of life itself, broken for us.

Today as we partake of communion, let's remember that He who is the mediator of the covenant is also the executor of the covenant. He is the one who brings us into agreement with the Father and the very place where humanity and God can come together. He took on our nature so that we could take on His.

> *Jesus, we thank You for making the way for us to be brought into fellowship and agreement with God. You laid down Your life as the perfect sacrifice. It was the cutting of Your body that resulted in the establishment of the everlasting covenant with us. You were broken so we could be whole. We remember and give You thanks and praise. Amen.*

For further study: Genesis 17:1–27, 22:18; 1 Samuel 18:3–4; Isaiah 61:10; Ephesians 6:10–17; Hebrews 9:1–28; 1 Peter 2:9.

MARCH 17
Christ Be with Me

Be strong and of good courage, do not fear nor be afraid of them; for the Lord your God, He is the One who goes with you. He will not leave you nor forsake you. (Deuteronomy 31:6)

SAINT PATRICK OFTEN prayed a prayer for protection that flows along the theme of "Christ with me." It goes in part like this: "Christ with me, Christ before me, Christ behind me, Christ in me, Christ beneath me, Christ above me, Christ on my right, Christ on my left, Christ when I lie down, Christ when I sit down, Christ when I arise."[1]

"Christ be with me" can certainly be a heartfelt prayer for protection. Who is stronger than God to walk with us and protect us? It's empowering to think of Christ with us wherever we are and wherever we go. But I think this prayer is about much more than protection. It's a reminder that Christ *is* with us. He is with us whether we walk along the path He's called us to or if we're straying from His teachings. He is there, calling us back to the right road. When that difficult person is trying our patience, Christ is present, listening to our heart and conversation.

He has made His home with us, and we have welcomed Him into our hearts. The Holy Spirit of God is our companion and helper. God with us. As we face the difficult person or situation, God is with us and in us, and He is able to love and act through us in a way that we can't ourselves. We can yield to His prompting and let Him work through us, or we can go our own way. The choice is ours, even while He's still as near as the mention of His name.

As we partake of communion, we remind ourselves that Jesus came to earth to pay the price for our sins. He took our shame and gave us His righteousness. He also made us His body—His hands and feet on this earth. He is with us to lead us, guide us, protect us, and live through us. "God be with me" means more than "God protect me as I walk into this situation." It means "God live through me in this situation." Often we fail and go our own way, but we pick up the bread and remind ourselves that He dwells in us. We pick up the cup and remember that He has opened the way for forgiveness, to us and through us. We are tested in this world and sometimes we fail, but He is with us to pick us up again and set us back on the narrow road. He will never abandon us.

Today, let's take a moment and ask the Holy Spirit to show us any area where we've forgotten that God is with us and gone our own way. As we confess our failures, He cleanses us again, renewing the closeness of our relationship with Him.

> *Holy Spirit, reveal to us any area where we've fallen short of God's glory and forgotten that He abides with us in this earthen temple. Help us to let Christ be manifest in everything, because God is with us. Amen.*

For further study: Deuteronomy 30:19; Psalm 84:11; Isaiah 30:21; Matthew 7:13–14; John 14:23, 15:26–27; 1 Corinthians 3:16; 2 Corinthians 1:20, 4:7; Colossians 1:27.

---

[1] "The Prayer of St. Patrick," The Turquoise Table, accessed March 10, 2025, https://theturquoisetable.com/the-prayer-of-st-patrick/.

MARCH 18
Grace for the Humble

For thus says the High and Lofty One Who inhabits eternity, whose name is Holy: "I dwell in the high and holy place, with him who has a contrite and humble spirit, to revive the spirit of the humble, and to revive the heart of the contrite ones." (Isaiah 57:15)

I WAS REMINDED recently of a past sin and failure. It caused me to wonder why I'm still so troubled by memories of sin and shame. Some would say it's all under the blood. Forget those things that are in the past and have been forgiven. I know I'm forgiven, but still the shame returns with the memory. It occurred to me that the memory of past failures isn't necessarily a bad thing.

In Luke, we read the parable of the tax collector and the Pharisee. The Pharisee is proud of all the good things he does, and in prayer, he thanks God that he is so wonderful and not like the evil tax collector standing nearby. The tax collector, however, is of a contrite and humble heart. He knows he has sinned and will likely sin again. He doesn't even feel he can lift his head to heaven as he says, "God, be merciful to me, a sinner." Jesus says that the tax collector goes home justified, but not the Pharisee.

The Pharisee keeps no memory of his sins or shortcomings. He is proud and haughty. He thinks he's on good terms with God, but his pride is his god. He doesn't have a good or close relationship with the Lord of lords. The tax collector remembers his failures and comes to God, knowing that without God's grace, there's no hope for him. With his penitent heart, he finds the grace to save his soul and lift his eyes to heaven.

Let's go back to our own memories of failures and sense of shame. Without them, we'd be in danger of becoming haughty like the Pharisee. We could start to think we're okay. What a dangerous place to be. To have our sins come to mind, even though we know they're forgiven, reminds us that we are simple sinners saved by grace. It's not about us; it's all about Him! Only His grace makes us righteous. We can thank God when a memory returns of a past failure, because it also reminds us of all He's done for us.

Jesus ordained the communion table to remind us that He took our sin and failures on Himself. He took the bread, blessed it and broke it, reminding us that His body was broken for us. He took the cup and gave thanks and reminded us that His blood was poured out for us. We are reminded once again that we were broken, but He makes us whole. We come humbly before Him, and His grace is poured out upon us, setting us free from sin and death—not because of how good we are, but because of how good He is.

Jesus, we come before You with a humble and contrite heart, knowing we could do nothing to earn our salvation. We thank You for paying the price for us and lifting us up. It's a gift of God. Amen.

For further study: Psalm 3:3; Luke 18:9–14; Romans 3:10–12; Ephesians 2:8–9; 1 Peter 5:5.

MARCH 19
The Word Became Flesh

> And the Word became flesh and dwelt among us, and we beheld His glory, the glory as of the only begotten of the Father, full of grace and truth. (John 1:14)

WHEN WE THINK of the Word becoming flesh, we think of Jesus Christ, the Word of God, who took on the form of a man and walked upon the earth as a man. This can also reflect that Jesus manifested the Word of God in the same sense we might say someone is a man of their word—that is to say, their actions match up with their spoken words. There is no deceit or guile in them. If they say they'll do something, they'll do it. Their character matches their words. Jesus was the perfect embodiment of the Word of God in all He said and did. There was no discrepancy between His speech and His behavior.

Paul tells the Corinthians that we are epistles read by men. People will look at our actions and judge whether or not they see the Word manifesting in our flesh. They may not read the Bible, but they'll read our actions. They'll either see the writings of the Bible or those of the world in the things we do.

Psalm 119 is structured as an acrostic. The verses of each stanza start with a different letter of the Hebrew alphabet, and the whole psalm is an ode dedicated to the Word of God. In it we learn that the Word of God is the way to blessing, the means of keeping us from sin, and the means to make us unashamed. It is righteous and cleansing. It causes praise, rejoicing, and delight. It revives us, teaches us, gives us understanding, strengthens us, gives us grace and truth, and enlarges our heart.

Salvation is found in the Word. It is faithful, and we can trust it. It's eternal. It gives us hope and comfort in our affliction. It gives us life. It reminds us that our portion is found with God. It puts thankfulness in our hearts and brings fellowship with other believers. It brings us back when we stray. God's lovingkindness is manifested in His Word, which is settled forever and faithful to all generations. It gives us wisdom and understanding. It is a light to our path and our shield and hiding place, bringing us safety. His Word is pure and righteous, from everlasting to everlasting. It keeps us from stumbling. It delivers us and helps us, and oh so much more.

We could sum up all of the above by saying that the Word of God is manifested by love: love of God for humanity, humanity for God, and people for each other. In that love is manifested mercy, salvation, and every good thing. We also should manifest the Word in our flesh so that others will see God in us. Today, let's remember Jesus—the Word become flesh who brings us salvation, mercy, healing, and truth.

> *Jesus, we recognize that You are the Word become flesh. You brought us salvation and mercy. You came with forgiveness for sins, and healing for humanity. Thank You. Help us to also manifest Your Word in our lives. Amen.*

For further study: Psalm 119; 2 Corinthians 3:2–3.

MARCH 20
The Lord Bless You and Keep You

The Lord bless you and keep you; the Lord make His face to shine upon you, and be gracious to you; the Lord lift up His countenance upon you, and give you peace. (Numbers 6:24–26)

WHEN MOSES RECEIVED the instructions from God on setting up the tabernacle and priesthood, he was also given a prayer for Aaron to speak over the people to bless them. We know God never changes, and if this is a prayer He wanted spoken over His people years ago, it would still be appropriate for His people today. Jesus is the fulfillment of this prayer. Let's look at it.

The first sentence is *"The Lord bless you and keep you."* In John 17:11, Jesus prays also that God would keep us. This implies that we would be watched over and preserved. He is able to keep us from stumbling and is faithful to establish us and guard us from the evil one.

The next line is *"The Lord make His face to shine upon you, and be gracious to you."* This speaks of joy and a pleasure in seeing the beloved. We talk of how people's faces light up when they see someone they love. God smiles when He looks at you. Jesus also prays for us to have joy—His joy fulfilled in us. When we recognize God's joy for us and the fulfillment of that joy in us, we can love others, and our faces will light up at the sight of other people.

"The Lord lift up His countenance upon you." This speaks of looking at someone directly. You know how it feels when someone's mad at you and turns their back on you, or when you feel ashamed and lower your face to the ground. God says He is willing to look at us. He's not holding a grudge and turning His back on us, because He forgives us. We need not carry our shame; we can leave it at the foot of the cross. Without shame, we can lift up our face and look into the eyes of Jesus.

The final line is a prayer for peace. Jesus also gives us peace—His peace. The peace the Lord gives is so much more than freedom from war. It implies prosperity, rest, health, and wholeness.

Interestingly, in Numbers, God says He has given this prayer to bless the people and establish His name on them. As followers of Christ, we're called Christian. His name rests upon us. Jesus has come that we would be blessed, protected, and provided for. He keeps us in unity one with another. God smiles and lights up when He sees us, and His grace is upon us. We can look at God's face and have peace because of Christ's sacrifice on the cross. In turn, these attributes flow from us to each other. Just like the moon has no light of its own but reflects the light of the sun, so we reflect His light to others.

> *Jesus, we thank You for coming and providing for us protection, blessing, and peace. God, You smile on us and love us. You have shown by Your sacrifice on the cross just how much we are loved. Thank You. Amen.*

For further study: John 14:27, 15:11, 17:11; Ephesians 4:32; 2 Thessalonians 3:3; Jude 24.

MARCH 21
Purified Waters

And the people complained against Moses, saying, "What shall we drink?" So he cried out to the Lord, and the Lord showed him a tree. When he cast it into the waters, the waters were made sweet. There He made a statute and an ordinance for them, and there He tested them. (Exodus 15:24–25)

WHEN THE ISRAELITES came out of Egypt, right after God had divided the Red Sea for them to cross over on dry land, they came to the water at Marah, but they couldn't drink it. The water was bitter and wouldn't give life. They complained against Moses, becoming bitter themselves! God showed Moses a tree, and when Moses cast the tree into the water, the water became sweet. What had been death to them became a source of life because of the tree.

Here we are in this fallen world. The world at times is bitter, and the sin in us brings death and not life. But there is a tree on Calvary that brings us life where before there was death. Jesus died on that tree, in the form of a cross, and that tree is now our ever-present reminder of His sacrifice that brings us life. He has saved us from the bitterness of the world and the death of sin. He is our source of living water and life.

Later on, we read about Elisha, a prophet of God. Elisha comes to the Jordan River, rolls up his cloak, and strikes the water. The water parts, and he crosses over on dry land. He comes to Jericho, and the king there tells him that they have a problem. The water is bad, and nothing will grow. Elisha takes a bowl of salt and goes to the source of the water. He pours in the salt, and the water is healed. It's now a source of life and growth.

Jesus says that we are the salt of the earth. We represent the source of living water. James tells us that it's important to control our tongue, and he uses the example of a spring of water, which can't send both bitter and sweet water from the same opening. He states that if a man can control his tongue, he can control his whole body. What do we do if we find our mouth speaking bitter evil words of death? We go to our source—Jesus Christ and the cross. We remember the tree on which our Savior died. We recall that He said we are salt—a source for healing and life in this bitter world. At the cross, we find forgiveness for our sins. At the cross, we find His life abiding in us that we might extend forgiveness to others. At the cross where Jesus died, we find life. As we remember what He has done and believe in Him, out of our hearts flow rivers of living water from the gift of the Holy Spirit.

> *Jesus, we remember the tree on which You died. You bore our sins on that tree and bought us eternal life. You make this bitter world sweet. You give us life where there was death. We remember and thank You. Amen.*

For further study: Exodus 15:22–27; 2 Kings 2:1–22; Matthew 5:13; John 4:10, 7:38; James 3:2–12; 1 Peter 2:24.

MARCH 22
Son of Man and Son of God

> Jesus answered, "Most assuredly, I say to you, unless one is born of water and the Spirit, he cannot enter the kingdom of God. That which is born of the flesh is flesh, and that which is born of the Spirit is spirit." (John 3:5–6)

NICODEMUS, A RELIGIOUS leader, sought out Jesus one night. Jesus told Nicodemus that to see the kingdom of God, one had to be born again. This was confusing to the religious leader. How can one be born a second time? Jesus said that we need to be born of water—that is, born of a woman, a human being birthed into the world—but also born of the Spirit. He goes on to explain that He would be like the serpent on the pole Moses lifted up in the wilderness, so that those who'd been bitten by poisonous serpents could look at it and live and not die. Jesus also would be lifted up on a pole, and humanity, bitten by sin, would look to Him and live. This was being born of the Spirit, or born again.

In the book of Romans, Paul writes that Jesus was born of the seed of David, according to the flesh. This is what Christmas is all about—God coming to earth as flesh and blood, as the Son of Man. But in the next verse, Paul proclaims that Jesus is the Son of God, as proven by His resurrection from the dead by the Spirit of holiness. This is what Easter is all about. Jesus was the perfect embodiment of God in the flesh, fully human, while remaining fully God. Between Christmas and Easter stands the cross. All of us, born in the flesh, have been bitten by the serpent's poison of sin, yet we look to the cross and live, born of the Spirit to eternal life. We are born of water, born in the flesh, and born in the Spirit, or born again. Between being born of water and born of the Spirit stands the cross. Without the cross, we're lost; with it, we rejoice with joy unspeakable and full of glory. Through the cross we find grace, the precious gift of forgiveness for all our sins—the ones of yesterday, today, and tomorrow.

We come to the communion table to remember and repent of our shortcomings. At times, the sting of sin still bites, but we come to the cross and find grace. We come to remember we are born again of divine and incorruptible seed. We're not just born of water; we're born of the Spirit. We aren't who we once were. We are children of the King of kings!

> *Heavenly Father, we thank You for sending Jesus to be born as a man, and we give thanks to Jesus for dying for us. We give thanks to the Holy Spirit declaring Jesus as the Son of God. We are so grateful for the incarnation and the resurrection. The price was paid for us to be free. We are and will remain eternally grateful. Amen.*

For further study: John 3:1–21; Romans 1:3–4; Ephesians 2:4–6; 1 Peter 1:8, 23.

MARCH 23
Words — A Creative Force

Let no corrupt word proceed out of your mouth, but what is good for necessary edification, that it may impart grace to the hearers. (Ephesians 4:29)

IN THE FIRST chapter of Genesis, we learn how the world was created. The verses are populated by the phrase "And God said …" Whatever God spoke came into being, and it was all very good. The world was built by the Word of God. Jesus Himself is the Word of God in bodily form. As Lord of creation, He could multiply a small amount of bread and fish to feed thousands; He could walk on water; He could merely speak a word and a servant would be healed. Words are a creative force with God.

It occurs to me that our words matter. They too can be a creative force. We read in Ephesians that we shouldn't speak words that are corrupt but only those that edify. Corrupt words are destructive words. They're wicked and rotten, used to tear down and not build up. To edify is to build up—to use our words to create those things we wish to see. Our words should bring grace to the hearers. As we read on in Ephesians, we find that corrupt words grieve the Holy Spirit. Paul tells us to put away bitterness, anger, clamor, evil speaking, and malice; instead, we're to be kind to one another, tender-hearted, forgiving one another just as God in Christ forgave us.

When I think of all the words I've spoken, even this week, I don't necessarily see many that edify. I see where I let frustrations, anxiety, stress, anger, or selfishness show. I've spoken words that have torn down instead of built up. Proverbs 14:1 says, *"The wise woman builds her house, but the foolish pulls it down with her hands."* Given that our words build up or tear down, I wonder how many marriages have been torn down by words. What about other relationships? Are they built up or destroyed by our words? Have we spoken grace, truth, and light, or have our words been corrupt and darkened others? Do our words show us to be growing more like the image of Christ, or do we look more like this fallen world?

As we partake of communion, we remember how God in Christ has forgiven us; He took our sins in His own body on the cross so that we could be dead to sin and alive to righteousness. We are to reflect His image in our dealings with others and use our words to build up, not tear down. Today if the Holy Spirit brings to your mind where you have sinned in your words, pause and ask for forgiveness. Then let us all move forward, remembering that our words are a creative force. Let's use them to build His kingdom on earth.

Father, the world was framed with Your Word. You spoke and it was created, and it was all very good. Remind us this day that our words are meant to create, to build, to bring a bit of heaven here on earth. Forgive us for our corrupt words and lead us in righteousness. Amen.

For further study: Genesis 1:1–31; Proverbs 18:21; Matthew 8:8–10; Mark 6:30–51; John 1:1–5; Ephesians 4:30–32.

MARCH 24
Doubting Thomas?

And Thomas answered and said to Him, "My Lord and my God!" (John 20:28)

YOU'VE LIKELY HEARD about doubting Thomas, the disciple who wouldn't believe Jesus was risen until he could put his finger in the holes in His hands and put his hand in Jesus's side where the spear pierced our Lord. Maybe you've even been called a doubting Thomas, implying that you lacked faith in God. I wonder if this impression of Thomas is quite accurate.

In Luke 24, Jesus appears to the disciples for the first time after the resurrection. The disciples had been told Jesus was alive, but they didn't believe it was truly Him. Jesus had to tell them to look at His wounds, look at His body, look at His flesh and bone. A spirit doesn't have flesh and bone like He had. Still, they didn't believe, because it seemed too good to be true. Finally, Jesus asked for some food and ate it in front of them. A spirit can't eat food, so this was the proof they needed that He was indeed alive. Thomas hadn't been with them when this occurred, so when he said that he wanted to see His wounds and touch Him before he believed, he was really saying that he just wanted the same thing the others had experienced. They'd seen Jesus in the flesh, and he wanted it too.

Now here it gets interesting. When Jesus does appear to Thomas in John 20, He comes in the same way: appearing through closed doors and saying, "Peace to you." Doubting Thomas doesn't question Him for a moment. He doesn't need to see Jesus eat anything to prove that He's not a spirit. Instead, Thomas immediately says, *"My Lord and my God!"* Doubting Thomas seems to have quite a bit more faith than his fellow disciples. We get stuck on Thomas's doubt because Jesus takes this as a teachable moment. He says to Thomas that there will be those who believe in Jesus without seeing His flesh and bone, and these people will be truly blessed.

Here we are, the people who've been told Jesus is alive, even though we haven't seen Him in the flesh. Do we say, "I won't believe unless He proves Himself to me"? Or do we fall at the foot of the cross and say "My Lord and My God!"?

> *Jesus, we've spoken about Thomas being such a doubter, but he recognized You right away as Lord and God. Forgive us for attitudes that have kept us from acknowledging You in all areas of our lives. We remember that You took the wounds to set us free, and we worship You. Amen.*

For further study: Luke 24:13–43; John 20:24–29.

MARCH 25
Trust in the Lord

Trust in the Lord with all your heart, and lean not on your own understanding; in all your ways acknowledge Him, and He shall direct your paths. (Proverbs 3:5–6)

A NUMBER OF years ago, I went on a trip with Outward Bound. Outward Bound is an organization that aims to challenge people to overcome obstacles, real or imagined, to become something more than they are. On this particular trip, we participated in an exercise where we put on a climbing harness and were secured by a rope placed over a pulley and held by one of the expedition leaders. Our job was to climb a telephone pole that was purposely set in such a way that it swayed. At the top was a small, six-inch-wide board we were to stand on. When ready, we were to leap off, trying to reach out to ring a bell hanging in the air ten feet away. The person holding the other end of the rope would then safely lower us to the ground.

The girl ahead of me was more fit and more skilled than me, but when she got to the top, she was unable to stand up on the plank. Stuck on her knees in fear, she could neither stand up nor climb down. It was some time before she managed to let herself be lowered down. When I went, even though I was less fit and not as well-balanced, I was able to complete the task and have fun at it. Why was there such a difference between us? She should have done so well. The difference was in where we placed our trust. She put her trust in herself, but I put my trust in the person on the other end of the rope. I knew he wouldn't let me fall.

Nowadays it's not physical challenges I find myself trying to overcome but rather faults in my character. Over and over again I find myself stuck. Unable to advance or go backwards, I revert to the same fears and behaviors. I've put my trust in myself, believing that somehow I can make myself change. But my trust has been misplaced! Only by trusting in the Lord will I ever overcome my fears and be more than I am. He is faithful to complete the work He has begun in me. In myself, I'm helpless to effect lasting change. I have to know that He has the other end of the rope and won't let me fall. Only then can I be free of my fears and become all I can be.

As you partake of communion today, take a moment to reflect on areas where you continue to stumble and where you seem stuck. Are you trusting in yourself, or in the redemptive work of the cross? Are you submitted fully to Christ and putting your fears in His hands, knowing He won't let you fall? He is worthy of our trust, and He makes us trustworthy to others around us.

> *Jesus, we recognize that You are the author and finisher of our faith. You are the first and the last, the beginning and the end. You hold our life in Your hands, and You won't drop us. You proved Your love for us with Your death on the cross. Help us to trust You and become trustworthy ourselves. Amen.*

For further study: Romans 7:7–25, 14:4; Philippians 1:6; Hebrews 12:2; Revelation 1:17–18.

MARCH 26
Jehovah Nissi

We will rejoice in your salvation, and in the name of our God we will set up our banners! May the Lord fulfill all your petitions. (Psalm 20:5)

A BANNER CAN be used as a symbol on coats of arms and flags. An army would hold its banner high when it went to war. As long as that flag was visible, the troops knew where the other members of their army were and that victory was still within grasp. If the flag started to fall, victory was uncertain. The banner waved high was an encourager, a rallying point. It went before the army, declaring identity and victory. Similarly, the original coats of arms were simple symbols on the shield, so in the heat of the battle, a soldier would know who was on their side. The symbol of the coat of arms is owned by the head of the family. This leader determines who has the right to carry the authority of the symbol. The heraldic banner was a rallying point for the family to identify with, a symbol of pride and victory.

When the Israelites were on their way to the Promised Land, they encountered the Amalekites. Joshua led the army in battle, while Moses went up on the hill and held his staff high. The staff was the symbol, like a flag or banner, that God was with them. As long as the staff was held high, Israel was winning, but when Moses's arms grew tired and the staff started to drop, the Amalekites would start to gain ground. Aaron and Hur came to help support Moses's arms until the victory was won. Moses then set up an altar and called it Jehovah Nissi—The Lord Is Our Banner. He recognized that their victory, strength, and encouragement came from the Lord. His staff, the banner, reminded the troops that the Lord was fighting for them and was with them.

This also foreshadows the Lord as our ultimate banner. Jesus, the very Son of God, was nailed to a wooden pole. That pole was raised and anchored, standing high on the hill for all to see. The cross became our banner. Like the banner of heraldry, it represents the head of the family. Like an army's banner, it's our rallying point. We look to the cross and are encouraged. We recognize that the battle is the Lord's, and He has fought and won the victory over sin. Every Christian identifies with other Christians through the work and symbol of the cross bringing us into one body. The Lord is truly our banner, and His banner over us is love. It was for love He paid the price for our sins. Like Aaron and Hur, do our actions help lift that banner high, so that people are drawn to Jesus? Or do we strike out and wound our fellow warriors? When we're discouraged, do we look to the cross, or do we surrender to our enemy? Let's look to Jesus, the author and finisher of our faith—our hope, our shield, our strength, our banner, and our victory!

> *Jesus, we thank You for paying the price for our sins and giving us the victory over the enemy of self. Forgive us if we haven't lifted You high or helped our fellow soldiers. Help us to stay in the battle and continue to look to You as our source of strength and hope. Amen.*

For further study: Exodus 15:2, 17:8–16; Psalm 33:20–22, 60:4–5; Song of Solomon 2:4; Romans 12:4; Hebrews 12:2.

MARCH 27
Washing Feet

He restores my soul; He leads me in the paths of righteousness for His name's sake. (Psalm 23:3)

WHEN JESUS WAS at the Last Supper with His disciples, He did something unheard of for a master and leader to do. He took off His garments, put on the towel of a servant, and started washing the disciples' feet. In those days, as people traveled the dusty roads wearing light sandals, their feet would become dirty. A servant would be called to wash off this dirt. It was a lowly and unpleasant job. Jesus did this to show us that just as He was our servant, we are to serve each other. But it has even more significance. When He came to Peter, Peter was at first reluctant to allow it. It was shameful to allow the master to serve the servant, but Jesus said that if Peter didn't allow it, their relationship would be broken. Peter, wanting a deep relationship with Jesus, immediately repented his words and asked Jesus to also wash his hands and head! Jesus replied that there was no need. If you were clean, only your feet were dirty and in need of washing.

Jesus was saying that if we come to Him, recognizing the ultimate service of His death on the cross to pay the price for sins, and if we repent of our sins and ask Him into our heart, we are clean of our sins. It's an instantaneous and miraculous act that cleanses our soul. Nevertheless, we still walk in this world. Occasionally we even walk on paths of unrighteousness and once again take on the dirt of the world.

Have you noticed that sometimes you still sin, even after you become a Christian? Look at the Ten Commandments. Have you placed something—anything—ahead of God in your life? Have you cursed? What about neglecting to spend time with God? Are there times you've dishonored your parents in words or deeds? What about murder? God says that even thinking evil about someone is like murdering them. Adultery? To even lust after someone is the same as the sin of adultery. Have all your thoughts been totally pure? Stealing? Do you acknowledge when the clerk hands you the wrong change? Any lying? Exaggeration or distorting the truth? What about coveting? Sometimes it seems that even though we're saved and clean, we walk the paths that dirty our soul. What are we to do? Once again, we go to Jesus—our Savior, our master, and our servant! We must confess our sins and allow Him to wash those spiritual feet, washing away the stain and dirt of sin that still clings to us.

The purpose of communion is to remind us of the work of the cross and to come to Him often, even daily, allowing His righteousness to flood us and cleanse us again. Thankfully, He is faithful and His mercies are new every morning.

> *Lord, Your mercies are new every morning. You do lead us on paths of righteousness and cleanse us from all our unrighteousness. We remember that Your work on the cross was sufficient for all our sins—past, present, and future—and we ask You to forgive us and renew us. Amen.*

For further study: Exodus 20:1–17; Lamentations 3:22–23; John 13:1–20.

MARCH 28
More Than Enough

> So they all ate and were filled. And they took up twelve baskets full of fragments [of the bread] and of the fish. (Mark 6:42–43)

MARK 6 INCLUDES one of the accounts of Jesus feeding a multitude of people with only a small amount of food. Five thousand men, plus women and children, needed to be fed, so Jesus took the small offering of food, blessed it, broke it, and gave it to the disciples, who set it before the people. We read in verses 42 and 43 that *all* ate and were filled.

When I read this account, it comes to my mind that no one was left hungry. From the least to the greatest, all had enough to satisfy their hunger. Jesus didn't forget anyone. He didn't consider anyone too fat, too young, too old, too mean, too dirty, too rude, too challenged, too broken, too rich, or too poor for Him to reach out to meet their need for that day. He fed and cared for all, regardless of their current position in life or their attitude.

If you were sitting in the back of the field in one of the last groups, watching the food being distributed, you'd probably think there was no way there would be enough. If you were very young, homeless, or an orphan, you'd listen to your stomach grumble and think that this would not be the day that would satisfy your hunger. Maybe you'd have to go begging to those near the front, who had food. Would they kick you away like people had in the past? You might be surprised to see the disciples approach, still breaking off chunks of bread and having people pass it on. You might be surprised to find that you're not forgotten. There is more than enough. Plenty, in fact, with plenty of leftovers.

Would you realize that Jesus is more than enough? He is more than enough, no matter what our sins, our station in life, how people have judged us, or how we've judged ourselves. He is more than enough to provide forgiveness for our sins, to make us new, and to satisfy our daily needs.

As a disciple of Christ, would you also recognize that He takes the little we have, our measly little talents and gifts, and multiplies it to make it more than enough to bless the multitudes? He takes our broken bodies, our broken souls, our broken and contrite spirits and, through them, distributes blessings to our family, coworkers, and all the people we touch as we walk the deserted wastelands of this earth. No one is forgotten. No one is forsaken. He is more than enough for us and in us. He makes us more than enough to reach out to those around us.

> *Jesus, thank You so much for multiplying the little bit we can do and using it to touch thousands. Thank You also for meeting all our needs and hopes, for forgiving our sins, and for providing all we need. We came to You empty, and You made us full. We bless You. Amen.*

For further study: Mark 6:32–44; 2 Corinthians 9:8, 12:9.

MARCH 29
Being Present

> When Jesus therefore saw His mother, and the disciple whom He loved standing by, He said to His mother, "Woman, behold your son!" Then He said to the disciple, "Behold your mother!" And from that hour that disciple took her to his own home. (John 19:26–27)

WHEN JESUS WAS hanging on the cross, dying a slow, agonizing death, He was still looking around Him, present with the people He loved. He was still providing for them and arranging for their future care. That's rather remarkable, isn't it? Can you imagine being in pain, falsely accused and dying a sinner's torturous death? Would you be thinking about how to arrange care for your mother? Here He was in His greatest hour of need, feeling forsaken, yet still caring for those around Him.

Even when He walked the dusty roads of the highways and byways of Israel, He was present with people. He would stop and look them in the eyes. He would touch them. Thousands of people would be crowding around Him, but He'd take the time to interact with individuals personally, to give them His full attention. We know He is the same yesterday, today, and forever, and He said He will never leave or forsake us. Do we recognize that He's still giving us His full attention? He's not just sharing our space, but He is present. He's paying attention. He looks us not only in the eyes, but in our heart and soul.

We hear so much about distracted driving, but maybe we should be talking about distracted living. How often do we give people our attention? We're with someone, but our phone buzzes, and we reach to answer it. Maybe our attention is diverted to something else grabbing at us, some sight in the distance, some concern or worry. Maybe we're even too busy thinking about what we're going to say or do next to really listen to the person speaking to us. People come to talk to us, and we don't turn our eyes from our screen. Go to a restaurant and look at all the couples eating. How many are truly engaged with each other, and how many are watching the big screen TVs or texting on their phones? There's an old saying that goes, "Yesterday is history, tomorrow a mystery, but today is a gift—that's why it's called the present." Being truly present with people is a precious gift. It's a gift Jesus gives to us. He gave it even at the hour of His greatest need. Will we give this gift to others?

> *Holy Spirit, show us where we've been too distracted to be present with people, and forgive us. Help us to put aside our fears, concerns, and phones that we might give the gift of presence. Lord, You are present for us and with us. You give us the gift of communing with us. Help us to reflect You in this area as we walk and talk with Your children. Amen.*

For further study: Matthew 8:7, 9:2, 22–24; Mark 10:49; John 4:9–10.

MARCH 30
Sitting in His Presence

For by grace you have been saved through faith, and that not of yourselves; it is the gift of God, not of works, lest anyone should boast. (Ephesians 2:8–9)

WHEN JESUS FED the five thousand people, He had the disciples make everyone sit down on the green grass. Having them sit likely prevented any shoving or rioting as people pushed in, trying to get their needs met. There's something about waiting calmly in His presence for the bread to come your way. Jesus didn't tell them to all join in singing hymns, though we know He sang hymns with His disciples. He didn't bid them fall down on their knees in worship. He didn't command them to do any special work. The only thing He required was that they sit.

The world we live in is very performance-oriented. We work to earn our pay. We work at relationships. We work at being accepted. Sometimes, likely without realizing it, we may even try to work to earn our salvation. Perhaps we think in our heart that if we don't go to church or do something for some person, God may not accept us. Jesus, however, required nothing of the five thousand, yet He still met their needs. If there were any there who didn't believe in Him, they still got fed. They all ate and were filled, yet all they did was sit on the green grass. We know it's right to work and earn our living. Our employment may just be the crust of bread passed along to us from the hand of Jesus, but there's something about resting in His presence and being confident that He's going to come through. Working while staying calm in His presence is different from working with an attitude of striving to be fed by His hand.

There is nothing we can do to earn our salvation. The gift of Jesus's sacrifice on the cross for us is just that—a gift. We can choose to receive it or not, but we can't earn it. We're accepted just because we're human and choose to receive His gift. We don't have to strive for it, nor would our efforts do any good.

Have you ever found yourself pushing to get your needs met? Maybe you even push others aside as you try to put yourself first. Instead, maybe we should take a moment to sit, to pause and relax as we soak in His presence. We don't have to push others aside to get our needs met. The bread will be distributed to all, and our turn will come. In fact, when it's passed to us, are we not to break off what we need and pass the rest on to those sitting beside us? Let's take a quiet moment right now to sit down and enjoy His presence.

> *Jesus, we recognize You as our Lord and Savior. You provide for us. You have met our needs for salvation and forgiveness of sins. You also meet all our needs in soul and body. We take a moment to acknowledge You, to sit in Your presence and focus on You. You are all we need. Thank You. Amen.*

For further study: Mark 6:32–44, 14:26; 2 Thessalonians 3:10–12; 1 Peter 5:7.

MARCH 31
Being Let Off the Hook

Our soul has escaped as a bird from the snare of the fowlers; the snare is broken, and we have escaped. (Psalm 124:7)

MY GRANDMOTHER LOVED fly fishing. She'd load her orange dinghy on top of her truck and drive up old logging roads to pristine mountain lakes. There she would spend a quiet afternoon casting her line into the water, enticing a fish to bite. Once caught, it was just a matter of time before that fish was reeled into the boat. Sure, he may have fought against the tug, and my grandmother at times would let the line play out, causing the fish to tire as he tried to swim away, but the end was the same. That fish would become dinner, unless it was so small that she'd take it off the hook and release it in exchange for the next, bigger catch.

Satan cast a lure into the world, enticing humanity to take the bait and bite the hook. The bait of sin was grabbed, and humanity was caught on the hook. He could take his time while he reeled us in. He may have let us swim away for a time, letting us think we were free, before he once again jerked the line. No matter how much we fought, the end would be the same: we would be pulled into the devil's boat.

Jesus, however, came to Satan with a proposal. Wouldn't he love to take the hook off those puny little fish in exchange for a big fish—a really big fish? Satan took that bait. He let us off the hook by placing the hook securely into Jesus Christ, the Son of God. We no longer inherit death as the inevitable price of sin. Jesus took the penalty so that we could be let off the hook. The devil let us go so that he could reel in the really big fish of God Himself. What the devil didn't realize, however, was that He was powerless to reel Jesus in. Jesus wasn't forced into the boat. He leapt into the boat, but He's so big, the boat couldn't hold Him. He upset the boat as He rose from the dead to once again swim free, the firstborn from the dead.

Because of what Jesus did for us, we swim free, but sometimes we try to put that hook on others. Maybe someone has wounded us, betrayed us, or in any other way offended us. We want them to pay for their deed, so we put them on the hook, demanding they pay the price owed to us. But Satan still holds the rod. The line from that rod now wraps around us before reaching out to the person we've put on the hook. When the devil yanks that rod and spins the reel, the line cuts into our soul. We're snared by our unforgiveness. The solution to finding freedom is simple. We need only reach out and release the hook from the offender. This frees the line so that we can shake it off and once again swim free.

As we partake of communion, we remember that Jesus took our penalty and let us off the hook, and we need to let others off the hook, forgiving as we have been forgiven.

Jesus, we're so grateful that You set us free from the snare of the devil. You paid the price to give us eternal life. You often remind us to forgive as we have been forgiven. If we're holding on to any unforgiveness, reveal it now so that we may confess it to You and release it, being set free once again to walk with You in joy. Amen.

For further study: Genesis 3:1–7; Acts 2:24; Ephesians 4:32; 2 Timothy 2:24–26.

APRIL 1
Blind Bartimaeus

> And throwing aside his garment, he rose and came to Jesus. So Jesus answered and said to him, "What do you want Me to do for you?" The blind man said to Him, "Rabboni, that I may receive my sight." (Mark 10:50–51)

BARTIMAEUS WAS A blind man begging near Jericho. He heard a commotion and asked what it was about. When he was told Jesus was passing by, he started to cry out, *"Jesus, Son of David, have mercy on me!"* (Mark 10:47). The crowd told him to be quiet, but he cried out even louder. Jesus heard his cry and stopped and commanded Bartimaeus be called over. He cast off his beggar's cloak and hurried to meet Jesus. Jesus asked Bartimaeus what he wanted, and Bartimaeus asked to receive his sight.

We can learn a lot from this incident. "Jericho" means a place of fragrance. Bartimaeus is said to be the son of Timaeus, and "Timaeus" means highly prized. I'm pretty sure Bartimaeus didn't feel much like the son of the highly prized as he sat begging alms by the roadside. When he called out to Jesus, the others around tried to discourage him, only changing their tune when Jesus Himself said they should tell Bartimaeus to come.

When Bartimaeus did reach Jesus, he didn't ask Jesus for alms. He didn't just want his needs met for that day—he wanted his whole life changed. He asked to see. He wanted to be able to see Jesus, to follow Him, to be a new creation. He didn't want to beg for alms. He wanted to see! He wanted to be adopted into Jesus's family and truly be the son of the Highly Prized. In Luke's version, everyone around praised God when they saw this miracle of his healing.

Sometimes it's as if we sit by the roadside begging. We've heard of Jesus, maybe we even caught a whiff of the fragrance of His love. We can call for Him, and those around us may try to discourage us. Jesus, however, hears us. He stops and calls to us, asking us what we want. We have a choice here. We can ask just for alms. We might pull our beggar's cloak around us and ask for money for a current need, or maybe a new job or a better boss. Or we can cast off our beggar's cloak and cry, "Jesus, I want to see. I want to see You. I want to watch as You touch my family and neighbors, bringing them life. I want to see the road You're walking in order to follow You. I want to be adopted into Your family and be Your child, a child of the Highly Prized."

As we pause today to partake of communion, we're reminded that once we were spiritually blind, but now we see. We are a child of the Highly Prized, walking the road He walks. It's not always an easy road, but communion reminds us that it's a good road. It's the road to life. Those around us can't help but notice the change in us and give praise to God.

> *Lord, once we were blind, but You gave us sight. Help us to see what You are doing in, around, and through Your body today. Help us all to see how You want to reach out to people. Thank You for enabling us to cast off our beggar's cloak as we call to You and You call to us. Amen.*

For further study: Mark 10:46–52; Luke 18:35–43; John 1:12; 1 John 3:1–2

APRIL 2
The Truth Shall Make You Free

Then Jesus said to those Jews who believed Him, "If you abide in My word, you are My disciples indeed. And you shall know the truth, and the truth shall make you free." (John 8:31–32)

PEOPLE INVOLVED IN writing dictionaries often proclaim a "word of the year." In 2016, that word was "post-truth." It was said that we are now living in a society where truth isn't as important as how things make you feel. False news can be propagated and false beliefs advanced with impunity. After all, it really isn't important if things are true as long as it feels good for you and we all get along, right? Yikes! What a word!

Still, we have to ask ourselves: Doesn't truth matter? If truth exists, and of course deep down we all know it does, then there's only one Truth, and it's pretty important to know what it is. The different religions in the world are mutually exclusive if there's one that is true. How can we know which one it is? Can we decide what's true by the evidence around us, by how it makes us feel, how we're changed, or by what we're willing to die for?

If one investigates the evidence in creation, they'll see that it points to a creator. Nevertheless, this isn't quite enough to convince everyone that Christianity is true. Some scientists, rejecting God but accepting creation's evidence, have proposed that we were designed by aliens! What about how Christianity makes us feel? Many people have religious experiences and "feel the spirit," even those who aren't Christians. This won't be enough. Will we die for Christ? People of other religions die for their faith too.

How does our faith change us? Now there's something with a bit more weight. We know that before we were saved, we were living for ourselves, but after we accepted Christ, we wanted to live for God and others. Christians are the most motivated to run shelters, to help the elderly, homeless, and destitute, and to love the unlovely. As Christians, we felt the change in our heart and motives. Others can counter, however, with all the times Christians aren't so loving, and there are unbelievers who are kind and generous, so maybe that's not quite enough to convince our friends of the truth.

If we read God's Word, the Bible, and abide in it, we come to know Truth. Truth, it turns out, is a person—Jesus Christ. To become a Christian is to meet Truth in our heart, for Jesus is indeed the Way, the Truth, and the Life. The words of One we've always known to be faithful and true can be relied upon as true. Truth resides in a relationship with the One who is True. He leads us from serving self to serving others, from death to life, hatred to love, darkness to light. Only in knowing Him will anyone find real Truth.

> *Jesus, we take the bread and the wine in remembrance that You are the Truth. There is none true but You. As we abide in You, we do indeed know the Truth, and You have set us free. We thank You for who You are. Amen.*

For further study: Luke 6:35–37; John 14:6, 17:17; Romans 6:17–18; Galatians 5:13; Ephesians 5:8–14; 1 John 3:14–16.

APRIL 3

Good News!

The beginning of the gospel of Jesus Christ, the Son of God. (Mark 1:1)

THE WORD "GOSPEL" comes from the old English words meaning "good news." The gospel is the good news! Let's look at the first verse of the Gospel of Mark with this in mind. It says, paraphrased, "The beginning of the good news of Jesus Christ, the Son of God." Almost half of the Gospel of Mark is devoted to the last week of Jesus's life. This Gospel focuses on the speed and determination of Christ heading to His mission of the cross, and it's introduced as the beginning of the good news of Jesus Christ. The good news is founded on Jesus's death and resurrection. What is good about a brutal beating and death on a cross? Only what it accomplishes for us. It's the good news that God so loved the world He gave His only Son so that whosoever believes in Him would not perish but have eternal life. It's the good news that Jesus has paid the price for our sins so we can live for eternity with Him in heaven, and it's the good news of Christ in us, the hope of glory. The cross is indeed good news.

The last verse of the book of Mark speaks of the disciples and says *"And they went out and preached everywhere, the Lord working with them and confirming the word through the accompanying signs. Amen"* (Mark 16:20). The Word of God, the good news, was confirmed through accompanying signs. The biggest sign of all is the change in our hearts. We come to God as broken people, lost in our sin. We receive the good news and accept Jesus into our hearts, and then we walk through this world suddenly changed. We're not the same people anymore. We feel the wonder of being cleansed from our sin and find ourselves able to love the unlovely. The world becomes a brighter place because of the light of the gospel shining in and around us.

Everything is changed, even when nothing has changed. We still live in the same house, maybe with the same annoying relative. We still have the same crazy boss, or the same employees, and yet somehow, it's all different. Our worldview has changed by the good news of Jesus Christ, the Son of God.

We partake of communion to remind us that we are in the world and not of it. The world has a strong pull, and at times it can cloud our vision. It can cause us to focus on the bad news around us and forget the good news. Communion is a moment to remember who we are in Christ and what He has done for us. Good news indeed!

> *Father, we're reminded today of the good news—that Jesus Christ has died for our sins. His body was broken so that ours could be whole; His blood was spilled so we could be saved! He lives in us. We pause to remember we carry the good news with the sign of its presence in us! Amen.*

For further study: Mark 16:20; John 3:16, 17:1–5, 14–19; 1 Corinthians 6:20; Colossians 1:27; 1 John 1:5–7, 2:25.

APRIL 4
His Mercies Are New Every Morning

Through the Lord's mercies we are not consumed, because His compassions fail not. They are new every morning; great is Your faithfulness. (Lamentations 3:22–23)

WHEN WE'RE AT someone's mercy, we're indebted to that person. They have the authority to determine our fate. They may be compassionate and let us off from that debt, or we could be held to account. God, as our creator, is ultimately the one on whom we depend for mercy. He set laws in place, reflected in the Ten Commandments, that can be summed up in "loving the Lord our God with all our heart and soul and strength, and loving our neighbor as ourselves."

So here we are, born into a world entrapped in sin and, invariably, we fall short of loving God and each other. The penalty of sin is death. The truth rises up before us and we are guilty, but the judge, leaning over His heavenly bench, looks down with mercy. His expression is of compassion. We are at His mercy, and He is merciful. His compassions fail not. All who have come to the foot of the cross and confessed their sins have found mercy and forgiveness. He has made us righteous. The truth is not denied. We were guilty, but our Lord has paid the debt and set us free. Our soul is at peace. As it says in the psalms: *"Mercy and truth have met together; righteousness and peace have kissed* [each other]*"* (Psalm 85:10).

When we came to the cross on the day of our salvation, it changed us from sin to righteousness, but as we walk in this world, there are times we slip up. We may once again bear false witness, covet our neighbor's goods, fall into adultery, dishonor our parents, or commit any other failing in attitude or deed. We suddenly realize that we once again stand before the judge, guilty. We may want to put a spin on it and explain away our thought or deed, but the truth rises up before us. The accuser of the brethren, the devil, points at us and says, "And you call yourself a Christian!" As we hang our head in shame, Jesus motions to us. He invites us to come and sit at the table with Him. He takes the bread, blesses it, breaks it, and gives it to us, bidding us to eat His body. He picks up the cup and gives thanks, then passes it to us and says, "Take, drink, this is My blood given for You." He reminds us that we are in His family. His blood is sufficient, and His mercy and compassion are new every morning. As often as we turn to Him, He reaches out in forgiveness. As we come regularly to His table and recognize His wonderful love, we find it easier to move closer to the kingdom of righteousness and away from the land of sin. His love makes us new every morning. As we partake of communion, we drink of His love and are made just a little more like Him.

> *Father, we come today partaking of the body and blood of Christ in the elements of the communion table, and we give thanks that Your mercies are new every morning. Renew us again as we remind ourselves that we are children of Your righteousness. Amen.*

For further study: Genesis 2:15–17; Exodus 20:3–17; Luke 10:27; Romans 6:23; 1 Corinthians 11:26; Hebrews 9:12–14.

APRIL 5
The Life Is in the Blood

For it [blood] is the life of all flesh. Its blood sustains its life. (Leviticus 17:14a).

BLOOD IS SUCH an amazing thing. It circulates through our bodies, connecting to the vast majority of cells. It is a crucial element in the life of those cells. Cut off the blood supply and soon the tissue becomes black, dry, hard, and lifeless. When the blood flows, it brings life-giving oxygen and nutrients to the cells while also taking away waste products and toxins. The blood brings infection-fighting cells to heal wounds and disease. The tissue remains soft and healthy, and the body as a whole is full of life when the blood circulates as it should.

Jesus's lifeblood was poured out so we might have life. In a way, His blood now circulates through the individual members of His body. The life He gives us by His blood sacrifice brings us the life-giving oxygen of the Holy Spirit and takes away the toxins of sin. With His life in us, we're no longer spiritually dead and dry but instead are full of vitality. Because we are in the world, there's a constant need to be renewed by the life-giving nutrients He supplies and to drain away the waste products of disappointments, frustrations, anger, and wounds that occur in this fallen world. His grace needs to circulate continuously within us.

By pausing to remember His blood poured out for us, we take a moment to breathe in the rich nutrients of life and to give to Him all the waste products that would bring death to our soul if we held on to them. We need this renewal regularly. To withdraw from the life-giving blood is to head toward a dryness and hardness in our soul. Take a moment to breathe deeply, to listen to your heart beat, and to remember that His blood renews us spiritually, just like our natural blood renews us physically.

> *Jesus, we thank You for pouring out Your lifeblood so we could live. We have received Your Holy Spirit, and we give You all the wasteful things of our life: our unmet expectations, anger, brokenness, and sin. Thank You for cleansing us, healing us, and renewing us every day. Amen.*

For further study: Leviticus 17:13–14; Psalm 51:10; John 10:10; Romans 3:24–25, 12:2; 2 Corinthians 4:16; 1 Peter 3:18.

APRIL 6
The Rock Cleft for Us

And the Lord said, "Here is a place by Me, and you shall stand on the rock. So it shall be, while My glory passes by, that I will put you in the cleft of the rock, and will cover you with My hand while I pass by." (Exodus 33:21–22)

MOSES LONGED TO see the glory of God, but God told him it wasn't possible for a man to look upon His glory in its fullness. The sins of humanity can't withstand the holiness of God. God, however, had a solution. What God proposed was that He would hide Moses in a cleft in the rock; after He passed by, Moses would be able to see His glory in a muted form by seeing the back of God. Even in this subdued form, the glory was so bright Moses was forever changed. He came down from the mountain with his face reflecting that glory to such a point the children of Israel couldn't bear to look upon him. Forever after, Moses wore a veil over his face when he went out to talk to the people, because the glory shining on his face scared them.

Sinful people still can't abide the holiness of God; however, God provided a solution for us so that we can enter into His presence. He sent His Son. Jesus is the rock we stand on. The rock that is Christ was cleft or broken so that we could hide ourselves in Him. But this time, the price for our sins has been paid in full. He took on our sinful flesh, and we became the righteousness of God. We now have access to the throne of God. His broken body paved the way for us to be able to enter the very presence of God and behold His glory.

The Bible also tells us that there was a "rock" that followed the Jewish people wherever they were on their journey through the wilderness (1 Corinthians 10:4). When the rock was struck, a cleft opened and life-giving water flowed out. Jesus was struck when on the cross. The spear from the centurion pierced His side, and blood and water flowed out. This water and blood would give us spiritual life. When Jesus died, the veil of the Temple that shielded the Holy of Holies—the place where God's glory resided—was torn in two, signifying we now can enter into the very presence of God. Interestingly, Matthew tells us that when the veil was torn in two at Jesus's death, there was an earthquake that also broke open the rocks. The natural world showed forth what was happening in the spiritual—our spiritual rock being cleft for us.

As we partake of communion, breaking the bread and drinking the wine, let's remember that He was broken for us to pour out His life in order to give us eternal life. We can now see the glory of God and reflect it, freely and unveiled, in our own lives on this earth.

> *Jesus, You are indeed the rock cleft for us. Your blood was poured out as living water, giving us eternal life. Your body was broken to pay for our sins. We thank You and remember today that we now can enter into the Holy presence of God and carry Your glory. Amen.*

For further study: Exodus 33:11, 18–23, 34:29–35; Numbers 12:3; Psalm 18:2; Matthew 21:42, 27:51; John 7:38, 19:34; 1 Corinthians 10:4; 2 Corinthians 5:21; Hebrews 4:16.

APRIL 7
Open Heaven

And He said to him, "Most assuredly, I say to you, hereafter you shall see heaven open, and the angels of God ascending and descending upon the Son of Man." (John 1:51)

JACOB, GRANDSON OF Abraham, was headed to his mother's hometown to find a wife. One night, he lay down to sleep and put a stone under his head as a pillow. As he slept, he dreamt he saw a ladder reaching up to heaven, and angels ascending and descending upon it. The Lord appeared, who told Jacob of His promise to bless all the nations of the world through Jacob's seed. When Jacob awoke, he called the name of the place Bethel, which means "house of God," and he said surely he was at the very gate of heaven. He took the stone he was using as a pillow and poured oil on it and set it up as a memorial.

Jesus, born of the lineage of David, a descendant of Jacob, is the seed from which all the nations of the earth have been blessed. When Jesus was choosing disciples, He was impressed with how quickly Nathanael had faith in Him, and He told Nathanael that he would see great things, even the heavens opened and angels ascending and descending on the Son of Man. Does that sound familiar? Isn't that just like Jacob's ladder? Jesus, our rock, is called Jesus the Christ, and Christ means the anointed one—one consecrated to a heavenly purpose.

Jacob slept on a rock. We rest on our rock, Jesus Christ, and the heavens are open to us. Jesus paid the penalty for sin so that we could be considered righteous. We can now come boldly before the throne of grace. We have open access to heaven. Our sins are forgiven, and we find grace and help in time of need. Jesus has chosen to make His home in us. Bethel, the house of God, is now all the saints and believers.

God has given His angels charge over us to protect us. They come and go from the very throne room of God and do His word. Because of Jesus, there's an open heaven between us and the throne, and the path of communication is clear. Twenty-four hours a day, seven days a week, the house of heaven is always open to us. Communion is our reminder that we have an open connection to heaven's throne. Sin can block the path, but as we bring it to the foot of the cross, confessing it, the way is crystal clear again.

Jesus, we remember Your sacrifice. You laid down Your life to make an open path for us to heaven and eternal life. Without You, the way was blocked by our sin, but You paid the price for our sin and set us free. You are the anointed One. If anything is blocking us from You, any hidden sin, reveal it, that we may repent and have the pathway open and clear again. Amen.

For further study: Genesis 28:10–22; Psalm 18:2, 91:11; John 1:29, 43–51, 14:23; 2 Corinthians 5:21; Hebrews 1:13,14, 4:16; 1 Peter 1:10–12.

APRIL 8
Jesus Is the Door

I am the door. If anyone enters by Me, he will be saved, and will go in and out and find pasture.
(John 10:9)

JESUS TELLS A parable about a sheepfold, the place of rest, healing, and provision for His sheep. In it, He's referring to eternal life in heaven and abundant life on earth. In the passage, He speaks of thieves and robbers who come in over the wall, trying to call and entice the sheep and steal them away. These are false gods, false religions, and false ideas that would try to make us believe we could somehow do the right things or be good enough on our own to enter heaven and stand in the presence of a holy God. He calls us to come into His kingdom, but He also reminds us that there is only one way to enter. That way is through Jesus Christ Himself—He is the door. We must receive Jesus as Lord and Savior to enter the heavenly sheepfold.

One day, Jesus asked His disciples who men said He was. Some said Elijah, others, Jeremiah. Jesus then asked, "Who do you, my disciples, say I am?" Peter rightly answers that Jesus is the Christ, the Son of the living God. Jesus blesses Peter and explains that it was that revelation of the Holy Spirit on which the church would be built. A locked door can be opened by the key. Jesus tells us He holds the keys to the kingdom of heaven and will give them to us. Jesus is the door, the gateway to the kingdom of heaven. The foundation of the key that unlocks that door is the revelation that Jesus is the Christ, the Son of the living God. Recognizing who Jesus is and accepting Him as Lord and Savior of our lives sets us free from the chains of sin and death.

He who holds the keys has the authority to unlock the door and enter the chambers. We are allowed into the royal kingdom of heaven and have the authority as sons and daughters of the King to access all the blessings and favor of that kingdom. We're no longer slaves but free people. We're no longer common or unclean, but royalty. We once were paupers and beggars, unable to lift our heads without shame, but now we come boldly to the throne of grace. We approach the king as one approaches a beloved head of the family. We're not the same people we once were. We've been adopted into God's family and given the keys to all His blessings by the revelation knowledge of Him. We come to understand His goodness to us, His love for us, His care for us, and His purpose for us. That revelation knowledge opens the door to all He has for us.

> *Father, we thank You for giving us the Holy Spirit, who has revealed to us Your love and the greatness of the sacrifice of Jesus Christ. You have given us the keys and bid us welcome. We can now make our home with You. We take the bread and the wine today and remember that we are no longer who we once were; we are members of Your royal family. Help us to live as sons and daughters of the one true King. Amen.*

For further study: Matthew 16:13–19; John 10:1–18, 14:6; Romans 8:2, 15; 2 Timothy 1:9–10; 1 Peter 2:9–10.

APRIL 9

The Last Jedi

For God did not send His Son into the world to condemn the world, but that the world through Him might be saved. (John 3:17)

THE STAR WARS movies are a bit of a cultural icon. Not many people haven't seen them. In many respects, the theme is a common one in many movies and books—the classic struggle of good versus evil. In the episode titled *The Last Jedi*, one of the heroes is about to continue on a suicide mission, but a heroine knocks him off his trajectory. He's mad at her for stopping him from trying to destroy a weapon of the force of darkness, but she rebukes him and says, "I saved you. This is how we win. We don't win by destroying what we hate but by saving what we love."

There's something very powerful in that thought. Isn't that what Jesus did? He defeated once and for all the forces of evil by saving what He loves. It just happens that the thing He loves is us. Satan must have been rejoicing to see Jesus dying on the cross, thinking he had won the war—the Son of God totally in his evil grasp. He must have wondered why Jesus didn't call the angels of heaven to fight a big battle and wipe him out. That's what Satan was doing—destroying what he hated. Wouldn't Jesus do the same?

But Jesus had a bigger plan. In saving those He loves, the power of death, sin, and the enemy was forever vanquished. Sure, the final battle hasn't yet been fought and will come one day, but the enemy of our souls has already been defeated. It's just a matter of time. One day, we'll walk through heaven's gates into eternity with Him. He didn't come to destroy people who were evil but to save all those who would choose the life and love He had to offer.

Sometimes we're so focused on knocking down the forces of evil that we forget that those forces of evil are knocked down by our love one for another. It's for the love He had for us that He continued on the road to the cross. It's the love we have for Him that enables us to love our enemy, to do good to those who hate us, to pray for those who use us. By His love, great works of faith are done. Love conquers our fear of death and hell and opens our prison and sets us free. Love has rescued us out of the very grasp of the evil one.

> *Jesus, as we partake of the bread and wine, we remember that You went to the cross. You let Satan attack Your body and spill Your blood so that all who believe in You would be taken from the kingdom of darkness and set free in the kingdom of light. You didn't come to condemn the world but so that the world through You would be saved. We remember and thank You. Help us to let that love flow through us to others trapped in the darkness, that they too would see Your light. Amen.*

For further study: Isaiah 61:1–3; Luke 6:27–30; Romans 12:21; Hebrews 2:14–18; Revelation 20:10.

APRIL 10
Esteem One Another

Let nothing be done through selfish ambition or conceit, but in lowliness of mind let each esteem others better than himself. (Philippians 2:3)

PAUL EXHORTS THE Philippians to be humble, to look out for one another, walking together in a spirit of unity. Unfortunately, sometimes our pride can get in the way of reaching that goal. If we're honest with ourselves, we may discover that we think ourselves better than others. The boss often feels superior to the employees. An employee may feel better than that lazy co-worker. Others feel they're of more value than the drug addict living on the street. God, however, says that all have sinned and fallen short of the glory of God. There is none who does good. We're all made of the same fallible, human stuff. Paul reminds us that we should do no works for selfish ambition; rather, we are to consider others better than ourselves. Sure, we can look out for our own interests, but we can't forget to look out for the interests of others in the process. True humility isn't about knocking ourselves down; it's about lifting others up.

When the world is pulling at us to fight and claw our way to the top, how can we remember that the way to the top is by esteeming others? Paul gives us the answer in the next few verses. We look to Jesus and remember who He is and what He did. Here is Jesus, equal with God the Father, yet He humbled Himself and walked the road to the cross. By His obedience even unto death, we now have forgiveness of sins and new life. He is exalted to heaven and has enabled us to join Him in eternity. He is our example. He is God. He is better than us, yet He humbled Himself and gave Himself for us.

Communion is all about pausing to remember what Jesus did for us and how He allowed His body to be broken for us so that we could be healed. He allowed His blood to be poured out as payment for our sins because He esteemed us worthy to be saved. We pause to give thanks to Him for what He has done and to remember that He is our example of how to look upon others. He also gives us the ability to lay down our lives for others.

At the communion table, we pause to ask the Holy Spirit to show us where we've fallen short so that we can repent and once again walk in close fellowship with the Spirit of God. Is there someone you've looked down on as unworthy of God's love? Is there someone you've stepped on in your rush to the top?

Dear Jesus, thank You for going to the cross to save us from our sins. We remember what You have done and ask for forgiveness for our pride and attitudes of superiority over the people You felt were worthy enough of Your sacrifice. We repent and ask You to change our hearts. Let that same mind be in us—to humble ourselves and esteem others as better than ourselves. Amen.

For further study: Romans 3:10–12, 21–23; 1 Corinthians 11:28; Ephesians 1:7, 4:17–32; Philippians 2:1–11; 1 John 3:16.

APRIL 11
Not Yours to Carry

> But let each one examine his own work, and then he will have rejoicing in himself alone, and not in another. For each one shall bear his own load. (Galatians 6:4–5)

A FRIEND OF mine was devastated when she found out a dear friend was trapped in sin. She asked God to forgive her for not seeing it or doing anything to try to stop it. Suddenly, she felt God say in her spirit, "I will not forgive you for that!" My friend admitted that at first she was shocked. She understood, however, what the Spirit was saying. She was not God. She couldn't know the struggles in the heart of another, nor was it her job to be responsible for another's sin. Only God can carry the failures of people we know and love.

I had a similar experience in my own life. Someone I loved was trapped in anger that ran deep in their soul. I felt I should be able to say the right thing, or not say the wrong thing, in order to stop it. I too cried out to God, seeking forgiveness for being unable to stop the other person's transgression. In my spirit, however, I felt God saying that this person had the right to their actions. I knew He wasn't saying their actions were right, but rather that they had their own free will. I wasn't responsible for their sin. I was trying to carry a burden that was never mine to carry.

Paul tells us in Galatians that if we see someone sinning, we should restore them gently, keeping in mind that we also could fall. He tells us to bear one another's burdens. In the next breath, he says people have to carry their own load. So which is it? Do we carry each other's burdens, or do we carry our own? It's both. We do need to help our brothers and sisters as much as we can when they're struggling under the heavy weight of temptation, but it's also not our job to carry their sin. Each of us is required to bring our transgressions to the foot of the cross and hand them over to Jesus. No one else can do that for us.

The communion table is our time to remember that God is sovereign and holy. Only He could carry the burden of our sin. It's our job to bring it to Him at the foot of the cross. We can encourage others to bring their burdens to the cross as well, but we can't carry their load for them. We do what we can to help them, but we also recognize there are some things we were never made to carry.

> *God, only You know all that's in the heart of a person. Only You can carry the weight of our sin. Holy Spirit, show us where we have sins we have yet to bring to the foot of the cross. Also, show us where we have tried to carry the sins of another, as we recognize those were never ours to carry. Teach us to support each other even as we each carry our own load to You. Amen.*

For further study: Galatians 6:1–5.

APRIL 12
He Is Our Portion

Nevertheless I am continually with You; You hold me by my right hand. You will guide me with Your counsel, and afterward receive me to glory. (Psalm 73:23–24)

COMMUNION IS ABOUT our relationship with Jesus and with other people. We can think of this like the image of the cross—our vertical relationship with God and our horizontal relationships with others. In many respects, they're interconnected. When we realize how much God loves us and cares for us, it makes it easier to have patience with others who may not love or care for us. Conversely, if we're walking in offense, unforgiveness, and broken relationships with others, it affects our relationship with God.

In Psalm 73, Asaph speaks on this. In the first part of the psalm, he declares his frustration and how offended he is with the wicked. The ungodly seem to prosper, and their lives seem easy and full of riches. They seem to avoid trouble even though they're proud, boastful, and speak wickedly of God and men. Asaph is jealous of them and wonders why he bothers to serve God, since he experiences trouble and pain. His offense with others has caused him to be offended with God, but then Asaph goes into the sanctuary and is reminded of the goodness of God. He remembers that all will face judgment, and these wicked people are headed for a horrible nightmare, separated from God. Asaph remembers that God is with him always. God gives him wisdom and strength and will receive him into eternal life in the glory of heaven.

In remembering who God is, and the richness of His goodness to us, we can have compassion on the ungodly. We have no need to be jealous or offended with others, because God has provided all we could ever want or need. As we walk in the perfect love of our loving God who gave Himself for us, we become unoffendable.

In partaking of communion, we pause to ask ourselves if we're jealous or offended with anyone so that we might confess it, repent, and be cleansed. We also remember the great richness we have in Christ. God is always with us. He holds us by our hand and guides us with His counsel, and He will receive us into glory. What more could we possibly desire? We're also reminded of the horrible future for those who don't receive Christ so that we may have compassion on them and declare God's works and love to them. Without Him, all is lost, and they are without hope. May we always show others the love and glory we've found in Christ.

> *Dear God, we thank You that You are always with us. You do guide us and will receive us into glory. Forgive us for being offended or jealous with our brothers and sisters. Guide us in Your love and help us to love others. We remember all You've done for us. All we desire is You. Amen.*

For further study: Psalm 73:1–28; Matthew 16:26; Acts 4:12; 1 Corinthians 11:17–34; Ephesians 2:11–22; 1 John 1:9.

APRIL 13
The Irony of the Three in One

> Concerning His Son Jesus Christ our Lord, who was born of the seed of David according to the flesh, and declared to be the Son of God with power according to the Spirit of holiness, by the resurrection from the dead. (Romans 1:3–4)

OUR GOD IS a Triune God—that is, He is three persons, yet He is One. We're made in the image of God. We have our body, soul, and spirit—three aspects yet one person. There's an irony in being one yet being three—single yet many.

There are other ironic things about this Triune God. He's the Father but also the Son. He's the judge of the world to whom we will all give account, yet Jesus is also our advocate—the lawyer who pleads our cause and leads us to mercy. He's the Chief Shepherd, but He's also the lamb slain for the sins of the world. He's the Lion of the tribe of Judah yet the meek lamb laying down His life. He's the creator of all the universe, yet He was born on this earth from a woman and so appeared as one who was created. He's the Son of God but also the Son of man. He's the King of kings yet the servant of all. He's the high priest and the sacrifice. He was killed and died, yet He lives. He ascended to heaven and sits at the right hand of the Father in heaven, yet He lives in our hearts.

Similarly, when we come to Him realizing that we're sinners in need of a Savior, He makes us saints. We come to Him repentant and humble and are exalted. We come broken and are made whole. We come poor and gain all the riches of heaven. We acknowledge our weakness and find that our weakness is now our strength because in our weakness He is strong. We are His servant yet part of a royal priesthood. We receive Him personally as a single person yet are now His body, part of a great multitude on earth.

Partaking of communion today, we remind ourselves that He died for our sins, yet He lives and reigns in our hearts. We partake of the bread representing His body and recognize we are now the body of Christ, part of a bigger whole that contains the whole family of God. We come to the communion table to be reminded of all this and to ask the Holy Spirit to reveal areas where we may be in discord with His body, that we might find healing for our soul.

> *God, we recognize the amazing character of You, our Priest and our Savior, our Shepherd and our Lamb. You died yet You live. We thank You for all the wonderful grace and life You've bestowed upon us, that we would find ourselves covered in Your glory, washed from our sins, and now called to be saints and Your body on earth. Forgive us any trespasses as we indeed forgive others. Amen.*

For further study: Genesis 1:26; Isaiah 33:22; John 1:1–4, 34, 5:26–27, 10:11, 17:21–26; Acts 25:19; Romans 1:7, 3:23, 12:5; 1 Corinthians 5:7; 2 Corinthians 4:5, 12:10; Galatians 4:4; Philippians 2:5–8; 1 Timothy 6:15; Hebrews 4:14, 9:14; James 4:6; 1 Peter 2:9; 1 John 2:1–2, 5:7; Revelation 5:5.

APRIL 14
Counting the Cost

Knowing that you were not redeemed with corruptible things, like silver or gold, from your aimless conduct received by tradition from your fathers, but with the precious blood of Christ, as of a lamb without blemish and without spot. (1 Peter 1:18–19)

MOST PEOPLE, WHEN setting out to build or do something big, first sit down and think about the cost versus the benefit. How much time, money, and energy are going to be required to do this, and will we receive enough from it to counter that cost? If the benefit isn't worth it, we're unlikely to pay the price. Even Jesus, in Luke 14, talks about this. He says that if you're going to build a tower, you sit down and make sure you have enough to complete it before you start. If you're a king going to war, you ensure that you have enough resources to fight your enemy, and if not, you will instead send a delegation asking for the terms of peace.

Let's imagine a conversation between God the Father and God the Son. The Father says, "Now Son, you see those people we created. They've sold out to Satan. They are born in sin and die in sin. Unless they are holy, they cannot come into our presence, and they cannot be holy unless they are redeemed. Unfortunately, the price required to redeem them is a sinless, perfect sacrifice. The only way to get a perfect sacrifice would be if one of Us went down and was born of a woman, lived the perfect life, and laid down that life. The price of redemption for these creatures would be astronomical. It would cost us everything."

Jesus stands up and says, "Father, I will go."

The Father replies, "Are You sure? They will mock You, wound You, forsake You. Some will refuse to believe no matter what miracles You do. You will lay down Your life and still be forsaken, denied, and refused by many. Many will refuse to believe You are real, or they may say You're real but refuse to recognize You as God. You may pay that price, and there may not be many who accept it and receive that redemption. There may not be much benefit compared to the price You will pay."

Jesus then answers, "But even if only one is saved, I will go. I will pay that price. I will give up everything for that one lost soul who comes to Us and is redeemed."

Jesus is our redeemer, the one willing to pay the price, to give His all. Likewise, to truly follow Jesus entails a cost. In fact, it costs us everything. Jesus living in us should affect every aspect of our life. He loved us enough to give His all. Do we love Him enough to give our all? To give Him everything?

> *Jesus, we recognize that You gave Your all. You paid the ultimate price to redeem us with Your blood. Reveal to us any area we hold back from You, that we may come to You for forgiveness and to receive Your power and strength to live a holy life for You. It may cost us everything, but You are more than worth it. You are the Lord and our Savior! We thank You for loving us enough to pay the price. Amen.*

For further study: Luke 14:25–35.

APRIL 15
Spiritual Triage

Love does no harm to a neighbor; therefore love is the fulfillment of the law. And do this, knowing the time, that now it is high time to awake out of sleep; for now our salvation is nearer than when we first believed. (Romans 13:10–11)

"TRIAGE" DESCRIBES THE sorting of people into different categories of urgency so that in attending to the wounded, the number of survivors can be maximized. Someone with a minor wound might wait a long time for treatment, while those with more urgent needs are seen first. It's a natural tendency to categorize things into different levels of urgency and severity.

We live in a fallen world that's in a constant war between the forces of good and evil. At times we become wounded or we wound others. We sin or are wounded by someone else's sin. As you sit on the battlefield, can you picture Jesus as a medic in an ambulance emblazoned with a large red cross, coming quickly to where we are? He screeches to a halt and jumps out, running to our side. He sees where we are wounded, His concern showing on His face. We look down at our wound and say, "Ah, it's just a graze from a stray bullet. It's not severe. Go to the others who are more seriously injured."

Jesus shakes His head and says, "No. Your wound may look small compared to others, but it's a serious wound. Left unattended, it will fester and destroy you. You need to come with Me to the front of the treatment line. This needs to be dealt with now."

All our sins and wounds to our soul are life threatening. We might look at ourselves and think a sin not very bad. A person who exceeds the speed limit will consider themselves less of a law-breaker than someone who commits murder. Yet in both instances, the law was broken.

It's not the size of the wound that determines the danger. The smallest prick from a thorn could fester and poison us, even if the wound from a sword cuts deeper. The good news is that Jesus came to take that poison from our soul. He came to overcome all the effects of the fallen world no matter the size of the failure. It's all important. All sin affects our relationship with God, and all wounds in our soul can be fatal if not dealt with. All of them bring us to the front of the line that has formed at the foot of the cross, covered in the blood of Jesus. Thankfully, God is big enough that everyone who comes to Him can instantly be transported to the front of the line. There is no need to wait. Now is the time. Today is the day of salvation. He is ready and able to deal with every wound, every sin, every failure, every fall right now. Don't delay. You don't know which wound will fester and destroy you.

> *Jesus, You came to redeem us from the effects of sin. We have all sinned and fallen short of Your glory, yet You reach out to us to heal and save us. We are Your priority. No wound is too small, no failure too great that You can't heal and restore us. We remember to bring to You all our failures and receive all Your grace, and we thank You. Amen.*

For further study: Romans 3:23, 13:8–14; 2 Corinthians 6:2; Titus 2:11–14.

APRIL 16
The Unleavened Bread

Therefore purge out the old leaven, that you may be a new lump, since you truly are unleavened. For indeed Christ, our Passover, was sacrificed for us. Therefore let us keep the feast, not with old leaven, nor with the leaven of malice and wickedness, but with the unleavened bread of sincerity and truth. (1 Corinthians 5:7–8)

THE UNLEAVENED BREAD served at Passover in a Jewish Seder meal is a flat, bland bread with rows of holes pierced in it. The small burn marks around the holes are called bruises. As a Christian, we can recognize immediately the symbolism here. Jesus, the bread of life, was without sin (symbolized by leaven). He was crushed (flat), striped (the rows of holes are like stripes), pierced (holes), and bruised (burn marks) in order to pay the price for our sins and set us free. In Isaiah 53, Jesus is described as nothing special to look at. He wasn't handsome to begin with, and after being bruised and covered by stripes from the whipping, the Bible says He was so marred that He was barely recognizable as a man. The Seder bread is broken during the meal, and Jesus was broken for us. He went to the cross and died, but the story doesn't end there. He also rose on the third day and is seated at the right hand of the Father. When He rose from the dead, He gave us the command to go and make disciples. Now all Christians corporately together act as the body of Christ here on earth.

In 1 Corinthians, Paul tells us to get rid of the old leaven—the sin that so easily grabs hold of us, our malice and wickedness. Instead, we're to become as unleavened bread, full of sincerity and truth. Because Jesus was sacrificed for us, we can put away sin and put on righteousness. He enables us to put away our old life and walk in a new life. Without God empowering us, we would never succeed. Even with His strength, we fail at times. We fall back into our old sinful habits. We may curse others or mistreat others, in our hearts if not in action. Communion reminds us that we are part of the body of Christ. Our job is to keep the Passover feast in our hearts at all times, remembering the bread of life broken for us, and that we too should walk a sinless life just as He did. The Holy Spirit may bring to our mind an area where we've fallen short, and this is the time for us to come to the cross once again to confess and repent. As we bring our failure to the foot of the cross, we're once again cleansed and free. We are now alive to righteousness and dead to sin, and by His stripes we are healed.

> *Lord, we bless You and thank You. You are the bread of life, broken for us. You were bruised, striped, and pierced as You paid the penalty for our sins. We now are to be like You and be without sin in our lives, but we still mess up. Please forgive us and make us new. Create in us a pure heart, clean and free of sin. Amen.*

For further study: Isaiah 53:1–12; Matthew 28:18–20; 1 Corinthians 15:4; Colossians 3:1–11; 1 Peter 2:24.

APRIL 17
Wounds from My Friends

And someone will say to him, "What are these wounds between your arms?" Then he will answer, "Those with which I was wounded in the house of my friends." (Zechariah 13:6)

THIS VERSE PROPHESIES of Jesus and the wounds in His hands, which came from His friends.

Have you ever noticed that nothing cuts so deep as a wound from someone you love? David wrote how hard it is to bear the betrayal of a friend. He said if it had been his enemy, it wouldn't have been so bad. You expect an enemy to treat you badly, but when it's your friend—now that wound penetrates deep into the soul! Jesus understood that kind of betrayal. Judas, one of His twelve disciples, betrayed the Messiah for a few pieces of silver. Not only that, but he betrayed Jesus with a kiss, a sign of love used to send Jesus to torture and death. Jesus's closest friends all ran away. Peter even denied having any knowledge of Jesus three times. Jesus calls us His friends, yet it was our sins that nailed Him to the cross. It was to pay for our redemption that He walked that road to Golgotha. The wounds in His hands and feet, the spear piercing His side and heart, are because of us, to save us.

Jesus asks us to forgive others just like we were forgiven. Sometimes it's easier to forgive strangers and enemies who have wounded us. Those wounds from our family and friends pierce our hearts, and we're more inclined to hang on to the hurt. We relive the abuse, the caustic or sarcastic comments, the times when our friends abandoned us in our time of need, the betrayal or any of a multitude of ways we've been wounded by friends and family. Jesus commands us to forgive just as we've been forgiven.

Think back on your past. Have we not at times made some sarcastic comment that cut someone to the heart, but then we said we were only joking, refusing to see the wounds we caused? What about times when a friend needed us, but we had other things to do? What about when our friend needed us to stand by them, but we were too afraid of others so we forsook our friend instead? We've been wounded by people, but we've also driven the spear of betrayal into the hearts of our friends, our spouse, and our family. We come to the communion table, remembering that He took the nails and the wounds to set us free. We also come to forgive others as He has forgiven us. When we come to the table, we find forgiveness for the wounds we caused and the healing for the wounds inflicted on us. We are made new and set free by His blood and grace.

Jesus, thank You for going to the cross, for giving Your body and blood to set us free. Amen.

For further study: Psalm 55:12-14: Matthew 25:31-46, 26:14-16, 50, 56, 69-75; John 15:12-17; Ephesians 4:32.

APRIL 18
The Son Still Shines Brightly

Every good gift and every perfect gift is from above, and comes down from the Father of lights, with whom there is no variation or shadow of turning. (James 1:17)

I WOKE UP today to a dreary day. Dark clouds filled the sky, and the wind blew strongly. Snow blew in sideways on the wind with a bitter cold temperature. It should be spring, but winter refuses to let go of its grip. The sun rose, but even at noon the world was shadowy and gray. It would be easy to believe the sun had lost some of its strength and warmth. If we jumped in a plane and flew above the clouds, we might be surprised to see the sun there, just as bright as the day before. When it's night on our side of the world, someone else has daylight. The sun never weakens, only our ability to see it changes.

Sometimes it seems like God doesn't have His strength or power like He once did. Our world seems dark and dreary, and we feel like He's changed toward us. Logic, however, tells us that the God who gave His life to save us, the God who made all creation and never changes, is still as powerful, as loving, and as wonderful to us as He's always been. Scripture reminds us that the God who made the stars in the sky is well able to give us good gifts. His Word proclaims His ever-faithful love. He demonstrated that love by walking the road that led to the cross. The God who gave His all for us is always shining just as brightly, even if at times we don't feel it or see it.

Pausing to partake of communion is to pause and remind ourselves of His great love. It's a reminder that He doesn't change like shifting shadows. He remains shining brightly with His love for us. The weather in our soul may shift and change; some days we feel the warmth, while other days are downright miserable, but He never changes. Maybe things haven't turned out as we thought they would. We thought it was going to be a warm springtime of our life, but instead we still feel winter's cold hand gripping our soul. To take communion is to remind us that our current circumstances don't really mean anything. Our God, who laid down His life on the cross and took it up again on the third day, is the only thing that truly matters. His power is not diminished. His love is no weaker. His grace is ever bright, shining to all eternity, reaching out to release us from our sins of the past, present, and future. Tomorrow may be a brighter day, but even if the clouds remain, His grace is ever present; His mercies are new every morning.

Jesus, we thank You for going to the cross for us. We thank You for preparing a place for us. You have made the way for Your grace to set us free from all our shortcomings and sins. You are not diminished by changes in our circumstances, and You remain ever-present, loving us, giving Your all to us. Help us to remember that one day we will be above the clouds with You forever. Amen.

For further study: Genesis 1:16; 1 Chronicles 29:10–12; Psalm 136:1–9; Isaiah 25:1; Lamentations 3:22–24; Malachi 3:6; Matthew 7:11; John 14:1–3, 15:13; 1 Corinthians 13:4–10; Revelation 21:23–24.

APRIL 19
Naked and Unashamed

> If we confess our sins, He is faithful and just to forgive us our sins and to cleanse us from all unrighteousness. (1 John 1:9)

WHEN ADAM AND Eve were in the Garden of Eden, before the fall of humanity into sin, they were naked and unashamed. Their innermost thoughts, feelings, and all their deeds were exposed and known, and they had no need to fear. There was nothing to be ashamed of. When they chose to eat from the tree of the knowledge of good and evil, their sin was exposed, and they were ashamed. In vain they tried to cover their sin and hide their nakedness; however, only God could cover them and restore their dignity. Animals were sacrificed to provide a covering for them. The sacrifice was repeated over and over again until Christ came once and for all and covered our sin with the blood of His sacrifice. We come to the foot of the cross, confess we are sinners, and He welcomes us into His family. We are now covered in His righteousness, and you would think that would be that. Unfortunately, we still sin and mess up. There are things hidden in our hearts that gnaw at our souls and hinder our relationship with God and others.

When we speak of baring our soul to someone, we mean that we're uncovering our innermost thoughts, fears, hopes, or dreams. Our soul is naked. So often we're guarded in what we reveal to people—often with good reason, but sometimes to our harm. Hidden in our soul remain secret sins and hurts that we fear revealing. How will people take that information? Will they still love us? Will we still be accepted? Will they expose our sin, or will they cover it with their love?

Jesus calls us to the table and tells us to bare our soul to Him. He knows us completely, but He wants us to confess our fears, our pain, and our sin so that we know in our heart of hearts He really does know. There is nothing hidden from Him. He wants us to know that He will still love and accept us. He will still cover us with His righteousness. He will still surround us with His love. As long as we try to hide it from Him, that failure has power over us to keep us from His glory. When we hold nothing back, we bare our soul and stand before Him as if we are naked, but we are unashamed. He has washed away our failings and made us new. We are sanctified and able to walk in intimate fellowship with God.

Today as we partake of communion, we remember that He died to pay for all our sins—past, present, and future. Let's take a moment and see if there is any hidden fault in us, and then expose it to the light of His love.

> *Jesus, we thank You for laying down Your life and shedding Your blood to pay the price for our sins so that we might be the righteousness of God in You. Your blood is sufficient, and we can stand before You, baring our souls, naked yet unashamed. Amen.*

For further study: Genesis 2:25, 3:7, 21; Psalm 19:12–13; Isaiah 61:10; John 1:12; Ephesians 1:5–6; Hebrews 4:12–13, 10:3–10.

APRIL 20
We Are His Workmanship

Know that the Lord, He is God; it is He who has made us, and not we ourselves; we are His people and the sheep of His pasture. Enter into His gates with thanksgiving, and into His courts with praise. Be thankful to Him, and bless His name. For the Lord is good; His mercy is everlasting, and His truth endures to all generations. (Psalm 100:3–5)

PSALM 100 TELLS us to give thanks to the Lord. We enter His gates with thanksgiving. We thank Him because He is good, merciful, and true. Communion in many churches is called the Eucharist, which is from the Greek word for giving thanks. It's called this because it was established at the Last Supper Jesus shared with His disciples when Jesus said grace, or in other words, gave thanks. Imagine that! On the night Jesus was going to be betrayed and handed over for torture and death, even knowing this, He paused and gave thanks. Because of His sacrifice, we are now accepted into heaven and welcomed into the kingdom of God. We see that God is good and merciful and we have much to be thankful for. We are now the sheep of His pasture and He is our Good Shepherd who laid His life down for the sheep.

In the book of Ephesians, Paul reminds us of how great the mercy and love of God are. Even when we were dead in our sin, He made us alive with Christ, purely by His grace. There is no work we could do to earn our salvation or make ourselves righteous before a holy God. God, therefore, did the work for us. Now we are redeemed from our sins, and He has given us power to do good works. The good works don't earn our salvation, but the sheer wonder and glory of His grace compels us to do good works. In fact, God ordained us to walk in good works. He has prepared the way for us to do this. He has planned it and enabled it.

In remembering what He has done for us with a thankful heart, it all becomes possible. We aren't overcome by evil, but we overcome evil by good. We're able to do good to those who are unkind or broken because we remember God was good to us when we were still sinners, unkind, and broken. Partaking of communion is all about remembering who we are and who we belong to by pausing to give thanks to Him.

Lord God, You are good and merciful. You are true. We acknowledged our sin and You set us free from the power of sin and death. We pause to give You thanks and to remember that we are Your sheep. We are Your workmanship, and You have ordained us to walk in good works. Help us to show others Your glory within us. Amen.

For further study: Psalm 100:1–5; John 10:11; Romans 12:21; 1 Corinthians 11:23–25; Ephesians 1:3–2:10; Hebrews 13:20–21.

APRIL 21
Passion

> Now it came to pass, as He sat at the table with them, that He took bread, blessed and broke it, and gave it to them. Then their eyes were opened and they knew Him; and He vanished from their sight. And they said to one another, "Did not our heart burn within us while He talked with us on the road, and while He opened the Scriptures to us?" (Luke 24:30–32)

WHEN WE SPEAK of someone being passionate, we mean that they have strong emotions, often of love, but it could also be anger. If they're really passionate, we compare them to being consumed by a burning fire. Have you ever wondered why the last day of Christ's life, when He suffered and died, is called the Passion of Christ? Certainly it evokes strong emotion in us. It reveals to us the great depth of His love, that while we were yet sinners, Christ died for us. Did you know the word "Passion" has its root and meaning in suffering? It's called the Passion because it's the time of Christ's suffering.

After Christ died on the cross, two of His disciples went on a journey to the town of Emmaus. They were sad and confused. They thought the Messiah would come and destroy their Roman enemies, but instead, the one they thought was their Savior had been tortured and died a brutal death. As they walked on the road, Jesus came alongside, but they didn't recognize Him. They told Him how their hopes had been dashed with the death of the one they thought would save them. Jesus then said to them, *"Ought not the Christ to have suffered these things and to enter into His glory?"* (Luke 24:26). In other words, He explained to them that true salvation is not physical salvation from a natural enemy but the spiritual salvation we're in such desperate need of. This ignites in them their passion! Their hearts burn within them. They start to understand what true love is and the depth of God's love for them.

In the book of Revelation, God rebukes the church of Ephesus. They seem like such a great church, but God tells them that they have lost their first love: they have lost their passion. He also rebukes the church in Sardis, because they look alive to others, but really, they are dead! He calls them to repent and reignite the passion. He rebukes the church of Laodicea as being lukewarm—without passion! He calls them to buy gold refined in the fire—the spiritual riches obtained through suffering.

Have you lost your passion? Have you lost the fire of love? Return to it by remembering the passion—the suffering of Christ—and reignite that passion of love for Him in your soul.

> *Lord, You walked the road of suffering so that You might save us from the suffering we deserve in the fires of hell. Remind us of the depth of Your love, and cause the passion of Your love to burn within us, directing all we say and do. Amen.*

For further study: Luke 22:14–20, 24:13–32; Revelation 2:1–8, 3:1–6, 14–22.

APRIL 22
The Gift of Grace

For by grace you have been saved through faith, and that not of yourselves; it is the gift of God. (Ephesians 2:8)

THE GREEK WORD *charis* means a gift. It also means grace. Grace—unmerited favor and blessing! What better way is there to describe a gift? It's the gift of the pardon of sins. It's also the thanks we give at meals for the gift God has given of our food, and the thanks Jesus gave on the night of His betrayal. *Charis* is intimately associated with the change in our hearts and lives from one of sin to one full of grace. It's a gift given willingly and freely. It can't be earned or paid back. *Charizomai* is rooted in the word *charis* and it means to pardon, to deliver, or to forgive. The ultimate gift of God is the pardon for our sins, in which we have received His grace. *Charis* itself is rooted in the Greek word *chairo*, the verb that means to be cheerful. There is joy and rejoicing at the root of gifts, at the root of grace.

Grace is ultimately the gift God has given us in the sacrifice of His Son, and receiving that gift births in us thankfulness and joy. Our behavior starts to change to be more gracious as it reflects the change in our hearts. Grace, gifts from God, gratitude, and joy are all wrapped up together.

Sometimes we can lose sight of the gifts of God. We lose our gratitude and joy. We forget about the grace we've received through faith, so we turn to communion. It's our reminder of the ultimate gift of God, the gift of His grace. It reminds us to give thanks, and in the giving of thanks, it reminds us to rejoice. As Jesus sat at the table, He broke the bread and said that His body was broken to make us whole. He took the cup and said that this was His blood being poured out to free us from our sins. As He said grace, He was bestowing grace upon us, the gift of Himself. From thanksgiving to joy.

The world drags us down and says, "Hurry, hurry, hurry. We have no time." The world says we are not enough. The world tries to break us and wear us down. But God tells us to pause. He bids us to sit at the table and pick up the bread that was broken for each one of us and eat. Take up the cup, drink, and remember. He is more than enough. His grace is sufficient. There is much to be thankful for. With His gifts come abundant joy and rejoicing. If we find ourselves in a place of dreariness, the pathway back to joy is in gratitude for His grace.

> *Heavenly Father, You have bestowed great gifts on us. You gave Your son to redeem us from our fallen condition. You have given us all things, and we thank You. Restore to us the joy of our salvation as we remember You. Amen.*

For further study: Psalm 51:12; Matthew 26:26–29; Mark 14:22–25; Luke 22:19–20; 1 Corinthians 11:23–25; 2 Corinthians 12:9; Philippians 4:4; Hebrews 12:2; 1 Thessalonians 5:16–18.

APRIL 23
Worship the Lord of Majesty

Give unto the Lord the glory due to His name; worship the Lord in the beauty of holiness.
(Psalm 29:2)

JOB WAS A prosperous man who walked with the highest degree of integrity. One day, Satan comes to God and says that Job only serves God because God protects him. God allows Satan to attack everything Job has to show that this isn't true. All Job's children die; all his animals and servants, his livelihood, are stolen and killed, and his body is struck with illness. Yet Job doesn't sin or curse God.

Job's friends come to comfort him, but they are miserable comforters. They say, "You must have sinned, so confess your sin and God will heal you." Job defends himself. He is angry and bitter and says he'd like to see God in a court of law, because God isn't fair. Here he is suffering even though he's a righteous man. Finally, a young man steps in and says, "Here's your problem, Job—you're self-righteous."

Then God Himself enters the conversation. He speaks of His great majesty, how He has fashioned the world, His intimate knowledge of every plant and animal, of the rain and sun. At first when I read these chapters, I heard God's tone of voice like He was angry. As I thought about God and His great mercy and how much He loves us—enough to die for us—I suddenly heard the voice differently. It was the tender voice of a loving Father saying something like this: "Job, you've thought yourself to be a pretty big man, and somewhere along the way, you stopped serving Me as an act of worship and started serving Me to save yourself and your family. You are exhausting yourself, and still you're not able to save yourself or them. Only I can save you and your family. If you were Me, the creator of the world, maybe then you could save yourself, but you're not." God had to bring Job to the end of himself to recognize there is no salvation by works; it is a gift of grace.

In this I saw myself. Going to church, serving in the church, even partaking of communion because it's something I do and not as an act of worship, is exhausting. These things become just another chore, another demand on an already busy life. Sure, we still believe we are saved by grace, but if we quit seeing our jobs, our service to our family, our service in the church as acts of worship to a God who loves us, then they become a demanding taskmaster in our lives. They exhaust and drain us rather than energize and fill us. Communion is all about pausing to remember our relationship with our heavenly Lord. Are we doing this because it's what we do, or is it an act of worship to our majestic Lord, the creator of heaven and earth and the Savior of our souls?

> *Lord, we bless You and worship You. You have created us. You know all about us. You know our sin, our failures. We repent of partaking of communion as another job or chore but see it as a reminder of who You are—the body and blood that saves and heals—and we worship You even in this. Amen.*

For further study: Genesis 1:1–2; the book of Job; 1 Peter 1:7–9.

APRIL 24
The Snare Is Broken

Our soul has escaped as a bird from the snare of the fowlers; the snare is broken, and we have escaped. (Psalm 124:7)

DAVID KNEW WHAT it was like to be hunted by an enemy, to be trapped in their snare. In Psalm 124, he writes that it was only by God fighting for him that he survived. The enemy had totally overwhelmed him; there was no hope in the natural. But God, the maker of heaven and earth, delivered him from the enemy's grasp.

David's poetry gives us a beautiful image of God's deliverance. He writes of being like a bird trapped in a snare, but before the bird dies at the hand of its enemy, the snare is broken and the bird soars free. There is no better image of freedom than a bird rising up into the heavens. When trapped in the snare, the bird faces death; he can't see anything but his fear. He can't move. He is helpless and wounded, but when the snare breaks, he is free. He rises high on the wind's breath and is able to see far into the distance. He's unhindered by the things of the world. There are no constraints on his flight as he dips and spins in the air.

Likewise, we were caught in the snare of the fowler. Our sins held us fast in the enemy's clutches. Certain death awaited us, and there was no hope outside of God. God in His mercy inserted His nail-pierced hands into the snare and broke it. We are free! We no longer face death but eternal life. This is so much more than just freedom from death. Jesus has granted us freedom to soar.

The wind of the Spirit blows and raises us up to the heavens. We aren't just released from the hold that fear and anxiety have on us, but we are free to rise up in faith. It's not only about being taken out of Satan's clutches but about entering into the embrace of our loving heavenly Father. We're not just freed from the power of sin; we now have the power to live for righteousness. We haven't just been taken out of the kingdom of darkness; we've been translated into the kingdom of light. We were blind, but now we not only see but have vision for the future. We're no longer held back; now we have purpose and destiny.

If the only thing Christ's sacrifice on the cross did was to save us from our sins and give us eternal life, it would have been enough, but He did so much more than that. He truly gave us life, and that life is one of great abundance and full of all things that are good.

Heavenly Father, we thank You that You didn't just save us from our sins. You gave us life. You gave us hope. You gave us purpose, strength, faith, love. You don't just break the snare of the fowler, but You teach us to soar on the wind of Your Spirit. We reach into the heavens and find safety, strength, and life in Your presence. We thank You for loving us that much to give us freedom to be all You created and desire us to be. Amen.

For further study: Psalm 124:1–8; Isaiah 40:29–31; Jeremiah 29:11; John 10:10; Ephesians 2:12–14, 3:20; Colossians 1:9–14; Hebrews 2:14–15; 1 Peter 2:24; 1 John 5:14.

APRIL 25
Last Things

And He took bread, gave thanks and broke it, and gave it to them, saying, "This is My body which is given for you; do this in remembrance of Me." Likewise He also took the cup after supper, saying, "This cup is the new covenant in My blood, which is shed for you." (Luke 22:19–20)

ON THE NIGHT when Jesus was betrayed, He sat at the table eating a Passover meal with His disciples. You have also, no doubt, heard it referred to as the Last Supper, since it was the last meal Jesus ate with His disciples before the crucifixion. I don't suppose when they were at the table, the disciples ever considered that it was the *last* supper. They likely thought tomorrow would continue on much the same as it had the day before. Even though Jesus had told them things were going to change and He was going to be betrayed, I'm sure they still thought their lives would continue unchanged. I wonder, if they had known this was truly the last night they would have with Jesus before His death and resurrection, would they have been humbler and more attentive to His words? Would they have clung to Him even as He washed their feet?

If we had known when we said goodbye at the door that this was the last time we would see our friend or loved one, would we have paused to treasure the moment? Would we speak words of grace rather than frustration if we knew that maybe moments later something would happen, and these would be the last words we would speak this side of heaven? Would we treasure the simple pleasures of life, the gifts given by God, if we knew this was the last time we would experience them?

We live in a fallen world. Life is fragile in this place. Just as the disciples didn't know that meal was going to be the last supper, we don't know what times are our last. Which hour is the last one to tell people we love them? Is this the last moment we have to show others the fruit of the Spirit—love, joy, and peace? This may be the last moment we have to show someone the grace of God. It may be the last moment we have to receive the grace of God. Peter tells us that the angels long to understand the wonders of God's grace that He freely bestows on us. This may be our last chance this side of heaven to be amazed by the wonder and glory of that grace.

Partaking of communion is about remembering His grace given to us. It's also about remembering the body of Christ around us and giving grace to others. Jesus knew that if we didn't pause and remember, life's circumstances would cause us to forget; therefore, one of the last things He did was to give us a way to remember so we would always walk in grace. We don't know which moment is the last time we have to offer someone grace this side of the grave, so let's remember to always walk in it.

> *Jesus, thank You for giving us a way to remember the grace we've received and can give. Help us to walk through life experiencing it and giving to others, like this is the last moment we have on earth to show forth Your grace. Amen.*

For further study: Luke 22:7–34; John 13:1–16; Galatians 5:22–25; 1 Peter 1:12–15.

APRIL 26
Agree with Your Adversary

Agree with your adversary quickly, while you are on the way with him, lest your adversary deliver you to the judge, the judge hand you over to the officer, and you be thrown into prison. Assuredly, I say to you, you will by no means get out of there till you have paid the last penny. (Matthew 5:25–26)

IN THE SERMON on the Mount, Jesus sat down to teach the multitudes what it means to be a Christian. He explained that it meant more than just keeping the Ten Commandments. "You shall not murder," say the commandments, but then Jesus said that if you're angry without cause, or curse your brother, it amounts to the same thing as murder. He talked about being reconciled with your brother before offering your gift to God, and He finished this passage with the advice to agree with your adversary quickly, lest you end up in prison and suffering.

Satan is the accuser of the brethren, our adversary. He's the prosecuting attorney coming to God and saying, "Did you see that? He cursed his brother! He's guilty! Put him in prison. This man is a sinner. Look at that—how he has broken your commandments, God. He has lied. He has lusted. He has coveted. He's guilty! Put him in jail and throw away the key! You say that You're a righteous judge, God. You know the law, and he broke it."

As we hear our adversary rant and rave, we know he's right. We've dishonored our parents, lusted, coveted, lied, stolen, not kept God first in our lives, even murdered, since to mistreat our brother even in our hearts is like murder. We are guilty. We're not worthy of a holy God, and we deserve to be thrown to the torturers. Thankfully, in this passage Jesus gives us the solution to our guilt: agree with your adversary.

The cross is all about coming to Jesus and saying, "Yes, Satan, my adversary, is right. I am a sinner, but I raise my eyes to see You on the cross, Jesus, and I see You have paid for my sin. You've taken the punishment for me and gone to hell's prison in my place, paying the price for my freedom." When we do this, we're no longer prisoners of guilt and shame. Jesus has set us free.

As we kneel at the foot of the cross, His blood covers our sin, but His Spirit also empowers us to change. We come not to just fear the punishment for sin but to hate the very sin itself. He gives us the desire and the ability to reach out to our brothers and sisters in reconciliation, for that is the other half of the equation. Communion is remembering He's paid the price for our sin. By confessing our sin—agreeing with our adversary—we are set free from condemnation, guilt, and shame. Communion also means recognizing our brothers and sisters as fellow members of the body of Christ and being reconciled one to another.

Heavenly Father, we agree with our adversary. He is right—we are sinners, guilty as charged. But we're also saints, saved by grace, the gift of Your Son. Help us to walk in peace with all people as much as is possible on our part. Help us to walk in the grace that He has so freely given. Amen.

For further study: Matthew 5:1–7:29, especially 5:20–26.

APRIL 27
Friends

Greater love has no one than this, than to lay down one's life for his friends. (John 15:13)

WE MIGHT CALL many people friends, but not all share the same depth of friendship. Some people are mere acquaintances, someone we see once or twice a year at family gatherings. Others we meet to go to a movie or out for coffee, but they're not part of our inner circle. Some are much closer, and we speak to them often and get together regularly. They're the people we share our lives with. Then there are some who get truly close. They know our hopes and dreams. They know our failures. They know what we're passionate about. These are the ones who seek to know our hearts, the ones with whom we share intimate times.

Jesus calls us His friends. He also has different levels of friendship with His followers. Some come to Him rarely, maybe once or twice a year at family gatherings. Others follow Him and call themselves Christians but don't really want to be pressured to change. They'll leave if the relationship gets challenging. Some are content to go out and work with Jesus, but they still aren't part of the inner circle. Then there were the twelve apostles who stuck around and were part of His day-to-day life. Of those twelve, three were much closer and were with Jesus during some of the highs and lows that the others weren't part of. These three were with Him on the mountaintop when He was transfigured before them. They were part of the inner room when He raised a dead girl.

Of those three, one lay upon His breast and felt the beat of His heart. Think about that. Since John was leaning on Jesus's breast when Jesus leaned forward to hand out the bread and the wine, John would have been moved as well when Jesus reached across the table, since they were in intimate contact. Did John feel Jesus's heart quicken as He leaned forward to pass the bread even to Judas? Did John know that even as Judas would betray the Son of Man, Jesus would call him friend?

What kind of friend are we? Do we speak to Jesus once in a blue moon? Do we follow Him just until it gets hard? Do we work for Him but out of duty, not out of a place of an intimate relationship? Do we betray Him when we're in a situation where it's not to our benefit to be called a Christian? Do we hang around the Christian crowd but lack intimacy with Christ? Do we have a daily relationship with the Savior that is somewhat close, or do we have a deep intimacy with Him, one that seeks to feel the beat of His heart, an intimacy that's moved when He moves, even if it's to reach out to our betrayer?

> *Jesus, we long for that intimate communion with You, one that feels the beat of Your heart, that is moved when You move. Bring us deeper into relationship. Lead us into a depth of communion with You, sharing all aspects of life, our highs and lows. Forgive us for when we haven't reached out with Your hand of compassion to others who have hurt us. Lead us in Your ways. Amen.*

For further study: Matthew 17:1–2, 26:48–50; Mark 5:35–43; Luke 6:12–13; John 6:60–66, 13:21–26.

APRIL 28
Unseen Beauty

But if we walk in the light and He is in the light, we have fellowship with one another, and the blood of Jesus Christ His Son cleanses us from all sin. (1 John 1:7)

THERE ARE RESEARCHERS who travel to the deep depths of the sea, where the light from the sun doesn't penetrate. Fish at this depth appear to be a dull gray color, but if the researchers bring them to the surface, the fish display brilliant and beautiful colors. This is consistent with the character of our God, the creator of the universe. He has put beauty even in things that are unlikely to ever have that beauty seen by others. He Himself is light, and there is no darkness in Him. He has no difficulty at all seeing the beauty that we miss.

The company that makes Dove soap once made a commercial in which women described themselves to a police sketch artist who couldn't see them. Then they had strangers describe the same women. The difference in the images was striking. When a woman described herself, she accentuated her flaws and failed to describe the beauty that a stranger clearly saw. The darkness in the world and in our hearts masks the beauty that should be plainly seen.

Have you noticed that when your world gets dark with stress, depression, anxiety, and trouble, it loses its color and appears gray? Instead of seeing the beauty in others, we are bitter and cynical, seeing everyone in that same gray, dim light. Isaiah said that even the Son of God was nothing special to look at in this dark world. The darkness in the world and in our hearts blinds us to the true nature of God and each other.

The cure for our blindness is to move toward the One True Light. Jesus is the light of the world. He gives light to everyone on this earth. If we let His light fill our hearts, the world and those in it regain their color and beauty. Our sins can cut us off from His light, but as John wrote, if we confess our sins, He is faithful to forgive us our sins and cleanse us from unrighteousness, restoring us to the light (1 John 1:9).

Communion is pausing to remember what He's done for us. It's about coming and confessing our sins so that we are restored to the light, and the darkness of the world no longer clings to us. It restores our ability to see the true color of love that before was hidden in the darkness. We can once again see the beauty even in the stranger we pass, the co-worker, the demanding client, the irritating, broken-hearted member of our family, and in ourselves. He has made all things beautiful, and only in His light can we see it.

> *Father, we thank You for sending the Light into the world to cure us of our spiritual darkness. The darkness blinded us to the beauty You have created and placed in each one of us. We thank You for that beauty in our body, soul, and spirit. You are amazing, God. Thank You for giving us eyes to see and the Light to see by. Amen.*

For further study: Isaiah 53:1–3; John 1:1–13; Hebrews 4:13; James 5:16; 1 John 1:5–9.

APRIL 29
Pass the Bread

> For as we have many members in one body, but all the members do not have the same function, so we, being many, are one body in Christ, and individually members of one another. (Romans 12:4–5)

TRAVEL WITH ME through time. Let's go back to a time even before the birth of Jesus and take our place at the table of the showbread in the tabernacle of Moses. On that table is unleavened bread, made of fine flour—crushed and bruised grain, mixed with oil, pierced and broken. There is wine also on the table to be poured out as a drink offering. We take our place at this table and eat the bread. We are the Lord's priests.

Now let's travel to the time of Christ. We walk with the Master and listen to His teachings. As Passover comes around, we sit at the table with Him. He leans over and hands us the bread and the wine and bids us to eat and drink. We are His disciples.

Once again, let's get in our time machine and speed forward to the present day. We sit at the table with our friends and family. We pick up the basket of bread in front of us and pass it across the table to the others sitting there. We are His body.

We are His body now on this earth. As Jesus walked along on His earthly journey, different opportunities to reach out to people presented themselves to Him. The multitudes came to Him seeking healing, provision, His teaching, His presence. Likewise, as we walk the earth and go about our daily life, different opportunities to reflect Christ are presented to us. Will we pass along His blessing, His provision, His strength, His grace, His love, or will we selfishly turn away? Which opportunities that come to us today will we say yes to? In which of those encounters will we take the time to pass the bread and wine of communion? Which ones will we reach out to and, with our actions, show other people that we see them and care? Sometimes as we travel along on our busy schedules, we lose sight of the fact that we're the only epistle some people will ever read. Will they read about Jesus in our actions? Let's try to remain aware and mindful of the opportunities that are presented to us every day to reflect His love.

> *Heavenly Father, sometimes we forget that we're the hands and feet of Jesus in this world. Holy Spirit, help us to notice those opportunities where our actions can reach out to the world with the love of the blessed Savior, who laid down His life for us. Amen.*

For further study: Leviticus 24:5–9; Matthew 26:26–29; Romans 12:3–21; 2 Corinthians 3:2–3; James 2:14–26.

APRIL 30
Dismember or Re-member

That there should be no schism in the body, but that the members should have the same care for one another. And if one member suffers, all the members suffer with it; or if one member is honored, all the members rejoice with it. Now you are the body of Christ, and members individually. (1 Corinthians 12:25–27)

HAVE YOU EVER had a serious injury or illness? It can take a long time to heal. Maybe you had to wear a cast and protect a limb, or go to physiotherapy. A lot of care, time, and effort might be needed to heal. In serious cases, a part of the body may even have to be removed or amputated. Amputation makes some things harder to do. Parts of the body that aren't ideally suited for a task have to be trained to take on the task of the lost limb. Things aren't always as smooth or as easy when a part of the body is missing. Sometimes people experience altered sensations in the remaining part of the body, such as phantom pain, decreased sensation, irritations, and sensitivities.

We are the body of Christ, yet sometimes when a member of the body is sick or injured, it seems we're not willing to do the hard work to bring healing to the body. We don't protect them or care for them. We don't participate in the necessary therapies or treatments, as they seem too hard or too long, and we think it's much easier to just cut that part of the body off. Unfortunately, with every member that's lost, tasks become a bit harder. Other people whose gifts maybe aren't ideal for the position must be recruited to do that work. Things are more difficult.

There's also lingering pain or altered sensation. We become numb in our hearts to the pain we should feel, and we feel too much pain when we shouldn't. Definitely there are times when a member becomes like a cancer and removal is best, but if we look around the world, we see that often we just don't make the necessary effort to bring restoration. People get offended and gossip flies, and people are shunned instead of being reached out to. We don't seem to give the same care to members of Christ's body as we would to members of our own physical body.

Healing is hard work. It takes time and effort, but in the end, it's so much better than dismemberment. Communion is a command to remember what Christ has done for us and that we are His body. In remembering this, we can work to re-member those who have been dis-membered.

> *Jesus, we remember that You gave Your life so we could be whole, personally and corporately. Help us to do the work needed to bring healing to Your body. Amen.*

For further study: 1 Corinthians 12:4–28.

MAY 1
The Haunted Man

In Him we have redemption through His blood, the forgiveness of sins, according to the riches of His grace. (Ephesians 1:7)

IN CHARLES DICKENS' short story "The Haunted Man," we meet Mr. Redlaw, a man tormented by the memories of someone who had done him wrong. He is desperate and pleads to be free of his painful memories. This wish is granted, along with the ability to give this "gift" to others. He thinks it will make life so much better for all if there's no memory of sickness, pain, betrayal, or hardship. Instead, the world for everyone with this "gift" becomes much worse. Along with the loss of the memory of the pain, they also lose the memories of the goodness and the grace that brought them through the pain. Songs lose their joy. Light becomes darkness. Mr. Redlaw discovers that in the memory of the evil done, there is beauty and grace that come through the healing. By giving up the memory of the pain of a fallen world, he had unwittingly given up all the true beauty, joy, and grace found at the foot of the cross.

Milly, a godly woman, comments to him that it's important to remember the wrongs done to us so that we may forgive them. Mr. Redlaw, in recognizing all the evil he did to others, finds that compassion grows in him as he also finds forgiveness at the foot of the cross.

There is much pain and distress in this fallen world, but where sin abounds, the grace of God abounds much more. This isn't an encouragement to sin but rather a call to walk in grace and to be instruments of righteousness. By recognizing all that we've been forgiven of, we can more freely extend grace to others. We bring our own sins to the foot of the cross and find redemption through His blood because of the richness of His grace.

We also bring the sins that others have committed against us to the foot of the cross and find His grace in us to extend to others. As we forgive, the memory of the evil is no longer the painful torment it once was, but now it's the path to greater grace. By the fellowship of His sufferings, we're conformed to His death and will come to know Him and the power of His resurrection. Having died with Him, we will live with Him. Through the memory of the torment, the sin can now be forgotten by the abundant overshadowing of the grace obtained through the trial.

As we come to the communion table today, we must examine ourselves. Are there sins we've kept hidden within us, holding their memory in a secret place to torment us? Let's bring them to the light at the foot of the cross, recognizing that God's grace is sufficient for us. One drop of the precious blood of the Savior is enough to cover our transgressions and bring us peace.

> *Holy Spirit, reveal to us any memory that torments us, whether pain we have caused or received, and lead us to the Spirit of grace and truth found at the cross. Jesus died and rose again that we might die to sin and be alive to righteousness. Help us, Lord, to walk in Your grace and truth. Amen.*

For further study: Matthew 6:12; Romans 5:20–21, 6:8, 13; 1 Corinthians 11:28; Philippians 3:10; Colossians 1:19–20; 2 Timothy 2:11; 1 Peter 4:8.

MAY 2
The Greater One Calls Our Name

And they heard the sound of the Lord God walking in the garden in the cool of the day, and Adam and his wife hid themselves from the presence of the Lord God among the trees of the garden. Then the Lord God called to Adam and said to him, "Where are you?" (Genesis 3:8–9)

IN THE BEGINNING, the Lord God made humans and put them in a garden. In that garden there was an abundance of provision. There was work, relationship, love, and the presence of the Lord walking with them and communing with them. There was also one tree that they weren't to eat of. We know how the story goes. Even though they had all the greatness of the garden except for that one tree, they chose to go to the lesser fruit of the tree of the knowledge of good and evil. They saw the enticements of that one tree—it was good for food (lust of the flesh), pleasant to the eyes (lust of the eyes), and desirable to make one wise (pride of life). They chose the lesser life of sin, while the Greater One was calling their name.

Jesus came into this fallen, sinful world to live a perfect life and die on the cross in order to redeem us from the effects of our sin. In a sense, He has prepared a new garden for us, as He gives us all things that pertain to life and godliness. In our little garden there is provision, work, relationships, love, and the presence of the Lord in our hearts. However, in this world there are also temptations. There is the lust of the flesh—unhealthy relationships, drugs, alcohol, and the excessive pull of food. There is the lust of the eyes—wanting that big house, cottage, pool, big screen TV, or anything else your neighbor has that you don't. And there is the pride of life—desires for affirmation, financial blessings, success, and popularity. Sometimes we find ourselves chasing after the rewards of these lesser things, even while the Greater One is calling our name.

Partaking of communion is an opportunity to examine ourselves and ask the Holy Spirit to reveal where we've sacrificed the Greater for the lesser. Where have we chased after lust and pride instead of turning back to the one who gave His all for us? It's a reminder that the Greater One gave His life so we could live. The Greater One calls our name and bids us fellowship with Him in the garden of His blessings. If we remember that, we'll be less likely to fall prey to the temptations of those lesser things that won't bring satisfaction to our souls.

Holy Spirit, we ask You to reveal to us where we've chased after lesser things and turned away from the one true God. We thank You, Jesus, for giving Your life for us and providing us with all we need, but particularly for Your communion—Your fellowship—where we can walk with You and talk with You. Thank You so much. Amen.

For further study: Genesis 1:26–3:7; John 10:10; Romans 8:11; Ephesians 1:7; 2 Peter 1:3; 1 John 2:15–17.

MAY 3
Pick Up the Phone

> Therefore, King Agrippa, I was not disobedient to the heavenly vision, but declared first to those in Damascus and in Jerusalem, and throughout all the region of Judea, and then to the Gentiles, that they should repent, turn to God and do works befitting repentance. (Acts 26:19–20)

MY ELDERLY MOTHER has been getting long-distance phone calls from scammers. They have disturbed her greatly and caused her to be reluctant to answer the phone when it's a long-distance number. I've learned to make sure to give it a lot of rings when I call so she has time to look closely at the number and recognize it as mine before she picks up. I will tell you, I was very angry with the scammers who would prey upon the elderly and vulnerable. I had the audacity to tell God I didn't want to see these people in heaven!

As soon as that thought was in my heart, it was closely followed by a reminder of what Greg Stieg wrote in *Unlikely Fighter*. He was challenged to go to the mall and watch all the people that walked by. As each person passed, he was to picture a sign over their heads saying "going to hell." As he sat, he suddenly saw that all these people were headed to physical hells as well as a spiritual hell. His heart swelled with compassion for them.

I recognized that the scammers too could have that sign over their heads. I doubt any of them dreamed when they were little kids that their future would be in scamming the vulnerable. Their life is hell now, and there is a hell that awaits. I also realized that God's got their number. He is calling them, pleading with them to answer His call. He's the only one who can give them a real future and a hope. Maybe they see Him trying to call them but are afraid to pick up the call. What demands might He place on them? What shame will they feel when they speak with His Holiness? It may seem easier to ignore the call than to venture into the unknown.

Peter was called to bring the good news to the Gentiles. This was unknown territory for him, and he may have been tempted to ignore the call, but he picked up and answered it instead. As a result, Cornelius and all his household were saved, and the gospel was spread to Gentiles around the world. Paul also answered the call to take God's message around the world.

As we travel this world, we may hear our spiritual phone ring. God wants us to help others hear His call. Will we let the heavenly call derail our agenda, or will we ignore the ringing in our hearts?

As we partake of communion, we should pause to reflect on the great blessing we have received by our salvation. Let's also pause to remember that there are those who have not experienced His grace. They're headed to hell, but Jesus is calling to them. We are His body, and that call rings through us. Will we pick up the phone?

> *Jesus, thank You for Your sacrifice that brought us salvation and abundant life. You have called us to be Your hands and feet, to be Your body on this earth. Help us to be obedient to the heavenly call. Open our ears to hear the call, and open our hearts to fulfill all You ask of us. Amen.*

For further study: Acts 9:1–19, 10:1–11:18.

MAY 4
Buy the Truth

Buy the truth, and do not sell it, also wisdom and instruction and understanding. (Proverbs 23:23)

THE PASSAGE ABOVE uses an interesting choice of words. After all, it's not like I can walk into the ideas store and ask the clerk for a pound of truth to add to my shopping cart. What on earth is this Scripture saying? We do talk about getting "buy in" for concepts or ideas. If someone says something we don't agree with, we often say "I don't buy that." To buy truth would be to believe it, accept it, grasp it, and act on it. What about selling? If someone gives up on their ideals and compromises their morals, we say they have "sold out." The natural question that follows is whether we've bought the truth or are purchasing lies.

I think many of us over our lives have bought into the lies of the enemy, such as "You are not lovable," "No one cares," "Your nose is too big, your hair too straight, or too wavy," "You can't do it; you're not good enough." Or how about these ones: He will never change. She will never learn. They can't do anything right. The situation is hopeless.

When we pause in our day to partake of communion, we are reminded that Jesus is truth personified. We have bought that truth, and we shouldn't sell it by forgetting or compromising that truth. When Jesus stood before Pontius Pilate on the eve of the crucifixion, He said, *"… For this cause I was born, and for this cause I have come into the world, that I should bear witness to the truth. Everyone who is of the truth hears My voice"* (John 18:37). Pilate answered somewhat cynically with *"What is truth?"* (v. 38a). He had Truth standing in front of him, yet he didn't "buy into" it.

When we partake of communion, we recognize the truth of Scripture, that Jesus came to seek and to save that which was lost, that He gave His life so that we might live, and that He loves us and paid the price for our sins to give us eternal life.

When this truth is central in our lives, we draw close to Him and find out other truths: We are precious and loved. We are perfected in Him. We can do all things in Him. We are the righteousness of Christ. He can change. She can learn. They can do what is right. The situation is never hopeless, but all things are possible with Him. He inspires us to buy the truth and not sell it. He reminds us not to sell out to the lies we hear in our head. Walking in communion with Him means walking in His truth. Always. Pausing to take communion is to pause and remember, to buy the truth and not sell it, to hold it, to act on it, to keep it dear to our hearts.

> *Jesus, we thank You that You only speak truth. It's not possible for You to lie. You say we are loved, and You proved it by dying for us. Help us to live in the truths You have told us and demonstrated to us. Amen.*

For further study: Matthew 19:26; Luke 12:6–7, 19:10; John 3:16, 14:6, 18:33–38; 2 Corinthians 5:21; Philippians 4:13; 1 John 2:3–6.

MAY 5
Incurvatus In Se

> Let nothing be done through selfish ambition or conceit, but in lowliness of mind let each esteem others better than himself. Let each of you look out not only for his own interests, but also for the interests of others. (Philippians 2:3–4)

THE LATIN PHRASE *incurvatus in se* means to be curved in upon yourself. Martin Luther adapted this phrase to describe a man curved in upon himself not only physically, but also one who bends spiritual goods toward himself, seeking to hoard them up and fulfill his own desires.

Many plants start out curved in upon themselves, but as they pop their heads above the soil, the curl starts to unfold. They begin to stretch up and open their developing limbs as they reach toward the sun. We also develop in the womb *incurvatus in se*, and when we're born, as babies we're still all about ourselves, getting our own needs fulfilled. We remain *incurvatus in se* in a sense in the early years, but if we're healthy, we should start to stretch up and grow, to reach out with our arms and stand up. We should start being able to give and not just take. As an adult, we speak of receiving people with open arms if we're welcoming them and receiving them with joy. Conversely, we may do the equivalent of curling into ourselves if we close off our heart to them.

Jesus was born as a baby, curled in body, but He demonstrated the polar opposite of *incurvatus in se* even at His birth. To be born as a human, He had to give up everything as He humbled Himself, being obedient even to death on the cross. The cross itself is a physical demonstration of that polar opposite of *incurvatus in se*—all limbs stretched out to the point of joints being dislocated, arms fully open as He gave completely of Himself to save us from our sins.

As new Christians we're like babies, taking in all the spiritual blessings and pulling them into ourselves. However, just as the baby grows physically to stand up straight, we should start to grow spiritually to stand up for others, to stretch out our arms and give of ourselves, to uncurl and open up, reaching toward the Son and to each other. Partaking of communion reminds us that He broke the bread and used it as an image of His body broken for us. We are to remember and, like Him, stretch out our hands across the table to one another to receive and to give. As He reached across the table, passing the cup of wine, we remember that His blood was poured out on the cross. We also stretch out our arms to pour our life into others. He has called us to open our hearts to others like He opened His arms for us.

> *Jesus, we acknowledge that we start out incurvatus in se, curled in on ourselves, hoarding up blessings and grace. Help us to mature and to grow, to stretch upward and outward to You and others. Show us where we have curled in on ourselves, and help us stand up and reach out to others. Amen.*

For further study: Deuteronomy 15:10–11; Luke 2:8–14; Romans 15:7; 1 Corinthians 3:1–6; 1 John 3:16–17.

MAY 6
Surrender

Then he said to Jesus, "Lord, remember me when You come into Your kingdom." (Luke 23:42)

ONE DAY, I really hope I grow up spiritually. Once again, I find myself coming to the communion table, my head hung in shame. I didn't manifest His love to my coworkers; instead, I let them feel my frustration. The day was long, the breaks non-existent, the cases difficult, and now it's the end of the day. It's late, and I'm hangry and tired. I still have a pile of paperwork inches thick to go through. The staff hover, wondering if there's anything they have to do in the pile of work I have yet to sift through, or if they can head home. My humanity readily overcomes my spirituality.

As I ponder my failure to be considerate or kind, I realize that I'm not surrendered to Jesus. I had an agenda, a plan to finish work on time and not hours later. My time wasn't surrendered to Him, so when the hours slipped by, my frustration and anger broke forth. My agenda, not God, controlled me. It occurs to me that whatever I refuse to surrender to Him will become my taskmaster, and it will be a cruel master. If I don't surrender my need for approval, it will control me, making me seek it through whatever means my soul thinks it can be satisfied. Social media may become an addiction, and lies may flow, all to seek the acceptance I crave.

I become like the thief on the cross next to Jesus, yelling at Him, "If You are really God, save Yourself—and me! Get me out of this mess! Prove Yourself to me by making things go my way." His sin and guilt are his taskmaster, making him use his final breath to rage against all that is good and holy. The thief being crucified on the other side of Christ might start out the same, but he comes to a place of surrender. He lays his guilt before Jesus and gives it to Him. *"Remember me, Lord,"* he says, and Jesus uses His final breath to welcome another soul into the kingdom of heaven.

As I pick up the wafer and raise the cup to my lips, remembering His sacrifice, I say, "But Lord, I'm not capable of surrendering my will. I don't want to be crucified with You. I want to rage against my pain." And He answers, "I know. That was why I had to go to the cross."

The one thief looked only at his pain, but the second changed his view from his own suffering to the suffering of the one who had committed no sin. He looked to the Man that was holy, dying for the sins of humanity, and he surrendered. In his surrender, he was set free. We can do no better. Only with our eyes on the Man, arms outstretched on the cross, can we surrender all to Him so He might set us free.

> *Jesus, we come to You, our eyes fixed upon Your precious sacrifice for our sin. Help us come to that place of surrender. May we hold nothing back. We don't want to be controlled by that evil taskmaster and our prideful ways anymore. Only You can set us free. We look to You and say "Remember us, Lord." Amen.*

For further study: Matthew 27:38–44; Luke 23:32–43; Romans 7:1–8:5; Galatians 2:20.

MAY 7
He Stands at the Door

> Behold, I stand at the door and knock. If anyone hears My voice and opens the door, I will come in to him and dine with him, and he with Me. (Revelation 3:20)

IN THE BOOK of Revelation, Jesus tells John to write to the church at Laodicea. He says that they are lukewarm, neither hot nor cold, so He's not impressed with them at all. They believe that they have everything they need, and they're rich in their own minds. Jesus says that in reality they're poor, blind, naked, and miserable. He counsels them to buy gold from Him that they may be rich, clothed in white raiment, with eye salve to heal their eyes so they can see. It seems this church had fallen into the sin of self-sufficiency. They couldn't see their spiritual need.

If we've been a Christian for a long time, it can be easy to lose sight of our continual spiritual need for our Savior. We can get to a point where we feel that our hand achieved our wealth. After all, didn't we pray and believe in just the right way to receive His blessings? Our life is good. We lose sight of our sin nature that continually tries to claw us away from the cross. Our vision is settled on how good things are instead of on that sin trying to rise up. We feel like we can walk in truth and light without the help of the Holy Spirit.

Jesus reminds us that we can't walk this walk on our own. We can't save ourselves from our sin. We may think our good works are earning us brownie points, but no matter how good our works are, they're not enough to deliver us from our sinful selves. We need our vision healed to see our spiritual poverty. When we recognize our impoverished state, we can buy the gold that Jesus offers. He can clothe us with His righteousness, and now we're dressed in white raiment. As long as we think we're doing it ourselves, we are lukewarm and lost. When we recognize that only by His grace are we saved, we can start to walk in the true riches.

He stands at the door and knocks. I don't think He's just softly tapping on our hearts. I think He's pounding, as He desires so strongly for us to crack the door open. His knuckles are bloody as He tries to get us to hear Him over the noise of the world. When we open the door, He comes in and sits at the table—He communes with us. We are reminded that it's by His grace, His work, and His ability that we come into His kingdom. Keeping that in the forefront of our mind keeps us from drifting off to the lukewarm nature of self-sufficiency.

> *Jesus, You have given us ears to hear. The ears of our heart hear You knocking, begging us to let You in. We come and open the door. Let Your light and truth flood our hearts and spirit. Come in and sit at the table. Pass the bread and wine as You remind us it is by Your grace and Your sacrifice that we are forgiven. Amen.*

For further study: Deuteronomy 8:1–18; Acts 4:12; Ephesians 2:8–9; Revelation 3:14–22.

MAY 8
Buen Camino!

A man who has friends must himself be friendly, but there is a friend who sticks closer than a brother. (Proverbs 18:24)

THE BOOK I'LL *Push You* tells a story of two very close friends. Justin is confined to a wheelchair, but he would love to travel the Camino de Santiago. The Camino de Santiago, or the Way of Saint James, is an eight-hundred-kilometer pilgrimage through the mountains in Northern Spain. It's as much a spiritual journey as a physical one. Justin's friend Patrick, when told of this walk, says, "I'll push you." And so begins the journey of these two close friends through rugged terrain, trial, and hardship.

Patrick literally does the heavy lifting on this trip as he pushes and pulls his wheelchair-bound friend through mud and rocks, peaks and valleys. This is no walk in the park. Others on the trail wish a *"Buen Camino"* as they pass—this is the typical greeting for pilgrims that means "Have a good walk." Still others stop and help push and pull, taking some of the strain from Patrick. As a tribute to their close friendship, this journey makes them closer still. They are brothers in faith. Proverbs talks of such a friend. It says it's one thing to act friendly and have friends, but there is a friendship that is closer than that of a brother.

Think about it. Sometimes in our families we're not so supportive. Sometimes selfish natures take over. Buttons get pushed just because we can push them, and not for any good reason. This isn't the way brotherhood should be. Jesus demonstrates true brotherhood to us. He sticks closer even than family. He lays down His life for us. If He ever pushes our buttons, it's only so that He can reveal and heal them. He pushes our spirits to continue when we want to quit. He is our companion through the mountaintops and down in the valleys, through rough ways and smooth. He walks with us on our journey, which is as much a spiritual journey as a natural one. He never quits, never fails, never gives up, never abandons us. He is with us step by step.

Others who pass us on the journey have different reactions when they see our struggle. Some walk by without a word. Some wish us a good journey. Some walk beside us for a ways, keeping us company, but some stop and take some of the load from us.

Jesus is always with us, in communion with us and helping us. Let's think about how we interact with others on their journey. Do we walk by, barely giving them a glance, or do we wish them *Buen Camino*? Do we keep them company, or do we take the pack from their shoulders for a time until they're able to shoulder it again on their own? Do we inspire others to love and good works? Jesus is our example, who laid His life down that we might walk in newness of life. We remember Him and endeavor to follow Him.

Jesus, thank You for being our companion, a friend who sticks closer than a brother. You push us. You carry us. You inspire us. May we reflect Your goodness in us to those around us as we walk this rugged trail of life. Amen.

For further study: Psalm 46:1; Matthew 28:20; 1 Corinthians 13:4–8; Galatians 6:2; Hebrews 10:24–25; James 2:14–18.

MAY 9
Shoulder to Shoulder at the Foot of the Cross

There is neither Jew nor Greek, there is neither slave nor free, there is neither male nor female; for you are all one in Christ Jesus. (Galatians 3:28)

THIS IMAGE CAME into my mind one day. There I was kneeling at the foot of the cross in utter devotion to my Savior. Someone else came to the foot of the cross, and as they knelt beside me, there was barely room, so they pressed in close to me as they tried to get closer to the cross. There we were, shoulder to shoulder, knee to knee. I looked over, and it was someone I don't really like. It was uncomfortable, and I wanted to put some distance between me and this person. To do that, I had to back away from the cross.

The vision is striking. There are many people in this world whom we might not like or get along with. Maybe there's an obnoxious person who attends our church. What about that homeless guy always begging on the corner? Don't forget the drug addict, the prostitute, the convicted pedophile, the thief, the broken, the physically challenged. Jesus welcomes all these to the foot of the cross. He's willing to redeem them all. As they work out their salvation, it will take time, and they won't always appear to us as a welcome friend. Yet they're still a member of the body and welcomed at the foot of the cross. If we want to distance ourselves spiritually from them, we must be the one to move, but the direction we move in will be away from Christ. Our judgment of others pushes us away from grace.

Of course, we need to have boundaries with others, but that doesn't negate the need to walk in love. We're called to rejoice with them as they press into grace, just as we're called to press into grace ourselves. We need to keep our eyes centered on Jesus and not be so concerned about judging those pushing into grace beside us. It's not for us to say who should and shouldn't be a member of His body.

Much of the rite of communion involves pausing to examine ourselves to see if there's anything in our hearts against members of His body. It's about keeping our hearts focused on Him and His grace. Communion is about receiving His love and acceptance but then letting it flow through us to others—even those we don't like. Paul admonished the church at Corinth when they were partaking of communion to pause and discern the Lord's body. The whole context concerned being willing to put others' needs ahead of our own desires. That's what discerning the Lord's body is really all about—seeing Him in all the others who are shoulder to shoulder with us at the foot of the cross.

Lord Jesus, we thank You for dying for us, saving us, accepting us. You have united us in one body. Help us to walk in the grace we've received and to keep ourselves focused on You and not in judgment of others in the body. Amen.

For further study: Romans 2:1–4, 14:1–4; 1 Corinthians 11:17–31, 12:4–27; Philippians 2:12–13.

MAY 10
Walk in the Light

> But if we walk in the light as He is in the light, we have fellowship with one another, and the blood of Jesus Christ His Son cleanses us from all sin. (1 John 1:7)

HAVE YOU EVER looked at a beam of sunlight shining through a window? When you look at it, you see all the dust and dirt swirling around in the air that was invisible in dimmer light. It can make it seem like a clean house is still pretty dirty. In fact, in dim light, a really dirty place can seem clean, but turn on the lights, and the stains and dirt are more visible. The brighter the light, the more visible it is.

When we're in the world, we don't see the sin in our life so easily, but when we come to Christ, we recognize our sinful nature. The sins of our past can loom larger than life. As His grace washes over us, we become clean. The stains of sin are washed away, and we put on the dazzling white robe of righteousness. We start walking in the light as He is in the light. We feel so clean.

But then a funny thing happens as we become closer and more intimate with Christ. It seems like our sins start to loom large again. As we approach brighter and brighter light, those specks of sin's dust can't help swirling around us in the world and become visible. Our spiritual house may be quite clean, but it starts to look dirty again. Here's the good news, though—where sin abounds, grace does much more abound. For certain, we don't sin on purpose to make grace abound, but we can rejoice that when sin becomes visible to us, we can still approach the cross and find the grace we need. As it says further in 1 John, if we say we have no sin, we are deceived, but if we confess our sins, He is faithful and just to forgive us and cleanse us again. We don't want to sin, but sometimes righteousness seems to slip further away from us the closer we are to Him. This is the brightness of His glory exposing the smallest fault.

That realization of our continued sin is discouraging. Instead of despair, however, we should rejoice. We've come close enough to Him to see things as they really are. We start to recognize the sin that still surrounds us, which in dimmer light wasn't visible. As long as we're in this world, sin's dust will cling to us; however, His grace and glory will also show up. Communion is both recognizing He has cleansed us from our sins and clothed us in righteousness, but also knowing that He covers us with His grace daily, cleansing us over and over again as the need arises.

> Jesus, sometimes it seems like we'll never be free from sin. Just when we think we start to get it right, more sins become visible to our eyes. We pause today to be grateful for Your light showing us the dirt that remains. We recognize that Your grace will cleanse us even from these sins. You enable us to walk in the light just as You are in the light. Thank You for setting us free from the dirt of the world. Amen.

For further study: Psalm 51:2; Romans 5:20–6:14; 1 John 1:5–10.

MAY 11

Sonship

And suddenly a voice came from heaven, saying, "This is My beloved Son, in whom I am well pleased." (Matthew 3:17)

HENRI NOUWEN WRITES about his friend Adam in his book titled *Adam, God's Beloved*. Adam was a severely challenged man who lived at L'Arche Daybreak community, where Henri spent time as a pastor. Adam touched a great many people with his gentle spirit that exuded the love of God, despite being so severely challenged. He could do little on his own. He wasn't even able to speak, yet he could teach Henri much about God's love.

Henri compared Adam's life to that of Jesus. He wrote:

> He (Adam) died as poor as he was born. Still, both Jesus and Adam are God's beloved sons—Jesus by nature, Adam by "adoption"—and they lived their sonship among us as the only thing that they had to offer. That was their assigned mission. That is also my mission and yours. Believing it and living from it is true sanctity.[2]

Jesus's value is that He is the Son of God, beloved by the Father yet given to us. We see Him at His baptism rising out of the water, the Holy Spirit descending on Him, and the Father speaking out, *"This is My beloved Son, in whom I am well pleased."* The favor of the Father rested on Him. He was upheld by the Father. He was chosen by the Father. Loved by Him.

Adam's value as a human being, beloved by God, wasn't diminished one bit by his severe physical challenges. His value rested in his sonship, just as Jesus's value was in being the Son of God. Our value, too, lies in the fact that we are sons and daughters of the Most High God. We also are His beloved child, in whom He is well pleased. His favor rests on us. We are beloved by God, chosen by Him, upheld by Him. Our value rests not in our performance but in our position as children of God.

How do we know He loves us for who we are, regardless of our performance? We know it because He sent Jesus, His beloved, to pay the price for our sins so that we might be eternally adopted into His family. No greater price could be paid, and He was willing to pay it for us—for you and for me. The price needed to buy our soul was more than all the riches of the world—so much more—yet He paid it readily. You are more valuable than everything this world has to offer because you are His beloved child. It has nothing to do with what you accomplish and everything to do with who you are.

> *Heavenly Father, thank You for adopting us into Your family and for loving us so much. You willingly paid the price to redeem us from our sins. We rejoice in being Your beloved child on whom Your favor rests. Thank You for loving us. Amen.*

For further study: Psalm 2:7; Isaiah 42:1; Matthew 17:1–5; Mark 1:9–11; Luke 1:35, 3:21–23; Ephesians 1:3–6; 1 John 3:1.

---

[2] Henri J.M. Nouwen, *Adam: God's Beloved* (Maryknoll, NY: Orbis Books, 1997), 37.

MAY 12
You Are What You Eat

Your words were found, and I ate them, and Your word was to me the joy and rejoicing of my heart; for I am called by Your name … (Jeremiah 15:16)

HAVE YOU EVER heard the phrase "You are what you eat"? The nutrients we eat get incorporated into our body. If we eat poorly, we are sickly and unwell. If we eat healthy food, we can also grow strong and healthy. If we fill up our stomach on junk, who'd want broccoli? Doesn't this principle apply to so many more areas of our lives? We talk about devouring a good book. We didn't eat the book physically, yet we took the contents of the book into our soul. The people and things we hang around with and pay attention to become a part of us. Jesus spoke to His followers and said they had to eat His flesh and drink His blood. Many were disgusted at these words and left. He asked if the twelve closest disciples wanted to leave, but Peter answered, *"Lord, to whom shall we go? You have the words of eternal life"* (John 6:68b).

Jesus indeed is the Word of God. He said those who feed on Him will live and have eternal life. So how do we eat His flesh and drink His blood? We must devour Him. The more time we spend with Jesus, with the Word, in His presence, focusing on Him, loving Him, and being with Him, the more we'll become like Him. We will devour the Word, and the Word will become a part of us. It will fill us and change us.

And here is where we come back to communion. The act of eating the bread and drinking the wine is the reminder that we are to open our hearts to Him, that yielding to Him is a daily process. We can't eat for only one day and expect to live for years after that on the energy from the one meal; rather, we have to take in nutrition regularly to keep our body strong and healthy. So it is with this Christian walk. We need to daily take in nutrition for our spirit and soul. We make thousands of small choices every day—some that make no difference in our lives, some that are harmful, and some that are life-changing in a good way. Will we choose to eat the things that enrich us and make us someone more like Christ, or will we choose the food that makes our soul unhealthy? Remembering Him and what He has done can help us make healthy choices in our day-to-day walk with God.

> *Jesus, thank You for giving Your body and blood to save us and give us eternal life. Sometimes we're so caught up in the world, we forget to spend time eating of Your Word, devouring Your presence. Sometimes we don't even want it, we're so full of the world. Help us to fall in love with You all over again, to be hungry for You instead of full of the delicacies the world has to offer. Amen.*

For further study: John 6:47–69; 1 John 3:16.

MAY 13
They Wounded Me Deeply

For it is not an enemy who reproaches me; then I could bear it. Nor is it one who hates me who has magnified himself against me; then I could hide from him. But it was you, a man my equal, my companion and my acquaintance. We took sweet counsel together, and walked to the house of God in the throng. (Psalm 55:12–14)

IN THIS FALLEN world, often people hurt us, either intentionally or unintentionally. Some of those wounds are deep and hurt a lot. The worst ones are those that come from a friend. Even David said in the Psalms that had it been an enemy who'd hurt him, it wouldn't have been so bad, but when it's a friend, that really stings. Jesus knows all about that, having been betrayed by His treasurer, one of His twelve closest followers. The betrayal led to a crown of thorns pushed on His head, His body whipped, His hands and feet pierced by nails, His side driven through with a soldier's spear. Every one of those wounds caused pain. He felt it all. Yet He uses one of His final breaths as a man on earth to say, *"Father, forgive them, for they do not know what they do"* (Luke 23:34).

As we go through life, people wound us. We talk of people who "tie our hands" or "trip us up," who "stab us in the back" or "cut us to the quick." Some of those wounds feel like the prick of a thorn, and some like the sting of a whip. Others feel like the piercing of a nail, and some like a spear driven through our hearts. They hurt. We can try to ease the pain of the whip, saying that others have gone through so much more, but that won't take the sting away. The pain of the wound can only be healed by giving it to the one who endured all for us. It goes away by the recognition that what was done to us was really done to Him, and through His grace we also can say, "Father, forgive them."

We also either intentionally or unintentionally have wounded others—sometimes like the prick of a thorn, sometimes like the sting of a whip, and sometimes like a spear driven through their hearts. When we recognize what we've done to the least of these His children, we have done to Him, we can only fall on our knees and shout, "Father, forgive me, I didn't know what I was doing."

Communion reminds us that He has been wounded for us. His desire is to set us free, to take away the sting of the whip and to heal our hearts. It's a reminder to forgive those who have wounded us and to seek forgiveness for the wounds we've caused others. All must be brought to the foot of the cross. Even the pain of the thorn has to be given over to Him, not just the piercing of our hearts.

> *Father, please forgive us for all the wounds we've inflicted on others. Forgive us for our failure to love people in the way You love them. Also, we ask for You, Jesus, to forgive others through us. Help us when we're unable to proclaim in ourselves, "Father, forgive them, for they know not what they do." Jesus, thank You for bearing the wounds for us that we might be free. Amen.*

For further study: Matthew 25:31–46, 26:47–50, 27:26–37; Mark 14:53–65; Luke 23:26–34; John 13:21, 19:1–6.

MAY 14
Neither Do I Condemn You

Neither do I condemn you; go and sin no more. (John 8:11b)

A WOMAN CAUGHT in sin is dragged by her accusers and thrown at the feet of Jesus. She should be stoned, they cry. Jesus ignores them and writes on the ground. As they continue in their cries, He stands and says, "He who is without sin can cast the first stone" (John 8:7, paraphrased). One by one, they drop their stones and leave. When none remain but the woman, Jesus asks if anyone is condemning her. She says they all have left, and Jesus answers, *"Neither do I condemn you."*

This is an amazing demonstration of God's forgiveness for us. The world, our conscience, our enemies all scream at us that we are sinners caught in the very act of our sin. The accuser of the brethren drags us to Jesus and yells in our ear that we deserve death, yet the only one without sin, who has the right to cast the first stone, says, *"Neither do I condemn you."* This is indeed what communion is all about: recognizing ourselves in this woman, condemned by the world but forgiven by Christ.

Communion is also about recognizing ourselves in the religious people yelling condemnation at those around us. We bring our frustrations, our anger, our complaints to Jesus, demanding He do something. Yet He calmly stoops down and writes in the sand. I imagine Him writing my own sins in that sand, and I realize that the rock in my hand that would condemn others is there because of my own guilt. I may be the woman dragged before Jesus and proclaimed guilty, but I'm also the one who drags others in the dirt, proclaiming their guilt. I suddenly see that I carry a heavy load of rocks, every one a prior wound or area of shame that I'm ready to pull out and throw at someone. Every evil word and angry frustration I voice about my fellow humans is a rock heaved from my storehouse.

Jesus calls me to drop my rock. In fact, He calls me to set down the backpack full of rocks and to empty my pockets. And just when I think I've dropped all my rocks, He quietly points out that if I would take the rock out of my shoe, I would find it easier to walk. So communion is also about seeing where we carry rocks in our soul, and it's about learning to throw those rocks into the sea of forgetfulness rather than at others. He writes my sins in the sand, ready to blow them away and wipe my soul clean.

Communion is more still. It's learning to become more like Jesus. Therefore, it's not just about dropping our rocks but about learning to be an anti-rock-thrower, to be one who says and does the things that cause others to drop their own rocks. The pathway lies in knowing we are fully loved and forgiven—then we're able to love and forgive others, as well as encourage others to do the same.

Jesus, thank You for writing our sins in the sand, ready to blow them away. Thank You for forgiving us, loving us, for gently and kindly teaching us to drop the rocks we carry. Because we are loved by You, we can learn to love like You do. We bless You and thank You. Amen.

For further study: John 8:1–11; Colossians 3:13; Revelation 12:10.

MAY 15
Walking in Harmony

The cup of blessing which we bless, is it not the communion of the blood of Christ? The bread which we break, is it not the communion of the body of Christ? For we, though many, are one bread and one body; for we all partake of that one bread. (1 Corinthians 10:16–17)

IT'S POSSIBLE TO be very different from others yet united as one. Consider a large orchestra. There's the horn section, the string section, and the percussion section—all very different, yet all playing the same tune. What would happen if every musician decided to play the music they liked best and refused to follow the leading of the conductor? The discordant noise would please no one—not the conductor, the audience listening to the program, or even the players themselves. But without a reminder, don't we tend to do just that? We try to march to our own drum, without considering we are part of an orchestra.

Jesus promises that where there is unity, He is there in the midst. The Greek word for agreement in these verses is *sumphoneo* (where we get our word for "symphony"), and it means to agree together and be in one accord. We can walk in harmony even when we are very different from one another or when we disagree on some points. Harmony is the way the differences are blended together in agreement to make a pleasing sound in the Lord's ears.

Communion with Christ is also communion with all who are in Christ. We're all one body. Everyone has a different function and comes with unique talents, yet it's the conductor who calls the tune. Jesus is the conductor and sets the members of the body in their proper place. There is a higher call on our lives than to spend it marching to the beat of our own drum. He hopes for so much more from us. We must take our place in His orchestra, playing by His direction, in harmony with His other players. The amazing thing is that when we take our place as part of the whole body, the music refreshes our own soul just as it refreshes all who are around us.

Unity in the body of Christ is music to all of our ears. Does that mean we won't make mistakes? Of course not. Sometimes people hurt us, or we hurt others. The sound can be discordant instead of sweet musical harmony. Before the real music starts, a tuning takes place. As everyone tunes their instrument, the sound is a little rough. Communion is a chance to look for where we're out of tune and reset our instrument. It prepares us for the Conductor to step up to the podium and tap his baton on the music stand to get everyone's attention. The world around us grows quiet, and then he raises His arms, and the music begins!

Lord, we remember today what You have done for us, Your blood that was shed for the remission of our sins, and how You have united us all together in the body of Christ. Help us to strive to walk in harmony with one another, playing our part as You have directed us to play. Amen.

For further study: Matthew 18:15–20; 1 Corinthians 10:16–17, 12:12–31; Ephesians 2:11–22; Colossians 1:24–29.

MAY 16
Choose Life

I call heaven and earth as witnesses today against you, that I have set before you life and death, blessing and cursing; therefore choose life, that both you and your descendants may live. (Deuteronomy 30:19)

QUITE A FEW years ago, I was driving some teenagers home and I mentioned that God is always watching us. They responded by saying that was creepy. At the time, I couldn't think of how to explain the difference between someone who watches over you because they truly love you and someone who's a stalker.

A stalker is not in love with the other person. The stalker wants to control the other person. They will watch them in order to fulfill their own needs and feed their obsession, not because they want to bless the other person. We use the term "stalker" to describe someone who is silently hunting prey, and this fits the person who stalks other people. They are hunting them to fulfill their own desires, not to benefit the person being hunted. The hunted has no choice in the matter.

God, on the other hand, loves us. In loving us, He allows us choice. He pursues us with His love but in no manner tries to control us. He always allows us freedom of choice. He doesn't impose His own will on us. Love also means that sometimes He must endure the pain of watching us suffer the consequences of our decisions. He can try to show us His love. He can tell us about His love and encourage us to receive His love, but in the end, the decision is ours to make.

God modeled good choices. He instructed us about good choices and warned about bad choices, but in the end, in loving us, He couldn't stop sin from entering the world. The choice was ours. He is our beloved, not our stalker. He loves us and gave His life for us, but He won't control us. True love is love that we give to Him willingly and not out of compulsion.

When we partake of communion, we remind ourselves that God so loved the world He gave His only Son, that whoever would believe on Him would not perish but have eternal life. We are reminded that true love doesn't control or demand but allows free will. True love may go to great lengths and effort for the beloved, but it's to meet the needs of the beloved, not to satisfy the obsession of the lover. Communion also reminds us that the choice is ours to receive Him or not. We can choose life or death, blessing or cursing. Choose life!

Father, we thank You for giving Your only Son. You have always given, and You still give. You gave us free will. We are not robots with no choice, but people who can and do choose You. Thank You for giving us everything we need for life and godliness, for love and purpose. Thank You for giving Your only Son to set us free from sin and death. Amen.

For further study: Genesis 3:1–7; John 1:12–13, 3:16; 2 Corinthians 9:7–15.

MAY 17
How Badly Do We Want Him?

And He said to her, "Daughter, your faith has made you well. Go in peace, and be healed of your affliction." (Mark 5:34)

A VERY ILL woman pushed through the crowd to touch Jesus. She had a condition that had caused her to lose blood over the previous twelve years. She'd spent all her money, tried all the physicians, yet still grew worse. She would have been anemic, weak, and tired. Every step would be a struggle. Her legs would feel like lead. It would have been easier to just give up and lie down to die.

Thousands of people thronged Jesus. She would have to push through the crowd in her weak and debilitated state. People would knock her aside or maybe knock her down. Yet she got up and pushed herself harder. She knew He was the Son of God coming with healing in His wings. If she could only reach Him, she believed she would be well. She managed to touch the hem of His garment, and Jesus, thronged by people, felt her pull healing virtue out of Him. He asked, *"Who touched Me?"* (Luke 8:45). His disciples were amazed at the question, but Jesus and the woman knew what had happened. She confessed with fear and trembling. A woman who had an issue of blood was not allowed to be in public or to touch people. He could order her to be stoned. But our Savior wouldn't do that. He told her to go in peace and be healed of her affliction. Think of how badly this woman desired to touch Jesus. She could have been killed for doing it. She was weak and tired yet pushed through thousands to reach Him.

How hard do we try to reach Jesus with our prayers for our friends and family, for our city? Do we seek Him with our whole heart, pushing through all the things the world crowds in the way? Do we let ourselves be pushed aside by TV? Does our job knock us down? Just how badly do we want to touch Him?

How much does Jesus want to see us saved and healed? I can tell you how much. Enough to pray in the garden so hard He sweat blood. Enough to be beaten with a rod, spat on, and whipped. Enough to have a crown of thorns pushed on His head. To struggle through narrow streets, carrying a wooden cross as His blood stained the road. Enough to submit to nails being driven through His hands and feet. He loved us enough and wanted it badly enough to push through the pain and pour His blood out at the foot of the cross.

Sometimes we're so busy letting ourselves be pushed around by the world that we don't take a moment to recognize who Jesus is and what He's done for us. Communion is about pausing to recognize the Savior and the price He paid for us. In doing so, we find healing for our spirits, for our souls, and, yes, even for our bodies. Let's push aside the worldly distractions to focus on Him.

Jesus, we recognize You: our Lord, our Savior, our Redeemer, our Healer, the One True God.
We remember You and what You have done for us on the cross. Amen.

For further study: Isaiah 50:6; Matthew 27:29–30; Mark 5:25–34, 15:19–20; Luke 22:19–20, 39–44; John 10:17–18; 19:1–18.

MAY 18
Defeating Giants

> Then David said to the Philistine, "You come to me with a sword, with a spear, and with a javelin. But I come to you in the name of the Lord of hosts, the God of the armies of Israel, whom you have defied." (1 Samuel 17:45)

MANY PEOPLE ARE familiar with the Old Testament account of David and Goliath. David was a shepherd boy who fought the giant Goliath, who had all Israel shaking in terror. King Saul tried to get David to at least wear some armor, but David took it off because it didn't fit him. Instead, he went to the river for five smooth stones that he put in his shepherd's bag before confronting the giant. Goliath mocked David, but David ran at him, saying that Goliath had a spear, but he had the name of the Lord as his weapon! With his sling and a stone, and faith in his God, David prevailed.

Even today, you and I face giants that mock us. We have giants of despair, grief, fear, addiction, physical illness, mental illness, financial struggles, lack of self-worth, and the list could go on and on. These giants scream at us, speaking in our heads and thoughts, "You're not good enough. You'll never make it. I will destroy you. You have no hope." Maybe we see a counselor, but the advice just doesn't fit. It might feel like putting on Saul's armor. Maybe we go to another counselor and they say something that's like a stone, smoothed by the water of the Word of God, inspired by the Holy Spirit. We can put it in our shepherd's bag and hold on to it. Maybe we see our pastor and get another stone for our bag, or maybe a friend speaks a word that sinks into our heart and helps us.

These "stones" are helpful; indeed, they're critical for our success, but they're not enough. Israel's army knew the Scriptures and that they were the chosen ones of God, but it wasn't enough to face their giant. David had the Scriptures just like they did, but he also had a relationship with the Lord of hosts. He knew God was with him and would fight with him and for him. He knew he wasn't running to face his giant in his own strength but in the strength of a God who loved him. And the giant fell.

This is where the Old Testament tale of a boy facing a formidable enemy meets the New Testament ordinance of communion. Communion is, after all, about reminding us of the relationship we have with the King of kings and Lord of lords. Jesus loves us enough to die for us, and He is powerful enough to also live for us. He fights for us and with us. He let His body be broken so we could be whole. He let His blood drip from that cross so we could live with Him in victory for all eternity. With this relationship, we can use the "stones" He has provided to bring down the giants who mock us.

> *Jesus, we thank You for this special relationship with the God of all creation. You love us, are with us, and never leave us. We're so grateful for how You love us and help us. We remember today that we are not in this life alone. You walk with us every step of the way as we face our giants, and those giants will fall!*

For further study: 1 Samuel 17; John 10:17–18.

MAY 19
My Companion

The cup of blessing which we bless, is it not the communion of the blood of Christ? The bread which we break, is it not the communion of the body of Christ? For we, though many, are one bread and one body; for we all partake of that one bread. (1 Corinthians 10:16–17)

THE ENGLISH WORD "companion" has its roots in Latin from *com*, meaning "with," and *panis*, meaning "bread." It implies a companion with whom you break bread. It's someone with whom you share a meal and your life. A companion travels the same road as you. A companion is also described as something of the same kind that assists another, like a companion book to a series. A companion is a fellow worker or a friend.

This understanding of companionship is reflected in many Scriptures. In the book of Acts, the disciples go from house to house eating together and sharing things in common. They are companions to each other, sharing the same faith. I love the image of breaking bread together. It implies not just provision of a like-minded friend but an intimate sharing of experience.

When God created the earth, He could have stayed distant from us. Like a demanding father, He could have set bread on the table, but kept Himself apart from His children. But God wanted so much more. He wanted to be our companion, to walk with us, to share in life together, to sit at the table and break bread with us.

He prepared a table in heaven for us, but there was a problem. Sin cannot be in the presence of that which is truly holy. God, in His love, solved the problem. Jesus would come to earth, born as a man. He'd walk the same road we do, share life with us, break bread with us, and ultimately take death for us so that we might always be in fellowship with the Holy Trinity. He became our companion in every way, sharing in life and death. Jesus isn't just our God. He is our friend, fellow worker, and travel companion—someone made of the same stuff as we are, who assists us to be something better.

He used the Last Supper—the breaking of bread, the sharing of the meal—to give us a tool to remind us that even after He died, He would rise again and remain our companion. Paul also reminds us that just as Christ's body was the bread broken for us, we are now His body. We are the bread, companions to each other in unity in the faith. Our actions should reflect our desire to support one another and not cause others to stumble in the faith. We are fellow travelers, companions of the way, with each other and with Jesus Christ.

> *Jesus, You chose to be our friend and our companion, not just our Savior. You break bread with us, travel this road with us, help us, and love us. We thank You for that and remember that You chose to be made of the same stuff as us so You could lift us out of the mire and into heavenly realms with You. Amen.*

For further study: Psalm 23; Matthew 11:19; Luke 22:14–30; John 14:1–4, 15:12–15; Acts 2:42–47.

MAY 20
Lay Down Your Life

Let this mind be in you which was also in Christ Jesus, who, being in the form of God, did not consider it robbery to be equal with God, but made Himself of no reputation, taking the form of a bondservant, and coming in the likeness of men. And being found in appearance as a man, He humbled Himself and became obedient to the point of death, even the death of the cross. (Philippians 2:5–8)

JESUS DID AN amazing thing. He is God, creator, member of the Trinity, the Word made flesh who lived among us, yet He laid His life down so we could live. No one took His life from Him. He had all power yet chose to lay down His own will and was obedient even unto death. He laid down His life in other ways, too.

Picture Him as He sits at His last Passover celebration with His disciples. He's about to institute the rite of communion. As He sits at the table with them, He suddenly rises, puts on the garment of the lowliest of servants, and proceeds to kneel down and wash their feet. He was telling them to follow His example, to serve others and not to *lord* it over them. This is made even more poignant in that Judas was there at the table, having his feet washed by the one he would shortly betray. Judas was a traitor, an enemy. Jesus knew that yet served even this man.

We are asked to follow Jesus's example, to take up our cross and follow Him. Rarely, this could mean putting ourselves in physical danger to lay down our lives for another. More often, taking up the cross and laying down our life involves things like looking the homeless in the eye and greeting them rather than turning aside and pretending they don't exist. It may be letting other people in line ahead of you. It might mean blessing someone and doing them a good turn even if they're mean to you. It could be attending a family function where that one relative is going to really get on your nerves, but you take the time to serve and be kind to them. Do you have a friend? Lay your life down for them. Do you have a spouse? Lay your life down. Do you have a family member or neighbor? Lay your life down. Do you have an enemy? Lay your life down. This is the example Jesus left for us.

Partaking of communion is a chance to remind ourselves that He laid aside His own will and life for us. Every day we have the opportunity to do the same for those around us. This isn't always easy, but with Him in us, living through us, it will be done.

> *Lord, thank You for what You've done for us. You set aside Your own will so we could live, laying down Your life for us. Let that same mind be in us. We can't do it without You. We need Your life and Your grace in us. Thank You for making the way to do just that. Amen.*

For further study: Matthew 10:38–39; 26:36–39, 53; John 13:1–17, 18:6; Philippians 2:1–18; 1 John 3:16–18.

MAY 21
Overcoming Our Vampires

The thief does not come except to steal, and to kill, and to destroy. I have come that they may have life, and that they may have it more abundantly. (John 10:10)

VAMPIRES ARE POPULAR these days. They're featured in cartoons, movies, and books. There are even modern-day vampire slayers chasing down rumors of vampires. Vampires come from twists on old legends about people who didn't die or who rose from the dead to suck the lifeblood out of people. They can't see themselves in a mirror or handle daylight, so they stalk their victims in the darkness. The myth says they can be defeated by someone wielding a cross, or by a wooden stake driven through their heart. Movies and books often make them out to be amusing or harmless.

Of course, vampires are a myth, but we have modern-day vampires—things that suck the life out of us. Some of these things may be obvious, like addictions to drugs or alcohol that make us unable to look at ourselves in the mirror for shame. Others are more insidious and sneak up on us as innocent amusements, yet they can trap us. Something may be fine in someone else's life, but it drains us of our life, slowly destroying us. Some of our personal vampires may have even started out as something good in our lives that slowly took over, stealing our time, joy, peace, or life.

The good news is that our personal vampires can be defeated at the foot of the cross. A stake was thrust into Jesus's heart, killing Him in order to defeat our ultimate enemy, who would destroy us and steal our life. He tells us to come and lay down our life at the foot of the cross so that He can give it back to us, fuller and richer than we could imagine. He is the light of the world, chasing away the demons that would destroy us. The enemy of our soul stands no chance against the power of His grace.

We pause to take communion to remind us that He has defeated death. He has laid down His life to give us life. He was broken to make us whole. The enemy would steal our life, but Jesus has come to give life. When our own personal vampires stalk us in the dark places of our soul, we need only bring them to His light. We may have to return to the foot of the cross fifty times a day, but His grace is always sufficient to help us overcome. We can go to Him for wisdom on how to deal with the things that plague us. We can go for strength, to receive grace, and to be forgiven yet again and set free once more.

Jesus, we thank You for laying down Your life for us. You freely gave it so that we may receive life. You were broken so we could be whole. We thank You that Your blood is sufficient. Your grace is enough to overcome all the things that would destroy us. We come to You today asking You to forgive us our shortcomings and renew us again in the power of Your grace. Amen.

For further study: John 1:1–18, 10:1–18, 19:34.

MAY 22
One Blood

And He has made from one blood every nation of men to dwell on all the face of the earth, and has determined their preappointed times and the boundaries of their dwellings, so that they should seek the Lord, in the hope that they might grope for Him and find Him, though He is not far from each one of us. (Acts 17:26–27)

WHEN GOD CREATED the heavens and the earth, He took some of the dust of the ground and made Adam in His image. When it came time to make Adam's bride, He didn't pick up another clod of earth; instead, He took Adam's rib to fashion her. Both had the same blood cells coursing through their veins. One blood. Because they were of the same blood, only one Savior is needed for all humanity. Every human alive today is related by blood, however distant that relation may be.

Recently there's been a lot of racial tension in North America, with news reports of injustice against Black and Indigenous people being brought to the forefront. The statement "Black Lives Matter" has become popular. Some take offense at this and reply with "All lives matter." The proponents of Black Lives Matter have responded that of course all lives matter. They're not saying that White lives don't matter but rather that Black lives matter just as much. Sadly, many people have underlying biases that suggest in their hearts, if not in their minds, that some lives don't matter as much as others. Their actions show that they look on some lives as having less value, such as Indigenous, Black, mentally/physically challenged or ill, the unborn, criminals, LGBTQ people, Muslims, or any manner of person that doesn't fit into their lifestyle.

A large movement of people is advocating for dying with dignity (assisted suicide) to alleviate suffering. I wonder if we valued people enough to focus our resources on helping people live with dignity if there would be the same demand for dying with dignity. If there were sufficient resources to really support and help women who were pregnant, would they feel the value of the unborn? I don't know the answers to these questions, but I do know that Christ died for all. He is our blood relative willing to pay the price so we might live.

He breathed life into all when He breathed life into Adam. He desires all to be saved. He reaches out to all, calls all, and gave His life for all. So today as we partake of communion, let's examine our hearts for any hidden bias. Is there a person or group of people that in the depths of our heart we don't want to see get saved and enjoy eternal life in heaven? Do we devalue anyone, or do we recognize that all people are of one blood, made in the image of God? Do we desire salvation for all, or just the ones like us? Let's have the same heart for people that Jesus has, willing to give our lives so others can live.

> Father, we recognize that You made people in Your image and of one blood. We're all the same race—the human race. Help us to value others as You do. We can't do it on our own. Holy Spirit, we need Your help to truly love others. Forgive us where we have had hidden sins and renew us in Your love. Amen.

For further study: Genesis 2:7, 21–22; Matthew 5:43–48; 1 Corinthians 10:16–17; 1 Timothy 2:4.

MAY 23
Follower or Disciple?

> And Jesus took the loaves, and when He had given thanks He distributed them to the disciples, and the disciples to those sitting down; and likewise of the fish, as much as they wanted. (John 6:11)

THE GOSPELS RECORD Jesus feeding five thousand men, plus women and children with five small loaves of bread and two fish. The disciples were tired and Jesus had suggested they go to a deserted place to rest, but the great mass of people followed them. The hour grew late and the disciples asked Jesus to send the people away to go buy food. Jesus, however, replied that the disciples should feed the people. The disciples were shocked. It would take tremendous resources to do that. Then Andrew said there was a lad willing to give up his lunch, but he didn't think it would help much.

This was what Jesus was waiting for! He blessed that small amount of food, broke it, and passed it to the disciples. They passed the pieces on to the crowd, and a great miracle took place. The small amount of food multiplied into enough to satisfy everyone, as well as have leftovers to continue to feed the disciples for many days.

Did you notice the different people in this story? There were the followers who came to receive. They just wanted to sit by the Master to be healed and fed. There was the lad willing to give what he had, even though it wasn't much to offer. Then there were the disciples who had to bring that offering to the Lord but then take back what Jesus gave them and give it to others, serving the people even though they themselves were tired and hungry.

It strikes me that we can be a follower or a disciple. We can be someone who goes to church to sit down and be fed, or we can go to church to stand up and serve. We can walk into a room wondering if our needs will be met, or we can walk in looking for whom we can serve. Sometimes we need to just be a follower, to sit in the presence of the Lord and let Him meet our needs through the hands of His disciples. Other times, even when we're tired and we feel like our soul is in a deserted place, we need to give what little we have to the Lord. He then can bless and multiply it and give it back to us to pass on to others. When we do that, He's able to cause enough fragments to come back to us to meet our needs for many days.

This is the miracle of our communion with Jesus. He blesses and breaks the loaves and passes them to us to pass on to others, causing the blessing to multiply to satisfy great needs. We can choose to be a follower or a disciple at any given moment of any day. Which will you choose?

Jesus, we want to be Your disciple, not just Your follower. When we're tired and feel like we're in a deserted place, it can be hard to believe You are presenting opportunities to bless us as we bless others. Take the little we have to offer You and bless it so that we can pass Your blessings on to others. Encourage us to stand up and serve. Amen.

For further study: 1 Kings 17:8–16; Matthew 14:13–21; Mark 6:31–44; Luke 9:11–17, 21:1–4; John 6:1–14.

MAY 24
Filled and Spilled

How God anointed Jesus of Nazareth with the Holy Spirit and with power, who went about doing good and healing all who were oppressed by the devil, for God was with Him. (Acts 10:38)

PICTURE A JAR, ready for use. It's clean and empty, but the lid is screwed on tightly. As long as that lid remains on, the jar will stay empty. But what if we remove the lid? If we take the lid off, we can fill the jar with whatever we desire. Once we fill it, we can put the cap back on and store it up, or we can leave the cap off. If we leave the cap off and jostle or shake the jar, the contents inside will spill out. The harder we shake the jar, the more of what's inside will spill out.

Jesus was filled with the Holy Spirit, but like a jar without the lid, the grace and power inside of Him spilled out on everyone He met. At the Last Supper, He told His disciples, "This is My blood shed for you." His blood was spilled out for us. Jesus may be like a jar filled with the Holy Spirit and grace, but He keeps the cap off. He was so filled to the brim with love that none of the world's dirt could get in the jar to contaminate it. His love compelled Him to pour out His blood as an offering for our sin.

Paul writes to the Corinthians that we have this treasure in earthen vessels. Adam was made out of the dust of the earth, so we are like a clay jar. The treasure inside of us is Jesus Christ, Lord of all creation. We too are filled with the Holy Spirit and with grace. We have a choice to make. We can screw down the cap on this jar, hoarding the grace, or we can remove the lid and fling it far away. Sure, the grime of the world might get in, but so can more grace. When our jar is jostled and bumped, that grace can spill out onto those around us.

Spending a bit of time in Holy Communion, partaking of the bread and wine, is an opportunity to remind ourselves of what Jesus has done for us and the grace that fills us. It's a chance to once again be cleansed from the world's grime that has contaminated the grace in us. It's a chance to once again fill our jar to the brim with His love so it can spill out everywhere we go. We need not fear the jostling of this earthly jar, but we can rejoice in the grace that flows from the shaking.

> *Holy Lord, we are so amazed by Your grace and love. You have filled us with a great treasure. You value us even if we are but jars of clay. Forgive us for the contamination of the world that got into our jars and cleanse us. Fill us anew with Your grace and love so that we overflow with Your presence, letting it spill out onto all we meet. Amen.*

For further study: Genesis 2:7; Luke 22:19–20; Romans 5:3–8; 2 Corinthians 4:6–15; Galatians 5:22–26; 1 John 4:13.

MAY 25
Tuck In

> He who dwells in the secret place of the Most High shall abide under the shadow of the Almighty. (Psalm 91:1)

HAVE YOU EVER gone to someone's house to eat, and as everyone pulls their chair up to a table piled with food, the host says "Tuck in"? "Tuck in" is a phrase that originated centuries ago in Britain. It's like the more common American phrase "Dig in." In other words, fill your plates, eat up, there's lots of food. There is more than enough to satisfy everyone's hunger. It originates in the thought of hiding something in a secure place. After all, you're hiding the food in your stomach. You might think of tucking a child into bed by folding the blankets around them, making them warm, secure, and comfortable. Or you could tuck a book under your arm, protecting it and bringing it close to you.

Many books and resources try to help us picture what it would be like to walk with Jesus in the first century, to sit at the rough wooden table, wearing a robe and sandals and listening as He says, "Here, take this bread and eat; it's My body." There's nothing wrong with picturing ourselves being invited to join Jesus's first-century life, but I think what Jesus really wants is to be invited to our twenty-first century table. It might be more helpful to our day-to-day life to spend a moment picturing Him joining our life in the here and now.

For example, picture us all gathering around the table, Jesus in the place of honor. The table is piled high with all our favorite foods. Jesus stretches out His hand as the master of the feast and says, "Tuck in!" Tuck in to His provision; tuck in close to His breast, listening to His heart beat for the people. Tuck in to His presence. Come into the protected place under the shadow of His wings. Feel the comfort, warmth, and security He provides. Dig deep into His love. Consume His Word. Press in deeper in your relationship with Him. You can always get closer. His supply is never-ending. His love is eternal. His mercies are new every morning.

> *Jesus, we tuck in to You, taking a moment to sit and notice Your presence, Your goodness, Your love. Thank You for loving us enough to give Yourself as the sacrifice to make us free. Help us to dive deeper into Your love. Amen.*

For further study: Psalm 57:1, 100:1–5; Lamentations 3:22–24; Mark 14:22–24; John 6:53–58, 13:23; 2 Corinthians 1:3–4; Hebrews 4:16.

MAY 26
Lord, Cross Out the "I"

I have been crucified with Christ; it is no longer I who live, but Christ lives in me; and the life which I now live in the flesh I live by faith in the Son of God, who loved me and gave Himself for me. (Galatians 2:20)

NOEL PIPER, IN her book *Faithful Women and Their Extraordinary God,* tells the story of Helen Roseveare, a doctor and missionary to Africa. With great pressures and demands on her life, she found herself often losing her temper. She blamed it on being tired and overworked, but eventually it became obvious that she wasn't representing Jesus the way she should. She was in a spiritual crisis.

Pastor Ndugu called her over to the fire and gave her some wise advice. He drew a line in the dirt with his heel. This, he said, represented the big capital I of self. Next, he mentioned how she would take a moment and hold her coffee, waiting for it to cool down to drink. He suggested that at that time, she take a moment to pray, "Please, Lord, cross out the I." He took his heel and drew a line across the first line he'd drawn in the dust. There she saw, laid out in the dirt, the cross.

This is, after all, what living for Christ is all about. We recognize we are sinners, but by the grace of God we are saved. Only by the work of the Holy Spirit in us can we start to behave in ways so that people will see more of Jesus and less of the "I" of self. We are crucified with Christ, and now Christ lives in us. By faith in Him, who loved us and died for us, we can live in the flesh in a way that honors Him. We can't do it by works or effort or by trying to be a good person; it's a work of grace through faith in Him. There is no other way to cross out the "I" but by coming humbly to the foot of the cross.

Communion is a small activity to cause us to pause and remember He was crucified for us. It's a time to remember that He has crossed out the I. Jesus now lives in us, and we live for Him. It's a work of grace through faith, not of human works. He has done it all for us. Like Helen learned to do with every cup of coffee, take a moment now as we lift the bread and wine to our lips to pray, "Jesus, cross out the 'I.'"

> *Lord Jesus, we come to You recognizing the work You did on the cross. You were crucified so that we could have new life with You. We cannot earn it. We cannot pay the price it took to buy our souls; only Your blood was able to do that. So Lord Jesus, please, in our lives today, cross out the "I." Amen.*

For further study: Romans 6:1–14; Galatians 2:20; Ephesians 2:8–10; 1 John 4:7–16.

MAY 27
The Prodigal Brothers

> And he said to him, "Son, you are always with me, and all that I have is yours. It was right that we should make merry and be glad, for your brother was dead and is alive again, and was lost and is found." (Luke 15:31–32)

JESUS TELLS THE parable of the prodigal son. A man has two sons. The younger one demands his inheritance, which the boy then wastes on parties and harlots. Soon the money runs out and he finds himself alone and starving. Then he comes to his senses and decides to try to go home. When he's still a long way off, his father runs to him, welcomes him, and throws a big celebration. When the older brother finds out, he is livid! He's been a good son his whole life—working the farm, doing what he's been told, yet the father never had a party for him. The father goes out and pleads with the older son, trying to get him to understand.

This parable is about how God loves us. Even when we were sinners, He ran to us to welcome us home. This parable, however, is as much about the older brother trying to earn his Father's love by good works instead of receiving it by faith. God gives us an abundant inheritance of grace and love. The younger brother wasted it by selfish living; the older brother wasted it by burying it in bitterness and self-pity. Both ended up outside the house at one point and could choose to return to the father's table or stay in their lost condition. We know the younger brother returned, but we never find out if the older brother chose to go inside.

We may find ourselves in either of those positions. We may be consumed by selfish desires, or eaten up by bitterness. But what if we chose to be a different child? What if we were a child who came in from the fields, sat at the table, and as the bread and wine were passed around, we talked with the Father: "You know, Dad, my friend really wounded me. It hurts so much. I know you've been through that. Can You help me to forgive? I don't want to bury Your love in my pain." Or maybe we sit with the Father who is grieving His prodigal son and say, "Hey, Dad, I heard that my brother is really suffering. He's made some bad choices and now his spirit is starving. Is there anything I can do to help bring him home? Is it okay if I sit here with You and watch for his return?"

Which child will we be? We sit here at the communion table to remember the abundance of grace we've been given. All that He has, He has given to us. It's our reminder to not waste the abundance of His grace and love.

> *Father, You gave Your all to us, even Your very Son sent to earth to allow His body to be broken so we could be whole. We have sinned at times in our lifestyle, at times in our attitude toward others and to You, yet You run to us to forgive us again and again. Help us to share Your love and Your grace even with our lost and broken brothers and sisters. Amen.*

For further study: Luke 15:11–32; Romans 5:8.

MAY 28
Feeding the Pigs

Then he went and joined himself to a citizen of that country, and he sent him into his fields to feed swine. (Luke 15:15)

IN THE PARABLE of the prodigal son, the boy wastes his inheritance and finds himself out of money and out of food. He ends up joining himself to a citizen of the country, who sends the boy out to feed pigs. Pigs were an unclean animal to the Jewish boy, so this was adding insult to injury, and still he was starving. At one point he comes to his senses and realizes that his father's servants are better cared for, so he returns home, seeking to be taken in as a servant, not a son. When he's still afar off, his father sees him, runs to him, and rejoices in the return of his child. The father puts the best robe on the boy, a ring on his hand, and sandals on his feet.

Sometimes we find ourselves in a position where we've joined ourselves to the ruler of this world instead of to the Father of heaven. The devil sends us out to feed the swine in our souls. These swine are all the thoughts and habits that plague us. Maybe it's the thought we're not good enough, not pretty enough, or that we're unloved, unwanted, unneeded, useless, good for nothing. We are broken, damaged goods; we've failed and screwed up. Maybe they are the pigs of bitterness, unforgiveness, or anger that we feed. We feed these thoughts and they grow fatter and stronger, while we grow weaker.

However, if we pause and come to our senses, we realize there is a better way. We should no longer stay there feeding the pigs but return to our Father. As soon as we make that decision, He runs to meet us. We arrive in filthy rags, weak and helpless. He covers us with the robe of His glory, removing our shame. He gives us the ring that signifies a new authority. The things of this world no longer reign over us, but we are in control over them. The Father puts sandals on our feet, giving us the protection of His peace from the things in the world that would wound us as we walk. We are accepted into the family, where the table overflows with His provision, enough to meet all our needs.

Sometimes this world gets us down. We forget who we really are and start feeding the pigs again, making them fat while our soul grows lean. Communion is a chance to bring us back to our senses, to remind us that we have a place at our Father's table. We are welcomed there. We may have arrived in bad shape, but now we're washed and clean. We're dressed in His glory and walk with authority and peace. No matter what's in our past, we have a future with Him. There is no longer any need to feed those pigs. Instead, we can take our rightful place at the banqueting table.

Thank You, Father, for providing for all the needs of our spirits, souls, and bodies. Thank You for welcoming us to Your table even though we were in a bad place and arrived in a poor state. You have cleansed us and set us in a high place with You. Remind us when we forget just who we are in You. Amen.

For further study: Isaiah 61:10, 64:6; Luke 10:19; Romans 5:6–8; Ephesians 1:3–6, 2:4–22, 4:17–32, 6:15; Philippians 4:19.

MAY 29
He Went the Distance

And he arose and came to his father. But when he was still a great way off, his father saw him and had compassion, and ran and fell on his neck and kissed him. (Luke 15:20)

I READ ONE day about a young girl who went on a mission trip with her church. They traveled to an impoverished community. As she handed out a bag of food to a destitute man, she said, "God loves you."

The man answered, "It appears He loves you a little more than He loves me."

I was really struck by that comment and wondered if I were in her place, what I would say to that man. After all, here I am, living a good middle-class life in a blessed country with good health care, lots of support systems, and plenty of food on my table. What would I say to someone who struggles for their very existence from one day to the next? I recognize we live in a fallen world; the choices people make affect every one of us, some more than others. Yet I know God loves us all deeply.

Then the answer came to me. I would say, "God most certainly loves you as deeply as He loves me. He never sent someone hundreds of miles just to give me lunch, but He did that for you. He'll go to any length to let you know how much He cares. There's no greater distance than the distance between heaven and hell, between holiness and sin, yet God willingly crossed it to bring you and me life. There's no greater price that could be paid than the blood of Jesus to bring us salvation, yet He willingly paid it."

God went the distance needed to meet us where we were. The price didn't matter; the distance didn't matter. The only thing that mattered was our great need. That's the real manifestation of love. God put our desperate need ahead of His own life. No matter how far away we get from God, He will run the distance to bring us His love.

> *Father, the depth of Your love is amazing. You gave Your all to give us life and bring us to You. We are truly eternally grateful. Amen.*

For further study: Luke 16:26; John 3:16–17; Ephesians 4:7–13; 1 Peter 1:16–21; 2 Peter 1:3–4.

MAY 30
We Don't Deserve It

> But I see another law in my members, warring against the law of my mind, and bringing me into captivity to the law of sin which is in my members. O wretched man that I am! Who will deliver me from this body of death? I thank God—through Jesus Christ our Lord! So then, with the mind I myself serve the law of God, but with the flesh the law of sin. (Romans 7:23–25)

I USUALLY GET up in the morning feeling like I want to be a hero today. I will serve God, give to others, be encouraging, and reflect Christ well in my dealings with people. Alas, however, when things start going wrong, expectations remain unmet, or difficulties arise, I find deep in my heart that what I really want to be is the villain, the one demanding my own way, wanting others to bend to my needs. I start out the day thinking all I want to do is love people, but what I really want is for people to love me. I say I want to give to others, but I really want others to give to me. I want to be selfish, rude, and angry when things aren't going the way they should. It's my right! Others would be selfish, rude, or angry in the same situation, so why should I have to be the one who's kind?

I'm in good company. Paul complained of the same thing in the book of Romans. There's a war going on between my flesh and my spirit, and my flesh really wants to win. Paul reminds us that we can't do it on our own, but Christ in us will help us. Jesus, our Savior, is the only true hero. He was sinless yet took the penalty for our sin as if He was the villain. He loves us even when we don't love Him. He gave His all, holding nothing back. He had a perfect right to be selfish, rude, or angry as He was mistreated, but He took the abuse silently.

In some ways, I want to be able to stand like a Pharisee before God, saying, "Look, I did great today. I wasn't mean or selfish. I gave and loved freely. I was a hero!" Instead, I find I stand before God with the publican, my head hung low, saying, "Be merciful to me, a sinner."

Thankfully, Jesus said in Luke that it was the publican who went home justified, while the Pharisee was praying only with himself, unable to find forgiveness for his soul. We don't deserve His grace, but in recognizing this, we're able to receive it. The more we receive His love, the easier it becomes for our spirit to win the war over the flesh, and the better our actions become.

We come to the communion table recognizing that as long as we're in this world, we'll mess up no matter how good our intentions. We come recognizing that we don't deserve the invitation to the table, yet in recognizing His love and grace for us, we know we are welcome there. Only through His grace can we hope for our spirit to win over our flesh and for our actions to change. The cross reminds us that He lived the perfect life and now lives in us.

> *Thank You, Jesus. You lived the perfect life and carried our sins to the cross to be nailed there. We come to You justified because of what You've done for us. We may hang our head in shame, saying, "Be merciful to me a sinner," but You then lift up our heads. Help us to let Your love be manifested in our lives. Amen.*

For further study: Isaiah 53:7; Luke 18:9–14; Romans 7:7–8:11; 2 Corinthians 5:21; Hebrews 11:6; 1 Peter 2:23.

MAY 31

> But God demonstrates His own love toward us, in that while we were still sinners, Christ died for us. (Romans 5:8)

DISNEY DID A movie loosely based on the fable of the *Snow Queen* by Hans Christian Anderson. In this movie version, Elsa, the older sister to Anna and heir to the throne, has a problem. She can touch things and freeze them. It gets worse when she's afraid. She is fearful of hurting people after she accidentally wounds her sister by sending a shard of ice into Anna's head. This causes Elsa to withdraw and become cold in all her relationships, isolating herself from those who love her.

The fear and anger grow until a second accident sends a shard of ice into Anna's heart. This wound will kill Anna unless she finds true love. In typical Disney fashion, Anna thinks this means finding her Prince Charming. The man she thinks is her savior, however, ends up being someone deceptive, who would rather see her and Elsa both dead so he can have the throne. Anna manages to escape the deceiver's trap and heads out to look for another man she thinks will save her.

On her way, with her "true love" off in the distance, and as her body is turning to ice, she sees the deceiver about to kill her sister. In a not-so-typical Disney fashion, Anna forsakes running for the man she thinks will save her, and in the few steps she has left before she turns to ice, she throws herself between the deceiver and Elsa, taking the fatal blow and saving her sister. As Elsa weeps, realizing the depth of her sister's love, the ice starts to melt and Anna is restored to life. Elsa suddenly realizes that love is the force that enables her to control the cold in her and turn it to good.

I love how this movie turned from the older Disney style of the Prince Charming who comes to the rescue with love's first kiss. Rather, it shows how true love is all about sacrifice. The deceiver comes to us, enticing us with the things of the world, when really his desire is only to destroy our soul. Jesus comes between us and the deceiver and takes the fatal blow. Our hearts, which have been stone cold, can now warm and become hearts of flesh. Jesus rises from the dead to take His proper place in the kingdom. The deceiver has been defeated and we are truly free by the power of God's love, demonstrated by His sacrifice.

> *Jesus, we thank You for demonstrating Your love for us by Your death on the cross. You took the punishment meant for us in order to set us free once and for all from the power of sin. This world sometimes makes us cold and distant, but You have come to give us life and a heart of flesh. We pause today to remember what You've done and to let Your love once again melt the cold attitudes that have tried to grip our hearts. Amen.*

For further study: Ezekiel 36:25–27; 2 Timothy 1:7; 1 John 4:7–21.

JUNE 1
In the Shadow of the World

Do all things without complaining and disputing, that you may become blameless and harmless, children of God without fault in the midst of a crooked and perverse generation, among whom you shine as lights in the world. (Philippians 2:14–15)

HAVE YOU EVER walked outside into a dark night and, looking skywards, were struck by the beauty of a crescent moon with Venus shining so brightly nearby? The darker the night, the brighter they shine. The beauty can take your breath away. Have you considered that neither Venus nor the moon have any light in themselves? They're both rocky balls, not even stars, yet they glow in the darkness, reflecting the light of our sun as they rise in the shadow of the earth.

I remember as a child once being outside and wearing special glasses, watching as the moon obscured the sun during a total eclipse. What struck me the most was that as the sun's light was hidden, suddenly the sky was full of stars and planets. They'd been there all along, of course, but until the sun's light was obscured, the brightest stars were all but invisible.

Until we cross to the other side of the grave, we live in the shadow of darkness. Evil reigns in so many areas in this world. It can be depressing to watch the news, to see the pain all around us. As Christians we know how bright the light of the Son is. He shines so brightly that even the greatest deeds done by the world's brightest stars will seem as nothing in His presence. Yet in the shadow of the earth, where darkness reigns, even though we have no light in ourselves, His light can reflect beautifully to all around us. No matter how deep the darkness, His glory will shine ever brighter in the members of His body. Maybe we won't be a star like Mother Teresa or one of the great heroes of the faith, but His light will still be reflected to all around us. Once we're on the other side of the grave, we'll find that the greatest hero on earth won't be bright enough to eclipse His light. It's enough for us to be where He has called us to be, reflecting His glory to those who live in the shadow of the world.

> *Jesus, You are the Son of glory, the Light of the world. The evil of this fallen world tries to obscure Your light, but the work of the cross makes it possible for Your light to be reflected in us. No matter how deep the darkness, Your light can be seen in us. Remind us always not to let the darkness overwhelm us but to look for Your reflection in others, and in ourselves. Amen.*

For further study: Proverbs 4:18; John 1:1–13; 1 John 1:5–7.

JUNE 2
I Love You, Seeker of Plastic Planes

If you then, being evil, know how to give good gifts to your children, how much more will your Father who is in heaven give good things to those who ask Him! (Matthew 7:11)

WHEN I WAS a child, I would run to greet my dad when he came home from a business trip. I didn't really want to see him; I selfishly wanted the small plastic plane he'd pick up at the airport. I couldn't wait until he dug into his pocket and pulled out the little gray piece of plastic. I still see him smile as my own face lit up to receive this silly little thing.

As I grew, I'd receive gifts from Dad, although I knew it was my mom who had purchased them. My dad would jokingly ask, "So what did I get you?" since it was also a surprise to him.

When I was older still, I no longer needed to receive a gift from my dad at all. Still, my dad would often throw a few books or puzzle magazines into care packages sent by my mom. These gifts, the adult equivalent of the plastic plane, thrilled me. They spoke of our relationship, that he knew me and what I'd like. It didn't cost him much, but it spoke volumes and was such a blessing.

We often come to God selfishly demanding His gifts rather than His presence. Still, I don't think He's offended when we run to Him asking that He reach into His pockets to find something for us. I think He smiles to see our face light up with the little token. As we mature, He continues to provide gifts, usually through the hands of others. God isn't surprised. He has provided and orchestrated the gift to bless us and meet our needs. He's not offended if we don't see His name on the gift tag. He's just happy to see us unwrap it and use it. As we really mature, we start to see the gifts not for their own value but more because they speak of the beautiful relationship we have with the God of the universe, the one who loves us, knows us, knows what we'd like and need, and is happy to give us good gifts.

What better gift could we possibly have than His grace? The salvation given to us by the gift of Jesus's death on the cross surpasses all other gifts. In coming to the foot of the cross to receive His grace, we recognize the giver of the best gift there could ever be. We come to treasure His presence. We recognize that the real value of those gifts is more for the relationship they represent than for the gift itself.

> *Jesus, we thank You for Your willingness to die in order to bring about our salvation. Father in heaven, You have given the most awesome gift we could ever receive. We're so amazed and grateful for Your love for us. Thank You for loving us, even when we seek the gifts more than the giver. Help us to seek You first and foremost, loving You like You love us. Amen.*

For further study: Matthew 6:19–34, 7:7–11; John 3:16; Romans 5:12–21; 2 Corinthians 9:15; Ephesians 2:8; James 1:17.

JUNE 3
Flawed or Unique

But now God has set the members, each one of them, in the body just as He pleased. (1 Corinthians 12:18)

WHEN I WAS on holiday one time in England, I purchased a mug in the gift shop at the Tower of London. Weeks later when I was back at home and using the mug, I felt a tiny flaw in the glaze on the handle. I sighed and thought, *Of all the mugs there, I picked one with a flaw*. In my spirit, however, I heard God say, "What, you want one just like everyone else has?"

It reminded me that God loves how unique we are. Even identical twins have unique fingerprints and personalities! Each cell in the body may have the same DNA, yet they are unique. Cloned cells can lead to cancers, not health.

Yet we so often spend our youth trying to be like everyone else, and our adulthood trying to make everyone else be like us. It's the rare person who has learned to celebrate their uniqueness and not try to force others to think and act the same way they do. I used to get into difficulties because I was so headstrong and stubborn. People would see that as a flaw in my character. But that stubbornness also has enabled me to stick with things even when they got tough and every bit of me just wanted to throw in the towel and quit. Others would call that determination and say it's my super power. I would see people who were meek and let others walk over them as having a personality flaw, but others would recognize them as peacemakers and call it a gift.

In 1 Corinthians 11, Paul admonishes the believers for not treating other members of the body with respect when they partook of communion. Then in chapter 12, he goes on to explain that all the members of the body have different roles and responsibilities. It doesn't make them any less important. All have their part to play. We all have different gifts—different super powers. Then in chapter 13 he reminds them that all the spiritual gifts are worth nothing unless they are rooted in love.

Here we are, about to partake of communion. Communion is all about how much God loves us, and it reminds us that we're now the body of Christ. We're all unique yet all part of the same body. The key is to do everything from a heart of love. The love He has given us resides in us and can flow out from us to each other.

Jesus, we're so grateful You allowed Your earthly body to be broken so we could be whole. Your presence in us enables us to love one another and accept each other as unique, as we all are. We are still Your body now on earth. Live in us and through us. Help us to celebrate each other and recognize everyone's super powers, whatever they might be. Amen.

For further study: 1 Corinthians 11:17–13:12

JUNE 4
Personality Types

> For we do not have a High Priest who cannot sympathize with our weaknesses, but was in all points tempted as we are, yet without sin. Let us therefore come boldly to the throne of grace, that we may obtain mercy and find grace to help in time of need. (Hebrews 4:15–16)

YOU MAY HAVE seen those different personality tests and assessments. They're sometimes done to show how different personality types fulfill different roles and purposes. One form slots people into the four types: choleric (bossy types), melancholy (introspective, perfectionist), sanguine (fun loving), and phlegmatic (agreeable types). John Trent has a version that uses animal characters (lion, beaver, otter, and Golden Retriever, respectively) to discuss the same idea. These tests can also help you recognize how your personality can be a strength or a weakness. I think of it every morning when I'm hauling a wheelbarrow full of manure outside. I prefer the wheelbarrow with one wheel instead of two because it's easier to dump, so this is its strength. When I accidentally dump the wheelbarrow in the barn passageway, I recognize the wheelbarrow's strength is also its weakness!

We sometimes have trouble relating to people with different personalities, but we can be assured that Jesus has no problem understanding us. He was the perfect Man. The Gospel accounts of His life show that He reflected all personality types. When He turned over the tables of the money changers, He was the lion using His strength of personality to set things right. When He made sure to spend time alone in prayer, and when He fulfilled perfectly every prophesy made about the Messiah, He reflected that personality of the beaver, doing all things to perfection. When He attended weddings and had a reputation of hanging out with winebibbers, He reflected the otter personality, which has no problem enjoying life and celebrations. When He laid down His own will and let Himself be oppressed and afflicted, letting love for others take precedence over everything else, He reflected the loving nature of the Golden Retriever. Jesus is the perfect Man, the perfect embodiment of all personalities. He's able to use the strength of all personality types at the appropriate time so that they are never a weakness.

As we grow in the faith and become more like Him, we become more understanding of others, and also better able to control our natural personality. We can let our less dominant traits shine through when needed. Also, we're more likely to recognize when we've failed to let our behavior be ruled by love. Thankfully, at these times we can go boldly to the throne of grace to find mercy because of who Jesus is and what He has done for us on the cross.

> *Jesus, You are perfect and understand all aspects of humanity. You get it. You know that our different personalities are our strength and our weakness. We bring to You our failures, where we haven't walked in love with others, and we thank You that as You live and grow in us, we become more like You. Amen.*

For further study: Isaiah 53:1–12; Matthew 5:48, 11:19, 21:12–13; Romans 16:25–27.

JUNE 5
Fear, Guilt, and Shame

And I will put enmity between you and the woman, and between your seed and her Seed; He shall bruise your head, and you shall bruise His heel. (Genesis 3:15)

MOST OF US deal at some point in our lives with the emotions of fear, guilt, or shame. The religions of different cultures put different emphasis on each of these as well. For example, a lot of Eastern cultures are based on honor. To dishonor the family is to bring great shame. Honoring their god is paramount to their actions. Many African and Indian cultures are based on fear. They will perform rituals and sacrifices or carry talismans to protect against harm caused by their gods. In North America, we tend to be guilt-based. We are guilty of sin. We focus on how we mess up and fail.

In our personal lives, many of us deal with one or more of those emotions. Adam and Eve can relate. God placed them in the Garden of Eden and told them that they could eat and enjoy everything—everything, that is, except the tree of the knowledge of good and evil. That one tree they couldn't eat.

One day Adam and Eve were looking at that tree when the devil enticed them, saying, "Look how good this fruit is. You should eat it. It will make you like God." They eat it and suddenly notice that they're naked. I wonder why they only knew they were naked then. My thought is that before they sinned, they were clothed in the glory of God, and once they sinned, the glory departed, exposing them to the shame of their nakedness.

Adam and Eve now had knowledge of good and evil. Before they had only known good, but now they knew what it was to do evil. They felt their guilt. They looked on their nakedness and felt ashamed. Then they heard God calling to them, but they were afraid, so they hid. There we have it all—fear, guilt, and shame. Their descendants have had to battle with those emotions ever since.

But there's good news. Really good news. God wasn't surprised by their sin, and He had already prepared a remedy. The Seed of the woman, Jesus Christ our Savior, born of Mary, would be wounded by the devil, but He would crush Satan and forever set us free. Jesus came to the cross to take away the fear of death. We know we have a place in heaven and don't need to fear any longer. He is perfect love and casts out our fear. He has taken on our sin and carried our guilt so that we can stand before Him justified despite our failures. He has carried our shame in His own nakedness on the cross. He restores us to a place of honor. We come to the foot of the cross to find the remedy for all our fear, guilt, and shame.

Jesus, we praise You. You are glorious and amazing. We were the ones who sinned. You never did, yet You took the sting of that sin and carried all our fear, guilt, and shame to the cross to set us free. We are so thankful. We remember today that You have set us free. Amen.

For further study: Genesis 3:1–24; Romans 3:9–31; 2 Timothy 1:7–10; Hebrews 2:5–17; 1 John 4:18.

JUNE 6
Pearl's Great Escape

And the Word became flesh and dwelt among us, and we beheld His glory, the glory as of the only begotten of the Father, full of grace and truth. (John 1:14)

A NUMBER OF years ago, I fulfilled a childhood dream and bought a small hobby farm to provide a home for my horse, Coco. Knowing it wasn't right for him to be alone, since herd animals really need a herd, when I brought him home, I also brought Pearl, an elderly, retired school horse. Other horses needing to be retired to a safe home soon followed, and a small herd was established. These horses enjoy being outside all day with unlimited hay and no demands placed on their lives.

One day as I put them out in the main paddock, Pearl decided to slip out the gate and escape into the yard. Because she'd previously been caught and put to work as a school horse, she's pretty impossible to catch. As soon as she glimpses a halter or rope in your hand, she walks away. Even treats don't entice her. I struggled to catch her with no success. Finally, she managed to wander into a secondary paddock, where I quickly closed the gate, trapping her where she was at least safe. Pearl was not at all happy with this arrangement, because the rest of the herd was too far away for her comfort. She was so upset, calling out and pacing, wanting to be with the others. I'm sorry to say I didn't have a lot of sympathy for her. She'd made her bed and she was going to lie in it! I had things to do. It was her own fault she was in such a mess, suffering in her loneliness.

A short time later, she was quiet and I went out and found out why. Coco, my trickster, is very adept at escaping paddocks. He walks through the fence as easily as I do. This horse had left the main paddock and gone in the secondary paddock, where he was hip to hip and neck to neck beside Pearl. They both had their heads down in the hay, enjoying a good snack as he comforted her.

I was instantly struck by the thought that this is what Jesus did for us. We were in difficulty due to our sin. It was no fault of His. We'd brought the trouble on ourselves and were condemned to separation from our holy God. Jesus was willing to step into our situation. He came as a man and took on our punishment so that we could now be forever with Him. He invites us to eat with Him at His table as we draw comfort from His very presence. We were in anguish and He brought us His peace. He continually comforts us in our distress and calms our troubled soul.

Jesus, thank You for being willing to come to where we were. You took what we deserved so we could be forever with You. You want to be with us, side by side, loving us. Thank You. Amen.

For further study: John 14:23–27; Romans 10:6–13; 2 Corinthians 1:3–4.

JUNE 7
How Do You Eat an Elephant?

Not that I have already attained, or am already perfected; but I press on, that I may lay hold of that for which Christ Jesus has also laid hold of me. (Philippians 3:12)

I WENT WITH an organization called Outward Bound one year on a hiking trip on mountainous and rugged terrain, carrying heavy packs. I was one of the least fit of the group, and I was really struggling. We paused for a brief rest, and I sat on a rock, unable even to take my pack off. The leaders had said that we would make it or not make it as a group, and I was feeling so guilty. I was sure I couldn't go on. As I sat crying in pain and shame, one of the guys in the group came and sat beside me. He said to me, "How do you eat an elephant?"

I was a little confused and didn't know what he was getting at, so I just shrugged my shoulders.

"One bite at a time," he answered. I didn't have to walk far. I just had to do one more step. After doing that step, I just had to do one more. So I got up and took that step, and another, and another for two kilometers! We made it! I won't say the rest of the trip was easy, but it was definitely easier. I had learned that I didn't have to walk the two kilometers before me. I just had to walk the next step.

Sometimes on our Christian walk the way gets difficult. We stumble and fall. We think we can't go any further. We feel like we're letting everyone down. Paul wrote about this to the Philippians. He said his goal was to know Jesus *"and the power of His resurrection, and the fellowship of His sufferings, being conformed to His death"* (Philippians 3:10b). Then he says he isn't there yet, but he presses on. I think being conformed to His death means laying down my own will to do the will of God. Often my will fights back, wanting its own selfish desires. To fight against my selfishness to the end of my life is overwhelming. I don't think it can be done. Then I realize that I don't have to struggle until I come to the grave. I just have to fight the battle in front of me at this moment. One step at a time. One good decision at a time. I need to press on one step at a time until the entire elephant is consumed. One step at a time, we will get there as we lean on His grace for each step of the way.

Every day by coming to meet Him in communion, I am reminded that today is a new day. He has washed away the sins of yesterday and provided enough grace for the struggles of today.

> *Jesus, thank You for walking with us, encouraging us, helping us take each step on the path laid out before us. You lead us, guide us, and help shoulder the load so that we can press on to the prize of the high calling we have in You. Thank You. Amen.*

For further study: Matthew 6:33–34; 2 Corinthians 12:7–10; Philippians 3:1–21.

JUNE 8
Taking Out the Trash

I say then: Walk in the Spirit, and you shall not fulfill the lust of the flesh. (Galatians 5:16)

I WAS READING that many recyclable products aren't really recyclable but end up in landfills, so I decided to try limiting my purchasing of products wrapped in plastic. I suddenly found that there were a lot of things I had to scratch off my shopping list. Yogurt comes in plastic containers. Granola bars may be in a box, but they're individually wrapped inside the box with non-recyclable waste. Perogies? Well, they come in plastic too, and so do mustard and ketchup. The list goes on and on. The end result is that I've learned to make these products.

I've discovered that these things aren't actually hard to make, so there's been a side benefit to the process. Not only do I have much less garbage, but these products taste so much better. There's also a lot less sugar in them, so my body appreciates the change too. It's better for me and the environment. Win/win. I find it easier and easier to make the good choices because of the great benefits I've gained in the process.

Living in this fallen world, it's easy to pile up the garbage in our lives. In Galatians we read about the works of the flesh being adultery, fornication, uncleanness, licentiousness, idolatry, sorcery, hatred, contentions, jealousies, outbursts of wrath, selfish ambitions, and so on. It's a pretty long list. The works of the flesh are everywhere, piling up in our spiritual landfill.

In that chapter, Paul goes on to talk about the fruits of the Spirit: love, joy, peace, longsuffering, kindness, goodness, faithfulness, gentleness, and self-control. As we walk down our spiritual grocery aisle and look up and down our choices, we see lots of opportunity to buy unhealthy food, throwing those contentions and outbursts into our cart. But we can make another choice. We can turn to the whole food of the Word of God and fill our spiritual cart with good ingredients that we use to mix up a big batch of love and joy and peace for our life. We don't have to buy the trash in the first place. And every time we make that better choice, our life tastes better, we feel better, and we have no left-over garbage taking up space in our life. Each time we make the better choice it becomes easier to do it again in the future, because we've reaped the benefits of our choices.

We come to the communion table acknowledging the pile of garbage we've collected, but also sweeping it away at the foot of the cross. We lean into Him and the help of the Spirit in order to make better choices for the future that will avoid the garbage altogether.

> *Jesus, thank You for taking the garbage out of our life and loving us into better choices and a better life. Amen.*

For further study: Galatians 5:13–26.

JUNE 9
Wonder

Beloved, now we are children of God; and it has not yet been revealed what we shall be, but we know that when He is revealed, we shall be like Him, for we shall see Him as He is. (1 John 3:2)

I READ A novel called *Wonder*, about a boy born with a severe deformity in his facial bones. It tells how he must overcome prejudice, rejection, and bullying to make friends despite his appearance. In one part of the book, someone gives him a space helmet. The boy ends up wearing that helmet all the time for a while, since it hides his face. He's disappointed when the helmet suddenly gets lost. It turns out, however, that his father hated that helmet. He missed seeing the face of his beloved son.

I think of how many of us are camera shy, not wanting to see our face reproduced in photos. I used to use a long telephoto camera lens to get good photos of my family because if they knew I was taking a picture, they would hide or their appearance would be altered by the worry about having their picture taken. When I was able to capture them unawares, their natural beauty was so evident. So many people are ashamed of their appearance—buck teeth, pimples, nose too big, nose too small, eyebrows too heavy, eyebrows not heavy enough. The list is endless. If someone is injured or has a scar or birthmark on their face, it's especially hard for them not to feel self-conscious, since so many others startle or react badly to facial deformities. God, however, doesn't have a problem with our scars or appearance.

I think God looks at us differently than we look at ourselves. He sees our beauty no matter what our appearance, because we are His beloved child. He longs to look at our face. He loves every mark and blemish that reflect our unique beauty. The Bible also says that Jesus wasn't much to look at. Once He was beaten and scarred, He must have looked horrific. It would be hard to look Him in the face. But what could be more beautiful than His loving sacrifice. We welcome Him into our hearts, and we long to see His face.

As we come to the communion table today, we pause to reflect that He loves us. He loves to look on our face. He's not ashamed of us. In His eyes we are His beautiful beloved. We also seek His face and His heart, knowing there is nothing in the entire universe more beautiful than our Savior.

> *Jesus, You were marred so badly it was hard to even recognize You as a man, and You went through that so we would be free from the shackles of sin and death. There is nothing more beautiful, and we are so very grateful for all You've done and for who You are. Amen.*

For further study: Isaiah 53:1–12; Ephesians 1:3–6; 1 John 3:1–2.

JUNE 10
He Did It for You

> And He took bread, gave thanks and broke it, and gave it to them, saying, "This is My body which is given for you; do this in remembrance of Me." (Luke 22:19)

WHEN JESUS INSTITUTED communion, He said that His body was broken and His blood was being poured out for you. Now I recognize that this is "you" plural, as in all of us. After all, we know that God so loves the *world*. The fact that Jesus did this for all of us, however, doesn't negate the fact that He also did this for *you*—you personally. Christianity is a global faith, but it's also a personal faith.

What if we were to imagine ourselves sitting at the table with Him as He shares communion. What if we could see into the future to His crucifixion and that, by chance, we'd be the only person in the history of the universe to accept His gift of grace and be saved from our sins? I can imagine if we followed the pattern that many of us have, we would say to Him, "Jesus, I'm not worth the sacrifice You're going to make. If only I will be saved, don't go through with it."

Jesus would look at us and say, "No, even if you're the only one who receives Me and accepts what I'm going to do, I will finish what has begun."

"But Jesus," we'd continue, "don't you see? Don't You know they will whip You, mock You, beat You, and tear You to shreds before hanging You on a cross to slowly suffocate?"

And He'd answer, "Yes, I know. But you will receive My grace and dance with Me in glory."

You see, God so loves the world that even if only one sinner would come to grace, He would pay the price. Thankfully, many have come to grace. Many have been saved and, praise God, many more still will come. There's something about knowing that He loves us enough to take the journey to the cross, even for just you or me, that encourages us to walk in His light in the midst of a dark world.

> *Thank You, Jesus. You allowed Your body to be broken and Your blood shed to save me. Despite my failures, I am worth it to You. The depth of Your love is beyond amazing! All of us globally thank You, and I personally thank You. Amen.*

For further study: Luke 22:19–20; John 3:16, 19:1–3, 17–24, 33–34; 1 Peter 2:9.

JUNE 11
Unbroken

> Therefore, if anyone is in Christ, he is a new creation; old things have passed away; behold, all things have become new. (2 Corinthians 5:17)

LAURA HILLENBRAND WROTE a biography of Louis Zamperini called *Unbroken*. Louis was an Olympian who was adrift at sea for over a month after his plane crashed during World War II. He was then captured by the Japanese. He suffered terribly and barely survived. We use the word "unbroken" to describe someone who overcomes difficulty without losing their true nature, like a horse who's still wild and unbroken by man's attempts to train him. The title implies that his spirit wasn't broken by the severe trials he endured, but this isn't quite true for Louis. When he returned to the United States, he was a broken man. He was angry, bitter, and an alcoholic. His wife convinced him to attend a Billy Graham meeting that ended up changing his life entirely when he answered the call to give his life to Jesus. His life became an inspiration to many as God healed all the broken places.

The title of the book really struck me as being even more true than our traditional use of the word "unbroken" for people who've endured difficult circumstances. When we come to the cross, we acknowledge that we are broken people in a broken world. As we humble ourselves before Jesus in our brokenness, He takes that brokenness for us and we are now un-broken. We can take on His righteousness, since He has taken on our sin. We're now justified and at peace with God, as though we'd never been broken in the first place. It's not like He just fit the pieces of the clay pot together by gluing the seams; it's more like He has taken the clay from which we are made and remolded us into a brand-new vessel to carry His glory. Louis was indeed un-broken by the Lord of Glory.

> *Jesus, thank You that You were broken that we might be un-broken. Your blood was spilled so we could be saved. You heal us spirit, soul, and body, making all things new. Thank You. Amen.*

For further study: Psalm 147:3; Isaiah 61:1–3; Jeremiah 18:1–6; 2 Corinthians 4:6–7.

JUNE 12
Better than New

And I heard a loud voice from heaven saying, "Behold, the tabernacle of God is with men, and He will dwell with them, and they shall be His people. God Himself will be with them and be their God." (Revelation 21:3)

HAVE YOU EVER noticed that we don't always appreciate what we have until we don't have it anymore? I spent a few weeks in Uganda riding around on an old bus, having to pick up water in big bottles and shower using a bucket of water. Compared to the people who lived there all the time, we had it really good, but compared to middle-class North American life, it was challenging. When we arrived back in Toronto and sank into the seat of a cab, I was struck by how incredibly comfortable it was. Of course, the seat in this cab was no different from the seat in any other cab in Toronto, but compared to the seats on the rickety bus in Africa, these seats were like a royal throne! My perspective had changed. I became thankful for being able to walk to a tap and turn it on for potable water. Having a real shower rather than pouring a bucket of water over my head was an incredible luxury that I hadn't appreciated before.

In the Garden of Eden, our ancestors had it really good. All the food they could eat, no death or disease, all the animals were friendly, and they walked with God every day. You'd think they would have been so grateful, able to resist the devil's temptation. God, of course, was not surprised by their fall from grace. He'd already made provision for our salvation.

It seems to me this is just like God. He can take a bad situation and make it something even better. Once the world became a fallen world, the contrast between heaven and hell became real. By experiencing life without God beside us, we can really grasp the wonder and beauty of having a relationship with the Lord of Glory. The contrast makes us appreciate our salvation and makes it something better than if the world had never fallen in the first place.

In the movie *Planes: Fire & Rescue*, a little crop duster plane has a broken part for which there is no replacement. He ends up crashing. When he wakes up from the crash, he finds the damage from the crash, including the broken part, repaired. He tells the mechanic that it's just like new, but the mechanic answers with his signature line, "*No!* Better than new!"

That's what our God has done for us. He makes us better than new. His solution to the fallen world is better than if the world had never fallen. We appreciate what He has done, because we know what it's like to walk without Him. We know what it's like to be dead in our trespasses and sins, so we rejoice ever more greatly when He makes us alive.

> *Father, we so appreciate what You've done. You gave Your only Son so we could have life. He took our sin, and now we're able to be with You, to walk in the presence of the Holy Trinity. It's a marvelous, miraculous remedy to our fallen nature. We are so grateful. Amen.*

For further study: Genesis 1:1–3:24; Ephesians 2:1–10; Revelation 21:1–22:5.

JUNE 13
Passing World

My soul shall make its boast in the Lord; the humble shall hear of it and be glad. Oh, magnify the Lord with me, and let us exalt His name together. (Psalm 34:2–3)

SOME TIME AGO, I heard a discussion on the radio about "passing White." This refers to someone who is bi-racial but looks like a White person, and they avail themselves of the privilege that can come to people who are not of color. This isn't really a new concept. During World War II, some Jewish people who looked to be of Aryan ancestry passed themselves off as non-Jews. For them it wasn't just about accessing privileges. It was about survival! Some people in our culture are able to be "passing White" but aren't hiding from their Indigenous or color ancestry; rather, they're embracing it. They use their privilege to show the fallacy of racism and to exalt their brothers and sisters of color.

Jesus, our Savior, was also bi-racial in a sense. He was fully God and also fully man. He was of the heavenly divine, but also born of human flesh in the world. He could "pass world" when He walked on the earth. Did not even the Pharisees judge Him as being just a man, the son of Joseph and Mary with brothers and sisters? Jesus didn't appear as a man to hide from His divine nature, but He embraced it, demonstrated it, and used it to exalt us, His human family, to His heavenly kingdom.

Now we have taken on His divine nature, but we are still able to be "passing world." The question becomes: Do we "pass world" to hide our divine nature? Is it a form of cultural survival to laugh at the off-color joke at the office, or to join with others in speaking ill of people? Will we hide because of our fear, or will we choose to embrace our dual nature? We can choose to bring grace to our workplace and families. We can show forth the light within us, bringing love and conviction but not condemnation. We can lift up those around us and point them to the higher call of life in Christ Jesus.

> *Jesus, Your death on the cross paid the price so we could put off our worldly sins and partake of Your divine nature. Help us to embrace the opportunity we have to show forth Your glory while we're still here on the earth among the lost and broken. Amen.*

For further study: Matthew 13:54–58; John 1:14; 1 Peter 1:3–2:17.

JUNE 14
What Is Between Us

For He Himself is our peace, who has made both one, and has broken down the middle wall of separation. (Ephesians 2:14)

I WAS DRIVING down the road one day and saw a father out for a walk with his little girl. I thought it was so beautiful. The girl's face radiated joy, but then the man's phone rang. He quickly answered it and was chatting on the phone, not noticing the now crestfallen face of his daughter. At restaurants I often notice people sitting with others at their tables, but all looking at their own phone. I saw the phone grow like a giant before me taking up my visual field, so I could barely see the outstretched arms of Jesus trying to reach to me from the other side of the phone.

So what drives us to let something like our phone come between us? I know phones cause a dopamine release, the neurotransmitter that triggers the pleasure-seeking centers in our brain. Intimate relationships also release dopamine. So why do we choose the dopamine from our phones instead of from real relationships?

My thought is that the pleasure release from an addiction is more certain, at least as far as the desire for pleasure. The addictive substance itself may quickly stop being pleasurable, but the thought that it might bring pleasure drives us onward. Real relationships are a bit messier and uncertain. Things can come between us and our close friends and relatives. Things can come between us and God.

Paul says in Ephesians that God has broken down the wall of division between us. I recognize that Paul is talking about the division between Jew and Gentile, but God has also broken down the wall between His holiness and our sin, His divinity and our humanity. I find after having been a Christian for some time that if I'm not careful, I can rebuild that wall brick by brick. I lay the bricks of disappointments from unanswered prayer or unconquered fears and anxieties. Let's not forget bricks of anger or unforgiveness. Ah, that last one can be a very large brick, especially when it concerns wounds from other Christians.

When we come to the communion table, we remind ourselves that God has broken down the wall between us by His death on the cross. It's an opportunity to ask Him which bricks we have placed while trying to rebuild the wall. It's the chance to once again let Him take the sledgehammer of His grace to smash those bricks to pieces.

Holy Spirit, reveal the things we have let come between us and the Holy Trinity. Is there anything blocking our intimacy?

I forgive now those who have hurt me, and I ask Your forgiveness for my desire to hang on to bitterness and unforgiveness, fear or anxiety. All is laid down at the foot of the cross.

Thank You, Jesus, for taking our sins and bringing us into relationship with You. Amen.

For further study: Psalm 16:11, 55:12–14; Matthew 6:9–15; Ephesians 2:1–22; 1 Peter 1:3–9.

JUNE 15

Today's Failure, Tomorrow's Success

I acknowledged my sin to You, and my iniquity I have not hidden. I said, "I will confess my transgressions to the Lord," and You forgave the iniquity of my sin. Selah. (Psalm 32:5)

WHENEVER A PLANE crashes, the cause is thoroughly investigated and brought to light. The purpose of this isn't to lay blame but rather to expose what went wrong so it can be prevented in the future. Investigation of a horrible crash today may result in the saving of thousands of lives tomorrow.

If someone has a rare illness, the initial investigations can be prolonged and take time to sort out. Once the diagnosis is made, the treatment can really begin. If the symptoms start to recur, the disease will be recognized more quickly and treatment started sooner. The process of getting to the root of the problem may not be pleasant, but it has great value.

There are many benefits to bringing things to the light. As long as we keep our sin secret and in the darkness, it has power over us. It can create fear and shame, eroding our faith. If we bring it to the light and expose it, we can then investigate root causes. The sin will lose its power over us. We'll also learn to recognize the symptoms of its recurrence, so we can deal with it more quickly. The process of confessing sin isn't pleasant. We fear the consequences, but to not deal with it will eat away at our soul. The hidden things can destroy us, but when we confess them, we find mercy. The quicker we deal with them, the shallower the wound and the quicker the healing.

Paul reminded the Corinthians that when they come to the communion table, they should pause to examine themselves to see if they've been treating their brothers well. He adds that if we judge ourselves, we won't be judged. When we make a habit of searching our hearts and exposing the dark places to His light, the process becomes easier and quicker. We can avoid problems in the long run. The pain of today's failure will become the successes of tomorrow as we avoid the things that once plagued and wounded us. So let's pause a moment and do just that. Is there anything that needs to be brought to the light so He may heal it?

Jesus, we come to You, knowing that You see all the dark places of our hearts already. Holy Spirit, show us what needs to be brought to light. Jesus, we confess our sins and seek Your mercy, which You have so willingly poured out upon us in Your blood that flowed down the cross. Amen.

For further study: Psalm 32:1–11; Proverbs 28:13; 1 Corinthians 11:17–34; 1 John 1:5–9.

June 16
Driving Life's Road—Look Well Ahead

For you had compassion on me in my chains, and joyfully accepted the plundering of your goods, knowing that you have a better and an enduring possession for yourselves in heaven. (Hebrews 10:34)

SOME YEARS AGO, I signed up for an adult refresher driving course with Young Drivers of Canada. At the time, that course had five main principles, or habits, it sought to develop in the driver.

The first one was to look well ahead. Looking as far ahead as you can enables you to see what's going on around you and plan your responses well ahead of time. Also, people tend to go in the direction they're looking. By looking far ahead, you stay in your lane better, and the driving is smoother.

We could say Jesus followed that principle on His route to the cross. He stayed on course no matter what obstacles came to Him by looking well ahead. Hebrews tells us it was for the joy that was set before Him He endured the cross. His joy came from looking far into the future and seeing you and me come to the foot of the cross. He wasn't focused on saving His physical life on earth that was immediately in front of Him, but He was focused on the eternal life we would receive by His sacrifice. He saw our eternal future and steered clear of all the obstacles the devil put in His way so He could fulfill the call to lay down His life for us.

When we come to the foot of the cross, we lift our eyes up into the distance and see the heavens opening with the offer of eternal life. As our eyes stay focused on that far distance, we can easily see the obstacles coming at us, but our eternal perspective keeps us from veering to the right or left. We can avoid the obstacles caused by sin. We are well positioned for our exit ramp when we come to it. If we take our eyes off Him and instead look just a few feet in front of us at our pains and problems, our faith veers all over the place. If we follow too closely to sin and anxiety, we can't steer clear of obstacles like unforgiveness. We lose our peace, and our road becomes bumpy.

So today as we partake of communion, we remind ourselves that we have walked to the hill of Golgotha, to the foot of the cross. From here we lift up our eyes to the heavens and see all eternity laid out for us. With the right perspective, the troubles of today aren't as big as they seem, and He will guide us in the way we should go.

Jesus, we ask Your forgiveness for the times we've taken our eyes off You. You are our example. You looked to the future of eternity and stayed the course, all the way to Your death on the cross. Help us to take our eyes off the problems of today and keep them firmly focused on You, so that You might keep us centered in the faith. Amen.

For further study: Joshua 1:7; Psalm 32:8; Matthew 4:1–11, 6:19–23; Acts 1:9–11; Hebrews 12:1–4.

JUNE 17
Driving Life's Road—Move Your Eyes

Having eyes, do you not see? And having ears, do you not hear? And do you not remember? (Mark 8:18)

THE SECOND HABIT Young Drivers of Canada taught me was to move your eyes. Sometimes when we're driving, we let our eyes fixate straight ahead, and then we miss things happening all around us. We might not perceive kids or people about to step into an intersection, or cars about to turn in front of us, or those speeding up behind us. Good defensive driving means regularly moving your eyes to scan areas around you so you can react to them.

Sometimes as I go about my business, I can fix my eyes on my destination. If there's a homeless person nearby, I purposely avoid looking at them so that my day isn't disrupted. Or maybe if someone is sitting at a table alone and sad, I go on my way, refusing to see it. After all, their problems are none of my business. What demand do they have on my compassion?

When I ignore those around me, I have forgotten that the Holy One lives inside of me. He is a man of great compassion. He stopped when people asked Him to. He halted when He noticed people who needed His touch. His day's agenda didn't take priority over the people around Him. Of course, nothing stopped Him from His ultimate plan to save us and make His home with us, but even on His way to the cross, He concerned Himself with others. When breathing was near impossible, He pushed Himself against the nails in His feet and spoke words to provide for His mother. "Compassion" is rooted in the words that mean to "suffer with others." Even His death on the cross was the ultimate act of compassion for fallen human beings.

We are His body on earth, and He sees the homeless, the broken, the sad, the rejoicing. He sees and is willing to step in. He's willing to provide food, comfort, prayer, or a helping hand. Are we willing to be His hands and feet to those around us? Are we willing to move our eyes and see them?

> *Jesus, thank You for Your ultimate gift of compassion to us all. Live big in us. Open our eyes to see. Holy Spirit, quicken our hearts with compassion for those around us and give us wisdom on how to live out being the body of Christ here and now. Amen.*

For further study: Matthew 9:10–13, 11:28–30, 15:32; Mark 9:20–22; Luke 7:13–14.

JUNE 18
Driving Life's Road—Spot the Problems

Therefore lay aside all filthiness and overflow of wickedness, and receive with meekness the implanted word, which is able to save your souls. But be doers of the word, and not hearers only, deceiving yourselves. (James 1:21–22)

ANOTHER HABIT TAUGHT when I took the Young Drivers of Canada course was to spot the problems: Are you in someone's blind spot? Is your vision hindered by parked cars? Is there someone sitting in a parked car who might suddenly open their door? The idea is to react in a way to fix the situation before you ever get into trouble. Can you get out of the blind spot? Do you see feet between the tires of the parked car, indicating that a child might run out into your path? If you look, you can stop or move over before they get injured. The sooner we react to the potential problems, the sooner we can move to a different path, and the better off everyone is on the road.

One day I was talking to a friend about someone from my past. I heard bitterness in my voice, even though what I was saying wasn't mean, nor was I angry. But my voice revealed that I still had a problem with unforgiveness. On another occasion, I caught myself rolling my eyes at a situation instead of dealing with things prayerfully and in love. Every day we have opportunities to notice where we're still tempted to sin, or where we're not walking in the perfect law of love. Sometimes I spot the problem but hang on to my attitude, continuing to drive into harm's way. However, at other times when I spot the problem, I take it to the Lord to help me deal with it. He is always gracious and good at providing a "way of escape."

A big part of communion is coming to the table with a humble heart, willing to examine ourselves to spot the problems. Now is the time to seek forgiveness and ask Him to change our heart to one that loves like He loves. In remembering His great sacrifice for our sins, we can remember to let go of our hurts and grief, laying it down at the foot of the cross.

> *Jesus, we come to You with the pain, unforgiveness, temptations, and grief that still live on in our hearts and lives. Help us to give it all to You. You carried our sin and shame and set us free. Help us to let go of the things that hinder our relationship with You and to lean into Your grace. Amen.*

For further study: 1 Corinthians 10:13; James 1:2–4:17.

JUNE 19
Driving Life's Road—Keep Space

I will run the course of Your commandments, for You shall enlarge my heart. (Psalm 119:32)

THE FOURTH HABIT promoted by Young Drivers of Canada was to keep space. This involved maintaining space around your car to allow time to react and to keep your vision from being impaired. You don't want to be boxed in by all the vehicles around you.

Naturally when I thought of this, I thought of the many Scriptures that warn us to be careful not to get boxed in with unbelievers. We shouldn't get into close relationships where we become influenced rather than being the influencer. Of course, we are in the world and must interact with it, but we're not of the world, so our behavior should reflect our higher calling as a child of Christ. We don't want to get so caught up in the world that we lose our vision and calling.

When I meditated on this thought, I felt the Holy Spirit whisper that there was another way we need to keep space. He reminded me that I have a tendency to close my heart off from others. Over the years, people I loved have deeply wounded me by their rejection. The natural reaction is to not let people into my heart to protect it from further wounds. If there's no space for people to move into, they can't get close enough to cause pain. Yet this isn't the example we learn from Jesus.

He loved deeply, and no one was wounded more deeply because of that love. Even after being so badly wounded, He has continued to open His heart to give and receive love. He hasn't closed it off or boxed it in. He hasn't erected barriers. He keeps space in His heart for each and every one of us. I also need to enlarge my heart to love others and to receive love from others. Sure, it's risky, but my Lord says it's oh so worth the risk! He has proven it over and over again for all eternity.

Jesus, thank You for setting the example. You were wounded and rejected, but You didn't close off Your heart. You enlarged Your heart enough to accept all who would receive You. Help us to learn to love and be loved just like You. Amen.

For further study: Matthew 5:43–48; John 17:13–19; 2 Corinthians 6:14–18; Philippians 3:17–21; James 1:27; 1 John 2:10, 3:13–21, 4:7–21.

JUNE 20
Driving Life's Road—Be Seen

Let your light so shine before men, that they may see your good works and glorify your Father in heaven. (Matthew 5:16)

THE FINAL GOOD driving habit promoted by Young Drivers of Canada was "be seen." This meant letting other drivers and pedestrians know you were there by communicating with eye contact or a light beep on the horn, and especially by keeping your headlights on at all times, even in the daytime. This was before daytime running lights were a thing in cars, so I developed the habit of turning on my lights as soon as I turned on the ignition.

Jesus told us in the Sermon on the Mount that our behavior was to be such that we would shine like a light in the midst of a dark world. People should realize that something is different in our lives. We should reflect the joy of the Lord. It should be obvious to others that we have something they need. This isn't accomplished by beating those around us into submission to God's laws; it's done by reflecting His glory. I traveled to Russia once with a missionary group. As we were crowded onto a bus at the airport, we laughed and enjoyed each other and the adventure that awaited us. A lady walked up to our group and said, "You guys are Christians, aren't you?"

We looked back at her and said that yes, we were. We asked if she'd heard us talking about Jesus. I was taken aback by her reply. She answered, "No, you guys are the only ones in this whole airport who are smiling."

When she said that, I looked around and noticed that she was right. Our faces were radiant, while everyone else in the area was downcast, under a heavy and oppressive cloud. As we traveled around over the next few days, I noted that Christians had a light others didn't possess. In that place, at that time, the difference was striking. Back home, it's not always as easy to let my light shine. Living in a culture rooted in Christianity, there's not the same degree of darkness in the world. But just like the headlights being on in the daytime make a difference for people to see my car, so I must still let my light shine for others to see the glory of God. It can be easy to slide into a grumbling and judgmental attitude, forgetting to turn on my light of joy in the Lord. Communion is my chance to come to the cross to be reminded to switch on the light, making sure it's not dimmed by past regrets and present troubles.

> *Jesus, You shone Your light, touching all in the world with Your love. Live big in us; shine through us and touch others through us. Forgive our failures and cleanse us anew that we may show forth Your glory. Amen.*

For further study: Nehemiah 8:10; Matthew 5:13–16; 2 Corinthians 4:17; Philippians 2:12–16.

JUNE 21
Regreening Our Soul

But those who wait on the Lord shall renew their strength; they shall mount up with wings like eagles, they shall run and not be weary, they shall walk and not faint. (Isaiah 40:31)

YEARS AGO, WHEN I told people I had accepted a job in Sudbury, many people responded with "Sudbury! Why there? It's a black hole."

It's true that when you drove through the area back then, in the late 1980s and early 1990s, there were few trees, and the exposed rocks were blackened by years of mining and acid rain. As the decades passed, things changed. The mines developed a scrubber system to clean the waste products from the smokestacks, removing the acid rain. The university developed ways to counter the acid soils and plant seeds for trees and grass to grow. Now when I drive the highway, I see that the area has been re-greened. Boreal forest grows where there had only been barren, blackened ground. It's hard to remember what it used to look like. It took time, but the area has been completely regenerated.

When we first come to Jesus, our hearts have been blackened by sin and the acid rain of abuse, fear, or bitterness. Jesus comes along with the scrubbers of faith and grace, stopping the old processes of pain. There are still visible signs of the disease that had once been in our soul, but as we renew our mind to His Word and walk with Him, He starts to renew our soul. Slowly, almost imperceptibly at times, we become new people. Our old habits wash away, and the life in the Spirit shines forth as the seeds of His love sprout and grow. The process can take time, but the finished product looks nothing like what we started with.

Today as we come to the communion table, we give our thanks that He is renewing us day by day by His love. The cross was just the beginning of the entire transformation.

> *Jesus, we are so grateful for the cross, but we are also so grateful that You continue to cause us to grow. We make mistakes, but we also improve. We're not the same as we were, and tomorrow will be better still. Thank You. Amen.*

For further study: Psalm 51:10; Isaiah 40:28–31; Romans 12:1–2; Ephesians 4:22–32; Colossians 3:5–11.

JUNE 22
The Fourth Man in the Fire

And the satraps, administrators, governors, and the king's counselors gathered together, and they saw these men on whose bodies the fire had no power; the hair of their head was not singed nor were their garments affected, and the smell of fire was not on them. (Daniel 3:27)

THERE WAS A time when the Israelites were carried away by their enemies to Babylon. Three of the Hebrew boys grew up and held positions in the Babylonian government while continuing to honor God. Now it came to pass that the king, Nebuchadnezzar, set up a gold image of himself and commanded his people to worship it. Shadrach, Meshach, and Abednego, the three Hebrew men, refused to bow to this idol. The king was infuriated and had the men bound and cast into a fiery furnace. The fire was so hot it killed the soldiers who threw them in, yet these three were unharmed. Nebuchadnezzar was astonished to see them walking around in the fire, unbound and free and talking with a fourth man, who looked like a god. The king commanded them to come out of the furnace, and all were shocked to see that their clothes weren't singed and they didn't even smell like smoke. King Nebuchadnezzar decreed that everyone should worship the God of the Hebrews, because no one else could deliver like that.

We don't have a worldly king demanding we worship a golden image, yet there are daily pressures that call us to bow our knee to other images of gold. We're pressured to fit in and live like those around us. We're driven to store up and hoard. Satan fans the flames to destroy us, flames of jealousy or desire for things other than God. Those flames lick at our heart, proclaiming we're not good enough, we won't fit in or survive the world's system unless we bow to the idol of this false god.

As we resist the world's idols and are tossed to its flames, we can rejoice and take hope. The fourth man in the furnace of Babylon lives in us and with us. We can walk around this world recognizing the touch of the Lord and hearing His voice. Those trials by fire will burn off the things that bind us, and we won't even smell like smoke! We'll perform our jobs well, but we won't bow down to the idol of gold, and our coworkers and neighbors will notice the difference. The three men in Babylon affected the whole nation with their faith, turning the king and all his subjects to the One True God. We can affect our nation in the same way, turning their hearts to the one who can deliver from the flames.

Jesus, we recognize that You died to set us free. You've set our sights on our heavenly home and have chosen to abide with us during our time in the world. You can hold us to the true path and keep us from caving to the world's call. Thank You for delivering us from sin and death and for walking with us every day, keeping us from being touched by the smoke of the world. Amen.

For further study: Daniel 1:1–21, 3:1–4:3.

JUNE 23

Unmet Expectations

Therefore, when they had come together, they asked Him, saying, "Lord, will You at this time restore the kingdom to Israel?" (Acts 1:6)

ONE DAY AT work I was thinking about my lunch break, planning to sit down and relax, and maybe do the crossword or the jumble puzzle. Sadly, as lunch time came around, and as so often can happen in a veterinary clinic, an emergency came in, causing all the plans in my head to be for naught. I felt angry and wondered why, but then I recalled that a common source of anger is unmet expectations. This wasn't a righteous anger fueled by mistreatment or abuse, nor was it anger triggered by fear. It was a thwarted selfish desire that had triggered the emotion. Knowing the cause enabled me to process the disappointment and move on in peace.

The disciples must have felt a range of emotions as they watched the Messiah breathe His last breath as His blood flowed down the cross. They had thought this man was going to re-establish the Jewish nation. Their hopes and expectations died with Jesus on the cross. Three days later, the disciples' hope revived as Jesus walked from the tomb. When they met with Jesus in the days after His resurrection, they asked Him if now He was going to restore Israel's earthly kingdom. They were still expecting a reign upon earth rather than the promises of heaven. Their hopes must have been dashed once again as they watched Jesus ascend to the clouds.

If the disciples had raged in anger at their unmet expectations, maybe you and I wouldn't have heard the good news of our Savior. Thankfully, however, they gathered together in the upper room to take their disappointment and fears to the realm of prayer. There the Holy Spirit met them in an astonishing way, and the nations heard the gospel proclaimed. Things hadn't gone as the disciples expected, but they went as the Lord intended. His kingdom was established in the hearts of people from all nations. It has continued to be passed down from person to person and will continue until He comes again to receive us all into Himself.

The cross was expected to be an instrument of destruction, not salvation, but the Father intended otherwise. As we come to communion today, we can thank God that things may not be going as we expected, but we can be sure that they're going as He intended. He has a long-term plan that we might not be able to see just yet. Regardless of what we experience, He will be with us, working things out for the benefit of all.

Father, thank You for giving Jesus to save us from our sins. You have provided an eternal home and call us to Your glory. You made the way when there was no other way. Your intentions for us are always for our good. We are truly blessed. Amen.

For further study: Acts 1:1–2:47; Romans 8:18–30.

JUNE 24
The Smoking Flax

> Behold! My Servant whom I uphold, My Elect One in whom My soul delights! I have put My Spirit upon Him; He will bring forth justice to the Gentiles. He will not cry out, nor raise His voice, nor cause His voice to be heard in the street. A bruised reed He will not break, and smoking flax He will not quench; He will bring forth justice for truth. (Isaiah 42:1–3)

SOMEONE ONCE TOLD me you could re-light a candle by lighting the smoke coming off it. The theory is that there are enough wax particles in the smoke that the flame can travel back down to the wick to relight it. Well, naturally we had to check that out, so we got a candle and, sure enough, were able to relight the wick by lighting the smoke curling up from the freshly snuffed candle.

The Bible says that Jesus wouldn't snuff out a smoking flax. Flax was the wick that allowed the burning of oil in lamps made back in the day. I can picture it—a Christian smothered by the world, their flame dying back with just the faintest curl of faith rising from them. Jesus comes to them and doesn't snuff them out but seeks to re-light the wick.

A friend of mine used to be a real firebrand for the Lord. Slowly his faith started to waver and die away. Oh, he was still a believer, but the passion had gone from his soul. I was praying for this person and hoping that when I saw him in church, I'd see the fire of faith burning bright again. Week after week, though, it was the same dull expression of going through the motions with none of the passion for the Lord. I was getting a bit frustrated with God. When would things change? When would he come in rejoicing?

It was then I saw in my mind an image of a flame about to go out, but a hand dropped a large log on it. Naturally, the flame wasn't bright enough to light the log, so the weight of the log snuffed out the last bit of fire. God was showing me that He couldn't just drop on heavy fuel for the flame—not yet, anyway. Instead, He was having to coax the flame back by lighting up the wisp of smoke still curling from the weakening grace. I shouldn't expect my friend to suddenly come in dancing, but I should watch for the slow growth back to faith.

At times in my own life, I falter. I let the world reach down with the snuffer to extinguish my flame. I can be assured, however, that slowly and carefully the Lord will tend the smoking flax I have become, to coax me back to vibrant life. It may not happen overnight, but it will happen.

> *Jesus, thank You for caring for us enough to re-ignite the flame. We confess that at times we've allowed the weight of the world to bruise us and weaken our faith, and we come to You confident that You always meet us with sufficient grace for today. Amen.*

For further study: 1 Thessalonians 5:5–11; Hebrews 10:19–25, 12:12–13.

JUNE 25

Give Thanks in All Things

In everything give thanks; for this is the will of God in Christ Jesus for you. (1 Thessalonians 5:18)

IN THE BOOK *The Hiding Place*, Corrie Ten Boom tells the story of her family's life under Nazi occupation during the Second World War. Corrie and her sister were imprisoned in Ravensbrück for hiding Jews and helping them escape the death camps. Even there, their faith shone brightly, and they routinely held Bible studies in their barracks. They marveled that their studies were never interrupted by the guards coming in on a surprise inspection.

One day as they held their study, they read the Scripture about being thankful in everything. Corrie's sister insisted they thank God for everything, even the fleas in their barracks. Corrie thought this was a bit crazy but went ahead with it because her sister was a great pillar of faith. Later, she overheard guards arguing about who would enter the barracks. It turned out they didn't like to go into that building because of all the fleas! It was the fleas that allowed Corrie and her sister to be able to proclaim the Word of God in relative security, free from discovery by the guards.

Now I don't want to get into a theological discussion on the difference between thanking God *in* all situations versus thanking Him *for* all things. In either case, when things aren't going as we'd like, it's easy to forget that God is worthy of our thanks regardless of our situation, and maybe even because of our situation. Some days it's more difficult than others to find things to be grateful for. If we look hard enough, we're sure to find His grace no matter where we are. An attitude of gratitude can change our outlook and bring us peace, as it helps us refocus on the blessings of God.

There is certainly no greater blessing than our salvation. Even if we have nothing else to be thankful for, we have His loving sacrifice that has saved us from destruction. As we partake of communion, we remind ourselves just how much we have to be grateful for in His wondrous gift of life everlasting.

> *Jesus, thank You for dying so we could live, for exchanging Your grace for our sin. Sometimes we forget just how blessed we are. Forgive us for complaining and losing sight of our blessings. Help us always to be thankful in everything. Amen.*

For further study: Psalm 103:1–5, 106:1, 47–48, 107:1–32; Colossians 3:12–17.

JUNE 26
The Other Prisoners Were Listening

But at midnight Paul and Silas were praying and singing hymns to God, and the prisoners were listening to them. (Acts 16:25)

WHEN PAUL AND Silas were in Philippi, the people there rose up against them after they cast a divining spirit out of a girl. They were badly beaten and put in the inner part of the prison, with their feet fastened in stocks. At midnight, they were singing hymns and praying when suddenly there was an earthquake. The foundations of the prison were shaken, the doors opened, and everyone's chains were loosened off. The prison guard, thinking the prisoners had escaped, was going to kill himself, but Paul called out that he shouldn't do that, as everyone was still there. The guard called for a light and fell down before them, asking what he needed to do to be saved. As a result, the guard and his family were saved. I imagine all the other prisoners were also changed in that moment upon seeing the power of God.

Paul and Silas had started out having a very bad day—falsely accused, beaten, imprisoned, chained, sitting in the dark—yet they weren't grumbling or complaining. They weren't demanding their rights or saying that this wasn't fair. They were praising God because He is worthy to be praised.

Not many people can sing God's praises when they're having a bad day. Sure, I like to think if I was being persecuted and falsely imprisoned for the gospel I'd shine forth with God's light. Honestly, though, how many times do I sing praise when my day isn't going the way I'd hoped? Most of the time I'm too busy complaining or taking my frustrations out on coworkers or the people I love. Do I really think I would sing praises when my circumstances are bad?

Many of us have days when we feel beaten by the world. We're chained by our anxieties and fears, imprisoned in our mind by our anger or frustration. What would happen if instead of complaining, we spoke forth our praise to God? Maybe, just maybe, we'd be set free, along with those around us. Maybe our city would be changed. Maybe people would come to know the Savior.

Regardless of our circumstances, God is worthy to be praised for who He is and what He did on the cross. Communion is our chance to pause and remember just that.

Lord, we give You thanks and praise. You are worthy of all our praises and adoration. There is no God like You. You have saved us and set us free. Even if our circumstances are bad, You are good, and we sing forth our praise to You. Amen.

For further study: Psalm 28:6–9, 68:3–6, 19–20, 32–35; Acts 16:16–40.

JUNE 27
Iron Shackles

God sets the solitary in families; He brings out those who are bound into prosperity; but the rebellious dwell in a dry land. (Psalm 68:6)

I LOVE LISTENING to my local Christian radio station. My favorite program comes on Saturday mornings. It's a kids program produced by Focus on the Family called *Adventures in Odyssey*. They always present great radio dramas full of things to learn, even though I'm thoroughly well past the age that would be considered a kid.

A series of these episodes shared the story of the Fisk University Jubilee Singers. Fisk University was started to bring education to recently freed Black people in the United States. They were constantly short of funds and in danger of having to close. One episode spoke of the students finding a bunch of old iron shackles and chains. Their teacher saw value in those old horrible pieces of iron. They could be sold for scrap metal to help provide for their needs for a few more days. This teacher also started a choir and took it on tour. Although the students didn't want to share with the White people the spiritual songs they'd learned in slavery, it was the singing of those spirituals that inspired people to give to the university, allowing it to survive and thrive. Just like the iron shackles that once had caused great pain now could serve a purpose in their freedom, so also could the songs that arose out of their struggle and agony be the means to provide for their future blessing.

Hopefully no one ever again experiences the shackles of bigotry and abuse. I certainly have no desire to minimize the horrible injustice of the past, but I do see that God takes the things that have bound us and caused us pain and uses it to provide for our future. We may not be shackled in irons, but we can be shackled by self doubts, fear, grief, anxiety, abusive relationships, defeating self-talk, poor self-image, or any number of other things that come from living in a fallen world. Jesus went to the cross to take the pain and set us free. He also helps us to rise into a new life. The old life may not be forgotten, but the struggles we've come through can shape our destiny and inspire others.

Jesus walked the path of pain all the way to the cross, knowing that path would be the thing that would set us free. The cross that tortured Him would become our symbol of grace and hope. We pause to take communion to remind us of His sacrifice and all it has brought us. We can bring to Him the pains of today, knowing He will bring us to the blessings of tomorrow.

> *Jesus, we thank You for setting us free. You provide for us and take those things that harmed us and make them into something special as a testimony of Your grace, just as the cross You hung on testifies of Your grace to us all. Amen.*

For further study: Romans 8:18–39; 2 Corinthians 4:1–7.

JUNE 28
Identity Theft

> Jesus, knowing that the Father had given all things into His hands, and that He had come from God and was going to God, rose from supper and laid aside His garments, took a towel and girded Himself. (John 13:3–4)

WE OFTEN HEAR about cases of identity theft in the news, where someone steals a person's identification to run up debts in their name and steal from them. Passwords are becoming more complex to avoid identity theft. It's a costly and very serious form of theft. Our true identity is not what the thief makes it out to be.

In this fallen world, an insidious form of identity theft happens all the time. The enemy of our soul uses other people—or even our own thoughts—to try to steal our true identity. He whispers that we will have to compromise, as there is no other way. Or maybe he tells us we can't admit an error, or tell the truth, because it will cause problems. Perhaps he says we're not accepted or loved. He tells us we have to pretend to be strong when we're weak. He tells us that if we humble ourselves, people will look down on us. There are a million ways he tries to steal our confidence and acceptance in Christ.

When Jesus was at the Last Supper with His disciples, before His betrayal, He humbled Himself and became their servant, washing their feet. The King of kings took on the position of the lowest of servants. John tells us Jesus could do this just because He knew who He really was. He knew the sacrifice He was going to make, and He was willing to do it and so much more. He knew the depth of the love the Father had for Him, and the depth of His love for us. The devil couldn't stop Him or steal His identity.

Remembering His love and sacrifice for us helps us to retain our own identity in Him when the devil comes whispering in our ear. We can hold fast to our integrity. We can humble ourselves when necessary, because we know He is with us and that He strengthens us. If we know who we are in Him, we won't be swayed by the lies of the enemy.

> *Holy Spirit, remind us who we are in Christ. We remember today that we are loved and He is with us. We know this because we know what He has done for us. He has given His body to be broken for us. He gave His blood to save us. We are loved and accepted. Amen.*

For further study: John 13:1–5; Romans 6:4; Ephesians 1:3–6; Colossians 3:12–17; 1 Peter 5:6–12.

JUNE 29
Verses Not on Your Fridge

For to you it has been granted on behalf of Christ, not only to believe in Him, but also to suffer for His sake. (Philippians 1:29)

A FRIEND TOLD me about meeting some people from a foreign country where Christians are persecuted. Four young people had been arrested for their faith. Three young men were badly beaten, but the young woman was released without being beaten. She was very upset about this and wondered if there was something wrong with her faith!

In North America, if you go into Christians' homes, many have Scriptures posted on their fridge, or hanging on their walls. These Scriptures are inspirational and speak of His power to save, heal, prosper, or lift us up to high places. We love all the Scriptures of victory and strength.

I don't think I've ever walked into a Christian home and seen Scriptures that say He has called us to suffer, or where Paul says he wants to be conformed to His death. How about where Paul talks about being beaten, left for dead, or shipwrecked? Paul even says he will "... *take pleasure in infirmities, in reproaches, in needs, in persecutions, in distresses, for Christ's sake. For when I am weak, then I am strong*" (2 Corinthians 12:10).

We love the verses where God says we are blessed, healed, and prosperous. I love those Scriptures too. However, if we only read those Scriptures and something bad happens, our faith is severely challenged. We start to question if God loves us, or we may even question if He really exists. If we focus on those Scriptures only, we lose sight of the fact that God never promised that we wouldn't have trouble in this life. Quite the opposite, in fact. But He did promise He would be there with us in the troubles. We don't live in the Garden of Eden, and we're still waiting for the New Heaven and New Earth He has promised. We live in that in-between place of the fallen world. Our circumstances don't prove His love for us—the cross does.

Because of the cross, we can rejoice and be confident of His love. Because of the cross, we know our sins are forgiven, and we have an eternal home with Him. Our circumstances may vary, but His love is sure.

> *Jesus, we thank You for taking our sins and setting us free. You gave Your life so we could live with You for all eternity. Help us keep our eyes on You, knowing regardless of what happens in this life, You are with us. Amen.*

For further study: Isaiah 65:17–19; John 16:33; 2 Corinthians 11:22–12:10; Philippians 3:7–14; Revelation 21:1–4.

JUNE 30
Pathways to the Miraculous

And the Lord said, "Simon, Simon! Indeed, Satan has asked for you, that he may sift you as wheat. But I have prayed for you, that your faith should not fail; and when you have returned to Me, strengthen your brethren." (Luke 22:31–32)

A BLIND PERSON One day came up for prayer. The prayer warriors instantly assumed that the person would want restoration of vision. This was not what the person wanted at all. Another physically challenged person said that whenever they walked into church, they felt as though others saw them not as a valuable member of the congregation, but as a problem to be fixed. Many physically challenged people have been healed, but many more haven't received physical healing. We know God loves us and wants us well, so what are we to make of the fact that not all will be well? Some situations are truly a trial.

Joni Eareckson Tada was paralyzed when young. Many people prayed for her physical healing, yet she remained destined to live life from a wheelchair. I'm sure she desperately wanted healing, but her quadriplegia has led to a worldwide ministry that has brought thousands, if not millions, of people to the Lord. It strikes me how as believers, even knowing how much God loves us, we assume that anything difficult is a problem to be fixed, when maybe it's a pathway to the miraculous.

When Jesus was in the midst of His betrayal, Peter saw a problem that needed to be fixed. Peter drew a sword and struck one of the members of the mob coming to arrest Jesus. Jesus, however, commanded Peter to put the sword away, and He paused to heal the ear that had been cut off. Jesus knew that the road He would soon walk was not a problem to be fixed but a pathway to the miraculous. It was this very path that would give the entire world access to salvation and eternal life.

Let's pause and remember that He chose the difficult path that led to the miraculous. He gave His life so we could live for all eternity with Him.

> *Jesus, we thank You that You didn't choose what was easy but what was better. You love us so much, You felt it was worth the price You had to pay—the price of Your blood poured out on the cross. Thank you. Amen.*

For further study: Matthew 26:30–56; Luke 22:47–53.

JULY 1
Fireworks!

> Through the tender mercy of our God, with which the Dayspring from on high has visited us; to give light to those who sit in darkness and the shadow of death, to guide our feet into the way of peace. (Luke 1:78–79)

JULY 1—CANADA Day up here in the north. It's a day to celebrate the founding of a nation.

As with many countries, the day is often celebrated with firework displays. When I was a child, the big one in Winnipeg took place at Assiniboine Park, a large park with lots of space. We would crowd in and spread out our blanket to sit and enjoy the show, which typically lasted longer than half an hour.

One memorable day, the fireworks were especially spectacular. The show started like usual, with a few large balls of color evenly spaced, before, suddenly, the sky lit up with one beautiful eruption after another, each one piling atop the last until the night exploded with color and light.

After about ten minutes, everything stopped. The sky became dark and quiet as the last tendrils of smoke drifted away. We all sat waiting.

If this had been the opening, what on earth would there be for the finale? Alas, nothing else followed. The show was over.

In the newspaper the next day, we read that the pyrotechnic specialists had accidentally set up the fireworks too close together. They ended up all going off at the same time, with one explosion setting off the next. Somehow, I don't remember anyone complaining about the show being so short that year, though. It truly was magnificent!

Jesus lived on the earth only until His early thirties. When we see an obituary today of someone dying in their thirties, we proclaim, "What a shame!" To die so young is a tragedy, a life cut short before they had a chance to succeed.

But is a person's success measured by the time they spent on the earth? Is success not found in accomplishing the purpose of the Father?

Jesus's life was short. It started out mundane, like any other, but it ended in a spectacular display of glory that would change all eternity. His light would be brilliant enough for the whole world to see. Future generations can look back to the cross and see His light illuminating the darkness that lay hidden in the soul.

Anyone willing can receive that light and have the darkness in their soul forever banished. When we partake of communion, we remember His light dispelling the darkness. We remember that He was a young man when He lived on the earth, yet with His final gasp, He proclaimed, *"It is finished!"* (John 19:30).

The purpose of the Father was complete. Salvation was brought to humanity. Salvation was brought to me. It was brought to you, too, and we are forever changed by His glory.

> *Jesus, You lived and died to change our lives in a spectacular manner, like an explosion of fireworks in our souls. We take a moment now to remember the glorious beauty of our salvation that You accomplished when you gave Your body and blood for us. You are truly glorious. Amen.*

For further study: Matthew 4:16; Luke 2:25–35; John 1:1–13, 12:35–36, 46, 17:1–5.

JULY 2
Weary and Scattered

> But when He saw the multitudes, He was moved with compassion for them, because they were weary and scattered, like sheep having no shepherd. (Matthew 9:36)

HOW OFTEN I can get irritated with people! Frustrations can abound and expectations remain unmet. People rush around, oblivious to those around them, hanging their heads and pushed down by the weight of burdens on their soul.

I often complain that there's no good customer service these days. Ask a store clerk to check something for you and they probably won't do it. When you try to signal a waiter or waitress, you may find everyone averting their gaze as you plead for someone to come and fulfill your request.

Consider the disciples being pulled in all directions by the multitudes of people. They were frustrated and being constantly interrupted. Did they, too, become skilled at averting their eyes so as not to catch the pleading needs of the people? Jesus, however, looked out and saw the lost people—weary and scattered, lost and broken, in need of a shepherd for their soul. He knew He had only a limited amount of time in this physical body and that it would take an army of people to reach the rest of the world through all the ages. He told His disciples to pray for laborers to go out and reap the harvest. The fields were white and ready, the weary seeking rest, the scattered wanting with all their hearts to focus on something good. The sheep are desperate to meet the Shepherd of their soul.

I often let myself be like those disciples, frustrated by the demands of life. I want the lost to behave like the found so I won't have to be the laborer who leads them to the Shepherd. If I can barely manage to avoid growing weary by today's distractions and demands, what hope do those without the Holy Spirit have? How can I expect them to be otherwise?

"God, give me Your eyes," I pray. "Your eyes are full of compassion."

Jesus was willing to reach out to the broken and hurting in Palestine, and He is still willing to reach out. He still sees the people. He longs for the harvest to be collected. But He's given that job to us. We are His body walking the earth today. We're the ones who need to reach out to those around us with His compassion, instead of complaining in frustration that the lost are acting like the lost.

As we break the bread, we're reminded that His body was broken for us, and also that we are His body. Will we let our hearts be broken for those among us, weary and scattered, lost sheep having no Shepherd? Or will we avert our eyes?

> *Jesus, You were broken and Your blood poured out to redeem us. You now send us out into the world to bring in Your harvest. Forgive us for being caught up in our own desires, and open our eyes to those around us in need of Your touch. Guide us, Holy Spirit, in the way of grace and compassion. Amen.*

For further study: Matthew 8:1–3, 9:35–38, 14:14–15, 28:18–20; Ephesians 1:17–23, 2:11–22.

JULY 3
BC/AD

> Therefore, if anyone is in Christ, he is a new creation; old things have passed away; behold, all things have become new. (2 Corinthians 5:17)

YOU'VE LIKELY ENCOUNTERED new initials used to mark the year. Instead of AD and BC, you may see CE (Common or Current Era) or BCE (Before Common Era). For hundreds of years, the date was referred to as BC (Before Christ) or AD (*Anno Domini*, the Year of our Lord). Jesus had such an effect that the world chose to count all of time based on His coming. But as the world moves further away from Christianity, those terms are a reminder of a faith people don't wish to be reminded of. This change maintains the same years marking all of history, but it removes the offense of Christ.

This change of name may be a convenient way for some to try to forget about Jesus, yet it doesn't negate the great effect He had, which was significant enough that the whole world changed its dating system to identify the years as either falling before or after His coming. Bad stuff still happens, and diseases, crime, and death remain, but the world chooses to mark the calendar with the knowledge that the Lord still reigns, even this year.

I rejoice in my own personal *Anno Domini*. Before a particular day back in 1985, I didn't really have a relationship with Christ, but from that date on, He's reigned in my life. My years are marked by His Lordship. Sure, I still mess up, and bad stuff still happens. Disease, death, and sin are still present, but He's still Lord. He's Lord of last year, this year, and next year also. He is Lord today. No matter what happens, I am still in my own personal *Anno Domini*, the year of my Lord. Time for me is marked by the date when I asked Jesus to be my Lord and Savior. His coming changed all of history, but His coming also changed me.

Communion is an opportunity to pause and remember. The crucifixion brought such changes, and enough of the world embraced the faith that all of time was marked by His presence on the earth. Communion is also an opportunity to remind ourselves that we've also come to and embraced the work of the cross. He has changed us and made us a new creation. The person I once was is no more. I live now in the year of my Lord, my own personal *Anno Domini*.

> *Jesus, we thank You for the work of the cross. That sacrifice changed the world enough to inspire people to mark all of time by Your coming. We recognize also that You being in us changed us, so we can also mark our time on this earth by before we knew You and after You came into our hearts. Thank You for forgiving our sins, for changing us, for being our Lord. Amen.*

For further study: Acts 17:6; 1 Corinthians 1:2–9; Galatians 2:20; Colossians 1:26–29.

JULY 4
The Pearl of Great Price

Again, the kingdom of heaven is like a merchant seeking beautiful pearls, who, when he had found one pearl of great price, went and sold all that he had and bought it. (Matthew 13:45–46)

JESUS OFTEN SPOKE in parables, using word pictures to explain what He was trying to say. In Matthew, He shares several parables to explain the kingdom of heaven. In one, He talks of a merchant seeking beautiful pearls, who sells everything he has to buy one particularly valuable pearl.

I've heard people say that this pearl of great price is Jesus. After all, He is of amazing value to us. He's also everything we could ever want. But I think this parable can be read with us as the pearl of great price. When we think of our sinful nature, this seems like it couldn't possibly be right, but let's think about it. A pearl arises because of an irritant that gets into the oyster shell. This wounds the mollusk, so layers of shell material are laid over the irritant to make it smooth and protect the animal. This shell material, also called nacre, or mother of pearl, is smooth, iridescent, and beautiful. This is what gives the pearl its value.

In this fallen world, the sins of others, as well as our own shortcomings, irritate our spirits and wound our souls. Thankfully, Jesus paved the way for the wonder of His grace to come and cover the painful irritant, coating it and making something smooth and beautiful in exchange. His grace makes us so beautiful that He was willing to sell everything to buy us. He sold His lifeblood. It cost everything, yet He was willing to pay the price.

The body of Christ collectively, and each one of us individually, becomes the pearl of great price, His bride without spot or wrinkle that He has purchased with His blood. We are valued beyond measure because of His grace. Our sins are covered and need no longer wound us, all because of our glorious Lord. Sometimes we forget our own value and the value He has placed on others. Communion is a time to pause and remember that you are precious and worthy, and so is the person next to you.

> *Jesus, we can't thank You enough for covering our sin with Your precious blood. You let that blood flow so that we could be protected by grace, forgiven and valuable in Your sight. We are so valuable that You gave Your all to buy us. Help us to see the value You have put in others and in ourselves. Amen.*

For further study: Romans 5:17–21; Ephesians 5:25–29.

JULY 5
Oil to Light Our Lamp

But the wise took oil in their vessels with their lamps. (Matthew 25:4)

JESUS TELLS A parable about ten virgins. All were waiting for the bridegroom. Five had brought extra oil for the lamps, and the other five had not. The bridegroom was delayed in coming, and the five who had no extra oil found their lamps going out. They tried to get the others to give them oil, but the first five said no, lest their own lamps go out. The foolish virgins had to go to the sellers of oil to try to buy some, and while they were gone, the bridegroom came. By the time they got back, the door was shut to them.

This doesn't sound very Christian-like of those five wise virgins. Couldn't they have shared their oil and prevented the horrible plight of the others being locked outside? Oil often stands for things like the Holy Spirit. It can also represent joy, unity, and especially grace. The five foolish virgins lacked grace. They were with the wise virgins, so they were in the church. They'd heard about the bridegroom, Jesus, and knew He'd be coming for them, yet they had no extra grace to keep their light shining. All they wanted was to take from their friends. Serving God was not a joy; it was a chore. They hung around the Christians, but the Holy Spirit wasn't part of their lives. They had no grace to rely on when things didn't go as they thought they would, or when God was late to answer their prayers.

The wise virgins knew that they needed to hang on to grace, even when life wasn't going the way they thought it would. They knew that everyone needs to come to Jesus for themselves. No one is getting into the marriage supper by relying on the faith of another. Going to church isn't enough. Hanging around Christians won't get you there. You need your own oil.

Communion is about letting God's grace fill us and light our souls. It's about knowing that Jesus's death on the cross has changed us, filling us with the fire of the Holy Spirit so that we can walk in grace, joy, unity, and faith. But it's also about asking ourselves if we've let our oil tank run dry. Have we started to rely on just going through the motions—going to church, hanging out with our Christian friends—but all the while, our oil has dried up and our lamp is going out? We've lost our joy and are no longer in unity with our brothers and sisters. Maybe we feel it's all God's fault. After all, He didn't show up when we expected Him to.

We can't take from another's oil; we have to go back to the source to fill our vessel. Partaking in communion today reminds us that we can't wait. Tomorrow it may be too late to refill our lamp.

Jesus, You have caused us to shine. Sometimes we let our disappointments in unanswered prayer steal the oil of grace that fuels the lamp. Restore unto us the joy of our salvation. Remind us of all You have done and the depth of Your love and grace. Amen.

For further study: Psalm 51:10–13, 133:1–3; Isaiah 61:3; Matthew 5:13–16, 25:1–13; 1 John 2:18–29.

JULY 6
Whom Are You Seeking?

Jesus said to her, "Woman, why are you weeping? Whom are you seeking?" She, supposing Him to be the gardener, said to Him, "Sir, if You have carried Him away, tell me where You have laid Him, and I will take Him away." (John 20:15)

JESUS HAD TOLD His disciples that He was going to be crucified and rise again on the third day, but they had trouble believing it. They'd seen with their own eyes Him being beaten and crucified. They'd seen the soldier drive his spear into Jesus's side and the blood flow out. When some women went to seek Him on the third day, they didn't go to find a living God; they went to bring burial spices to treat the dead body. When an angel asked them why they were seeking the living among the dead, they ran away, afraid.

Mary Magdalene saw Jesus, and He asked her whom she was seeking. Her answer indicated that she was still looking for a dead body, not a living Lord. *"Tell me,"* she asked, *"where You have laid Him, and I will take Him away."* Even though she had seen Jesus do the miraculous, she was still seeking a God who stayed where He was laid—a dead, powerless man, not a living God.

The Word of God whispers in my soul, "Whom are you seeking?" I know He's asking if I'm seeking a living God or one who stays where I put Him. Do I seek the Jesus who will get me a new car, restore a broken relationship, or take the pain away? Or do I seek the Jesus who says *"My grace is sufficient for you, for My strength is made perfect in weakness"* (2 Corinthians 12:9)?

I think C.S. Lewis summed it up well in the Narnia Chronicles. The figure representing Jesus is a lion. He is said to be a good but not tame lion. He won't perform tricks for us or jump through the hoop of fire at our command. He will not be caged or prodded.

Sometimes I want Jesus to be a tame lion. I want Him to stay where I put Him and do what I tell Him to do, but it's the dead who stay where they're put. The living rise up and move as they will. Do I believe He will restore the broken and take the pain away? Certainly. Do I know when or how? No. It's impossible to know all the things a living God knows and does. I can only be sure that He is good. He is love. And His grace is sufficient, whatever comes my way.

Whom do I seek? The dead body or the living Lord? Whom do you seek?

As we partake of communion, we recognize that Jesus chose to lay His life down for us because He is good and He loves us. It was of His own free will that He laid it down, and by His will He took it up again. We seek this living God who loved us enough to pay the price for us.

> *Jesus, forgive us for the times we try to put You in a box to perform tricks for our pleasure. Help us to recognize that You are working for our good even when we don't see it. You proved Your love and power when You laid Your life down on that cross. Help us to seek the living, loving God You are. Amen.*

For further study: Psalm 100:5; Matthew 16:13–23, 26:20–32, 27:1–66; Mark 16:1–13; Luke 24:1–12; John 10:18; 2 Corinthians 12:9; 1 John 3:1–2.

JULY 7
Distressing Disguises

Now it came to pass, as He sat at the table with them, that He took bread, blessed and broke it, and gave it to them. Then their eyes were opened and they knew Him; and He vanished from their sight. (Luke 24:30–31)

WHEN JESUS ROSE from the grave, He appeared to Mary Magdalene while she was at the tomb weeping. She didn't recognize Him and supposed He was the gardener. Imagine that, a woman who had followed Him, received miracles from His hands, and seen angels in His empty tomb, yet she still believed Him dead and didn't recognize Him when she saw Him. He was in disguise.

Mother Teresa was noted for her great works around the world but especially with the poor and destitute in Calcutta. She said she saw Jesus in a distressing disguise in the bodies of the poor. She reminded us that Jesus Himself told us that what we do to others, we do to Him, so with every person she interacted with, she was touching and treating Jesus in disguise. It gave her the strength to love and serve everyone, no matter how smelly and diseased.

This challenges me. Am I seeing Jesus in those around me, or do I fail to recognize Him? At times I find it easier to love a complete stranger than those in my own family. I fail to see Jesus in the people I know the best. He may come disguised as the frustrated or the angry, not just the diseased and broken. He may be the parent with dementia or the stubborn child. He could be the bored barista or the lazy coworker. Yet how I treat other people is how I treat Him. How often have I failed to see Him, to love Him in all His distressing disguises?

The disciples walking to Emmaus also met Jesus on the road, but they didn't recognize Him either. As He spoke to them, their hearts burned within them. They knew there was something different about this man. It was only when they sat at the table and Jesus took the bread, gave thanks, and broke it that they suddenly realized they were in the presence of the risen Lord. It was in partaking of communion with Him that they realized He was in disguise. This is indeed the purpose of communion—to remember Him. We take time to remember what He has done for us and look for Him in the faces of those around us. It reminds us to receive Him in all of His distressing disguises.

Jesus, forgive us for not recognizing You in the faces of others. We have treated Your people shamefully at times, so that's how we've treated You. We want to see You and love You. Help us see You even when You're in disguise. Amen.

For further study: Matthew 25:31–46; Luke 24:13–43; John 20:1–25.

JULY 8
Snuggle In

> And Jesus answered and said to her, "Martha, Martha, you are worried and troubled about many things. But one thing is needed, and Mary has chosen that good part, which will not be taken away from her." (Luke 10:41–42)

I FOLLOW A typical pattern when I rise in the morning. I make a tea, grab my communion bread, spend a bit of time with Jesus, then head out to the barn to take care of the horses and do the chores. After that, I feed the other pets, take a shower, make breakfast, and then get ready to go to work, all before 8:00 AM. Sometimes the time pressure can be intense, like when I have to leave home earlier than usual.

On one of those days, as I sat with my tea and bread and looked at the clock, I had only a brief window of time before I had to get out to start on those chores. But that day I had no thought or Scripture in my head for my communion time. My mind was blank, my soul too rushed, and God was not speaking! *Hurry up, God*, ran through my heart and head on endless replay.

My dogs, who had run outside when we got up, were now scratching at the door to come back in. I sighed and got up to let them in before taking my place back in my recliner, tea and bread still waiting on the table beside me. As soon as I sat down, one of my dogs leapt in my lap and snuggled into my shoulder. And he stunk! He had clearly rolled in something disgusting. I tried to push him away, but he leaned in closer. The cat then strolled in and claimed part of my lap. His warmth was so comforting, but he blocked my Bible, and I was yet to have communion with Jesus. The chores and duties of the day were still calling …

The animals were demonstrating, of course, what Jesus was trying to whisper in my soul. "Slow down, breathe, snuggle in. Isn't this what communion with Me is all about? Lean in close. Feel the warmth of My love. I don't mind that you sometimes smell because you rolled in the world's garbage. I know you can't wash yourself. Come to Me for cleansing as you receive My love."

Martha had opened her home to the Lord, but she also let busyness and duties claim her heart. Jesus gently reminded her that there are times when we need to just snuggle in to Him. This is the best part and what it's all about. John also leaned in on the Lord's breast as Jesus shared the first communion with His disciples, commanding all of us to remember Him when we also partake of communion. My chores and duties all got done, and I was out of the house in time, but with a better attitude after spending a moment thinking of Mary and John leaning on the Lord's breast, snuggling in, while they partook of communion together.

Let's lean into Him and snuggle up to His love as we break the bread today.

> *Jesus, thank You for loving us. You let us approach You and come close to You even when we've messed up. Cleanse us and hold us close. We thank You for Your amazing, deep, and wondrous love. Amen.*

For further study: Psalm 51:10–11; Matthew 11:28–30; Luke 10:38–42; John 13:23.

JULY 9
Look Up

Now when these things begin to happen, look up and lift up your heads, because your redemption draws near. (Luke 21:28)

WHEN I WAS a kid, I took western style horse riding lessons, but my good friend rode English style. My friend eventually convinced me to take lessons at the barn where she kept her horse so that we could ride together. As a result, I now take English riding lessons. The problem is, I've always been a bit of a chicken when it comes to jumping. As I've gotten older, I've become even more of a chicken, since I don't heal as quickly if I fall. Luckily, the instructor is patient and gets it, so she keeps the jumps set low and works on the basics to help build my skill and confidence.

I often mess up by spending all my time looking at that "big" scary jump. The more I stare at it as the horse trots to it, the more tense I get, and the more I throw off my balance. The more I'm off balance, the harder it is for the horse, and the problems build and build. This week the instructor spent a lot of time getting me to look up instead of at the jump. When I kept my eyes up, the horse carried me smoothly as we sailed over the obstacle.

As I'm writing these devotions, there's a lot of trouble in the world: war in Ukraine, war in Israel, violence, theft, home invasions, destructive floods and fires, earthquakes, and volcanic eruptions. It can be scary and an obstacle to our peace and faith. Jesus, however, warned us that it would be like this. When His disciples pointed out the beauty of the temple, He told them it wouldn't last and that the world would become even more troubled. But He also told them not to panic. When they saw those things, they would know He was coming back soon. God is still in charge no matter how many obstacles the enemy puts in our path. We need only look up, and He will carry us over whatever comes our way.

As we partake of communion today, let's remember that He is our sovereign Lord. No trouble is so big that it can stop the ultimate plans of God. Jesus's life was not taken from Him; He laid it down for us to save us from our sins, and He's coming back to receive us into His heavenly home. In the world there may be trouble, but we can be at peace because He has overcome the world.

> *Heavenly Father, we bless You and thank You that You love us. You sent Your Son to save us, and Your plans will all be fulfilled in the coming days. Father, Jesus, and Holy Spirit, three in one, nothing surprises You or catches You off guard. You are prepared for all things. Help us look to You, trusting You and not setting our eyes on the things that look so scary, since we know You will carry us through it all until we are wrapped in Your loving arms. Amen.*

For further study: Luke 21:5–33; John 10:18, 16:33; Acts 1:9–11.

JULY 10
Freedom from Fear

> Inasmuch then as the children have partaken of flesh and blood, He Himself likewise shared in the same, that through death He might destroy him who had the power of death, that is, the devil, and release those who through fear of death were all their lifetime subject to bondage. (Hebrews 2:14–15)

MANY YEARS AGO, I taught young kids in children's church. I usually brought a snack for them, and one day I picked up a box of donut holes. I had just enough for each child to have one apiece. One young fellow had chosen a filled donut hole. He bit into it and was suddenly very scared. I was having trouble figuring out what the problem was. One of the other children solved the mystery when they looked over at the jam oozing out from the middle of the donut and said, "Eeew, it's bleeding!" Thankfully, a little bit of education about jam-filled donuts was able to overcome that fear. Another girl was not so lucky.

One day when I was hiking, I saw a young girl who had to cross some rocks on a rope as part of a physical challenge with her school group. She was paralyzed with fear. You could see that she was unable to do it, even though the whole class was stuck waiting for her and everyone else had already proven it was safe as they crossed. All the education in the world wasn't enough to overcome her fear. Even though she felt shame before her peers, her fear of falling was the more powerful emotion, and she was in bondage to it.

When I look back over my life, I can see that every stupid thing I ever did was because of fear. Fear at times was debilitating and hindered my ability to interact with people. Fear would cause me to lie or sin. Fear kept me in bondage.

Jesus knew we'd be affected and controlled by our fears, especially the fear of death. By coming in the flesh and dying for our sins, He freed us from the bondage of fear. Death no longer has a hold on us because we know in our spirit that we'll live for all eternity with Him. He also fills us with His love so that we can interact with others in love for them. The fear is overcome by the love in our hearts. Do we forget this from time to time and still stumble in our fears? Certainly. That's why we pause today to partake of communion.

As we eat the bread and drink our wine, we're reminded that Jesus has overcome death. We're no longer in bondage to fear, for His love is poured out on us as His blood was poured out on the cross. He has set us free from the power of sin and death.

> *Jesus, You gave Your body and blood to set us free from bondage to fear. You have freed us from the power of sin and death and made the way for us to spend all eternity with You. You have poured Your love into us so that we can reach out to others. We are forever grateful. Amen.*

For further study: Romans 6:1–9, 8:12–17; 2 Timothy 1:6–10; Hebrews 2:9–18; 1 John 4:16–19.

JULY 11
Lost Senses

Oh, taste and see that the Lord is good; blessed is the man who trusts in Him! (Psalm 34:8)

MY FRIEND CALLED to let me know she'd caught the COVID-19 virus. She knew she had it even before she tested positive because she'd lost her sense of smell. My mom knows all about the loss of that sense. She was involved in an accident that caused a brain injury. Thankfully, she lived and the only permanent injury was the loss of her sense of smell. As a result, her taste was altered. Much of our sense of taste actually comes from our sense of smell. If there's no sense of smell, food tastes bland. Naturally my mom still eats her meals. Those meals still bring nourishment, even if they lack flavor.

When we first come to Christ and ask Him into our heart, our senses are filled with His presence. Life is more vibrant and filled with color and flavor. Sometimes, though, when we've been in the faith a long time, disappointments and failures can dull our senses. Reading the Word of God can become tasteless. It becomes a chore rather than a delight. Going to church can be dull. We wear a mask, pretending all is well, while we fight off the urge to close our eyes in sleep.

Some may say, "Why read your Bible if you don't want to? Why bother going to church when it's all a farce? Aren't you just being a hypocrite?" But even as tasteless food still brings nourishment to the body, these Christian disciplines still bring nourishment to our spirit and feed our soul.

When Jesus was in the Garden of Gethsemane, He wrestled with having to drink a cup that wasn't just bland—it was downright horrific. He prayed earnestly, asking if there was not some other way, until drops of blood came from His sweat. Then He looked beyond the cross. He looked to how the sacrifice of His flesh would save us. Our spirits would feed on His spiritual flesh and drink His blood, and we would find remission for our sins. He did what He didn't want to do so the greater good would come.

He is our example. As He pressed on, so can we. We can nourish our spirits even as we pray for the return of our senses. The process may seem dry and hard, but His truth remains. Today we pause to remember what He did for us and to press on in faith, regardless of our feelings.

Jesus, thank You for resisting the pull to abandon the cross. You pressed on despite the fact this was a distasteful job, bitter and cruel. Help us to keep You ever before us, remembering the greatness of Your sacrifice for us. Amen.

For further study: Mark 14:32–42; Luke 22:39–46; John 6:53–59; Philippians 4:10–13; Hebrews 10:19–25, 12:1–4.

JULY 12
Lift Up Your Head

I tell you, this man went down to his house justified rather than the other; for everyone who exalts himself will be humbled, and he who humbles himself will be exalted. (Luke 18:14)

IN THE BOOK *Under the Overpass*, Mike Yankoski tells the story of when he and his friend Sam Purvis decided to live for one year with the homeless and destitute. Their goal was to develop compassion for the marginalized people as well as bring God's strength to the broken. He writes about sitting on the concrete, hungry and cold, and watching people walk past, not even seeing the homeless around them. One person was even talking about how God calls us to help others, yet she gave Mike and Sam not a glance.

He explained that one of the hardest things to do when their year of homelessness ended was to once again look people in the eye. Shame can do that to people, with our heads hanging down, our eyes cast to the ground. Mike and Sam had nothing to be ashamed of, yet they felt the judgment of people who should have been reaching out with the hands of Jesus.

In Luke 18, Jesus tells the story of a tax collector, a known sinner, who stood at the temple, praying for the Lord to forgive him. He dared not even lift his eyes to heaven as the weight of his shame pressed down on him. A Pharisee was also at the temple praying. He thanked God that he himself was so unlike the sinner covered in shame. He tithed, and he didn't commit adultery or extortion. Jesus says the Pharisee was praying with himself, his prayers not reaching anywhere near heaven. Jesus also stated that the tax collector was forgiven, but the Pharisee was not.

The prodigal son in Luke 15 started off haughty, rich, proud, and entitled. It took a time of losing all, becoming homeless and destitute, to bow his head with humility. When he returned to his father, now humble and contrite, his father ran to him and received him with open arms. His father lifted him up, clothed him, and restored him to a place of blessing and authority.

Sometimes our lives seem filled with shame. We have sinned or are embarrassed by our situation, yet God lifts our heads. He looks us in the eyes and blesses us. When we walk in our pride, so confident that we're righteous, we walk on dangerous ground. Do we walk by the destitute, saying, "Thank God I'm not like them"? Or do we take a deep breath and say, "There but for the grace of God go I"?

Today as we partake of communion, let's ask the Holy Spirit to reveal any area where pride has a foothold in our lives. Have we judged others or sought instead to lift up their heads? As long as we're in this world, we'll have opportunity to sin. This is our chance to bow before our Lord in humble prayer as He lifts up our heads, restoring us to His fellowship and joy.

Thank You, Lord, for You are the glory and lifter of our heads. We had sinned, but You have justified and forgiven us. We are so blessed. Your grace is sufficient to redeem us from all our mistakes and failures, and we give You thanks.

For further study: Psalm 3:3; Luke 15:11–32, 18:9–14; 1 Peter 5:5–9.

JULY 13
For God So Loved the World

For God so loved the world that He gave His only begotten Son, that whoever believes in Him should not perish but have everlasting life. (John 3:16)

JUST ABOUT EVERY Christian has John 3:16 memorized. I remember a preacher once told us to scratch the word "world" out in our Bibles and insert our own name. It's true. God so loved us each individually that I believe even if you were the only person who was going to be saved, Jesus would have still gone to the cross.

As I write this, there has been another mass shooting in the United States. I was thinking, *God so loved those murdered people, that if they believed in Him, they would not perish but have everlasting life.* But then the next thought followed. *For God so loved the murderer, that if he would believe in Him, he would not perish but have everlasting life.* It occurred to me that we could insert anyone in place of the word "world." For God so loved the Israelites … For God so loved the Palestinians … For God so loved the Ukrainians … For God so loved the Russians … or even Putin or Hitler.

I have to admit, this offends me a little. Does this mean if Hitler was the only one in the world who was going to be saved, Jesus would have gone to the cross? What about murderers and child abusers? What about the person I know who's mean and vindictive? Would He really die for them too? I believe the answer to that is yes. A thousand times yes. For God is love. He loves each of us so much, He was willing to send His Son to pay the price for our sins. John 3:17 says, *"For God did not send His Son into the world to condemn the world, but that the world through Him might be saved."*

There have been wicked people who've come to the saving knowledge of Jesus Christ. Thankfully, when God gets a hold of them, His love changes them. Love replaces the wickedness. We've all sinned and fallen short of His glory. God's love for sinners challenges me. Can I love even the wicked person? Can I love the relative who grates on my nerves, or the co-worker who's so offensive? God loves them enough to lay His life down for them. Will I love them the same? Only by recognizing His love in me is this even possible. This is why we come to the communion table—to remind ourselves of His great love, that He laid down His life for me, for you, for the world.

> *Father, thank You for loving us so much. You desired our salvation so intensely that You sent Your only begotten Son so that we could have everlasting life. Help us to love others as You love them. Help us to seek their salvation as much as You seek it. Amen.*

For further study: Romans 3:19–31; 1 John 3:16, 4:7–21.

JULY 14
Would You Go?

> And Ananias went his way and entered the house; and laying his hands on him he said, "Brother Saul, the Lord Jesus, who appeared to you on the road as you came, has sent me that you may receive your sight and be filled with the Holy Spirit." (Acts 9:17)

SAUL WAS A persecutor of the early Christians. He jailed them and even stood by approving of the stoning of the martyr Stephen.

One day on Saul's way to arrest Christians, Jesus knocked him off his horse and asked him why he was persecuting the Lord. Saul was suddenly blind and had to be led by the hand. Jesus then went to a Christian named Ananias and told him to go and pray for Saul. Ananias said, "Wait a minute! This guy has been tracking us down and sending us to jail, and you want me to go pray for him!"

I wonder what Ananias thought when Jesus made that request. If he was like me, he'd be thinking, *Whoa, Lord, you can't be serious. That guy is coming here to throw us in jail and kill us. I'd be walking into the lions' den to go to him. That's just crazy! You can't possibly be serious. That was a good joke; you had me going there for a minute. Now can we talk about something else?*

Ananias may have been saying something to that effect when he reminded Jesus of just how badly Saul was harming the church. Was he expressing the incredulity of it all, or was he reminding Jesus of Saul's deeds in a spirit of fear, wondering if he'd be martyred at Saul's hands? Was he reminding Jesus of who Saul was because he didn't want to go?

Jesus answered Ananias: *"Go, for he (Saul) is a chosen vessel of Mine to bear My name before Gentiles"* (Acts 9:15a). We know how this turns out. Ananias must have found faith in God's words. When he approached Saul, he didn't address him roughly or say, "Hey, you, murderer and persecutor of the church!" He said, *"Brother Saul, the Lord Jesus … has sent me [to] you …"* (Acts 9:17). He called Saul his brother. Ananias had already accepted Saul into the faith, despite his past.

God has never asked me to go pray with a murderer, but there are plenty of people He could ask me to go to and I would hesitate. There's that person who treated me badly, or the one who betrayed me, the person who's a cheat, or a thief. If Jesus asked me to go to them, would I? If He asked you, would you go? I pray our answer is yes.

> *Jesus, we've met people who have wounded us. It's hard to approach these people with Your love. Help us to hear You clearly so that when You say to go, we know that the time is right and Your greater plans for these people will come to pass. Help us to trust you enough to call people our brother, even when in the past they were our enemy. We can't do it on our own; we need Your love in us. Today we pause to remind ourselves of the great depth of that love. Amen.*

For further study: Acts 6:9–15, 7:58–8:2, 9:1–31.

JULY 15
Come Forth!

Jesus said to her, "I am the resurrection and the life. He who believes in Me, though he may die, he shall live. And whoever lives and believes in Me shall never die. Do you believe this?" (John 11:25–26)

THE SHORTEST VERSE in the Bible is found in John 11:35: *"Jesus wept."* This is in the middle of the passage about Jesus's friend Lazarus, who had died. The people there believed that Jesus was weeping because His friend had passed away. I'm not so sure they had that right.

At the beginning of the chapter, Jesus gets word that Lazarus is sick, but He doesn't rush to the bedside. He doesn't make it to Bethany until Lazarus has been dead for four days. Martha comes running to Jesus and says, *"Lord, if You had been here, my brother would not have died"* (John 11:21). Jesus tells her that Lazarus will live, because Jesus is the Messiah, but Martha thinks He means Lazarus will live in the afterlife.

Mary then comes running to Jesus and says the same thing—that if only Jesus had been there, Lazarus wouldn't have died. And this is when Jesus weeps. Here were His close friends, and even they didn't understand He was the Messiah. He was the resurrection and the life, not just for some undetermined future time, but now and forever. How disheartening it must have been that even His close friends didn't recognize that in Him was life everlasting.

Jesus asks them to take away the stone, but Martha complains that by this time, the dead will stink. She still hasn't recognized that Jesus is the resurrection and the life. Jesus stands and prays so all can hear and believe, and then He shouts, *"Lazarus, come forth!"* (John 11:43b). Lazarus comes out of the tomb, bound in grave clothes, but very much alive. Jesus commands them to loosen Lazarus from his burial wrappings and let him go.

We are close friends of Jesus. We know He's the Messiah, but sometimes He doesn't seem to show up when we first call to Him. We think that if only He'd been here, the situation would have been different. The long days pass with our loved ones still unsaved and rejecting Christianity, and we start to think there's no hope. They've been dead in their sins for too long.

Maybe we're in a situation that truly stinks and there's no hope for change. Or we at one time had a dream, a calling, that seems dead, its hope unfulfilled. It's easy to forget that He's still able to step up to the tomb and call forth what was dead to new life. We can run to Him with either an accusation that things would have been different if He'd showed up sooner, or we can come to Him with faith, knowing He is able to resurrect that which is dead. Sure, there will still be work to do—grave clothes need to be removed to set everything truly free—but the heart will be beating again.

> *Jesus, we come to You, partaking of the bread and wine and remembering that You indeed are the Messiah. You laid Your life down willingly, and You were able to take it up again. You did this for us and for our families, our neighbors, our country. Your blood is powerful enough to save all who call on You. Resurrect our dead hopes and dreams for our loved ones, that we would see Your glory. Amen.*

For further study: John 11:1–44.

JULY 16
Golden Joining

> But, speaking the truth in love, may grow up in all things into Him who is the head—Christ—from whom the whole body, joined and knit together by what every joint supplies, according to the effective working by which every part does its share, causes growth of the body for the edifying of itself in love. (Ephesians 4:15–16)

LEGEND HAS IT that the shogun Ashikaga Yoshimasa broke his favorite Chinese tea bowl. He sent it to China to be repaired, and it was sent back with staples used to hold the pieces together. He didn't like the look of the staples and felt there must be a more aesthetic way. From that inspiration, Kintsugi was birthed.

Kintsugi is an ancient Japanese art that unites pieces of broken pottery using material mixed with gold or silver. *Kin* means golden, and *tsugi* means joinery, so the translation would be "golden joining" or "golden repair." The idea is that instead of hiding the brokenness or discarding the item as worthless, the broken parts are celebrated. The precious lines of gold highlight and bring attention to the beauty of those pieces being reunited to a glory even greater than what was in the original.

In the Garden of Eden, the beauty and perfection of God's world was shattered into a million fragments of broken relationship. Our relationship with God was broken as well as our relationship with each other. The former glory was smashed. God could have discarded everything. He could have swept up all the broken pieces and tossed the world into a heavenly garbage can, but He had a better plan. He would send His Son, born of a woman, to be a glorious unifier who could reunite humanity with their God and with each other.

We live in this fallen world and know firsthand the depths of brokenness. When we come to the cross and receive the Savior, we also experience the wonder and glory of His redemption. The final product is something even more glorious than the original unfallen world. The God of the universe, born into a fallen world, living a sinless life and shedding His blood for our salvation, covers us with His glory and unites us with His love. We can still see the broken parts, but we are once again made whole. And it's beautiful.

> *Lord, we thank You for Your redeeming work. We are reminded of what You did for us and that You have reunited us in relationship with the God of the universe and with each other. Help us to walk in unity, showing forth Your glory. Amen.*

For further study: Genesis 1:1–3:24; Ephesians 2:11–22.

JULY 17
Up!

> Walk in wisdom toward those who are outside, redeeming the time. Let your speech always be with grace, seasoned with salt, that you may know how you ought to answer each one.
> (Colossians 4:5–6)

THE MOVIE *UP* is about an old man whose life is full of misery, having lost the love of his life and now about to lose his home. He's angry and bitter and decides to fly his home to South America using thousands of helium balloons. Unfortunately, his plans are altered by an accidental stowaway—a young boy from a broken home.

They land in South America, where the old man meets his childhood hero but finds out that he's not the amazing person he expected to find. While processing all this information, dealing with the animal friends the boy makes, as well as trying to find a way to get the boy home, the old man finds the peace he needs to move on. He also finds the part he can now play as a role model for the fatherless boy.

When I mentioned watching this movie to a young coworker, she blurted out, "I love that movie! I laughed all the way through it!"

I have to admit, I was taken aback. You see, I was about to say, "I cried through the whole movie." Life experiences can do that to you. This coworker was half my age and hadn't yet experienced the loss of a loved one, a broken home, the difficulties of a world that would intrude on your peace and displace you from your home, the failures of your childhood heroes, or the disappointment of shattered dreams.

Thankfully, though, we have a Savior who knows all about loss, yet He redeems us. He comforts us in our loss. He heals the broken places. He restores our peace and gives us a purpose. He gives us fresh dreams for the ones that are gone forever. He is the one hero who will never fail us. Because of His redemptive strength, we can remember to walk in kindness to others in this broken world, even when things aren't going as we expected. Through the love we've found in Him, we can bring answers to a lost and broken world.

> *Jesus, thank You for redeeming us from our sins and preparing a future for us. Sometimes loss is overwhelming; help us to focus on You, that we might reflect You and Your redeeming grace. Amen.*

For further study: Psalm 147:3; John 14:27; Galatians 1:4; Ephesians 5:15–17; Colossians 4:2–6; Titus 2:11–14.

JULY 18
Mistaken Identity

> But it is written: "Eye has not seen, nor ear heard, nor have entered into the heart of man the things which God has prepared for those who love Him." But God has revealed them to us through His Spirit. For the Spirit searches all things, yes, the deep things of God. (1 Corinthians 2:9–10)

I WAS LISTENING to the news the other day, and they mentioned that someone thought a kangaroo was loose from a zoo, but upon investigation, it turned out that they were mistaken. The supposed kangaroo turned out to be a red fox. We laugh when we think of people making such a mistake, yet things like this happen all the time. Apparently, the thing most often mistaken for a UFO is the planet Venus. I heard of someone who painted the word HORSE on his horse so that hunters wouldn't mistake it for a deer and shoot it.

We aren't just limited to mistaking one thing for another. We might mistake one thing as being the cause of something else. Even insurance companies might label a bad storm as an "act of God," but did God really do that, or was the storm the result of sinful humanity causing the world to fall from its Edenic state?

Sometimes our limited knowledge in an area causes us to make mistakes in our understanding. God declares in the Psalms that sinful men sometimes think that because He's silent, He's sinful like them. People sometimes think that because they've had hardship, God must not exist. We mistake our unfortunate circumstances as meaning that God doesn't care, doesn't love us, doesn't exist, or if He does, He is mean or vindictive. We try to reshape His identity to fit what we experience.

Our thoughts and impressions at any given time aren't necessarily an accurate representation of God. Just because I think a fox is a kangaroo doesn't make it one. Thankfully, we have the Word of God to reveal to us His true nature. We know that God is good because He demonstrated His great love for us by sending His only begotten Son to die in our stead. We know He is just but that He is also merciful.

At times our circumstances might obscure our view, so we pause today to remind ourselves of His love. We pause to remember that His love was not just words spoken in vain, but He demonstrated that love when He stumbled down the narrow streets, His bloody back shouldering a wooden cross. Sometimes we need to be reminded that we only see in part right now what one day we will see more clearly. In the meantime, He has proven we can trust Him. He is honest and true. He is love.

> *Father, Jesus, and Holy Spirit, three in one, You are love and You love us. You have also revealed that love to us through the Scriptures and in our hearts. We thank You that even when we struggle, You remain faithful and true. We can trust You. One day our understanding will be more complete, but even now we can trust in Your love, so clearly demonstrated at the cross of Calvary. Amen.*

For further study: Deuteronomy 32:4; Psalm 50:16–23; Luke 6:36; John 3:16; Romans 1:18–23; 1 Corinthians 2:1–16, 13:12; 1 John 4:14–17.

JULY 19
How Long, O Lord?

And they cried with a loud voice, saying, "How long, O Lord, holy and true, until You judge and avenge our blood on those who dwell on the earth?" (Revelation 6:10)

IN THE BOOK of Revelation, John sees the souls of those martyred for the faith, who cry out *"How long, O Lord."* They're asking God when He will avenge their blood and when justice will reign. God tells them to be patient until all those who are going to be saved in these terrible end times join them in martyrdom.

Elijah also cries out "How long?" to the Israelites, who have forsaken their God for another idol. In 1 Kings 18:21, he asks the people how long they will falter between two opinions. They need to choose one God and one only.

The other day a good friend called to ask for prayer for their child, who was caught up in addiction. I found myself calling out to God in prayer: "How long, Oh Lord, will this go on? How long will friends and family suffer? How long until my unsaved friends and family recognize You, the Lord of Glory? How long?" I struggle with the days rolling into years without seeing any change in those closest to me. The lost still turn their backs on God; my loved ones still suffer with illness, addiction, pain, and trouble. I want to cry out to them like Elijah did. How long will it take before you see the One for whom you really seek!

When my soul quiets, after I have poured out my heart in prayer, I hear God also say to me, "How long?" He says, "How long will you continue to hold on to the offenses of your brothers? I have enabled you to walk in harmony, if you would only give the offense to Me. How long will you continue to turn for comfort to things that don't really give any comfort? You seek satisfaction in other things rather than turning to Me, the only one able to truly give you all you could ever hope for. How long will you continue to beat yourself up over the sins of your past? Those sins have been forgiven and thrown into the sea of forgetfulness, yet you continually fish them out. How long are you going to forget what I have done to set you free?"

The purpose of communion is to remind ourselves of the work He did for us on the cross and that we're forgiven, He lives in us and enables us to walk in righteousness, and He is all we could ever need. It also reminds us that although trouble is still present in this world, He has overcome the world. He alone knows the times and seasons for our friends and family. We come to Him in prayer for ourselves and for others, but with the reminder that He gave His all for us, and He has been victorious over sin and death. His blood is sufficient for all, and it's sufficient for each one of us personally.

Jesus, You reign victoriously. You are the lamb that was slain, and You are worthy. We thank You for dying for us so we could walk in righteousness, trusting You, free from condemnation. You are all we could ever need or even hope for. Amen.

For further study: 1 Kings 18:1–40; Psalm 103:1–22; Micah 7:18–20; John 16:33, Acts 1:6–8; 2 Corinthians 1:3–7; Ephesians 3:14–21; 2 Peter 3:9; Revelation 5:1–7:17.

JULY 20
A Different Flavor

I am the living bread which came down from heaven. If anyone eats of this bread, he will live forever; and the bread that I shall give is My flesh, which I shall give for the life of the world.
(John 6:51)

A FRIEND OF mine was buying a box of beef and asked if I wanted one too. She would drive far to pick up this box of a variety of roasts, steaks, and ground beef because she was buying it direct from a farmer who fed his cows only grass, no grain. I had a big freezer, so I thought I'd get a box as well. What surprised me was how very different the grass-fed beef tasted. I thought it would taste the same as store-bought beef, but it wasn't at all the same. I didn't like it at first, but luckily, since I had a whole box of it, my tastes changed over time and I grew to enjoy it.

Before we ask Jesus into our hearts, we're accustomed to feeding on the world and all its ways. When we come to the cross and receive the sacrifice of Jesus to redeem us from our sins, we now feed on the heavenly bread—the living bread that came down from heaven and gives us eternal life. Our tastes change, and the flavor we present to the world is different. Our friends and family may not like that new flavor, as it seems off to them. It's not what they're used to. Maybe they hope it's a fad we'll grow out of. Maybe they think we've been caught up in a cult and fed a field of lies. They may try hard to get us to come back and feed on the things of the world. It can be tempting to give in, to go back to our old ways, when everyone is expecting that from us. If we do, those old tastes will become familiar again. We can forget how much we like and enjoy the wonderful life we have with Jesus.

This is why Jesus told us to pause and remember. By stopping to partake of communion, we remind ourselves that our old nature has died and we've become a new creation, alive with Him. It's a chance to pause and meditate on the Word of God, to fill our spirits with all He has to offer. We are renewed day by day. Those old things that used to attract us lose more of their hold as we feed off His presence. As we become more like Him, even our friends and family will start to appreciate the new flavor we offer. We can only pray they will come to experience it themselves in all His wonderful glory.

Jesus, You said You were the living bread who would give us eternal life. We realize that it's in recognizing Your death for us that we partake of this body and blood You have given. We thank You for changing us and making us new, and we pray for our unsaved friends and family, that they too would experience Your saving grace. Amen.

For further study: Joshua 1:7–9; John 6:1–71; Romans 6:1–14; 2 Corinthians 5:17–21; Philippians 4:6–9.

JULY 21
What's in a Name?

And she will bring forth a Son, and you shall call His name Jesus, for He will save His people from their sins. (Matthew 1:21)

WHEN I WAS very young, my older brother went by the nickname "Moose." One day, a young man called the house and asked for Marcel. I answered, "I'm sorry, you have a wrong number." He apologized and hung up. Immediately the phone rang again and I answered. This time a young man (the same young man) asked for Moose, to which I replied, "Hold on, I'll get him."

I was young enough to have forgotten that Moose wasn't really my brother's name. The funny thing was that my brother's friend told us that when he called the first time, he was going to ask for Moose but thought he would need my brother's real name. Even to this day, more than fifty years later, it still makes me chuckle to remember the incident.

I've met quite a few people who have changed their name, either legally or just by convention. In the last chapter of Romans, Paul mentions many names of Christians he is sending greetings to. Some, I suspect, may have changed their names. Philologus means "lover of words." It's hard to imagine giving that name to a baby who couldn't yet read. With some names, I wonder why the person never chose to change them—Hermes, Nereas, Olympus—all names related to false gods. When they became a Christian, were their names offensive to themselves or others? Clearly God wasn't offended by the names the world had given to them, as He accepted them as He did the others.

At times God has chosen names and changed names of people. Abram became Abraham (father of multitudes). Saul (asked of God) became Paul (little), although we don't know if this name change was done by God Himself, Paul, or others. Yet Paul must have been reminded that he was the least in the kingdom every time someone called his name.

God Himself goes by a multitude of names. Whole books have been written about the names of God. Of course, the name we relate to the most is "Jesus." It's the name told to Joseph by the angel of God to give to Mary's first-born Son. Jesus means "Yahweh saves." And He does. It's a beautiful name. There is no other name under heaven by which we can be saved. There is power in His name. His name is amazing because of the depth of God's love, a love that sent Jesus all the way to the cross to shed His blood for our sins. That love provided eternal life for us all.

We come to the communion table to remind ourselves that Jesus indeed saves. We also know that regardless of what the world has named us, we are accepted in Him. We are called the beloved saints, the very ones He was willing to pay the price for to redeem us for all eternity.

Heavenly Father, we thank You for giving Jesus to save us. You have adopted us into Your family and You call us beloved. We are precious in Your sight. We are Your sons and daughters, and You call us by name, knowing even the very hairs of our head. We are forever grateful. Amen.

For further study: Genesis 17:5; Matthew 1:20–21, 10:30; Acts 2:17–21, 3:12–16, 4:5–12, 10:34–48, 13:9; Romans 16:1–24; 1 Corinthians 1–2; Ephesians 3:8; Philippians 2:5–11.

JULY 22
Mary, Mary, Quite Contrary

Then Mary said, "Behold the maidservant of the Lord! Let it be to me according to your word."
And the angel departed from her. (Luke 1:38)

DO YOU REMEMBER the old nursery rhyme that starts "Mary, Mary, quite contrary, how does your garden grow?" I have to admit, I never understood that rhyme. Why was Mary contrary? I've read that the name Mary does mean "obstinacy" or "stubbornness." I would have thought other names could have easily been the association for stubbornness. My grandmother was the most stubborn woman I ever knew, and I was more stubborn than her! That stubbornness enabled me to stick with the plan to make it to veterinary college, even when things got hard.

When I think of the name Mary, the last thing I think of is stubbornness. Mary, the mother of Jesus, was meek and obedient to the will of God. When I think about this, my imagination wanders, and I imagine a longer conversation Mary may have had with the angel Gabriel. It might have gone something like this:

"Why would God choose me to be the mother of His Son? I have such a reputation of being obstinate and stubborn. Wouldn't he want someone meek instead?" Mary asks.

"No, He wants you. Will you stick with the plan, even when it gets hard? Will you stay with it when your family and friends think you're an immoral woman? How about when the city doors are closed in your face and you have to sleep in a barn? Will you stay with the plan when people want to kill your baby, and you have to flee to another country? Will you continue on when you hear about the horrible loss of young children in your hometown—children killed in place of your Son? Will you stick with the plan when your other children want you to come collect your firstborn because they think He's gone insane? Will you stay with the plan when a sword of grief pierces your heart, even as you see the spear plunged into the side of your Son?"

Mary, I imagine, looks back over her life and all the times she's been determined and stubborn, pushing through pain and frustration to see things through to the end. She looks up and says, "Let it be to me according to your word."

Mary stuck with the plan. She didn't rally Jesus's disciples to fight a war with the Romans but realized Jesus's call was to lay down His life in the spiritual warfare for our very souls.

Sometimes life gets hard and things don't go as we plan. It can be hard to stick with it, to remember that this life is not our final home. We struggle to fulfill the destiny God has for us, but then we look to the cross. We see that Jesus also stuck with it. He persevered and brought us the peace and strength we need. He provided the grace for yet another day through His sacrifice on the cross.

Jesus, You didn't quit. Even when Your body and soul cried out in pain, You persevered. You looked to our salvation and said it was worth the cost. We need Your grace every day; remind us that You have provided more than enough, no matter what the day holds. Amen.

For further study: Matthew 2:13–18; Mark 3:20–21,31–35; Luke 1:26–33, 2:25–35; John 19:17–37; Hebrews 12:2–4.

JULY 23
Soaring Like Eagles

But those who wait on the Lord shall renew their strength; they shall mount up with wings like eagles, they shall run and not be weary, they shall walk and not faint. (Isaiah 40:31)

I ONCE WENT on a cruise to Alaska. Events on the ship ran late into the night, and the sunrise came earlier every day. I longed to get a good photo of the sunrise but generally overslept. On the last day, I arranged a wake-up call and finally did manage to rise early enough to get out to my sunrise. And what a sunrise! It was beautiful. I stayed out there for some time. As the sun rose higher in the sky, I saw an eagle floating on the warm currents of air rising off the ocean. He soared in big, lazy circles, going higher and higher. I watched as he entered a bank of clouds and then emerged above them, and still he continued to rise high in the air. I think he flapped only once, if at all. The whole time he just rested on the air currents. I watched until he became a black speck high in the sky, unrecognizable as the majestic bird he was.

Isaiah wrote that if we wait on the Lord, we will soar like an eagle. Waiting can mean a lot of things, including serving, but in this case, the word for wait means to hope. Hope—a confident expectation and desire based on His promises. I often feel more like a hummingbird, madly flapping my wings and not daring to even stop and perch. I'm flitting from flower to flower, trying to get everything done and feeling like I'm the only one working. I'm not saying there's anything wrong with that.

Hummingbirds are beautiful and serve a great purpose, but at times we're called to be eagles. I can't control everything or make things go according to plan. I find myself fatigued as I desperately run from one thing to the next, not stopping to rest in His grace. Things happen, maybe through no fault of my own, and I can't fix them. I can't heal my friend of cancer, or bring my loved ones to salvation, but I can awaken to my need to rest on the wind of His grace. I can have a confident expectation and desire that somehow, somewhere, sometime He will make things turn out all right. I can be sure of His love for me and for those around me because He proved it when He stumbled His way on the cobbled, narrow streets carrying His cross to Golgotha.

> *Jesus, help us to rest in Your grace, to let Your love carry us. Sometimes we get in a flap about things in life, but You remind us instead that we can be carried by Your grace, soaring on the wind of Your everlasting love. In You there is rest. We can trust You to lift us up above the troubles on the earth. You proved Your love when You died for us. We thank You for all You've done and for who You are. Amen.*

For further study: Isaiah 40:27–31; Matthew 6:25–34, 10:28–31, 11:28–30; Luke 10:38–42.

JULY 24
Lighthouses

For it is the God who commanded light to shine out of darkness, who has shone in our hearts to give the light of the knowledge of the glory of God in the face of Jesus Christ. (2 Corinthians 4:6)

THE YEAR I turned sixty, I met up with nine of my girlfriends from high school to reunite and celebrate this milestone year for us all. We'd been scattered around the continent and had all followed various paths. One of our group had moved with her family to Nova Scotia, so we decided to all meet up there and tour around that province for a week. We had a great time being together and enjoying the coast. We spent one day driving along the lighthouse trail looking at some of the lighthouses that still remain, including the iconic one at Peggy's Cove. When we got to Peggy's Cove, the fog had rolled in, which made the lighthouse even more poignant.

Nowadays many lighthouses are out of service, with sailors relying on GPS systems, but in past times they were critical for safe navigation through rocky shores. A lighthouse would be a beacon to others. It would point out the dangers and show the way to the port. Lighthouse keepers would not only make sure the light stayed shining brightly, but they also helped rescue others in case of shipwreck.

The cross is our lighthouse. It's the beacon that shows us the way. By looking at Christ on the cross, we're reminded of the dangers of sin that can cause our life to shipwreck. It also points the way to safety and freedom from sin and death. When we accept the amazing grace that saves us, we become lighthouse keepers. His light now resides in us. Our job is to make sure the light shines brightly, guiding others to safety. We can also reach out our hands to the shipwrecked, pulling them out of the deep waters that are overwhelming and freezing their soul.

When we forget the grace in us, when we walk in offense, when we're quick to judge others as we walk in self-righteousness, it's like we've thrown a black-out cloth over the light within us. Others no longer see the beacon to guide them through the fog that assails their minds.

We come to the communion table to bring our hurt and offenses to Him so that He can once again remove the black-out cloth that hides our light. We come to the table to be reminded of His grace and light within us. We come to get fresh oil so that our light may shine ever brighter, guiding those to the Savior's beacon—the rugged wooden cross lifted high on the hill for all to see.

> *Jesus, You are our guiding light. You direct our steps and lead us to the safe haven of Your love. Forgive us for hiding Your light, and renew us that it may once again shine brightly for all to see. Help us to reach out a hand to those who are shipwrecked, instead of sitting in judgment over their peril. Amen.*

For further study: Psalm 119:105; Matthew 5:14–16; 2 Corinthians 4:1–7; 1 Timothy 1:12–19; 1 John 1:5–7.

JULY 25
Living in Awe

How great are His signs, and how mighty His wonders! His kingdom is an everlasting kingdom, and His dominion is from generation to generation. (Daniel 4:3)

IN THE MOVIE *Fifty First Dates*, Henry (played by Adam Sandler) is a veterinarian who meets and falls in love with Lucy (played by Drew Barrymore). The trouble is, Lucy has an inability to make new memories due to an accident. She keeps reliving the same day over and over again, so every time Henry dates her, it's like she's meeting him for the first time. Henry ends up making a video explaining what has happened in her life since her accident. The video serves as her memory, allowing her to move on. The interesting thing to me is the beautiful sense of awe that Lucy demonstrates at the start of each day as she contemplates the wonder of her life.

Living out in the country, I'm often in awe of God's creation. As I head out to the barn late in the evening, the Milky Way cascades across the sky. I'm amazed as the constellation Orion, the hunter, marches his way across the horizon, his trusty dog, Canis Major, at his heels. The sun rising over the hills, its rays breaking through the trees, is no less stunning than the night sky. The leaves on the trees, the flowers of summer, and also the beauty of the fresh snowfall in winter captivate me. At least they do when I remember to stop and take them in. Often, I'm too busy running from one chore to the next to remember to stand in awe of God's marvelous creation. The days crowd in on each other, and the individual beauty of today gets lost in the thoughts of tomorrow or the regrets of yesterday.

Whether we've been saved for a few days or a few decades, sometimes we can forget how incredibly amazing it is that the God of all creation loves us so much that He was willing to give up everything to save us from this sinful nature. The one who stretched out the heavens and set the earth on its axis, who calls all the stars by name, came to earth as an infant to grow up, live, and die among His creation. This sets Christianity apart from all other religions. In the others, humanity has to work to be saved, trying to please a demanding god. In Christianity, the one true and mighty God came down to do the work for us because He loves us with a pure love. As we go about our day-to-day lives, we might forget just how amazing and awe-inspiring that is.

Today as we partake of communion, let's pause to remember the wonder we felt on the day of our salvation. It's still just as amazing today as it was the day we first believed.

> Jesus, when we think of the beauty around us, the amazing things You have created, we are in awe of You. Even more so, we're in awe that You would choose to redeem Your creation, paying the price for our sins. There's nothing more beautiful than what You've done for us. We thank You and stand in awe and wonder of our amazing God. Amen.

For further study: 1 Chronicles 16:7–15; Job 36:22–39:30; Psalm 19:1–14, 33:1–22, 104:1–35, 119:161–168; Isaiah 40:21–26.

JULY 26
Fight for Them

And I looked, and arose and said to the nobles, to the leaders, and to the rest of the people, "Do not be afraid of them. Remember the Lord, great and awesome, and fight for your brethren, your sons, your daughters, your wives, and your houses." (Nehemiah 4:14)

NEHEMIAH WAS A Hebrew man living in Babylon and working for the king. One day, he learned that Jerusalem was in ruins and the people who had escaped captivity were in distress. His heart was broken. The king gave Nehemiah permission to depart to Jerusalem to repair the city.

Some people were vehemently opposed to the rebuilding of Jerusalem and were willing to use deception, discouragement, and even physical threats to stop the work. Nehemiah was not to be deterred! He rallied the people and got them working on restoring the walls and gates. Because of the threat of attack, the people worked with a weapon in one hand and a trowel in the other. The jewelers worked alongside the merchants, always ready to rally to fight their enemies if need be.

God calls us to build up others, restoring people to relationship with Him and each other, but we have an enemy vehemently opposed to the restorative work. The enemy is not flesh and blood but will do all in his power, using deceit and discouragement, to stop us. When we fall for the enemy's tricks, we turn our swords on one another. We squabble with our family, neighbors, and coworkers. We spend time looking at what they're doing and complain about how they're building their portion of the wall instead of focusing on our own restoration work. Maybe we even get frustrated with God. We may think, *I'm a jeweler, not a builder or a soldier. Why does He have me doing this work? It is so not me! Someone else needs to work to bring restoration. It's not my job! Why should I have to feed the homeless or be the one who makes the first step toward reconciliation? After all, my neighbor wounded me wielding his trowel. He needs to apologize first.* What has happened to cause my bitter and complaining attitude? I've forgotten my Lord, who is great and awesome. I've taken my eyes off Jesus and believed the lie that my enemy is the person beside me. I started fighting *with* other people instead of fighting *for* them.

God calls us to wield our sword against our real enemy, Satan, and to fight for our families, homes, neighbors, and cities. Our job is to go about our restoration work, wielding the Word of God in prayer as our sword. We remember our Lord, awesome and true. We remember that He has won the war, even though there are still battles He calls us to fight. Let's keep our eyes on our real enemy and fight for one another.

Jesus, we remember You. You proved Your awesomeness when You fought Satan's deceptions and won the war for our souls. Remind us to wield Your Word against our real enemy and not each other. Help us to be ministers of reconciliation, pointing people to You. Amen.

For further study: Nehemiah 1:1–6:19; 2 Corinthians 5:11–21; Ephesians 5:15–21, 6:10–18; 1 Thessalonians 5:11; 1 John 3:16.

JULY 27
Plastic Christianity?

If we confess our sins, He is faithful and just to forgive us our sins and to cleanse us from all unrighteousness. If we say that we have not sinned, we make Him a liar, and His word is not in us. (1 John 1:9–10)

I HAVE A good friend who grew up in a florist's shop. Her family owned a greenhouse, and their home was attached to the business. She knew all about various plants and flowers, their health and diseases. I was out for lunch one day with this friend and I commented on a beautiful plant the restaurant had on a shelf. She glanced at it and said, "It's plastic."

I was shocked. It was such a beautiful plant. I asked her how she knew it was plastic. Her answer was quick and clear and has enabled me to spot plastic plants from a distance. She said, "It's too perfect. Real plants have flaws." Of course, plastic plants lack dead leaves and broken branches, but they're also cold and lifeless. Real plants brighten the room *and* benefit our health and environment.

In this day and age of social media, we see images of what looks like someone's perfect life. There has been a rise of dissatisfaction with people's own lives as they fall into a trap of thinking other people have it better. Of course, the lives we see in edited images are fake, plastic. Real lives are often messy. I'm not saying we should proclaim our sins and failures to the world, but there is grace found in acknowledging our less-than-perfect life. In Hebrews 11, the writer talks about heroes of the faith. Half the chapter is about people who were blessed and prosperous, but the other half concerns those who were persecuted, beaten, and martyred.

Some aspects of our walk of faith are beautiful, but some are a trial. Some things cause us to bloom, and others break our stems and kill our leaves. We all have flaws, we all sin, and that's why we needed the one perfect man to come and die for us, saving us from our sins. Life was real for Him too, and it got really messy, through no fault of His own. It damaged Him physically, but He bloomed magnificently as the Rose of Sharon, paving the way for our salvation.

When life gets messy, we need to remember that it's real life. It got messy for Jesus too, but the end result was our salvation and eternal life. There is nothing wrong and everything good with that real life.

Jesus, You were beaten, stripped, mocked, and killed, but it was Your plan. You came down to be born and live as a man in this messy world to save us because we couldn't save ourselves. You set us free from sin and death, and we are eternally grateful. Amen.

For further study: Song of Solomon 2:1; Isaiah 35:1–10; Romans 3:21–28; Hebrews 11:1–12:4; 1 John 1:8–10.

JULY 28
Onesimus

> But if he has wronged you or owes you anything, put that on my account. I, Paul, am writing with my own hand. I will repay—not to mention to you that you owe me even your own self besides. (Philemon 1:18–19)

PAUL WROTE A short letter, included in the New Testament, to a friend named Philemon. A slave named Onesimus was owned by Philemon, but something happened and Onesimus ran away. It's quite possible that Onesimus robbed Philemon before escaping. We're not told the details, only that he had proved unprofitable to his master.

Onesimus met Paul in prison, and through that encounter became a Christian. Paul wrote to Philemon to ask him to welcome Onesimus back, now as a brother and not just a slave. Paul also told Philemon to put any debt he held against his former slave on Paul's account. Paul reminded Philemon that he owed Paul a great debt as well, so he should keep that in perspective.

Of course, this epistle mirrors our Christian life. We are like Onesimus. Once we were unprofitable to God (our master) because of our sin nature. We owed God a great debt, but Jesus came as an intermediary between us and the Father. He put our debt on His account. We are now received not as slaves but as free men.

There's another side to this, however, as we also tend to hold debts against people. The other day, I was talking with friends about baking something, and they mentioned learning to cook in home economics class in school. I immediately started ranting about how I'd wanted to take shops, but our junior high principal didn't allow the girls to take those classes. They had to take home economics instead. The Holy Spirit quietly reminded me that for almost five decades now, I've held the debt against that principal, and Jesus has asked me to put it on His account. Who knows, maybe I bake today because of those classes I hated in junior high! Maybe if I'd taken shops, I would have been ridiculed and never again taken up a drill and hammer to build things, like the deck I so enjoy. In any case, Jesus asks me to remember the huge sin debt I have been forgiven of and to release the small debt owed to me. I hold other debts against people, but God reminds me to give those up too. He doesn't deny that I was wronged. Some of those debts were large ones in the world's eyes, yet that debt is still nothing compared to the one I owe Jesus. I have received more than enough grace and so should be able to extend grace.

> *Jesus, we recognize the debt we owe You for taking on our sins. Help us to release the debts we are holding on to, knowing we have received the greater grace. Amen.*

For further study: Matthew 18:21–35; Philemon 1:1–21.

JULY 29
Spirit Life

Who also made us sufficient as ministers of the new covenant, not of the letter but of the Spirit; for the letter kills, but the Spirit gives life. (2 Corinthians 3:6)

I SAW A post on Facebook the other day of a beautiful Indigenous girl celebrating her life in Jesus Christ. She wrote that some of her family members were offended when she became a Christian because of the trauma they'd gone through in the residential school system. Eventually her mom also became a Christian, and she said that had the teachers in the school shown them this Jesus she now knew, everyone would have welcomed Christianity.

There are many movies, books, and personal stories about traumatic experiences people have had with Christians who were able to quote Scripture but didn't reflect the heart of Christ. Scripture can be on our walls and in our mouths, but if Jesus isn't in our hearts, the word will kill. It will kill people's hope. It will kill culture. It will kill dreams. It will break people's spirits and wound their souls. It will bring condemnation, not salvation. But where the Spirit of the Lord is, there is life and liberty.

Paul wrote about this in his letter to the Corinthians. He explained that Moses delivered the Ten Commandments, written on stone, and it had enough glory to make Moses's face shine. He also wrote that this was a ministry of death, and Moses covered his face with a veil so others wouldn't see the glory, which was fading. However, if the ministry of condemnation had glory, how much more glorious is the ministry of righteousness brought about by Jesus's sacrifice on the cross? There was glory to what is passing away, but even more glory in that which remains for eternity. Once our hearts were veiled to the glory of the gospel, but in Christ, the veil is removed and we can look on His glory. We have hope, freedom, and life as we are being transformed into His image by the Spirit of the Lord. The Word of God can be used to kill, but *The Word* of God, Jesus Christ Himself, brings life and life everlasting.

Partaking of communion reminds us that we are now His body on earth. We're being transformed into His glory. The Scriptures aren't written in stone as a means to condemn our sin, but they are written in our hearts so that we no longer desire to sin. We reflect the glory of His righteousness. There is a power and beauty in that reflection that will never pass away. The Word of God lives in us, His Spirit bringing life to others where the words of God alone could be used to bring condemnation and death.

Jesus, we thank You for Your glorious grace. You have given us Your righteousness. Help us to show the world the glory of Your presence instead of using the Word of God to condemn. May we reflect You always. Amen.

For further study: Exodus 34:1–35; John 1:1–14; 2 Corinthians 3:1–18.

JULY 30
There's Room at the Table

> Then Ziba said to the king, "According to all that my lord the king has commanded his servant, so will your servant do." "As for Mephibosheth," said the king, "he shall eat at my table like one of the king's sons." (2 Samuel 9:11)

I WAS VISITING my mom and noted a small wooden bench in the garden. It looked vaguely familiar. Suddenly, I recognized it as one of the two benches that used to be on either side of the kitchen table when I was a young child. I was struck by how small it was. It seemed bigger when my siblings and I were small and fighting for room at the table. My left-handed sister and I were always bumping elbows and pushing at each other to get the other to move over.

As we grew, we learned to make room at the table. The bench was replaced by chairs, and a leaf or two would be added to the dining room table. The house could accommodate large numbers of family members over the holidays.

David made room at his table for one who should have been his enemy. Mephibosheth was the son of Jonathan. He was living at Lo Debar, which means a place with no pasture. He was in hiding, really; after all, he had a claim to the throne. God had given the kingdom of Israel to David, and not Mephibosheth. When David inquired if there were any relatives of Jonathan around, Mephibosheth must have felt frightened. He would have thought he'd be killed to remove any heirs to the throne. David's intent, however, was to honor his friend Jonathan. He gave Mephibosheth good pasture lands and servants, but David also made room for Mephibosheth at the king's table. Mephibosheth was treated as if he was one of David's own children. I wonder if some of David's own sons weren't a little put out by making room for Mephibosheth.

We once were in a dry and barren place spiritually. God came seeking us in order to invite us to eat at His table. We were children of His enemy, yet He sought to bless us and not destroy us. He made room at His table. There is room for the left and right-handed, for people from all nations and cultures. There is room for the graduate and the school dropout. There is room for the strong and the weak, the brave and the fearful, the people who have it all together and the ones who have been broken in pieces. God calls us to push over and make room on the bench for all who would join, even if they're different from us. Let's rejoice with Him as we find yet another leaf for the table so that we can make room for our neighbor to join the feast.

> *Jesus, remind us to push over and make room because You welcome all to Your table. You ask us to break the bread and pass it down, to drink from the cup and pass it along. Just as You welcomed us when we were Your enemies, so You welcome all who will come. You died for whosoever, not just the people we like. We partake of Your body and blood to remember the welcome to all of us, and to push over and make room for others. Amen.*

For further study: 2 Samuel 4:4, 9:1–13; Matthew 8:11; 1 Timothy 2:1–4.

JULY 31
Red Rover

> I, therefore, the prisoner of the Lord, beseech you to walk worthy of the calling with which you were called, with all lowliness and gentleness, with longsuffering, bearing with one another in love, endeavoring to keep the unity of the Spirit in the bond of peace. (Ephesians 4:1–3)

WHEN I WAS a child, all the neighborhood kids would often play together. One of the games we would play was Red Rover. We'd form two lines on either side of the yard, our arms linked together to form a wall, and one side would call out, "Red rover, red rover, we call *(child)* over." We'd call out the name of a child from the other team, and that child would run at the opposite line of children and try to break through the line. If they managed to break through, they'd take a child back to their own side, growing their team. If they couldn't break through, they'd join the opposing team. Of course, kids would try to spy out the weak spots. If there was someone smaller and weaker in the line, the stronger ones nearby would pull in and hold on tighter to defend the living wall, knowing the opposing team would target that very spot.

As Christians, we link arms to make a wall to defend against the enemy—or at least we should. We're not like a wall made with bricks, all from the same mold. We're more like a dry-stone wall in Scotland. These walls are made of stones of a variety of shapes and colors. The master builder fits them together, creating strength and unity of purpose without mortar. If we as living stones look at the one next to us and complain they're not like us, or if we pull away from each other, the strength of the wall is weakened. Our enemy could break through the line. In fact, the enemy will target those weak spots. Instead, those who are strong need to support and draw closer to the weak, maintaining the unity of the faith. Those Scottish dry-stone walls have withstood the test of time. They've remained standing from generation to generation because of the skill of the builders. We have a much more amazing master builder who has fitted us together, united by His body and blood. We can rejoice to know He has placed us in the body just where we need to be to defend the faith and help grow the wall.

> *Jesus, You have united us with other Christians into Your body. Remind us to strengthen those who are weak, to pull in tighter together when the enemy attacks our brothers and sisters. You gave Your life so that we could be one with You, and we remember this and are grateful. Amen.*

For further study: Psalm 133:1–3; Acts 20:35; Romans 12:3–18, 15:1–7; 1 Corinthians 12:4–27; Ephesians 4:1–16.

AUGUST 1
Grace to You

Grace to you and peace from God our Father and the Lord Jesus Christ. (1 Corinthians 1:3)

HAVE YOU NOTICED how many times Paul blesses his readers by saying *"Grace to you, and peace from God the Father and the Lord Jesus Christ"*? Most of his writings to the church start and end with these or similar words. It's easy to just slide over them, like our letters of old that began with "Dear *so-and-so*" and ended with "Sincerely" or "Yours truly." Yet this wishing grace on people means so much more.

Grace is gratitude, joy, and rejoicing for a gift received. People have described the grace of God as being God's righteousness at Christ's expense, yet it's more than that. Grace means to have a debt canceled. It implies being overwhelmingly thankful for this beautiful and indescribable gift. It means we rejoice in this gift that we didn't deserve; in fact, we deserved the very opposite of grace. We are guilty and have no excuse. We owed a debt we couldn't pay. We should have received condemnation, but God extended grace. We can live in peace now and in the life to come because of the grace extended to us by the sacrifice Jesus made on our behalf.

I wonder what the world would be like if I bookended each interaction with others by praying for them to receive grace and peace from God the Father and our Lord Jesus Christ. As I go about my day, I realize that I don't fully comprehend the grace of God. Some people with whom I interact annoy me. At times I have to have a difficult conversation with someone. There are people who cross my path who are downright nasty. I'm not really keen on praying for them to receive grace.

So I sit here with my little wafer of unleavened bread and my communion cup, and I remind myself of the grace I have received so that I can extend grace to those around me, no matter what the circumstances. And I pray "grace and peace to you" as images of my family, friends, co-workers, and neighbors march across my mind. Grace and peace to all I will encounter today. It's a bit harder to be ungrateful and unkind to those around me when I've framed our interactions with His grace. As I receive His grace, I can extend His grace, and oddly enough, I find His grace and peace multiplied back to me again. What a wonderful, glorious circle of grace.

> *Heavenly Father, we are so astounded and awed by Your grace. While we were yet sinners, Jesus died for us. You invited us into Your kingdom of righteousness even though we weren't worthy. We are grateful and rejoice in the grace extended to us. Help us to extend grace to all around us. Amen.*

For further study: Romans 1:3–7, 3:21–26, 5:1–11, 16:20, Ephesians 2:1–10.

AUGUST 2
Beloved Kinsmen

Greet Urbanus, our fellow worker in Christ, and Stachys, my beloved. Greet Apelles, approved in Christ. Greet those who are the household of Aristobulus. Greet Herodian, my countryman.
(Romans 16:9–11a)

THE LAST CHAPTER of the book of Romans is a long list of people Paul wishes to send greetings to, interspersed with various descriptions of those people. He calls them sister, brother, kinsmen, fellow workers, his beloved, beloved in the Lord, fellow laborer, fellow prisoner, approved in Christ, chosen in the Lord, mother, host of the church, and helpers.

When I was reading this chapter one day, I was thinking of us all as the body of Christ—fellow workers, kinsmen, sisters and brothers in the Lord. Suddenly it occurred to me that the descriptions Paul gives to these people in the body of Christ, Jesus also gives to us. He is our kinsman. He was born in this world as a human being to be one with His creation so He might pay the price to redeem us from this fallen world. He is our beloved, but we are also His beloved. He works with us and through us, making us His fellow workers. He has chosen us. We are fellow laborers, in some cases also fellow prisoners. We are approved in Him. We host His Church and are His helpers, showing forth His grace to the world. We are of His household, and one day we'll go home to the place He has prepared for us in eternity.

There is comfort in knowing that even as I call Him my beloved kinsman, He calls me the same. I am beloved not because of anything I have done but simply from my position as a member of the body of Christ, redeemed by His grace. He has chosen me. Amazing! I'm not sure I would have chosen me, yet He had no hesitation in receiving me. He pours out His love on each of us abundantly and with no reservation. He proved it when He walked the narrow road to the cross, blood staining every step He took. He greets us, calls us by name, and welcomes us into His family. You are loved and the beloved of Christ. You are His kinsman, even as He is yours. What a wonderful family!

Jesus, thank You so much for becoming our kinsman redeemer, for choosing us, for loving us, for calling us by name. Thank You for calling us Your beloved. Amen.

For further study: Ruth 4:1–6,14; John 14:1–4; Romans 16:1–27; Ephesians 1:3–6, 2:19–22.

AUGUST 3
Treasurer of the City

> Gaius, my host and the host of the whole church, greets you. Erastus, the treasurer of the city, greets you, and Quartus, a brother. (Romans 16:23)

IN ROMANS 16, Paul lists people to whom he and those with him are sending greetings. One of those people is Erastus. He's described as the treasurer of the city. Did you catch that? He was the treasurer. This was a pretty high position. He was responsible for collecting money and paying bills. In a sense, he was the keeper of the treasure. He wasn't the treasurer of some small enterprise but of the city. Certainly he was a trusted individual in a high government position.

This is one of the really cool things about Christianity. In Jesus, the rich and the poor, the high and the low, are united in one body. It's not just a religion for the broken and weak but also for the wealthy and strong. This also shows how quickly faith in Jesus had spread, reaching even to high government officials in mere decades after Christ's sacrifice for us on the cross.

When I think on this verse, I hear God whispering in my heart, "Will you be the keeper of My treasure?" God's treasure, of course, is people. He loves people, and it was for people that Jesus gave His life. We're called to give our lives for people in following the example of our Lord. Will we keep our family, or will we tear it apart with our words? Will we care for our neighbors, or turn a blind eye when the thief comes to steal, kill, and destroy them? Will we lift up our city in prayer, or complain about the government to all who will hear? We all can be treasurers, keeping the treasure of our homes, neighborhoods, and cities by bathing the people in prayer, watching over them, loving them, and greeting them with the grace of Jesus.

Cain killed his brother Abel out of jealousy, and when God confronted him and asked where Abel was, Cain replied, *"Am I my brother's keeper?"* (Genesis 4:9b). God told him that Abel's blood cried out from the ground. How much more does Jesus's blood cry out as He longs for all people to come to a saving knowledge of His sacrifice. We can turn our backs on our brothers and sisters, or we can say, "I will be the keeper of this treasure on behalf of Christ. I will pray for them and love them even when I'm angry or disagree with them. Even when I'm jealous or hurt, I will love them and believe for them to be saved. I will be my brother's keeper because I also have Treasure inside of me."

> *Jesus, You are our treasure, and You are in us. Your treasure is also people, and You call us to keep Your treasure, to love them and pray for them. We are reminded of Your sacrifice for us all as we partake communion. Help us to love others even when we don't want to. Amen.*

For further study: Genesis 4:1–10; Proverbs 14:1; 2 Corinthians 4:6–7; 1 John 3:9–21.

AUGUST 4
Re-Joice

Rejoice in the Lord always. Again I will say, rejoice! (Philippians 4:4)

GRACE IS SUCH a marvelous thing—forgiveness, gratitude, and rejoicing all wrapped up in one concept. To rejoice in our salvation is beyond wonderful.

When verbs have "re" at the beginning, it often means to repeat the action. Examples would be words like reaccept (to accept something again) or reacquire (to acquire something again). I recognize that joy is a noun, so to rejoice is more of an emphasis on being joyful as opposed to finding joy again. At the same time, I like the idea of having a reminder to re-joy when the world has weighed us down. And the world can be weighty. Sickness, persecution, fights with neighbors, fights with family members, financial troubles, trials at work, household chores that never end, the fast pace of life as we rush from one duty to another, elderly parents, wayward children, people who just don't understand how you feel—the list is never-ending. No matter how good your life is, you'll bump into struggles in this fallen world at some point or another.

Jesus tells us to rejoice and be exceedingly glad when we're persecuted. We're told to rejoice in trials. The disciples rejoiced to suffer shame for His name. In many places of Scripture, we're told to rejoice. Paul tells the church at Philippi to rejoice. Philippi was where Paul was falsely imprisoned, beaten, and held in stocks in the darkest place of the prison, yet at midnight, he and Silas sang praise songs to the Lord. He knew something about needing a reminder to find joy in the midst of struggles. We need to remind ourselves from time to time to find our joy again by looking to the source of all joy—the one who saved our souls by His death on the cross.

Today as we partake of communion, let's pause to find joy, and re-find joy if need be. Let us re-joy again in our heart and soul, speaking our thanks to the God of all creation.

Jesus, we are forever grateful for all You have done. Sometimes we forget the joy Your grace provides, so we pause today to rejoice in You, the source of all our joy. Amen.

For further study: Matthew 5:11–12; Luke 6:22–23; John 17:13; Acts 5:29–42, 16:16–31.

AUGUST 5
The Ultimate Superpower

> For the message of the cross is foolishness to those who are perishing, but to us who are being saved it is the power of God. (1 Corinthians 1:18)

A VERY POPULAR type of movie involves someone being born with, or through some freak of nature acquiring, super powers. Probably my favorite movie in that genre is *The Incredibles*. In that movie, Bob Parr is trying to balance family life and use his superhuman strength to defeat an enemy bent on destroying all those with super powers, while at the same time living in a world that wants to pretend that those with super powers don't even exist.

Maybe having superhuman strength, lightning speed, laser-beam eyes, or the ability to fly would be cool, but we have an even greater super power. Christians have received the super power of grace, which empowers us to forgive those who wound us. We need a good amount of grace to navigate a world that increasingly believes that the story of a God who sacrifices Himself for humanity is a myth. We need grace to not be overcome by evil but to overcome evil with good. We need grace to turn the other cheek and walk an extra mile. Grace is critical to reaching out to the broken and lost. It enables us to maintain joy in our spirit even when our circumstances bring sadness to our heart. Grace has the power to save us from our sins and give us eternal life in His glory. Grace is the ultimate super power!

As we walk in this world, with our enemy bent on destroying followers of Jesus, we need to remind ourselves that we have the power to overcome. When we partake of communion, we come to the foot of the cross to remember the sacrifice that saved our souls and changed our lives forever. Nothing in this world is stronger than the power of God's amazing grace. We pause to remember that we have the super power of His grace working in us and through us.

> *Jesus, we are so amazed by Your grace. It's the power that saves us and changes us. It's the power that overcomes the world. We are reminded that nothing is impossible with You. Thank You for empowering us with Your grace. Amen.*

For further study: Isaiah 61:1–3; Matthew 5:38–42; John 10:10, 16:33; Romans 12:21; Ephesians 2:4–8.

AUGUST 6
Survivor!

> Blessed be the God and Father of our Lord Jesus Christ, the Father of mercies and God of all comfort, who comforts us in all our tribulation, that we may be able to comfort those who are in any trouble, with the comfort with which we ourselves are comforted by God. (2 Corinthians 1:3–4)

FOR A SHORT time, I ended up at a gym that had TV screens everywhere. The sound was off, but I could tell the show was pitting people against one another. Facial expressions were harsh and only joyful when someone else failed. I discovered that this show was called *Survivor*. The goal was to get everyone else eliminated and be the last one left. I wasn't impressed.

I can contrast that wilderness reality program with the wilderness experience I had with a company called Outward Bound. We entered that journey with the instructions to either make it all together or not at all. I was definitely not in good enough shape to carry a heavy pack up and down the rocks north of Lake Superior. At one point I didn't think I could go on. I was upset thinking I was going to be the cause of the group not making it. My body hurt intensely, but my soul hurt even more. One of the guys in the group came and sat beside me and encouraged me.

Later on in that trip, I was doing well and was at the front of the group instead of the back of the line. Another girl was struggling like I'd been days before. Tears were in her eyes, and you could tell she didn't think she could go on. Sadly, I was too self-centered and glad that it wasn't me this time at the back of the line to be the one to comfort or encourage her. Someone else had to take on that job.

Paul rebukes the church at Corinth for just this kind of thing. They had started thinking only of themselves instead of the body of Christ as a whole. Partaking of communion is a reminder that it's not about us but about His body. This is not a survivor religion where we don't care if everyone else gets eliminated as long as we make it to the end. This is about waiting for one another, helping and encouraging one another in the love and grace of God so we all make it together. We are to come alongside each other when one of us feels they can't go on. We walk with them, step by step, just like Jesus walks with us, step by step by step.

> *Heavenly Father, You have comforted us, encouraged us, strengthened us. You made the way for us to live a life that is abundant and full of grace. We remember today that it's about us, but not just about us. Help us to comfort and encourage others like we've been comforted and encouraged. Amen.*

For further study: 1 Corinthians 11:17–34; 2 Corinthians 1:3–7; 1 John 4:7–21.

AUGUST 7

Wish

> For I know the thoughts that I think toward you, says the Lord, thoughts of peace and not of evil, to give you a future and a hope. (Jeremiah 29:11)

I LIKE TO watch movies from time to time, either in the theater or at home. I particularly like animated movies and have quite a DVD collection. The other day, a friend and I went to see a movie put out by Disney called *Wish*. It's about a kingdom that's ruled by a sorcerer who takes everyone's deepest wish and keeps them in his castle. He tells them he's keeping their wishes safe until they're granted, but in reality, he isn't planning on granting any but the most trivial of wishes. Asha (voiced by Ariana DeBose) discovers the darkness of people's lost hopes and seeks to restore the wishes to her family and others.

When I walked away from the movie, I was thinking about my deepest wishes and hopes. I joked with my friend that I should wish for a bunch of talking animals to come and keep my house clean. Sure, everyone wants good things and an easy life, but really, my most sincere wish is for my family and friends to know and receive the love of God. I wish for godly relationships where right now relationships are more broken and worldly than whole and heavenly. Is there anything more desirable than that? I want it for them, but I also want it for me so that we can share in this faith walk together.

Sometimes it feels like God has gathered my wish and kept it. But I know that if He's taken my wish and held on to it, it's not to prevent it from coming true. He keeps my wish in His heart because it's His wish too. Both of us long for the day when this wish can be fulfilled in all His glory. He desires that all should come to salvation. He proved that when He gave His body and blood to save humanity from their sins. Sometimes it seems like we'll never see the desire of our hearts fulfilled. It may seem impossible to believe that certain people will turn to Christ. We can trust, however, that He's doing everything possible to draw them to life and freedom. By God coming as a man and sacrificing Himself, He has already done the impossible!

> *Jesus, Your heart is for people, and You long for them to know the wonder of salvation. Sometimes we feel the situation is hopeless, but it's not. With God, nothing is impossible. We remember all You have done to get people to know You. You stopped at nothing. We put our hope in You and thank You for all Your grace. Amen.*

For further study: Psalm 37:3–6; Matthew 19:16–26; 1 Timothy 2:1–8.

AUGUST 8
Who Is Your Source?

For He satisfies the longing soul, and fills the hungry soul with goodness. (Psalm 107:9)

WHEN I WAS young, the two school subjects I really disliked were geography and history. My interests were in science and math, and I didn't want to have to take those other subjects at all. Oddly enough, as I've aged, I've discovered how very interesting those subjects are. I love books of all kinds, but I've especially developed an interest in biographies. It's fascinating to see how people have overcome struggles and risen above their trials.

Some biographies, however, I find discouraging, especially those of unsaved famous musicians and actors. Often they turned to alcohol, drugs, or illicit relationships, and my heart aches for them. They've tried to find comfort for their souls with things that can never truly satisfy their hearts. They may have lots of money and fame, but their lives remain empty.

All of us at times try to find comfort with the wrong things. Some people reach for alcohol when their heart aches. Some reach for drugs. Some use retail therapy, running out to buy something new. I have a weakness for tea and cookies, or I might find my emotions numbed while scrolling through Facebook. In all these situations, we're searching to satisfy our hearts' aches with things that can't do the job. Only one can truly satisfy. Jesus, the bread of life and living water, is the only one who can replace emptiness with hope.

Jesus is priceless, yet we come to buy His bread without money. He gives freely to all who come to Him. His grace is endless, His mercies new every morning. In this fallen world, it's easy to forget that He's the source of all goodness and comfort. We may run to the wrong things, but He calls us back to that which is true. Herein lies the essence of our communion with Him. We remember that He is the living bread broken for us. We remind ourselves that His blood is the drink that satisfies the deepest thirst of our soul. We recognize that we've tried to satisfy our soul with the wrong things, so we turn back instead to the Savior of our soul. He is the only way. His is the only path to freedom.

> *Jesus, You are the bread of life and the living water. You are the only one who truly satisfies. We repent of trying to find comfort in the world's ways and turn to You, looking unto You, the Author and Finisher of our faith. Amen.*

For further study: Psalm 107:1–43; Isaiah 55:1–3; John 4:4–14, 6:22–66; Hebrews 12:1–4.

AUGUST 9
The Greatest of These Is Love

And now abide faith, hope, love, these three; but the greatest of these is love. (1 Corinthians 13:13)

IN 1 CORINTHIANS 13, Paul speaks of love. He describes all that love is and what it isn't. This chapter finishes with the statement that faith, hope, and love abide, but the greatest of the three is love.

Faith is a belief or trust in someone or something, with the implication that actions based on that trust will follow. It's about having an assurance of something and being completely convinced in it.

Hope is a confident expectation. It means to look forward to something good and beneficial. The thing we hope for is yet unseen, but we are looking to the day when our hope is fulfilled.

Faith and hope go hand in hand. The Bible tells us that faith is the substance of the thing hoped for, the evidence of what we do not see. We can hope in the future because we have faith in the One who holds the future. We can hope because we have faith in the power of His love. We have faith in His love because His past actions prove that His future actions can be totally trusted. His love has been proven by His blood poured out on the cross. He showed His love in that while we were yet sinners, He died for the ungodly. Our faith is not a blind faith. Our hope is not a futile hope. They are based on His incredible love. The love is the greatest of the three because the other two are founded on His love.

Jesus, we are so grateful for Your abundant love. We have faith in You and hope for our future because of the depth of Your wondrous love, which You poured out upon us. There is no love greater than Yours, and we are eternally thankful. Amen.

For further study: Romans 5:1–8; 1 Corinthians 13:1–13; Hebrews 11:1–3.

AUGUST 10
Peace of God

Peace I leave with you, My peace I give to you; not as the world gives do I give to you. Let not your heart be troubled, neither let it be afraid. (John 14:27)

I RECEIVED SOME sad news recently. Someone I love dearly was passing out of this life and into the next. My heart grieved at the loss of their presence, yet I felt the peace of God. I wonder if this was what the disciples felt as they sat at the communion table with Jesus on the night He was betrayed.

On that night, Jesus had broken the bread and passed it to His disciples, telling them His body was about to be broken for them. He passed the cup and explained that His blood would be poured out. He washed their feet and reminded them to humbly serve one another, and then He spoke to them at length. He told them of His departure. He comforted them, telling them He would send the Holy Spirit to remind them of all He had said to them. And He told them He was giving the disciples His peace—a peace that passes all understanding. They would have peace in the midst of trials and suffering. He finished His long discourse by praying for Himself, His disciples, and all believers yet to come to the faith. Jesus was about to experience excruciating pain; the disciples were about to experience excruciating loss, but He reminded them that they would have peace and God will be glorified. Amazing.

This is why we can walk in peace. We know in our hearts the depth of His love. His prayers for us bring comfort when the world has none to offer. We can reach out to our heavenly Father and know He hears us, just as He heard Jesus. We can place our grief in His hands and rest in His love.

Jesus, on the night You were betrayed, You gave thanks. You shared the communion meal with Your disciples and gave us this practice as a reminder that the sorrows of this world are not the end of the story. There is a glory on the other side of the cross that brings peace in the midst of loss. Thank You for loving us and giving Your life for ours. Amen.

For further study: John 13–17; Philippians 4:6–9.

AUGUST 11
Drink from Your Roots

For I determined not to know anything among you except Jesus Christ and Him crucified. (1 Corinthians 2:2)

WE HAVE A decent crop of wild blueberries growing this year. The last few years haven't been so lucky. Last summer started out looking great. The plants were getting green and there were lots of flowers, but then the weather became hot and dry. The flowers dried up and fell off. The plants withered. Sure, we had a bit of rain here and there. The drops on the leaves were so pretty, but not enough moisture made it to the ground to nourish the plant. A plant has to drink from its roots to stay alive. Its foundation is the part that's in the ground, not the branches that wave in the air.

Likewise, for buildings to stay strong no matter what the weather, their foundation must be solid and sure. The Leaning Tower of Pisa leans not because the top was poorly built but because the foundation on which it stands is weak.

Paul explained to the Corinthians that God laid the foundation for the Christian faith—Jesus Christ and Him crucified. Others would build on this foundation. Some would build well; others, not so much. At the end of the age, everyone's work will be known for what it was. Still, the foundation had to be kept sure and strong. No other foundation can be laid than Jesus Christ, crucified for our sins. From that foundation, nourishing living water flows up to the parts that people can see, and we can stay strong when the winds of trouble blow. Happiness, prosperity, a good life, a good job, and great relationships are wonderful. They can bring beauty to our lives like water on the leaves, but they won't truly nourish our souls. The lasting fruit of the Spirit comes from strong roots that drink deeply of the living water.

We come to the communion table to remember our foundation in Christ. It's the basis from which all else flows. Without a strong foundation, our faith can topple in the storms of life; our fruit may wither and die before it has the chance to nourish those around us. We pause to take of the bread, remembering His body was broken so we could be whole. We lift the cup to remember His blood was spilled so that we could have everlasting life. From this foundation, our faith is established and sure.

> *Jesus, we're so grateful for Your sacrifice to save us from our sins. We rejoice in Your gift of salvation and we remember it today. It's our foundation on which all else is built. In remembering this, we receive Your life-giving water to the very roots of our faith, keeping them healthy and strong that we might produce fruit to nourish those around us. Thank You. Amen.*

For further study: 1 Corinthians 2:1–5, 3:6–11; Galatians 5:22–26.

AUGUST 12
Trustworthy

Blessed is the man who trusts in the Lord, and whose hope is the Lord. For he shall be like a tree planted by the waters, which spreads out its roots by the river, and will not fear when heat comes; but its leaf will be green, and will not be anxious in the year of drought, nor will cease from yielding fruit. (Jeremiah 17:7–8)

WHEN I FIRST started out with my own veterinary clinic, I went in on an emergency call one day for a dog with an injured eye. The owners of the dog said that in their rush, they'd forgotten their wallet. Since I wanted to recheck the dog in a few days, we agreed they could pay then. Sadly, they didn't show, and when I tried to reach them at their phone number and address, it turned out that the information they'd reeled off so easily was false. They had purposely cheated me. I was angry and upset. I had come in after hours. It had cost me in supplies, overhead, and time with my family, and I had trusted them.

When I reported it to the police, the officer laughed at my naiveté. I was upset until I felt the Holy Spirit say it wasn't necessarily a bad thing I was cheated. It showed that I'd believed they'd be honest because I would have been honest in that situation. It may have been a bad reflection on their character, but it was a good one on mine. Still, I had to set up further boundaries to prevent occurrences like this in the future. After all, unlike God, people aren't completely trustworthy.

I'd like to think I'm always trustworthy, but if truth be told, I can't even trust myself to do things in my best interest. I may eat too much, spend too much, listen to feelings that speak lies about who I really am. Thankfully, God is trustworthy, and He has our best interests at heart. We can't put trust in people or even in ourselves, but we can put our trust in Him. When we put our trust in His Word, we find nourishment for our souls. He leads us on straight paths and guides us to His glory. He causes us to bring forth good fruit that will nourish others, even when all around us is dry ground.

We can know 100 percent that He is trustworthy and has our best interests at heart because it was proven at the cross. He said He would save us, and He did. He says He loves us, and He proved it abundantly when He walked the Via Dolorosa—that painful path to the cross. He could have walked away. He is God and didn't have to continue on that path, but He looked to us and said we were worth the cost. He would pay the price for our redemption. Putting our trust in people may be misplaced, but it's always the right thing to put our trust in Jesus.

Jesus, Word of God, You are the one in whom we put our trust, and that trust is not misplaced but proven reliable and sure. We thank You for who You are and all You have done. Amen.

For further study: Psalm 33:1–22; Proverbs 3:5–8; Jeremiah 17:5–9; Matthew 26:51–54.

AUGUST 13
Talk Is Cheap

> Jesus answered and said to them, "Go and tell John the things which you hear and see: The blind see and the lame walk; the lepers are cleansed and the deaf hear; the dead are raised up and the poor have the gospel preached to them." (Matthew 11:4–5)

WHEN JOHN THE Baptist saw Jesus, he was absolutely convinced that Jesus was the Christ. He said things like *"Behold! The Lamb of God …"* (John 1:29) and *"And I have seen and testified that this* (Jesus) *is the Son of God"* (John 1:34). As the saying goes, talk is cheap, and you don't really know if people mean what they say until it's tested. It was only a short time later, as John unjustly languished in a prison cell, that he sent a couple of his disciples to ask Jesus if He was the Messiah. What had happened to his assurance and faith? I don't know what went on in John's heart and head, but I suspect he was disappointed that he was left in his own personal hell. After all, wasn't the Messiah to set the captives free? Jesus was John's own cousin, yet nothing was being done to stop Herod from keeping John captive. Where was the Messiah when John needed Him?

Jesus tells the disciples to go and tell John the things they had seen and heard as they followed Jesus among the crowds of people. The blind received their sight, the deaf heard, the lame walked, the lepers were cleansed, the dead were raised. Jesus was reminding John of the prophecies of what the Messiah would do, and He was declaring that He was fulfilling these prophecies. It wasn't just talk: Jesus was all action.

Sometimes life doesn't go quite as we expect. It isn't always sunshine and roses. Sometimes the clouds are thick and all we see on the rose bushes are thorns. We may wonder where our Messiah is. Did He forget us? Was He ever real? Or was our assurance in times past mistaken? What if, as we languish in the prison of our mind, the expected encouragement never comes?

At those times, we need to make our way back to the foot of the cross and be reminded that once we were blind, but now we see. Our ears were deaf to His love, but then we heard His voice calling our name. Our walk was hindered by sin, but He strengthened our weakness and caused us to walk on the paths of righteousness. We were diseased by sin, but He cleansed us. We were captives to sin, but He set us free. We were dead, but He raised us to everlasting life. This world can crowd in with its darkness, but remembering all He has done restores the light.

> *Jesus, You have set us free. Sometimes our circumstances can cause us to forget all You've done to demonstrate Your great love for us. We come to You today, being reminded once again that we were blind but now we see. Thank You for all You have done and who You are. Amen.*

For further study: Isaiah 35:3–7, 61:1–3; Matthew 11:2–6; John 1:29–36, 3:26–30.

AUGUST 14
The Doctor Will See You Now

Let us therefore come boldly to the throne of grace, that we may obtain mercy and find grace to help in time of need. (Hebrews 4:16)

AS I AGE, many friends and family members have developed serious illnesses. Some have had to travel great distances to see specialists to find help for their condition. They sit in the waiting room in some trepidation, waiting and wondering when their name will be called. Will the doctor really be able to help, or is this all futile? There's a mixture of relief and dread when the receptionist says to them, "The doctor will see you now." They're relieved that now they'll have answers, but they dread that the answers may not be what they hope for. They might hear that the sickness is very bad, even terminal. Will this specialist be able to bring the longed-for cure?

I was thinking of God as being a specialist for the sickness in our spirit. The wonderful thing about God, though, is that this doctor is always in. He abides in our hearts, so there's no long journey needed to find Him. His door is always open. When we approach Him, we'll always hear, "The doctor will see you now." We step into His throne room, maybe even with a mixture of dread and relief. Will we hear the answers we long to hear? As we sit in His presence, we find He is not in a hurry. He has no need to rush off to another patient but gives us His full attention. No matter how long it takes, He will listen to our story and complaints. He won't rush us or cut us off. He's not offended by anything we bring to Him. He might nod His head wisely. When we're done, I imagine Him saying, "Yes, that sickness is very bad. In fact, this sin-sickness is 100 percent terminal."

We look up at Him, tears in our eyes, and ask, "Is there any hope for me?"

And this is when we see Him smile and answer, "Absolutely. You came to the right place. This disease, untreated, would be terminal, but I have good news. These holes in my hands—they hold the cure. Open heart surgery will be performed; it will be successful, and you'll live! My death and resurrection have guaranteed it."

No matter what we're experiencing, we can go to Him. His scarred hands take ours, and we can find relief for whatever ails us.

Jesus, You are the doctor of our soul. You arranged the cure for the worst disease ever to affect humanity. We rejoice in Your presence and take a moment today to spend time with You at the throne of grace. We are so blessed by all You have done, and we thank You. Amen.

For further study: Romans 6:23; 2 Corinthians 1:19–22; Hebrews 4:14–16; James 1:14–21.

AUGUST 15
"Peace to You"

So Jesus said to them again, "Peace to you! As the Father has sent Me, I also send you." (John 20:21)

I LOVE DOGS. No other creature with whom we share our lives greets us so exuberantly no matter how long we've been gone. My dogs are over the moon with joy when I come home from work, but also when I come back in after just fetching something from the car! No one else is as consistently happy to see me. It's easy to be just as happy to see them. Their joy breeds joy in my heart. It's so contagious.

People are a bit trickier. I have an acquaintance who's like my dogs. Every time she sees me, she rushes over and hugs me with joy. It's life-giving. Others aren't quite so generous with greetings. Another friend tends to be down on life in general. If she greets anyone at all, it's with a frown. If you say hello cheerfully, you may get a grunt back or some complaint about the day. I struggle to try to stay upbeat when I meet her. Sometimes we greet someone with fear in our hearts. If a mother says, "Just wait until your father gets home," a child knows trouble awaits them.

When Jesus was arrested, His disciples fled in terror. Peter even denied knowing Jesus. When Jesus rose from the dead and appeared to His followers, He didn't greet them harshly. He didn't accuse them of letting Him down, nor did He remind them of their failures. He told them to rejoice. He proclaimed peace to them. He greeted them with love—a love that was proved abundantly when He laid His life down so we could live.

We may struggle to love others at times. In fact, sometimes it's only possible if we remember the love of Jesus that resides in us. This is why we pause to take communion. We're reminding ourselves of His great love, and that His love abides in us so that we'll be able to walk in that love with those around us. We remember that our failures don't hinder His love. When we come to Him, He always greets us with joy, whether we've been gone from Him for minutes, days, or decades. His love is consistent and true. May we absorb His love so deeply into our hearts that it pours out joyfully to all we greet.

Jesus, thank You for Your great love. Thank You for always desiring to see us, for rejoicing when we come to You. Thank You for always greeting us with Your peace. Amen.

For further study: Matthew 28:9–10; Luke 24:33–43; John 20:19–29; Romans 15:13.

AUGUST 16
He's in Our Boat

And they came to Him and awoke Him, saying, "Master, Master, we are perishing!" Then He arose and rebuked the wind and the raging of the water. And they ceased, and there was a calm. (Luke 8:24)

ONE NIGHT, JESUS said to His disciples that they should all cross to the other side of the lake, so they loaded up the small boat and headed out. When they were in the middle of the lake, a great storm arose. Water filled the boat, and these experienced fishermen were certain all was lost, but Jesus was asleep in the back of the boat. The disciples woke Him and asked if He knew or even cared that they were perishing. Jesus then rebuked the wind and waves and there was great calm. Then He chastised the disciples for their lack of faith.

I once heard a preacher say that Jesus rebuked His disciples because He'd been training them, and any one of them could have stood up and calmed the storm. I heard another preacher say that the disciples should have just trusted that when Jesus said they were going to the other side of the lake, that's where they would end up. Honestly, I don't know whether it's either of these or something altogether different that Jesus was trying to convey. Personally, I think as long as Jesus was in the boat, they didn't need to give in to their fear. Easier said than done. Logic would have said there was much to fear.

We sometimes encounter storms in our own lives. Some storms are small and expected. Others are sudden and large. They rip at our sails and can be a struggle to row against. Waves of loneliness may swamp our soul. Maybe sickness washes over us or a member of our family. The winds of loss may rip at our hearts. Our hopes and goals may seem to be on a shore that's impossible to reach. There was a time when even though I was surrounded by a sea of faces, I felt lost and alone on the waves. Jesus appeared to be sleeping, and seemed not to care that I was perishing. I mistook His peace for His absence. I had forgotten He was still in my boat. When I recalled He chose to come down and get into humanity's boat in order to get us safely to the other side, the storm in my soul subsided to a peaceful calm.

I don't know if in the midst of my storm I'm supposed to speak to the storm myself, wake Jesus up, or just trust that He'll get me to the other side, but I do know He is sharing my boat. He sails with me through every struggle and trial, and He's in your boat too. Communion is all about remembering that He chose to come and join humanity in all its brokenness. He stepped into our storms so He could calm them and bring us into His heavenly realm. Life's trials have a way of making us forget we're not in this alone. Sometimes we need a reminder so we don't panic in the storm but trust in His everlasting grace.

Jesus, we're so thankful You joined humanity's boat to save us. We were perishing in our sin, yet You brought us calm within our souls. We pause to remember Your amazing grace. Amen.

For further study: Deuteronomy 31:6–8; Isaiah 41:10; Matthew 8:23–27; Mark 4:35–41; Luke 8:22–25.

AUGUST 17
The Cheerful Giver

> So let each one give as he purposes in his heart, not grudgingly or of necessity, for God loves a cheerful giver. (2 Corinthians 9:7)

I ONCE ASKED a friend for a favor. She did it but so begrudgingly I was sorry I'd even asked. I would rather she had just said no if she was going to complain so much about it. It wasn't really a favor anymore, since that would have implied that I was thankful for being supported and blessed by her action. Her reluctance negated any benefit I received by the action itself. I don't know if she felt compelled to do it because we were friends, although I had no intention of forcing her. I suspect you've experienced similar situations yourself. Maybe you were even compelled to do a favor for someone. Being forced to give a gift makes it no longer a gift but a chore. The blessing is gone, and in its place only resentment remains. The relationship isn't enhanced but rather diminished.

Paul wrote to the Corinthians that he didn't want them to give out of compulsion but willingly, for that's what God loves. This makes sense, since God desires a healthy relationship with humanity. Our relationship with God grows out of grace and gratitude. It's not forced. He gave us the example by willingly laying down His life for us. No one could force Him to the cross. He walked to it of His own accord. He also doesn't force or compel us to receive His free gift of grace. We choose it willingly or not at all.

Paul also writes that we reap what we sow. If we sow a little, we only reap a small harvest. If we sow a lot, we reap an abundant harvest. Jesus gave His all. He held nothing back, and His harvest is still being brought into the kingdom. His harvest stretches out to all eternity. We can follow His example in giving. He gave His all willingly, and we can choose to willingly give back to Him in our love for others. He won't stop us if we withhold our love or give it only grudgingly, but then our harvest will be wilted by resentment. But if we give freely as we have freely received, what a wonderful harvest is in store! Our ability to freely give is proportional to how well we remember the grace so freely given to us. We partake of communion to remember this very grace we've so freely received.

> *Jesus, thank You for giving Your all, willingly and not by compulsion. We're so blessed by Your grace. Help us to remember all You've done for us so that we might freely give to others just as You gave to us. Amen.*

For further study: Matthew 10:7–8; John 10:7–18; 2 Corinthians 9:6–18; Philippians 2:1–18; Hebrews 12:1–2; 1 John 3:16.

AUGUST 18
Seasons Change

> While the earth remains, seedtime and harvest, cold and heat, winter and summer, and day and night shall not cease. (Genesis 8:22)

JUST BEFORE THE rains come in countries with dry and rainy seasons, the plants can be so dry they appear dead. It looks hopeless, but past experience has shown that as soon as the water comes, life arises.

We can get into dry seasons too. Whether spiritually or emotionally, our soul feels withered, like it can't go on. I remember one time in particular when I was having trouble finding a place to stay, so I was living in a tent at a campground. The people who owned the campground had just bought it and set up the tent spaces where the community launched their boats. I came "home" from work one day to find the entire community fighting with the campground owners over my little tent.

As I sat on the picnic table eating some dinner and listening to the fight, I could also hear music playing in the distance that sounded familiar. As the discussion over the tent wound down, the words of the song "It's Beginning to Rain" came into my head. That church chorus was just what I needed to hear. Sure, things looked bad. I was essentially homeless and knew I was going to have to pack up my tent and find a new place to stay, but I also knew that the spiritual and emotional drought I was in was going to change. God had a plan and a place for me. He poured out His grace, and the season changed.

Most of us have likely experienced dry seasons. At times like that, you wonder if faith is dying. Can it rise again, even if the rains come? Is it too late? Thankfully, we can rest in God's faithful promises.

There could be no drier time than the time before we knew of His redeeming grace. The death and resurrection of Jesus changed everything. Where everything seemed dead and gone, suddenly as He poured out His Spirit on us, there was abundant life. God has promised that the dry seasons on the earth will change, and we can also trust that the seasons of spiritual dryness will also change. No matter how dead our faith may look, it can spring back to abundant life. God abundantly proved His ability to bring the dead to life when the stone was rolled away from the tomb to show that Jesus had conquered sin and death once and for all.

> *Jesus, You died yet You rose again. Sometimes our faith is dry and seems almost dead, but we recognize that You bring us life, and life that is abundant. Even our friends or family members who have fallen away from the faith can be resurrected to new life. Let the rain of Your grace fall on us all. Amen.*

For further study: Genesis 8:1–22; Joel 2:28–32; Acts 2:1–41.

AUGUST 19
Unfathomable

> My mouth shall tell of Your righteousness and Your salvation all the day, for I do not know their limits. (Psalm 71:15)

IT'S BEEN SAID that we know less about the ocean than we do about the moon. The depths of the ocean are hard to explore and much is unknown of the deep. The deepest depth of the ocean is deeper than the highest heights on the earth. At the bottom, all is dark and cold. The pressure of the water column is intense enough to crush all but the sturdiest of objects. There is so much we don't know about these deep places.

In Psalm 71, the psalmist writes that he hasn't found the limits of God's righteousness and salvation. He's not been able to sound out the depths of God's grace. I believe only Jesus truly understands the weight and depth of God's grace and glory. He went to the very depths for us, crushed by the weight of our sin, but then reached up to roll away the stone from the tomb to release the fullness of God's grace to the world.

Sometimes we feel the weight of this sinful world. It brings us to a dark and cold place, and our soul is crushed by the pressure all around us. It may look hopeless, but we can look to the cross, reaching our hands up to be grasped by the nail-pierced hands of our Savior. He has the strength to pull us back to the warmth and the light because He has already lived it and done it. By His strength, not ours, we are returned to the surface to come up with a gasp, breathing in the breath of His Spirit. Once again, we feel the warmth of the Son as our soul expands with His love.

> *Jesus, we bless You and thank You for the grace so abundantly given to us. You have redeemed us from our sin and set us free. We bask in Your glory and are refreshed by Your love. We're so very grateful for all You have done and all You are. Amen.*

For further study: Psalm 71:1–24.

AUGUST 20
Pockets with Holes

"The glory of this latter temple shall be greater than the former," says the Lord of hosts. "And in this place I will give peace," says the Lord of hosts. (Haggai 2:9)

WHEN I LANDED at the airport after a trip, I found out my car had been stolen. The police had recovered it, but it was still upsetting. I was tired and frustrated, and now I had to deal with insurance and reports and all the other things that ate away at my time, money, and emotional resources. As I drove home in subzero temperatures with a broken window, causing cold air to sting my cheeks, the last thing on my mind was grace. In fact, I felt like grace was something that had been put into a bag with holes in it.

A verse in Haggai talks about that. God tells people that they're working hard, trying to have abundance for themselves, but He's blown their money away and put it in sacks with holes because they've neglected His temple. In other words, they were neglecting their relationship with God as they went about with a "me first" mentality. I also had that attitude. Why should I have to deal with theft and damage of my goods? The thief should be caught and punished! Why do I have to pay the price for their sin? Why doesn't God ensure that nothing bad happens to me? Questions like these can sink us into a cynical place where grace is nowhere to be seen.

Jesus had a right to complain. He had committed no sin yet was beaten and murdered for the sins of others. As He hung on the cross and looked at the perpetrators of this horrible crime, He said, *"Father, forgive them, for they do not know what they do"* (Luke 23:34). He offered grace, not vengeance. He didn't complain that it was the sins of others that brought Him to that place. He freely walked to it so He could buy us all back from the brink of hell.

The thief doesn't realize the evil he's playing with, the path to hell he's on. He doesn't know what he's doing. He's blinded to the eternal ramifications of a soul apart from God. We may not be building a temple of stone, but our bodies are now the temple of the Holy Ghost. We can choose to offer grace to build others up, restoring the temple, or we can neglect the temple by focusing on ourselves. Cursing others will result in the grace we wish to receive slipping from us like it had been poured into a bag full of holes. We can end up cynical and broken instead of full of peace and love. Remembering what Jesus did, how He forgave our sins, encourages us to extend forgiveness. Truly, for those living apart from God, they know not what they do.

Jesus, You forgave us our many sins. If we withhold Your grace from others, we lose out on the grace we desire to receive. Thank You for reminding us that we can give grace just as much as we can receive it, and it won't slip through holes in our pockets when we have extended grace to build others up. Thank You for Your abundant peace in the midst of our struggles. Amen.

For further study: Haggai 1:4–2:19; Luke 23:33–34; 1 Corinthians 6:19–20; 2 Corinthians 6:16–18.

AUGUST 21
He Sees Us

> Let us therefore come boldly to the throne of grace, that we may obtain mercy and find grace to help in time of need. (Hebrews 4:16)

CAROL OFF IS a Canadian journalist. In her book *All We Leave Behind*, she mentions a brief time during her work in Afghanistan when she wore a burka. She explained that others seemed to forget there was a person under that bright blue cloth. She was forgotten in cars and had doors shut in her face just because others forgot there was another person with them.

Over on this side of the world, Michael J. Fox wrote something similar in his book *No Time Like the Future*. He'd had spinal surgery and had to use a wheelchair for a time. He wrote that when he was in it, people seemed to see only the chair and not the person in the chair. I was struck in both these accounts of how easy it is for people to lose sight of others right in front of them. A piece of cloth, an assistive device, and like magic they've been dehumanized. I know I've been guilty of doing that to people who look different. There have also been times in my life when I've felt invisible. No one saw me or the struggle I was having. We can be surrounded by people yet oh so alone.

In the book of Hebrews, the author writes that nothing is hidden from God's sight. He sees all of us, and He sees all our failures. All things are naked and open to the eyes of Him to whom we must give account. It's a comfort to think that He sees us when no one else does, but when we think of our failures, we hang our heads in shame, knowing He has seen it all.

In the same breath, the writer continues his words to the Hebrews. Yes, God sees it all, but we have an amazing high priest who understands fully. He can sympathize with us, since He came as a man to the earth and endured the same temptations we experience. He understands how weak we are, yet He remained sinless to be the perfect sacrifice to atone for us. Now we can walk boldly to the throne of grace. With all our hurts, with all our weaknesses, with all our failures, with all our pain and joy, we are received with grace. Because of our Savior, we hold our heads high. He sees us. He knows us. He loves us still, and He reaches out with nail-scarred hands to receive us into His glory.

> *Jesus, thank You for being the perfect sacrifice to pay the price for our sins. You understand our weakness and our shame, but You receive us with grace and help. We're so blessed by all You have done and who You are. Amen.*

For further study: Psalm 73:21–24, 90:8; Hebrews 4:12–16.

AUGUST 22
Knit Together

> But, speaking the truth in love, may grow up in all things into Him who is the head—Christ—from whom the whole body, joined and knit together by what every joint supplies, according to the effective working by which every part does its share, causes growth of the body for the edifying of itself in love. (Ephesians 4:15–16)

MY SISTER IS a great knitter. She makes all kinds of beautiful things for family and friends. On a recent visit, I asked her to show me how to knit. I spent as much time pulling everything apart and starting over as I did on my attempts to knit a few rows of a simple scarf. I'd end up with these weird tangled knots or dropped stitches. Extra loops would appear from nowhere. I had no idea where I was going wrong. As often as not, when I'd see it messed up and go to pull it all apart again, my sister would stop me. She'd say she could fix the mess I'd made, and she could! She would move bits of yarn around, grab a bit here, move a bit there, and soon it would all be nice, even rows of stitches. I have no idea what she did to correct all my screwups, but I had the finished product to prove that she had indeed made everything turn out right.

God is a master knitter. He's been knitting the hearts of His people together to make us into His beautiful body. Sometimes we resist His efforts. We jump off His needles, or our enemy comes in with a pair of scissors, snipping away at the stitches connecting us. Sometimes we watch as our relationships unravel, and we feel helpless and hopeless. At any moment we expect God to pull out His needles and just pull the whole thing apart so He can start over. But God is a true master. He looks at the mess we're in and says, "Wait, I can fix that!" He moves people into our lives, tugs at our hearts here or there, and pulls us back into alignment with His body. Where the devil has slashed us, God comes along with His yarn of golden grace to weave a pattern into all the broken places, creating something beautiful.

When all of creation started to unravel because of the fall of humanity into sin and destruction, God already had the plan to restore us to relationship with Him. Christ would come and live a sinless life and die on the cross to knit our hearts together. The resulting grace woven in our lives results in something even more beautiful than the original creation. He continues to work His magic, knitting and repairing our tangled relationships, and He will continue to do so until we all come into the unity of the faith. He's not a quitter, and He never fails.

> *Father, thank You for loving us. You gave Your only begotten Son so we could become the body of Christ on earth. How beautiful is the body that was broken for us! How glorious the blood shed for us! And how beautiful is His body now made of every person who calls Jesus Lord. Help us to grow in unity of the faith, united with You and with each other through Jesus Christ, the head of the body. Amen.*

For further study: Genesis 3:15; 1 Corinthians 12:12–13:10; Colossians 1:15–23, 2:1–3.

AUGUST 23
But Then There Is Jesus

> Now there is in Jerusalem by the Sheep Gate a pool, which is called in Hebrew Bethesda, having five porches. In these lay a great multitude of sick people, blind, lame, paralyzed, waiting for the moving of the water. (John 5:2–3)

MANY SICK PEOPLE would spend their time hanging out by the pool of Bethesda. They were waiting for a chance to be healed by being the first one in the pool when the water was stirred by an angel. When Jesus comes to this pool, He sees a paralyzed man and asks him if he wants to be well. The man answers that there is no one to help him to the water. Someone else always reaches the water before him. His condition seems hopeless. For him to be healed, it would mean all those other desperate people would hold back and let him arrive first to the water.

Jesus tells the man to take up his bed and walk, and immediately the man is completely healed. He obtains the mercy He seeks from the man who came to him, and not from the miracle he'd been waiting for. There was a very remote chance of finding healing in that place through a random miracle, but then there was Jesus, the miracle worker Himself. People were waiting at the house of mercy hoping to find grace, when the very person able to extend mercy was walking among them.

Sometimes I find myself waiting. I'm waiting for someone to come and solve my problems, to make my life better. I'm waiting for someone to apologize first. I'm waiting for the situation to change. I sit in the house of mercy, nursing my hurts, waiting for someone's heart to be stirred to come to my rescue. I've lost sight that Jesus, the miracle worker, lives in me. Jesus, the one who through His death on the cross has purchased my very salvation, stands with me. He knows my pain and how long I've held on to it, waiting, and He asks me, "Do you want to be well?"

Will I look at Him and say, "I'll just keep waiting for someone to pull me to the pool." Or will I look into His eyes and say, "You know, I've been waiting a long time, but then there is You, Jesus. I trust You."

I'm sure He reaches His hands out to me, and to you, and tells us to take up our beds and walk! We need not wait to find mercy. We need not put our hope in a person to come and apologize to us first; we can walk in the path of forgiveness. We need not complain that others push us aside, because we walk with the healer of our soul. He gives us the ability to walk away from the place of waiting for everyone else to fix our circumstances and make our world right. It is Jesus who makes our world right, regardless of our circumstances. No matter what's happening in us and around us, there is Jesus.

> *Thank You, Jesus, for enabling us to get up and walk the walk You've called us to. You have forgiven us so that we can walk in forgiveness. You have healed our emotions and freed our spirit. You have redeemed us from the curse of sin and death by dying in our place. Because of what You have done, there's no need to wait to walk in this freedom. Amen.*

For further study: John 5:1–16.

AUGUST 24
Justice and Mercy

He has shown you, O man, what is good; And what does the Lord require of you but to do justly, to love mercy, and to walk humbly with your God? (Micah 6:8)

LATELY, I'M HEARING a lot of people crying out for justice, and rightly so. Our hearts recognize injustice, and we desire that the perpetrators be held to account. We wouldn't think much of a judge who would accept a bribe and proclaim an obviously guilty person innocent. We're enraged when a criminal gets off on a technicality. Yet if we were the one called before the bench, we wouldn't stop our lawyer from using every possible means to set us free. When our own faults are in question, we want mercy, not justice.

How can a holy God possibly reconcile the need for justice against sinners while still allowing for mercy? We're called before the judge's bench, and our sins are paraded openly for all to see. We may hope our lawyer will look for some technicality. In our hearts, we say we had to sin like that. We had no choice. Consider our ancestry, our heritage, our upbringing. Or maybe we hope the judge can be bribed or will turn a blind eye. We may promise to never do it again, even swearing on the Bible that we're done with sin, all the while knowing that as soon as we're released, we'll slip back into the same old patterns and behaviors.

Instead, our lawyer stands up and says, "It's true. My client is guilty of all, and he has no excuse."

The judge looks at us and says, "Guilty as charged. The penalty of sin is death!"

As we cast our eyes down, broken in our sorrow, knowing what we're destined for, our lawyer once again approaches the bench. "Father," He says, "I know You are just and holy. We can't bribe You. The sentence can't be commuted to life in prison, because the correct penalty is indeed spiritual death. However, I'd like to offer My blood instead. Let Me face the death penalty on behalf of My client, even though I've committed no sin."

The gavel falls down with a bang and the Father says, "Let it be so. Justice will be tempered with mercy by Your perfect sacrifice."

We tend to see others' sins as worse than our own. Often, we feel our mistakes are reasonable or understandable, but communion is about remembering that we are guilty as charged. We come to the throne room of God knowing justice must be served. By partaking of communion, we're reminded that we deserved the punishment but received mercy instead through Jesus's death on the cross. For this we are thankful.

> *Father, You are a just God, and we are so grateful that Your justice is met with Your mercy. Both are perfectly fulfilled in the death of Your Son on the cross. Holy Spirit, help us to remember that we're not as good a people as we think we are but You are perfectly good, and Your love is poured out upon us to set us free from the power of sin and death.*

For further study: Leviticus 11:44–45; Psalm 11:7; Isaiah 30:18; Romans 6:15–23; Ephesians 2:4–10; 1 John 2:1–2; Revelation 6:9–11.

AUGUST 25
Restoration

He restores my soul; He leads me in the paths of righteousness for His name's sake. (Psalm 23:3)

I'VE HAD THE privilege of seeing some famous artwork up close, having visited the Hermitage in Russia, the Louvre in Paris, and some of the galleries in Italy, including the basilica in Rome. The work is truly amazing, and you can readily see why it became so valuable. These pieces truly show the skillful touch of the master artist. I am shocked at times when I hear of people vandalizing the art. People have attacked art by throwing acid or paint at it, or by slicing at it with sharp knives. Some have vandalized art by kissing it and causing the lipstick to destroy the work. The art is also damaged by the ravages of time. The paintings in the basilica have been damaged by candle wax, smog, heat, and humidity.

It takes teams of amazing people to restore damaged art. They carefully clean off debris and stitch together the torn pieces, touching up areas to try to carefully match the original. It's painstaking and careful work. To try to protect the works from further damage, some pieces have been sealed behind bulletproof glass after being restored.

God is the ultimate master artist, and the value of His creation is beyond price because of the tremendous value of the artist. He created us perfectly, but the fall of humanity into sin brought about horrible destruction. Now we are damaged, sometimes by willful acts of violence; some have been wounded by the kiss of a false love. At other times, damage comes just by the ravages of time, living in this fallen world. As long as we live on this earth, we risk further damage. We're not sealed away behind bulletproof glass but interact with each other and the world.

Jesus came to clean us up and restore us from the effects of sin and death. He took on the damaging effects of the fallen world, being abused and beaten, betrayed by a kiss, so He could restore us to glory. He also cleans us up from the day-to-day grime that sticks to our souls.

Communion is about coming to Him, recognizing the amazing work of restoration, as well as bringing our faults and failures of today to His table so He can clean us up and restore us again. As long as we live in this world, we have need of His grace to restore us to glory. He stitches our torn hearts, wipes away the dirt, and paints fresh color over all that has faded, over and over again as the need arises. We are never so damaged that the master artist can't restore us to glory.

> *Jesus, thank You for saving us. You restored us from the spiritual death we inherited from our forefathers and also cleanse us day by day from the sin-dirt that clings to us as we move around in this fallen world. You are the master artist and restorer. Thank You for renewing us in Your grace and glory. Amen.*

For further study: Psalm 23:1–6, 51:1–17; Matthew 26:47–49; John 13:1–17; 2 Corinthians 5:21.

AUGUST 26
Timing

Then Jesus said to them, "My time has not yet come, but your time is always ready." (John 7:6)

THE TIMING OF when things happen can be really important. A rosebud has a set time to bloom, a bird's egg must hatch at the right moment, and a butterfly needs to emerge from the chrysalis to spread its wings. The rose bush can't bloom when winter's snow lays on the ground. If the egg is opened before the chick is ready, the baby bird will die. The chrysalis prematurely opened will not bring new life but rather destruction.

Even if things happen at the appointed time, there can still be loss. The rosebud may be ready to bloom, but if it's not given water, it will dry and shrivel before its beauty can be seen and enjoyed. The bird that hatches on time but stays in the nest will never enjoy the freedom of flight. The butterfly that pushes through the chrysalis but then just sits there in the sun will never find a mate and reproduce itself.

Jesus had an appointed time to come and give His life. His death for our sins was planned from the beginning of the world. It took place at the perfect time, enabling the gospel to spread across the globe. He didn't permit His life to be taken before that time, nor did He forgo the destruction on the cross to set up an earthly kingdom. He stayed true to His call and purpose to save us from our sins. He did all that was necessary for us to receive grace.

Jesus, the Rose of Sharon, bloomed on His appointed day, but if we don't receive His grace, the beauty is lost to us, as our hearts shrivel and dry without the living water to nourish His grace. Even if we receive His grace but then just stay self-centered, thinking only of our own salvation and nobody else, we'll never learn the amazing glory of soaring on the wind of the Spirit. If we refuse to step out to follow Him, His life won't be reproduced in us, nor will we be able to reproduce it in others.

Jesus came as a man to live and die at a specific time, but as He told His brothers, it's always our time to receive Him. It's always the right time to receive the beauty of His salvation. It's always the right time to soar, spreading His grace to those around us, and to let His character develop in us so we can reproduce it in others. Our appointed time to accept Him, live with Him, walk with Him, love with Him is always now.

Jesus, You had an appointed time to come as a man. There's also an appointed time for us to die, but You came so we could have abundant life today, and life for all eternity. We revel in Your glory and thrive on Your grace. We mess up from time to time, but we come to You to once again soar with You on the wind of the Spirit and to fulfill all You call us to do.

For further study: Psalm 95:6–8; Song of Solomon 2:1; Isaiah 40:31; 2 Corinthians 6:1–2; Hebrews 3:7–15, 9:27.

AUGUST 27
A Threefold Cord

> Though one may be overpowered by another, two can withstand him. And a threefold cord is not quickly broken. (Ecclesiastes 4:12)

LAST SUMMER I was walking part of the Camino de Santiago in Spain. I met many people on the trail, and most of the walkers carried at least one walking stick. The walking stick was really useful. Parts of the path are steep and rocky, so the stick helps keep a stumble from becoming a fall. Even on the easier parts of the trail, the stick gives that extra rhythm and stability to the walk, especially when one gets tired from the many kilometers covered over the course of the day.

Solomon wrote in Ecclesiastes that one person could be overpowered by another, but two could withstand the attacker. I think of this as us alone versus us with Jesus. Alone, we're no match for the devil and his tricks. Our sin easily overpowers us, but with Jesus in our heart, we can withstand the enemy of our soul.

Solomon then adds that a threefold cord is not quickly broken. If two strands of the cord are my love for God and His love for me, the third strand is our love for each other. Like the walking stick, our love for each other helps us support and encourage each other. Sure, I can walk really well with just God and me, but when the heat of the day and the long journey fatigues me and the road gets rocky, I can stumble and fall. The way is harder. I have less rhythm and stability. With the support of others, my walk is steadier when the road gets rough. When I hold a grudge and refuse to forgive, it's like throwing away my walking stick at the time I need it the most. My walk with God can falter and I may fall. The road isn't always easy, and our love and support for each other can make our footsteps more sure and the walk more enjoyable. The more we want to pull away from others, the more we need to find people we can draw close to who will be like a true and steady walking stick.

When we partake of communion, we pause to remind ourselves about the beautiful relationship we have with Jesus, but we're also reminded to pause and examine our relationship with the body of Christ—each other. If we've tossed away our walking stick of relationships, this is our chance to bring our failures and losses to the cross to be bathed in grace. We can start out clean and fresh once again, ready to continue on our journey.

Jesus, we're so blessed by the beautiful relationship we have with the Trinity because of You. Thank You for walking with us in this life. Help us to see where we're at fault in our relationships with Your body and to bring us all into the unity of the faith. Amen.

For further study: Leviticus 26:12–13; Ecclesiastes 4:9–12; Amos 3:3; Hebrews 12:12–15.

AUGUST 28
Surely Goodness and Mercy

How God anointed Jesus of Nazareth with the Holy Spirit and with power, who went about doing good and healing all who were oppressed by the devil, for God was with Him. (Acts 10:38)

THERE'S A JOKE about a young boy who was determined to walk to school without his mother accompanying him. His mother was worried, so she asked a neighbor who often walked with her daughter in the mornings to discretely follow the boy and make sure he got to school safely.

One day on the way to school, the boy was walking with a classmate who asked, "Who is that lady always following you to school?"

The young lad quickly answered, "That's Shirley Goodness and her daughter Mercy. The Bible says they will follow me wherever I go."

Psalm 23 was written by David, who was at one time a shepherd to a flock of sheep. This psalm compares the Lord to a good shepherd carefully watching over and providing for His human sheep. The final verse says, *"Surely goodness and mercy shall follow me all the days of my life; and I will dwell in the house of the Lord forever"* (v. 6). The whole psalm is about God's tender loving care for me. When I come to that final verse, I think of how the Lord's goodness and mercy bless me every day in every way. I realized recently that this last line could also be thought of in a different way. Because I'm part of the Lord's flock, I should leave a trail of goodness and mercy for others wherever I go.

Jesus went about doing good because God was with Him. God is with me, so do I also go about doing good? When I leave work, or the grocery store, or the neighbor's house, or church, have I left behind memories of the goodness of God? If I'm honest with myself, I'm aware that this isn't always the case. Often my fatigue, anger, or outright peevishness leave harsh words that hang in the air and follow me, rather than reflecting the loving nature of God.

Only by keeping a steady reminder of the goodness of God dwelling within me do I have any chance of that same goodness following me as I go about my day. This is what communion is all about. It's a sure and faithful reminder of the goodness and mercy we've received so that we can express that same goodness and mercy to others. It's also a chance to bring our failures to the foot of the cross to find healing and mercy for our souls.

> *Lord, forgive us for the times we mess up, letting our hurt and anger follow us around instead of letting Your goodness and mercy fill us and follow us. Thank You for loving us and being the Good Shepherd who laid His life down for the sheep. We are truly blessed. Amen.*

For further study: Psalm 23:1–6, 37:3–8; John 10:1–18; Colossians 3:12–17.

AUGUST 29
Little Foxes

These things I have spoken to you, that in Me you may have peace. In the world you will have tribulation; but be of good cheer, I have overcome the world. (John 16:33)

I WAS AT church today, and it seemed like everyone in the congregation was struggling in one form or another. One lady had lost a dear relative. Another was going for surgery; one was ill, and another had financial troubles. I also felt like I was under attack—literally! I'd been bit by three different species of animal in that one week. Little problems may not be a big deal in themselves, but when a bunch of little problems mount up, it can feel like the whole world has come against you.

Solomon wrote in the Song of Solomon that the little foxes can spoil the vine. It doesn't always take a big storm to cause a crop failure. One of the bites I received, although minor, became infected, and the condition could have been serious if that small wound was neglected. The grieving woman needed support from the body of Christ; the sick needed our prayers as well as appropriate medical attention. The body of Christ needed to come together to deal with all those little foxes that would spoil the fruit of the Spirit in the hearts of the people.

Jesus knew all too well how injuries can become compounded. The Pharisees mocking Him would have hurt. The blows of men's fists and the plucking of His beard caused pain physically and emotionally. The cruel strokes of the whip, each one by itself not enough to kill Him, but taken together enough to wound Him so badly He was no longer recognizable. Jesus knows what it's like for His body to feel one blow after another.

Sometimes when we face little difficulties, we tend to ignore them. We feel that they're too insignificant to bring to the body of Christ for prayer; they aren't enough of a concern to bring to the foot of the cross. If we let this little difficulty, this little fox, chew away at our heart, the fruit of the Spirit in us becomes damaged. Our love, kindness, longsuffering, peace, and joy can be eroded and weakened until the whole crop fails. The crop insurance lies in bringing all our hurts and wounds to the foot of the cross and to each other. Christ knows more than we can ever understand just how each blow to our heart wounds us, yet He reminds us that He has overcome the world. Our peace rests in His loving sacrifice. We all stand together at the foot of the cross, supporting each other in our trials. This is the beauty of communion—communion with Jesus and with each other as His body.

Jesus, You understand how each wound hurts, no matter how big or small the injury. We bring all our cares, worries, heartaches, and physical and emotional pain to You. Our trouble in this world is temporary; our life with You, eternal. Thank You for reaching out to us, helping us, healing us, and giving us peace no matter what our circumstance. Amen.

For further study: Song of Solomon 2:15; Isaiah 50:6, 52:13–53:12; Matthew 27:27–32; Romans 8:35–39; 2 Corinthians 4:8–18; Galatians 5:22–6:2; Colossians 1:24–29.

AUGUST 30
Love and Be Loved

My beloved is mine, and I am his. He feeds his flock among the lilies. (Song of Solomon 2:16)

HAVE YOU EVER asked that age-old question: "Why am I here?" This is a really deep question. People often wonder if they have a purpose, a reason for being. I believe we remain on this fallen world for three reasons: to learn to love others, to learn to love ourselves, and to learn to receive love. All of these can be a challenge. It can be hard to love the unkind and broken people around us. It can be even more difficult to love ourselves. We know all our own failures. Our own flaws glare back at us when we look in the mirror. Even more difficult is to let ourselves be loved. After all, to love and be loved opens us up to being hurt. We have to let ourselves become vulnerable and trust that people will respond to our love and not reject us. We have to hope and trust they won't let us down. There's no greater pain than being wounded by the one you thought loved you like you loved them.

Jesus understood this really well. He was equal with God and was God, yet He let Himself become vulnerable. He gave up His omnipotence to become a man. He trusted those closest to Him, even though He knew that one of His friends would be His betrayer and all the others would run away at the time of His greatest need. He came knowing that the religious leaders who should have welcomed Him would arrest Him and surrender Him to be beaten, abused, mocked, and crucified. He did this knowing that the people He did it for—you and me—might reject His love and turn away. Jesus knows just how painful it is to love. He also knows the beauty and wonder of love received and returned. Jesus was willing to pay the price for our sins so we would join Him in glory as His bride. The glory of God shines forth in all its splendor because of love given, love received, and love returned.

Loving and letting ourselves be loved is scary. If we're honest with ourselves, most of us could say we feel like God has let us down at times. Our head knows it's not true, but our heart sometimes listens to lies. If a perfect God can let us down, how much more likely are our friends and family to fail us? Loving others might mean your love is rejected, just like some reject the love Jesus gives to us all. Letting ourselves be loved means being vulnerable and at risk of deep wounds to our heart, just like Jesus was wounded by those who should have recognized His sacrificial love. Loving and being loved carries a very high price, but the cost is worth it. Loving and letting ourselves be loved reveals the glory of God in all its splendor.

> *Jesus, You have shown the amazing depth of Your love for us. You've called us Your bride, Your beloved. Let Your glory be revealed in the love You have given us and Your love that flows out of us. Amen.*

For further study: Matthew 26:20–25, 30–35; Mark 14:27; Philippians 2:5–10; Revelation 21:9–27.

AUGUST 31
Blowing Fuses

> Let all bitterness, wrath, anger, clamor, and evil speaking be put away from you, with all malice. And be kind to one another, forgiving one another, even as God in Christ forgave you.
> (Ephesians 4:31–32)

MY PLACE OF work is moving to a new custom-built location. There will be a lot of great things about the new building, but one of the things I'm really looking forward to is that we'll be able to use the kettle and the microwave at the same time. Every time we do that in our current location, we blow a fuse—or more accurately, trip the breaker. At least the breakers are easy to reset.

I used to rent a home where every time I used the kettle and toaster at the same time, I'd blow a fuse—a real old-fashioned fuse. I'd have to go downstairs, unscrew the old one, which was now garbage, and replace it with a brand-new one bought from the hardware store. It was the price I had to pay for overloading the circuits and causing the connection to the source of power to be lost.

We still sometimes talk about people blowing their fuse. In other words, they get so overwhelmed and emotional that they blow their top, ranting and raving and generally carrying on in anger. They've lost their connection to the source of real power, the power to love.

In the book of Ephesians, Paul talks about putting away our old nature with its wrath and evil speaking and putting on a new forgiving and loving nature, just like God. This may be easier said than done at times. Life can seriously overload our circuits. Situations and circumstances can be overwhelming. It may only take one more small demand to cause us to blow a fuse. One of the ways we can combat the old nature is to take a few moments to quietly reflect on the love and forgiveness bestowed on us through Jesus Christ and His sacrifice for us on the cross. To pause and give thanks for all He has done can keep the connection to the source of love and power strong and stable. If we've blown a fuse emotionally, bringing our failure to the foot of the cross is also the way we reset the breaker and re-establish the connection. Let's take a moment to do that right now.

> *Jesus, we remember Your sacrifice. We're awestruck by the depth of love poured out on us. Forgive us once again for our failures to walk in that love, and keep our connection to You open and strong. Teach us to recognize when we're getting overloaded, and help us to take the time to focus on all You've done and who You are. Amen.*

For further study: Proverbs 19:11; Ephesians 4:17–5:4; James 1:19–22.

SEPTEMBER 1

Family

God sets the solitary in families; he brings out those who are bound into prosperity; but the rebellious dwell in a dry land. (Psalm 68:6)

WHEN I FIRST moved across the country away from all my friends and family, I really struggled with loneliness, but a couple of families really helped me adjust. Whenever I was bored or lonely, I'd go to them and join in with whatever they were doing that day. It might be household chores or a board game, but those families welcomed me into their homes. Their presence encouraged me and helped me to get settled in this new place.

The word "family" refers to parents and their children certainly, but it also means all those related by blood or being similar in kind. All people trace their lineage back to Adam and Eve, so all are blood relatives—one big family. Also, all Christians are related in kind. We have the same head and are all part of the body of Christ—one close family. The church provided me with people who would become as close as family members, people who would help get me through the rough spots.

I like to think of a herd of muskox. When they're threatened by a predator, the stronger members of the herd form a circle around the weaker ones. The strong ones face outward to danger, while the young are protected in the center. Sometimes we're so weak we need to be in the center of the circle, protected by our church family. Sometimes we have to take our place in the outer ring, guarding the herd. At other times, we feel weak, but in taking our place in the outer circle, we're brought back to a place of strength as we're energized by the fulfillment of our purpose.

When Jesus passed through Samaria, He stopped to rest at a well. Tired, hungry, and thirsty, He stayed put while His disciples went to buy food. While Jesus was waiting, He ended up talking to a woman about Himself, the Living Water. That conversation would minister to the woman and as a result bring her into the family of God. This would affect many others from the village as well, bringing them hope and salvation. When the disciples got back with food and water, Jesus was no longer hungry, tired, or thirsty. By ministering to others, He was strengthened Himself.

God has placed us in families—not just our natural family of parents and siblings, but in the family of God and the family of humanity. Within those families, sometimes we're the strong one and the protector, sometimes we're the one in need of help and protection, and sometimes by taking our place in helping others, we find ourselves helped in the process.

Jesus, by Your sacrifice on the cross You have united us all by Your blood into one family. Bring us into relationships one with another that we might each be encouraged and strengthened for the task You have for us. Amen.

For further study: John 4:1–42; Acts 17:24–28; 1 Corinthians 12:12–26; Ephesians 3:14–21.

SEPTEMBER 2
Ain't God Alive

And He is the head of the body, the church, who is the beginning, the firstborn from the dead, that in all things He may have the preeminence. (Colossians 1:18)

SOJOURNER TRUTH WAS a woman in the 1800s who fought for the abolition of slavery and for women's rights. In a famous speech, she said, "Ain't I a woman." There's some question if these were the exact words, because although she was born into slavery, her first language was Dutch. Nevertheless, that phrase is captivating and serves as a good tool to help people remember her speech for women's rights. She went around preaching and speaking and also shared the podium with other great abolitionists. One of those was Frederick Douglass. After one of his speeches encouraging people to fight slavery with violence, Sojourner Truth said to him, "Is God dead?" It was a reminder that violence wasn't necessary and that their fight against slavery wouldn't rely only on the works of people. "Is God dead?" was even put on Sojourner's tombstone.

When I first heard about Sojourner Truth, in my head I didn't hear "Is God dead?" but rather the same thing said another way: "Ain't God alive?" That sentence now jumps into my spirit. There's much wrong in this fallen world. Slaves may have been set free, but people of color are still oppressed in many ways. Women are still often paid less than men and have to work harder to prove themselves. People feel hopeless. Many die from drug overdoses. Some steal from others. People cheat on others. Relationships are struggling. Many are broken and lost. But we are not without hope, because ain't God alive!

God lives. He brings light to the darkness. He reaches out to the lost and lonely. He's in us to guide us. His love reigns in our hearts. He leads us in paths of righteousness and teaches us to forgive as we have been forgiven. Even if our circumstances are unchanged, we know the amazing change He has done in our hearts. We've felt the freedom that comes from the forgiveness of our sins. We can rejoice that our names are written in the Book of Life. All eternity awaits us with joy and anticipation. Our situation is never hopeless, because ain't God alive!

The irony, of course, is that God came to die in our place so we could live for eternity. Thankfully, the grave couldn't hold the living God, so He rose again, the firstborn from the dead, able to conquer the death that reigned in us all through sin. We serve a living and powerful God. We rejoice because "Ain't God alive!"

Jesus, You died for us and conquered death so we might live. We give You thanks and rejoice that You indeed live. Our God is alive and powerful. Nothing is impossible for You. Amen.

For further study: Psalm 23:3; Luke 10:20; John 11:25, 16:13; Acts 2:22–36; Ephesians 2:4–6; Revelation 1:18.

SEPTEMBER 3
Run Your Race

> Therefore we also, since we are surrounded by so great a cloud of witnesses, let us lay aside every weight, and the sin which so easily ensnares us, and let us run with endurance the race that is set before us. (Hebrews 12:1)

I HAVE A friend who runs marathons. She's trained for many years and is leaner and fitter than I'll ever be. Our city hosts a marathon annually, and I always mark the date on my calendar—not to participate but so that I take an alternate route to church instead of getting stuck in traffic waiting for the runners to cross the road.

There's always an amazing variety of people who run. I've seen some pushing strollers, some walking and chatting, and some running all out. Along the way are support crews. Every few blocks there's someone manning a table with glasses of water to hand out. There are people directing and stopping traffic as needed. Cones, pylons, and signs mark the route so the runners don't go off course. I applaud the participants. They show determination to complete their race at whatever pace they're moving at.

God has set our own race before each of us. My route may not be the same as yours. My challenges will be different, as will my successes. Some days I struggle to put one foot in front of the other in my walk of grace. Other times grace empowers me to run with speed. Nevertheless, my goal is to finish my race. Until I cross that finish line, I'm going to need a support crew. I need the people reminding me to take a drink of the Living Water. Others come along to direct traffic and mark out the route so I don't go off course. You need those people too as you run your own race. All of us also need that crowd standing by, watching us race and cheering us on so we don't quit when the way gets hard. Sometimes our race puts us in the position to be the support crew for other people running their race. We're participants in the race and also those standing on the sidelines cheering on others who are running their own race. The writer of Hebrews wrote that all the great people of faith who have gone before us are cheering us on, helping us run our own race.

One of the greatest acts of faith we can do is to encourage someone else when we're struggling with the aches and pains of our own race. Encouraging others gives us new energy as grace flows between us. We have Jesus as our example. He ran His race, which led to the cross. Even while fighting for each breath, He spoke to the man on the cross beside Him, welcoming him to paradise. Even when broken and bruised, His blood flowing down the cross, grace was encouraging others and flowing out freely to all who would receive Him.

> *Lord, we thank You for all You've done. Help us now to run the race You've set before us. Give us strength to help and encourage others along the way. Amen.*

For further study: Proverbs 11:25; Matthew 10:38–42; Luke 23:39–43; John 1:12–17; 1 Corinthians 9:24–27; Hebrews 12:1–3.

SEPTEMBER 4

Goodbye

Therefore you now have sorrow; but I will see you again and your heart will rejoice, and your joy no one will take from you. (John 16:22)

MANY DECADES AGO, I moved far away from my family as I followed where God was leading. At least once a year, I'd take a trip home to visit with everyone I'd left behind. Often when the day came for me to leave them and return to my own city, I'd end up in a fight with my family. After a few years of this, I realized I was picking a fight because I didn't like saying goodbye. I was hoping it would make leaving easier. Of course, it didn't make it easier at all. I think it would have helped had I known then the origin of the word "goodbye." The word is a contraction of "God be with you," which is a prayer saying that even though we're apart, we're united in the Lord and He will be with you. It's a blessing.

At times in our lives, we have to say goodbye, either to friends and family, but also to people who are a bad influence on us. David certainly experienced this. He had to run away from Saul in order to save his life. David's best friend was Saul's son Jonathan. When they parted, they wept and pledged their friendship to each other and each other's descendants. It was a true "God be with you" goodbye.

As David hid from Saul, there were occasions when he had opportunity to kill Saul, but David was an honorable man and refused to harm Saul. When Saul realized David had restrained his hand from murder, he called to David and apologized for the harm he himself had intended to do to David. He asked David to return and take his place in the kingdom. David was wise enough to realize Saul's remorse would only be temporary, so he said goodbye. David did not return to Israel until after Saul had died in battle with the Philistines.

Just before Jesus was crucified, He also paused to speak to His disciples and say goodbye. He told them He had to depart for now but it was a good thing. Their separation would be only for a little while. Because Jesus was going to say goodbye for now with His death on the cross, the Holy Spirit would then be able to come and dwell within them, and in us. For now, there would be sorrow, but afterward, there would be unending joy. This is what we remember as we pause to take communion. We're reminded that He died for us to enable God to be with us. We're also reminded that with God in us, we can speak and be a blessing to those around us, even when we have to say goodbye for the time being.

Jesus, thank You for blessing us, for enabling us to have the Holy Spirit within us, reminding us of the love of God that dwells in us. Help us to bless everyone around us and seek to say "God be with you," even when we must say goodbye. Amen.

For further study: 1 Samuel 20:1–42, 24:1–22, 26:1–25; John 16:5–7, 16–24.

SEPTEMBER 5
The Mystery

> Now we have received, not the spirit of the world, but the Spirit who is from God, that we might know the things that have been freely given to us by God. (1 Corinthians 2:12)

I OFTEN HEAR people quote 1 Corinthians 2:9— *"Eye has not seen, nor ear heard, nor have entered into the heart of man the things which God has prepared for those who love Him."* They quote that verse to highlight that God has mysterious ways that we can't fully comprehend. If one reads on, however, the next verse says, *"But God has revealed them to us through His Spirit"* (v. 10a). This doesn't mean that we can't understand what God has for us, but rather the opposite. He has revealed it to us through His Spirit.

No one truly knows what's in the heart of a person except the spirit of that person; likewise, God's Spirit knows God's heart. The key to understanding this passage is knowing that God's Spirit resides in us because of the work of the cross. The mystery that eye has not seen and ear has not heard is the amazing grace that sees God become a man and die for us to redeem us from sin and death. The incredible love God has for humanity is a mystery, but it's a mystery revealed to us through the cross.

Because of God's Spirit in us, the gift of salvation is revealed to us. Paul goes on to admonish the Corinthian church that because this grace had been revealed to them, they should not be living carnal lives full of division and jealousies. Because God's Spirit is in us, revealing grace to us, He can also reveal that grace through us to those around us.

The Bible says that angels long to understand this mystery of God's love but are unable to fully comprehend it. People who are not yet saved can't really understand the depth of God's love. I was reading about Corrie Ten Boom witnessing to an SS lieutenant, Hans Rahms. He had trouble understanding how God could love the infirm, the broken, and ultimately those who had done great evil, himself included. Without God's Spirit, it's difficult to understand God's love for the unlovely. Corrie's witness influenced this man greatly. She let God's Spirit shine through her to try to reach this broken sinner.

This is the essence of communion. It's the reminder that God is in us and with us and to let that grace shine through us. We need reminders. It's easy to fall back into the natural world, forgetting the spiritual world we now live in. Let's pause to remember this amazing mystery, the love of God.

> *Jesus, we're so amazed by Your love and sacrifice. It's hard for people to understand how You could love us so much to come as a man and die for sinners. We're so grateful for the Holy Spirit within us, revealing to us the mystery of this amazing grace. Amen.*

For further study: Romans 5:8, 16:25–27; 1 Corinthians 2:2–3:3; 1 Peter 1:10–13.

SEPTEMBER 6

Tune In

> Beloved, now we are children of God; and it has not yet been revealed what we shall be, but we know that when He is revealed, we shall be like Him, for we shall see Him as He is. And everyone who has this hope in Him purifies himself, just as He is pure. (1 John 3:2–3)

I'M DRIVING A rental car right now, and since I'm not used to this car, I find myself constantly hitting the radio tuning button by accident. This causes the radio frequency to move just a few points away, but it's enough to lose the signal from my favorite Christian station, leaving me with static until I can reset it.

A lot of things can interfere with a radio signal. When I was a child, we had a TV that had a "rabbit ear" antenna. If my mom ran the electric mixer, we'd get static on the TV, as it bounced around at about the same sound and frequency as the mixer. If one of us kids went to adjust the antenna, our body would extend the antenna's range and improve the signal, so the other kids would shout for us to stay there holding the antenna. The consistency of the picture improved a lot after we got cable.

Our Christian life can be a bit like my radio or those old TVs. God is sending out His signals of love and forgiveness, but my tuner needs adjustment. Maybe I've been knocked a bit off the signal as I go about my day. Perhaps all the worldly frequencies around me start to crowd in and muddle God's signal. The mountains in our path may block the signal, or life's storms may strike us, knocking out our ability to receive His love. Of course, others around us may reach out to the antenna, extending the signal and helping to clarify God's message. His message has been sent clearly, but our receivers sometimes need a little help or adjustment.

One of the ways we can tune in to His message is by pausing to partake of communion. As we remind ourselves of Jesus's death and resurrection, we tune in to the very proof and expression of His love. It's also a time to come to Him to confess the sins and failures of the day, when we let the world push in on us. By examining ourselves and confessing our sins, we come to the foot of the cross to receive forgiveness. Our receiver of His love gets re-adjusted and back in tune with His Word. With the reminder of all He's done for us, we can also be a voice of clarity and truth to others, to help them better receive the signal of God's grace and mercy.

> *Jesus, we thank You for Your love. Help us to hear You clearly and to proclaim Your amazing grace to all around us, that they might see You clearly. Amen.*

For further study: Luke 22:19–20; 1 Corinthians 13:9–13; 1 John 1:8–2:2, 3:1–3.

SEPTEMBER 7
What Do You Have in Your House?

So Elisha said to her, "What shall I do for you? Tell me, what do you have in the house?" And she said, "Your maidservant has nothing in the house but a jar of oil." (2 Kings 4:2)

ELISHA, A PROPHET in the Old Testament, was approached one day by a widow in dire straits. Her husband had died and they owed people money. Her sons were going to be sold into slavery to pay the debt. Elisha didn't organize a fundraiser or give her a donation; instead, he asked her what she had in her house. She said all she had was one little bottle of oil. Elisha told her to borrow as many containers as she could and then use that small bottle of oil to fill the others. As the woman did this, the oil miraculously multiplied to fill all the containers she had borrowed. Elisha then told her to sell the oil, pay their bills, and live off the rest of the money.

This widow didn't need a handout. She needed a miracle. God used what she already had to work that miracle. Certainly, He used the support of her neighbors, who loaned her containers to make it all possible, but the main component was something she already possessed, mixed with her faith that the words of the man of God were true.

At one time we were slaves to sin, sold to Satan, to pay the debt of our failures, but someone preached to us Christ crucified. We grasped how He paid the debt for our sin and set us free. The Holy Spirit took up residence in us and we rejoiced. Life was good. Perhaps since then, struggles have come from the circumstances of life. There may be times when we feel stretched so thin there's nothing left. Our emotions are bankrupt. Perhaps we struggle with a recurring sin debt threatening to sell us back into slavery to the world. We feel destitute and without hope.

Then along comes someone to remind us that we're not destitute but have a treasure in the house. We have the oil of the Holy Spirit, who flows freely in our lives. He fills our container and can spill over into our neighbors' containers. We're reminded that our debts are paid in full and there is more than enough to live on. Sometimes we just need a reminder of all we possess. Communion is just that reminder. We remember that we've been redeemed from sin and death. The Holy Spirit resides in us and is sufficient to spill out from us to all around us, regardless of our circumstances.

> *Lord, we're so very blessed. We're forgiven and full of Your grace. We have more than enough grace to meet our needs for today and for tomorrow. Thank You. Amen.*

For further study: 2 Kings 4:1–7; Romans 8:9–11; 1 Corinthians 1:23–24; Ephesians 1:7–12.

SEPTEMBER 8

Interdependency

> As each one has received a gift, minister it to one another, as good stewards of the manifold grace of God. (1 Peter 4:10)

THERE'S A LOT of talk these days about reconciliation from colonialism. Colonialism is the practice of one group obtaining control over another group and exploiting them for economic or political purposes. It's been rampant in the past, and there are still many examples of colonialism today. As we hear about what occurred in the past, such as the Indigenous children being abused in residential schools, we are horrified and think that we'd never do that. The Pharisees said much the same thing. They said they wouldn't have killed the prophets of old, yet they went on to crucify the Lord of Glory.

As long as there are situations in which someone believes they're better than another, colonialism reigns. When we help out at the soup kitchen with the attitude that the clients need our service and our pity but not our respect, we're in danger of renewing colonialism. As the body of Christ, we're interdependent on one another. Paul says that there are parts of the body with honor and parts with less honor, but all have a purpose and value. If one hurts, all hurt. If one is blessed, all are blessed. I have a gift or ability to give to you, but you also have something that I need. The healing of my soul is tied up in the healing of your soul. Our relationship with others needs to be based on mutual respect.

In Paul's letter to the Romans, he discusses a situation in which some Christians believe eating food offered to idols doesn't matter, but other Christians feel this would be a sin. However, if someone entices them to eat this food, they'd be causing them to sin, as they wouldn't be eating it in faith. He says, *"Do not destroy with your food the one for whom Christ died"* (Romans 14:15b). I think we can expand this to say, "Do not destroy with your attitude of superiority the one for whom Christ died." Or do not destroy with your pity, your money, or any other thing in which you feel superior to others. This is the essence of communion, just as Paul wrote to the Corinthians. We partake of communion to remember Christ's death and the love we've received, and to examine ourselves to see where we're not walking in love with each other. If we realize we are at fault in some area, the good news is we can bring it to the cross and once again be forgiven and cleansed.

> *Jesus, forgive us for any area where we've treated others like we are their colonial masters instead of with mutual respect. We also forgive any who have "lorded" it over us, just as You have forgiven us our sins. Thank You for Your body and blood demonstrating Your great love. Help us to walk in that same love for one another. Amen.*

For further study: Matthew 23:29–31; Luke 23:13–25; Romans 12:3–16, 14:1–15:7; 1 Corinthians 11:17–34, 12:1–31; 1 Peter 4:8–11.

SEPTEMBER 9
Don't Just Do Something, Stand There

Come to Me, all you who labor and are heavy laden, and I will give you rest. (Matthew 11:28)

AS A VETERINARIAN, some days can be pretty stressful. Animals can be brought in with serious illnesses that may be a challenge to diagnose. There's strong pressure to do something, anything. Sometimes people say, "Don't just stand there, do something!" When I was in college, however, we had a professor who used to turn that phrase on its head. He'd say, "Don't just do something, stand there!" to remind us to pause and look at the whole situation. It was a reminder to take a deep breath and compose our thoughts so that our actions would be helpful and not just some knee-jerk reaction to the pressure.

At times life can pour on the pressure. As I'm racing around getting the animals settled and the chores done, trying to get ready for work, I also have to put dishes away, catch up on laundry, and do a thousand other things, all while behaving like a good Christian. I hear words in my head like a train: *Gotta be, gotta do, gotta be, gotta do, gotta be, gotta do*. That train seems to steadily gain speed as it pushes me to not just stand there but do something. God, however, whispers on the wind, reminding me at times to pull the brake cord on the train before it gets derailed. He reminds me to pause and look around to take in the whole situation. He says to take a moment to smell the flowers, to hear the birds chirp their happy song, to touch my loved ones, to look at the sun rising over the hill, to pause and breathe in the glory of God. We can taste and see that the Lord is good.

All our actions have to flow out of the love birthed in us by Jesus's sacrifice on the cross. If we try to be a good Christian and do good works without that foundation, we're doomed to fail. That high-speed train pushing us to perform is sure to get derailed as we start to resent all the demands on us. Keeping the train on the rails comes by taking a moment to stand there and remind ourselves of the glory and grace of God flowing in us and through us. It's a breath of fresh air to our weary souls.

Jesus, thank You for Your grace. You've given rest for our souls. We pause now to remember Your glory. We thank You for Your beauty and Your love that surrounds us, fills us, and empowers us. Amen.

For further study: Psalm 19:1–6, 34:8; Matthew 11:28–30; Hebrews 10:19–24.

SEPTEMBER 10

Belonging

> And when he comes home, he calls together his friends and neighbors, saying to them, "Rejoice with me, for I have found my sheep which was lost!" (Luke 15:6)

JOHN SWINTON WROTE about how the church relates to disabled individuals. He differentiated inclusion versus belonging. Inclusion means you have a right to be there. In other words, you're allowed to come in and there's a place for you to sit; people may or may not greet you. This is not the same as belonging. When someone belongs to a place, they're missed when they're absent, and others go looking for them. There's a world of difference between being included and belonging.

Jesus made the way for us to be included in the kingdom of heaven, but more than that, He made it so we can belong to heaven. In the parable of the lost sheep, Jesus described how the Good Shepherd notices when even one of His sheep strays, and He goes looking for it. He rejoices and tells everyone to rejoice with Him when He finds the little lost lamb. In the next parable, He spoke of a woman who has ten coins but loses one. She searches diligently for the one she lost, and when she finds it, she calls everyone to rejoice with her. This is the essence of belonging. We are missed if we stray, and we are sought after so that the relationship may be restored.

Sometimes when we don't know how to relate to people, we exclude them. At other times, we're unsure of how to help people feel like they belong, so we default to just letting them be included. We think that we've done something good because they weren't excluded. All of us have been on the full spectrum, from feeling excluded to being included only, or to belonging. We've also been on both sides of that coin, from being the one who feels like they don't belong, to the one who makes others feel like they don't belong. God, however, has proclaimed that we are the body of Christ. We belong to Him and to one another. God has His millions of sheep, and He diligently seeks after every one, but we also have our circle of people, all with value to us, whom we can seek after so they feel like they belong.

As we partake of communion, we give thanks that Jesus has made the way for us to belong to the heavenly kingdom. We also pause to examine ourselves. How have we treated those around us? Have we only included people, or have we helped them to know they belong to the body of Christ? If we haven't done our best, we can come to the foot of the cross to find forgiveness and also strength to reflect the beauty of His grace to all around us.

> *Jesus, we're so blessed and honored that You've made the way for us to belong. There's nothing greater than belonging to Your family. Help us reach out to those around us with Your love as we have received that love from You. Amen.*

For further study: Luke 15:1–10; Ephesians 1:2–6.

SEPTEMBER 11
What If?

Pure and undefiled religion before God and the Father is this: to visit orphans and widows in their trouble, and to keep oneself unspotted from the world. (James 1:27)

HAVE YOU EVER wondered what life might be like if Jesus hadn't come to the earth as a man to pay the price for our sins? Wherever Christianity has gained a foothold in the world, the culture has been impacted for the good. Christians established the first hospitals and universities. They look after the elderly and the poor. Widows and orphans have found food and shelter. Literacy has been promoted, and women raised up from oppression. Slavery was opposed. Good laws were established based on Christian principles. This came about because Christians recognize the value and dignity of all people, from the womb to the grave.

God sent His Son to the world, for the world. The Christian recognizes that as God has laid down His life for us, so we should lay ours down for each other. Sharon James in her book *How Christianity Transformed the World* quotes Basil, the Bishop of Caesarea, admonishing the rich to care for others: "The bread in your board belongs to the hungry; the cloak in your wardrobe to the naked; the shoes you let rot to the barefoot, the money in your vault to the destitute."[3]

What if Jesus hadn't come? What would the world be like? We've seen the effects where Christ hasn't been honored: Life is devalued. Some are considered to be of more worth than others. From the unborn to the elderly, to women, the disabled, or lower castes, people can be seen to lack worth and so can be disposed of. It was seen in the Holocaust and in acts of terrorism. It's seen in hopelessness and suicide. Without Christ, people who are devalued are denied education or advancement. Without Christ, people traffic drugs, or they may even traffic other people, since it doesn't matter the harm caused as long as the trafficker makes money. The Christian is rightly horrified by the acts of cruelty and violence that occur around the world. We understand that people are valuable because we've seen how valued we are in the eyes of God.

We have enough value that God was willing to sacrifice His only Son to save us from our sins. We have enough value that the precious blood of Christ was poured out on the ground to redeem us from a life without God. We have a value beyond measure. Knowing how valuable we are to God enables us to value those around us.

> *Heavenly Father, we're so blessed and valuable in Your eyes. Thank You for loving us enough to send Your Son to set us free. Birth a deeper love for others inside us so that we might reflect Your glory to all. Amen.*

For further study: Matthew 10:29–31; John 3:16; 1 John 3:16.

---

[3] Basil of Caesarea, as quoted in Sharon James, *How Christianity Transformed the World* (UK: Christian Focus 2021), 130.

SEPTEMBER 12
I Want More

> For I consider that the sufferings of this present time are not worthy to be compared with the glory which shall be revealed in us. (Romans 8:18)

IF I'M HONEST with myself, there are a lot of things I desire and want. Some things are frivolous, mere icing on the cake, and others are much more important. I'd like to replace some old furniture and renovate my bathroom. I'd like to read all the books on my shelf. I want to go to Australia at some point in my life. I want to lose twenty pounds and be stronger. I want my aging body to not have aches and pains. I want my friends and family diagnosed with cancer to be healed. I want my friend suffering from depression to find joy. I want the weather to be nice when I'm out walking. I want all the sermons at church to be vibrant and inspiring. I want so many things, but I also really want so much more.

More than having a nice house, I want my home to be full of the love of God. More than having a healthy body, I want to have a healthy relationship with Jesus. More than reading words, I want His Word deep in my soul. More than traveling around the world, I want Jesus visible in my life everywhere I go. More than physical healing for my friends and family, I so want them to know the Healer. More than joy for my friend with mental illness, I want her to know the Giver of Joy. More than a sunny day, I want the Son shining strong in me. More than a good church service, I want the pastor and congregation to have a vibrant relationship with the Savior of their souls. I want so much more than a good life; I want the Giver of Life.

It's easy to get distracted from what really matters, wondering when or if our desires in this world will be fulfilled. It's easy to focus on the things we don't have and lose sight of the One we will always have. Jesus said if we would seek after His kingdom, all the other things we need in life would be fulfilled. When our eyes stray and we lament not having all we want, we need to refocus on the cross and remind ourselves of all we have. As we seek that deeper relationship with Him, all the other things in life fade in significance. He will give us more than we could ever ask for.

> *Jesus, we want to know the depth of Your love. Increase our knowledge of Your great love so that we will walk in it. Reveal Your glory in us. Amen.*

For further study: Matthew 6:19–34; Romans 8:15–39; Ephesians 3:14–21.

SEPTEMBER 13
Betraying His Grace

And whenever you stand praying, if you have anything against anyone, forgive him, that your Father in heaven may also forgive your trespasses. (Mark 11:25)

IT'S FUNNY SOMETIMES the things God will bring into your mind when you're driving along, especially after you've had a challenging day. Sometimes when a vet is on call, we encounter people who aren't very nice. I had a call like that late last evening. One of the owners of the dog was nice, but the other was angry and ranting. He said some not very nice things and made some nasty accusations. I know he's just upset and in denial about his elderly dog's serious illness, but it still stings. I was having trouble keeping my temper in check. It didn't help that after authorizing the tests and therapies, it turned out he had no finances to pay for the procedures that had been done. The vet clinic is still a business, and this business was going to be out a substantial sum needed to pay staff and to finance those very procedures. As I drove home, I was more than a little ticked off.

As it also turns out, I'm currently reading a famous work called the *Inferno*. Dante, an Italian poet, wrote about how he imagined a trip through hell. He imagined nine circles, each successive ring getting closer to where Satan resides, and each circle documenting more serious sins. The Holy Spirit nudged my spirit to consider what Dante envisioned as the worst sin in his innermost circle. This circle is reserved for those who betray their benefactor. Judas Iscariot resides there, having betrayed the one who would be his Savior.

As I thought on all these things, I felt that my anger was justified. This client had been rude, disrespectful, and dishonest. He most certainly is not my benefactor. Then I felt the Holy Spirit whisper in my soul. Was I not betraying the grace I had received by refusing to forgive? Have I not benefited so tremendously from grace, yet I break faith with that grace by harboring such a grudge? This man had wronged me. In fact, there will be more struggles in the future as collection agencies or courts get involved. Holding people to account for their word, however, need not stop me from forgiving that same person. The two are not mutually exclusive. Loving someone also means wanting them to become more than they are. Encouraging this fellow to be a man of honor who keeps his word is a good thing and can be done with grace instead of anger. In my dealings with those who are difficult, I need to remain loyal to the grace I have received through Jesus Christ. Freely I have received of His grace, freely I need to give it.

Thank You, Jesus, for the grace You have poured out on us. We pause to remember that we have been forgiven and You enable us to walk in grace and forgiveness to others. Bless those who have harmed us, and lead us in Your footsteps. Amen.

For further study: Matthew 10:8; Ephesians 2:4–8, 4:30–32; Hebrews 10:19–24.

SEPTEMBER 14
Going Out of Your Way

Then the Spirit said to Philip, "Go near and overtake this chariot." (Acts 8:29)

SOME TIME AGO, I heard someone say that Jesus never went out of His way to help someone. My first thought was *Wait, what? That can't be right.* Jesus went to Samaria to speak to the woman at the well even though it wasn't on His way. Even though Jesus was being hurried along by Jairus to help his dying daughter, Jesus paused to speak to and help a woman who'd been bleeding for twelve years. The person who said Jesus never went out of His way to help people then explained that helping people was never out of Jesus's way.

I'm sure Philip had other things to do when an angel called to him and told him to go on the desert road from Jerusalem to Gaza. He must have wondered why he had to go out of his way to the road leading to Egypt. When Philip saw a chariot with an Ethiopian eunuch in it, the Spirit told Philip to join himself to the chariot. The man in the chariot was a high official of the Queen of Ethiopia, and he was trying to understand the book of Isaiah. The Ethiopian invited Philip to ride with him in the chariot and they discussed the Scriptures. Philip used that as the starting point to share about the Savior, Jesus Christ. The eunuch ended up committing his life to Jesus. By obeying the call to go on the road to Gaza, Philip was in a position to be used by God in a powerful way.

How many times have I noticed someone as I went along who looked like they needed prayer or an encouraging word, but I walked away, not willing to go out of my way to share the love of Jesus? It's so easy to turn away and pretend not to see the "chariots" in our path. It's easy to ignore the call to put aside our own agenda to follow God's agenda. If we understood that following God's agenda is never out of our way, we might reconsider taking that brief moment to reach out to those around us.

Jesus, of course, took the ultimate trip "out of His way." He left the glory of heaven and His position in the kingdom to come to earth as a man and walk the way to the cross. He chose to follow that path in order to save you and me and all who would believe in His name. He now is with us as we walk our path, and He will help us lead others to His glory.

> *Jesus, we're so grateful You came to save us. You didn't consider it out of Your way to pay the price for the sins of humanity. Help us to notice others around us in need of a touch from You. May we recognize that it's never out of our way to show others Your beautiful glory. Amen.*

For further study: Matthew 9:18–26; John 4:1–42, 11:1–44; Acts 8:26–40.

SEPTEMBER 15
"I Will Come."

And Jesus said to him, "I will come and heal him." (Matthew 8:7)

THE GOSPELS RELATE an incident of a centurion asking Jesus to come heal his servant who was paralyzed and in torment. Jesus said He would come to heal him. The centurion stated that he wasn't worthy enough for Jesus to come into his house, but if Jesus just said the word, he knew the servant would be healed. He recognized Jesus's authority and believed in Him. Jesus marveled at the centurion's faith. This is a story of Jesus's compassion and of a man's faith in Jesus being who He is—the Son of God.

My imagination wanders, and I see Jesus talking with God the Father and the Holy Spirit in heaven as they look upon the earth they created. The Father speaks of how sad He is that humanity, made in Their image, has become so evil. "Look at them," He says. "They're so sad and broken. They murder and cheat each other. They hurt the children and are lost in their sins. It would take a great sacrifice to pay the price to save them from their sins. A very, very great price. A price beyond measure."

Jesus looks at the earth, then looks up into the eyes of the Father and says, "I will go and heal them."

The Holy Spirit looks tenderly at Jesus. "You realize, of course, the price that must be paid. One of us would have to become one of them, live a perfect life yet be condemned to die for their sin."

The angels gasp. "But they are not worthy of such a price. They are so sinful! Could You possibly go to their place and be with them?"

Jesus stands tall, determination showing on His face. "Yes! I will do it. I will go to earth and live among them. My blood will pay the price to set them free and heal them."

The Father bows His head. "Go, My Son. You are the Word of God, and You will become flesh and dwell among them. All who receive the Word will be saved from their sins."

"Yes," the Holy Spirit adds, "and then we will come and make our home in them, and they will live with us forever, healed from the law of sin and death that has infected their souls."

It's the story of the compassion of God and the faith of man in recognizing who Jesus is and His amazing grace. He has come and healed us.

Jesus, thank You that You, the Word, became flesh and dwelt among us. You paid the price for us and set us free. We believe and acknowledge that You are our Lord and our Savior. Amen.

For further study: Matthew 8:5–13; Luke 7:1–10; John 1:1–17; Ephesians 2:8–9; 1 Peter 1:18–21.

SEPTEMBER 16
Friend of Sinners

> The Son of Man came eating and drinking, and they say, "Look, a glutton and a winebibber, a friend of tax collectors and sinners!" But wisdom is justified by her children. (Matthew 11:19)

I HEARD AN interview on the radio with a lady who used to call herself a Christian but no longer did. She had walked away from the church because of the failures and judgments of the people in the congregation. Her heart had been broken by injustice. The interviewer asked how people around her reacted when she told them she no longer considered herself a Christian, since she'd been so involved in various ministries before. Her answer made me sit up and take notice. She said that several had come to her, even those in her close family, who were relieved and said now they could talk freely to her, openly sharing things they'd been holding back. They no longer feared her judging them.

I thought about my own family and friends and asked myself if they held back from me. The answer was clearly and obviously yes. I could quickly think of many examples of people obviously holding their tongue or keeping me out of the loop. Did people fear I would judge them, or were they ashamed to share their struggles, thinking a Christian would disapprove of their choices? The way sinners flocked to Jesus, I don't think they had problems opening up to Him. I suspect it was because they knew He loved them.

I hope our love for people shines through strong enough to overcome their fears. After all, we can be totally free and open with Jesus. We never have to hold anything back. He knows it all anyway, so we might as well bare our hearts to Him in our prayers. There's something freeing about being fully known yet fully loved. We can be "naked and unashamed" in His presence, with all our shortcomings laid bare. We don't fear His judgment because He has already paid the price for our redemption.

> *Jesus, thank You that You know us intimately yet have still accepted us fully into Your family. We are so grateful. May Your love in us shine so strongly that those around us are free to bare their souls so that we may share the redemption story with them in all its glory. Amen.*

For further study: Genesis 2:25; Luke 18:9–14; Ephesians 1:3–6; Hebrews 4:12–13.

SEPTEMBER 17
He Reached Us

> For I am persuaded that neither death nor life, nor angels nor principalities nor powers, nor things present nor things to come, nor height nor depth, nor any other created thing, shall be able to separate us from the love of God which is in Christ Jesus our Lord. (Romans 8:38–39)

IT'S BEEN SAID that Yuri Gagarin, when he flew into space, stated that he didn't see God there. This was probably not true. Yuri was a religious man. Nikita Khruschev was the one who implied Yuri had said it, so as to defend atheism. When John Glenn flew in space, he said he was amazed by creation, and it strengthened his belief in God. I think the moral of the story is that if you don't have Jesus in your heart, you're unlikely to see Him, but if you do have Him in your heart, you see evidence of Him everywhere!

People without Jesus are still on the other side of a great chasm in their hearts. It's a huge hole that can only be filled by Jesus. The good news is that there's no hole so big that Jesus can't fill it. There's no height so high that Jesus can't reach it. There's no depression so deep that He can't heal it. You can't sink so low in your depth of sin that He can't raise you out of it. There's no loneliness so intense that He can't erase it with His presence. Nothing can block His love flowing to us.

How do we know this is true when depression, loneliness, or sin claw at our soul? We know it's true because there's no greater distance than that between heaven and hell, yet Jesus spanned it. There's no chasm deeper than that between God's holiness and our sin, yet Jesus crossed it—literally. Some days we can forget the depth of His love because of our circumstances or emotions. Pausing to partake of the bread and the wine is to pause and remember that nothing can separate us from His love. Ever. It's that powerful.

Jesus, we're in awe of Your great love. We had a huge hole in our hearts, but You filled it with Your love and presence. We were on the other side of the chasm from God, but You crossed that chasm to bring us to a new life with You. Nothing can change that. Thank You. Amen.

For further study: Matthew 12:40; Luke 16:19–31; Romans 8:31–39.

SEPTEMBER 18
Keep Pouring

Now hope does not disappoint, because the love of God has been poured out in our hearts by the Holy Spirit who was given to us. (Romans 5:5)

THE WORSHIP SERVICE at church this week was really special. Beautiful children danced with flags before the altar. The congregation's voices rose together, singing to Yeshua. It was anointed with the presence of God. As I raised my hands in praise, it felt like His glory was pouring out on us and filling the cup of our soul. In my mind, I spoke to God, thanking Him for filling my heart with His presence. Suddenly I had the thought that rather than telling Him I was full, I would pray that He keep pouring. If He would keep pouring His love and glory, our hearts would be so full that His love would fill to the brim and spill over. The more it would spill over, the more it would touch others around us. So yes, Lord, please keep pouring and pouring and pouring.

And He does. He has poured out His love for us as He poured out His blood for us. He has no limits to His love. He doesn't withhold it or stop its flow. We will not be disappointed. The more He gives, the more we have to give. The more we empty our hearts to those around us, the more room there is for Him to pour even more love in, letting it spill out over and over again. We need not fear any lack of His love. He will never be in short supply. His love has no limits. It can reach the worst sinner and the most righteous saint. His love penetrates to the deepest parts of the earth and reaches to the highest heaven. His love surrounds us and is within us. We can pray for Him to keep pouring it out, knowing He's more than willing to pour it on us, just as Jesus was willing to pour out His blood from the wounds in His body.

Jesus, You poured out Your blood in demonstration of the love of God poured out on us. We ask that You keep pouring it out. We know You don't withhold Your love from us. Fill our hearts so completely that Your love spills out on all around us. Amen.

For further study: Deuteronomy 28:1–14; Psalm 23:1–6; Luke 6:38; John 7:37–39; Ephesians 3:14–21.

SEPTEMBER 19
Restorer of Streets to Dwell In

Those from among you shall build the old waste places; you shall raise up the foundations of many generations; and you shall be called the Repairer of the Breach, The Restorer of Streets to Dwell In. (Isaiah 58:12)

WHEN I WAS a child, people spent a lot of time outside. Parents would sit on porches, and kids would play ball in the streets. Now it seems most of us don't even know our neighbors. It's easy to keep to ourselves, lost in our smartphones. We post nice Christian platitudes to our social media accounts and feel like we've done something good. We have virtual communities, but many people these days lack a real community around them.

In the book of Isaiah, God admonished His people for this kind of thing. In chapter 58, He talks about fasting. The Israelites were fasting in order to be seen by others as being good people. They may be fasting, but they would exploit the people who worked for them and do wicked deeds. God was not impressed. He says the fast He wanted was one that enabled people to have extra bread to give to those who had none. He desired for people to share their clothing and goods with the poor. He wanted people to break the hold of wickedness and help the oppressed be free.

God wants us to notice those around us and not hide from them. In other words, He was asking us to fast from our own pride and selfish desires. He was asking us to lay down our lives for those around us, just like He has laid down His life for us. The rest of the chapter focuses on the amazing blessings that come from putting aside our pride and self-righteousness. Our light will shine brightly. When we call, He will be there to guide us, satisfy us, and strengthen us. We will be a repairer of the breach, a restorer of streets to dwell in. By fasting selfishness and laying down our lives for those around us, we create a real community, one united in Christ.

I don't know about you, but sometimes I find it hard to do. My pride seeks to stand tall and fights against the humility I know I need. Instead of fasting, I give in to the hunger to be seen as someone good, even while evil hides in my heart. Thankfully, however, there is the cross and communion. I come to the table and confess my selfish will and He cleanses me yet again. Today becomes a new day, a new chance to fast in the way He has chosen. His light shines in my darkness and dispels it completely. He has repaired completely the breach that existed between me and His holiness. Only when His grace reigns in my heart do I have even a remote chance of walking the road of self-sacrifice. Thank God for that grace.

> *Jesus, thank You for repairing the breach between us and heaven's glory. Thank You for the community You've established. We are united by Your blood. Holy Spirit, bring to our remembrance the call to fast to self and walk the path of humility, just as our Savior walked. Amen.*

For further study: Isaiah 58:1–14.

SEPTEMBER 20
Purchased, Not Stolen

I have blotted out, like a thick cloud, your transgressions, and like a cloud, your sins. Return to Me, for I have redeemed you. (Isaiah 44:22)

HAVE YOU EVER stolen anything? When I was a child, I stole a piece of Double Bubble candy from the local corner store. I felt so guilty that to this day I still can't stand the smell of that gum. I wish I could say that I learned my lesson and never stole anything again, but that would be a lie. I remember being too shy to ask a church if I could have a copy of the music sheets they'd printed, so I just stole one. I felt so guilty that years later I mailed it back to them. Silly, I know, but it was what I had to do. It's hard to enjoy something when you know it's not rightfully yours. If you steal something, you're always looking over your shoulder, wondering when someone else is going to realize that you took it unlawfully. I've heard it said that you don't become a thief by stealing—you steal because you're a thief. How true that is. Our nature is reflected in our actions. Our nature is only changed by coming to Christ and being bought by Him.

Given that God is holy and not a thief, it's not surprising that the method He chose to redeem us from our sins was to purchase us. He had created us, as He created all things. If anyone had a right to consider us as belonging to them, He did. Even though we were created by Him, He let us choose whom we'd belong to, and we chose an evil master. If He stole us back, we wouldn't rightfully be His, and the thief could come and take us back again. Jesus, however, purchased us with His blood. We came lawfully under a new master, who loves us and set us free from sin and death. The thief cannot reclaim us. Guilt cannot hold on to us as we come and confess our sins, finding redemption at the foot of the cross.

As we partake of communion, we recognize that we've been bought at a price. The precious blood of the sinless Lamb was the price needed to buy us. We've put off our old master, our old nature, and taken on the new life in Christ. We are a new creation because of the price He paid.

> *Jesus, thank You for paying the price to redeem us from sin and death. We can walk in grace and holiness because of You. Thank You for forgiving us and setting us free. Amen.*

For further study: Leviticus 19:11; Isaiah 44:21–24; Romans 8:1–2; 1 Corinthians 6:19–20, 7:22–23; 2 Corinthians 5:17.

SEPTEMBER 21
Enriched

> While you are enriched in everything for all liberality, which causes thanksgiving through us to God. (2 Corinthians 9:11)

I CAME ACROSS a scientific study some time ago. The researchers had put water laced with a potent street drug in with some lab rats. Many of the rats became addicted to the drug. Someone had the idea, however, that a rat living in a bare cage wasn't living a very normal life, so they repeated the experiment with rats that lived in an enriched environment with access to outdoors. Things to do, see, and smell. In that situation, very few rats touched the drugged water.

This is the case with many addictions, I think. The addiction is how the person deals with physical, emotional, social, or environmental pain. It's not just drugs or alcohol that people may turn to in order to deal with pain. Some may reach for unhealthy food, while others may eat too much or not enough. Some may go shopping. Others may deal with pain by spending long hours at work, or getting involved in unhealthy relationships. Some may turn to social media, or spend hours watching one show after another. I'm not saying there isn't a time for these things, but sometimes we turn to these things to deal with pain instead of going to the one who can heal the pain. As long as we're in this world, there will be social, physical, emotional, and environmental pain. Eden is long gone, and the new heavens and earth aren't here yet. When faced with the pain in this world, we'll always have a choice. We can run to the things that distract or numb us, or we can run to the Savior, who enriches our soul.

Jesus paid the price with His broken body for us to be healed. He enriches every part of our lives. Our spirit is made new, our soul is filled with healthy thoughts, our body is physically touched. He can enrich our relationship with others in the body of Christ. His Word fills our hearts with all that is good. The cycle of sin and death is broken, and we are free to walk in His glory.

Jesus, sometimes we forget how much You have enriched our life, and we turn to other things to try to heal our hurts. We come to You, knowing You forgive us. Help us to turn quickly to You instead of distractions, for You are the true healer of our souls, the one who enriches us in every way. Amen.

For further Study: Psalm 147:1–20; Proverbs 10:22; 2 Corinthians 9:8–15; 1 Peter 2:24.

SEPTEMBER 22
From Darkness to Light

He has delivered us from the power of darkness and conveyed us into the kingdom of the Son of His love. (Colossians 1:13)

DARKNESS CAN'T REMAIN in the presence of light. Light overpowers and banishes it. Even if the light wants the darkness to stay, it cannot. The two are incompatible and can't inhabit the same space. Turn on the light, and darkness must flee. The only way darkness could remain in the midst of light would be if its very nature fundamentally changed.

Similarly, that which is unholy cannot inhabit the same space as the holy. The two are incompatible. If the holy wanted the unholy to remain, the latter would have to fundamentally change its very nature. What if the only way that nature could be changed would be for the holy to take on the banishment awaiting the unholy? It would be a tremendous sacrifice, yet God was willing to do it out of love for us.

God is light, and in Him there is no darkness. He is holy, and there is no unrighteousness in Him. On the other hand, we are born into darkness as children of unrighteousness. Jesus paid the price for our sin so that we could take on His righteousness and thereafter abide in the presence of all that is holy. Our very nature was fundamentally changed by His sacrifice.

One day we'll abide with Him where His light and holiness permeate everything, but right now, while we reside on the fallen earth, things block His light and create shadows. Pride and selfishness, sins committed by or against us, times we omit to do the good we should do … these things rise up in our souls like a thick cloud obscuring the light and warmth of the Son. By coming to the communion table, we bring our hurts and failures to the foot of the cross, where the wind of the Spirit blows the cloud away. His holiness again fills us and overcomes all that is unholy.

Jesus, we are so enamored with Your presence. We thank You for paying the price so that we may abide with You for eternity. Holy Spirit, reveal to us anything that comes between us and God's holy light so that our relationship with the Holy may not be hindered. Amen.

For further study: Acts 26:15–18; Ephesians 5:8–11; Colossians 1:9–14, 1 John 1:5–7.

SEPTEMBER 23
Mining His Glory

That their hearts may be encouraged, being knit together in love, and attaining to all riches of the full assurance of understanding, to the knowledge of the mystery of God, both of the Father and of Christ, in whom are hidden all the treasures of wisdom and knowledge. (Colossians 2:2–3)

I LIVE IN a mining town. Geologists scan the earth to find areas to explore to try to find the treasures hidden there. The minerals may be in large veins of wealth embedded in the rock. If they dig in the wrong spot, they'll miss the treasure they seek. The machinery could be digging a parallel course only feet away, but if it's outside of the vein, all their efforts will be for naught.

People search for the wealth of God's glory in many ways. Many people do good things and are a blessing to others, yet they can miss out on the glory that God would reveal in them. In ourselves, we fall short of the glory of God no matter how hard we try to live a good life. However, when we seek His glory by digging into His grace, we're overwhelmed by the abundance of His treasure, the riches of His grace. We've found the motherlode and will never be able to mine to the very end of the vein. The deeper we dig, the more we find. His Word reveals His glory.

We now have this treasure hidden in our hearts, our earthen vessel, as Adam himself was formed from the clay. We can carry this grace to the surface for all to see and tap into. We need to continue to mine His glory to add to the treasure in us. One of the ways we do that is in pausing to take communion. We remember the amazing, abundant wealth of His grace, refilling our hearts to carry with us through our day, shining out to all we meet.

Jesus, Your blood flowed, showing Your glory like a vein of gold hidden in the earth. Now Your great treasure is hidden in our own earthen vessels, Your very body. May Your glory shine for all to see, that they would be drawn to seek out Your glory for themselves. Amen.

For further study: Genesis 2:7; 2 Corinthians 4:1–7; Romans 3:21–24.

SEPTEMBER 24
Shake Us Up

> And when they had prayed, the place where they were assembled together was shaken; and they were all filled with the Holy Spirit, and they spoke the word of God with boldness. (Acts 4:31)

A COUPLE OF spots in the New Testament mention a place being shaken, like a small earthquake occurred. One of these occasions was after the apostles had been threatened and told not to speak of Jesus. The apostles, however, prayed for boldness and the power of God to be manifest. On another occasion, Paul and Silas had been beaten and imprisoned, yet they were praying and singing hymns. The shaking on that occasion was strong enough to break open their chains and all the prison doors!

I don't know anyone personally who has experienced an earthquake related to their prayers. I wonder if it happened today if we would find it inspiring or terrifying. I wonder what would happen if we prayed for boldness despite the threats we hear in our heads. I wonder what would happen if, in our worst circumstances, when we've been beaten down and chained by our thoughts, we prayed and sang hymns. The battle rages on. Much of the persecution we face today occurs in our own minds, where we must take those thoughts captive and replace them with prayer and praise. This can only be done by knowing we belong to Jesus. May our lives be shaken up by the knowledge of His love for us.

We pause to take communion to remind us of the depth of His great love. He was willing to pay the price to set us free from all that seeks to bind and destroy us. He gives us life and freedom from sin and death. He has shaken off all that is unholy from us so that we might walk with Him in His glory.

> *Jesus, shake us up. Keep us focused on Your amazing grace that has set us free. Remind us to turn to prayer and praise when wrong thoughts assail our mind. Keep us centered in Your love. Amen.*

For further study: Acts 4:23–31, 16:25–31; 2 Corinthians 10:3–7.

SEPTEMBER 25
Calluses

> For the hearts of this people have grown dull. Their ears are hard of hearing, and their eyes they have closed, lest they should see with their eyes and hear with their ears, lest they should understand with their heart and turn, so that I should heal them. But blessed are your eyes for they see, and your ears for they hear. (Matthew 13:15–16)

WHEN I WAS young, I decided to take guitar lessons. I was never very good at it, but it was especially hard at the beginning. Pushing the strings down onto the frets was painful. It was difficult to push hard enough to get any kind of nice sound. As I practiced, my fingers became callused, and it was easier to get a reasonable sound, but my sense of touch was dulled.

Sometimes in life we push down with our faith on our difficulties, but the sound we get isn't pleasant or harmonious. We push harder and we may build up calluses on our heart. Sure, we don't feel the pain now, and maybe the sound is a bit better, but we've been called to play in an orchestra where we need to feel the music of God in our hearts. The Holy Spirit lifts the baton to direct us and the music begins as the sound of Christ dragging His cross along the floor scratches into the tune. I find myself with a bit part. Maybe my job is only to hit the triangle one beat for each blow of the hammer that drives the nails into Jesus's hands and feet. The drums roll with thunder as the sky turns black. All feels lost. Then the trumpet sound calls out and Jesus steps from behind the curtain into the limelight. The Father, sitting in the front row, leaps to His feet. He starts to clap, slowly at first, but then with thunderous applause as He shouts, "Bravo! Bravo!"

As the orchestra rises to take a bow, Jesus turns to shake each hand of the orchestral players. As He comes to me, I am ashamed. I only had a small part, and I don't think I played it very well. As I look up into His face, I stumble over my words: "I didn't strike it quite right. I think my timing was off."

He motions to the Father and the Holy Spirit as they say, "No, it was perfect. You played with feeling. You heard the notes. We've invited so many to play in the orchestra who have refused to pick up their instrument and try. You did what you could, and with all of us together, it is enough."

Life can be hard. It's easy to become jaded, our hearts callused. We need to guard against that and remember that He is using each of us in this symphony. Our part may be small, but it's enough. He did the heavy lifting when He carried His cross up the hill to Calvary. Our job is only to keep our hearts tender and attuned to the leading of the Holy Spirit.

> *Jesus, thank You for all You've done for us. You've called us to play a role. We mess it up at times, but all You ask is that we keep practicing. You'll bring it all together in Your glory into a beautiful symphony of healed hearts. Amen.*

For further study: Matthew 13:10–17; Romans 12:3–11; Ephesians 4:17–23.

SEPTEMBER 26
Marred Beauty

> Let nothing be done through selfish ambition or conceit, but in lowliness of mind let each esteem others better than himself. (Philippians 2:3)

MY MOM HAS a really cool electronic photo frame. Anyone can email pictures to it and they show up on the screen in a slideshow. It's neat to see all the different photos people have sent her sliding by one after another. My eyes are always drawn to the images as they parade by. I noted a difference in facial expressions on many of us in these photos. When my family or I knew our photo was being taken, the facial expression was often strained and contrived. When we didn't know, however, our faces were beautiful. The smiles were large and the eyes showed the soul's light.

It seems when we're posing for a photo, we're so focused on how we might look to others that it mars the natural beauty within. It's a false humility or pride that makes us so concerned about what others might see. True humility doesn't knock us down; rather, it elevates others. With true humility we're more concerned about those around us than about ourselves. True humility shows the joy we feel in the presence of the other, and we're not ashamed of that joy radiating on our faces.

Jesus expressed real humility by putting aside His heavenly nature so that He might exalt us to His glory. His face was marred physically, but the beauty of His soul shone through to reach all generations. We see His beauty and rejoice in His presence. Being like Christ is to be more concerned with those around us than with the image we present to others.

Let's pause now to remember His sacrifice and the glory He will reveal in us as we in true humility start to resemble Him.

> *Jesus, thank You for laying down Your life to save us. You have revealed to us Your beauty and glory. Shine in us in all we do and help us to be more concerned with those around us than with the image we portray. Amen.*

For further study: Psalm 34:4–5; 2 Corinthians 3:17–18; Philippians 2:1–16; 1 John 3:1–3.

SEPTEMBER 27
"That's My Specialty!"

Therefore He is also able to save to the uttermost those who come to God through Him, since He always lives to make intercession for them. (Hebrews 7:25)

MANY YEARS AGO, I went to see a photographer about getting some wedding photos done. When I mentioned what I was looking for, he said, "Ah, weddings, that's my specialty!" He did a great job. Years later, I remember seeing photos of animals on the walls of his studio, so when I wanted professional photos of my dogs, I went back to him. When I arrived, another couple had just come in to talk to him about baby photos. As I patiently waited in the background, I heard him say, "Ah, baby photos, that's my specialty!" After the couple left, I went to talk to him about my pets. He said (you guessed it) "Ah, pet photos, that's my specialty!"

Recently, I was going through an emotional trial. Someone dear to me was entering end-of-life care. Cancer was causing pain that was hard to get under control. As I talked to God about the emotions and cares we were experiencing, I heard Him say, "Ah, but this is my specialty."

He does indeed understand all about death and resurrection. He's the specialist for everything we need and all we go through. He has walked it, lived it, died in it, and rose again. He lives for us and to make intercession for us. He's able to save us to the uttermost. Nothing is too difficult for Him. He is the ultimate specialist.

Jesus, we're so grateful for You. You're always making intercession for us, and You love us so deeply. Thank You for Your sacrifice on the cross and for leading us through to victory. Amen.

For further study: Jeremiah 32:17; Romans 8:18–39; Jude 1:24–25.

SEPTEMBER 28
You Can't Have It All

> But now having been set free from sin, and having become slaves of God, you have your fruit to holiness, and the end, everlasting life. (Romans 6:22)

I LIKE IT when we have nice, mild temperatures. It's good for walking and being outside. Warm temperatures, however, mean more bugs. When winter comes, if it stays mild, the snow is slushy and hard to walk in. Really cold temperatures make the snow hard and great for snowshoeing, but it's also harder to keep yourself warm. Cold temperatures make great ice for skating, but it's harder to skate when you're bundled up in lots of clothes. Rain in the summer waters the garden well, but it can cause flooding and sticky mud. We can't have it all. We can't have the green plants and colorful flowers without rain; we can't go snowshoeing without snow and cold. We can't go skating without cold enough temperatures to make good ice. We can't have the beautiful fall colors with the changing of the leaves, without the weather getting cold enough to stop the flow of sap.

We also can't have a resurrection without a death. We can't rise to new life without putting off the old one. We've all done things we're ashamed of, and it would be nice if we never failed, but then we wouldn't know the amazing power of His grace. Where sin abounds, indeed grace abounds much more.

As Paul reminds us, though, this isn't permission to sin. If we have truly found His grace, the last thing we want to do is go back to a dead life. We want to walk and live in the new one. This doesn't mean we never make mistakes. Walking in new life is a learning process, just like a toddler learns to first pull himself up using the help of furniture before stumbling into his loving parents' arms. Later, he's steadier and can stand and walk without as much assistance. Later still, he can run and jump to the best of his ability. He may be a track star, or he may struggle to make it across the room, but every step is a victory of faith. Such is our walk in this new life.

Jesus knew there could be no resurrection for us to new life without there first being a resurrection of His body from His death on the cross. His tomb had to be opened and His grave clothes set aside forever. We also instantly throw off our grave clothes of sin and death when we receive Him. We still need to go through the process of working out our salvation as we learn to walk all over again, but this time, it's by faith and not by sin.

Jesus, thank You for giving Your life so we might live. We're so amazed by the grace that brought You out of the tomb and went before us to lead us in this new life. Amen.

For further study: Romans 6:1–23; Philippians 2:12.

SEPTEMBER 29

Grace—Never Out of Style

Jesus Christ is the same yesterday, today, and forever. (Hebrews 13:8)

I STOPPED IN a traveler's rest stop not long ago and was surprised to see a bank of payphones. It had been such a long time since I'd seen a payphone anywhere. Even a hotel I stayed at last year had no phone in the room—just a sign saying landlines were passé. If you didn't have a cell phone and wanted a phone in your room you had to request one.

It seems so many things fade from fashion or common usage. Who would have thought back in the day that the time would come when the large video stores would all be shuttered and gone? Time marches on, and things come and go. Something that once seemed so necessary and permanent becomes a thing of the past that no one wants or needs. There is one thing, however, that we will always need and that will never go out of fashion.

The Bible says Jesus is the same yesterday, today, and forever. He doesn't need to be superseded by some new thing. He's already perfect and complete. He paid the price once for our sins, and it need not be paid again by some other or newer means. Things will never change to a point where we outgrow our need for His grace. Nothing can take its place. The newest high-tech gadget, the greatest medical development, will never be able to save us from the effects of sin and death. There is only one Savior, and His name is Jesus. Only one death paved the way for us to have new life. The cross can't be improved upon or done away with. Jesus is the same yesterday, today, and forever because He is enough. His grace is enough. We have no need for anything other than this.

Jesus, You never go out of style. We will always need You. Your grace is ever sufficient for us. You have saved us, and we are so grateful for who You are. Amen.

For further study: Joshua 1:5; Psalm 34:1–19; Hebrews 13:7–15; 1 Peter 3:18.

SEPTEMBER 30
Velocitized

You are the salt of the earth; but if the salt loses its flavor, how shall it be seasoned? It is then good for nothing but to be thrown out and trampled underfoot by men. (Matthew 5:13)

I WAS DRIVING home from a long trip and I became velocitized. This occurs when a driver is just going through the motions and starts to misjudge their speed due to prolonged travel at high speed. It was hard to slow down to make an exit to the rest stop. Luckily, I recognized I wasn't paying close attention and made the corrections to be a better driver.

While I was on this road trip, I'd met up with an old friend who spent some time complaining about the people she worked with. I could sympathize with her, but I also realized that as Christians, we can become velocitized in our daily lives. We're traveling with great speed from one day to the next, and it's easy to get caught up in the world's highway. We join with others in grumbling about our family or our coworkers, forgetting that we've been called to be salt and light to the broken and hurting people around us. We can go to church and just go through the motions. We're there to get a good sermon instead of to give of God's grace to others present. We stand in line at the grocery checkout annoyed that we've chosen, again, the slowest line, instead of pausing to pray for the harried mother with the unruly kids.

When we pause to partake of communion, we're pulling off into a rest stop to regroup and refocus. It's a chance to recognize where we've been distracted into mindless speeding along the world's highway, and then ask for His forgiveness. Our job isn't to get to our destination as fast as possible, flying by others without a care. Our purpose is to let our light shine in the darkness to illuminate the road for others to follow. Communion is a time to refocus and remember that on the road to our final destination, we're called to be salt, able to season the world with His grace.

Jesus, forgive us for when we've forgotten our true purpose for being here. At times we've sped along without thought of our purpose to shine Your light to this dark world. Help us to reflect You clearly in all we do. Amen.

For further study: Matthew 5:13–16; Philippians 2:12–14; 1 John 1:5–9, 3:13–21.

OCTOBER 1
Getting Stuck in the Mud

He also brought me up out of a horrible pit, out of the miry clay, and set my feet upon a rock, and established my steps. He has put a new song in my mouth—Praise to our God; many will see it and fear, and will trust in the Lord. (Psalm 40:2–3)

THIS TIME OF year can be challenging on the farm. The ground isn't cold enough to be hard, but the grass isn't growing enough to keep rain from making the field a soggy, deep pile of muck and mire. One morning as I wheeled two heavy bales of hay out to the field in a wheelbarrow, the barrow became mired in the muck, unable to go further. Grabbing a bale of hay, I slogged over to the feeder, my boots sticking in the mud and causing a sucking sound as I struggled with each step. I rejoiced as I made it to the feeder, swinging the bale up to toss it in, only to find my boots firmly stuck with mud up to the ankles. Unable to move my feet, I couldn't keep my balance as the heavy bale hit the edge of the feeder and fell back on me, causing me to fall deep into the mire. This mud—mixed with horse urine, manure, and old wet hay—soaked through my pants and ran down inside my boots. I had to push into the manure as I struggled to stand. My clothes stunk, and I was wet and uncomfortable from head to toe. It was all I could do to finish the chores and head into the house to get a shower before sitting down to breakfast.

Life has a way sometimes of knocking us down into the muck of the world. As we sit there contemplating our fate, Jesus comes and crouches beside us. He reaches out His hand and says, "Here, let Me help you up out of this mess." As He gets you back to your feet, you see His gaze look up and down your filthy clothes. Maybe you see His nose wrinkle as you start to smell your own stench from the manure of sin you've fallen into. Maybe you look into His eyes and say, "Jesus, sorry, I really stink."

I imagine He looks back at us, a twinkle in His eyes. "Yes," He says, "the way you treated your spouse, and the words you had with your coworker, were indeed pretty stinky. But come with Me into My house. You can have a shower in My grace. I have fresh, clean white clothes for you. Come, I've laid out the table, broken the bread, and poured out the wine. All is ready."

A part of pausing in your day to partake of communion is taking a moment to look back on your behavior and see where you've let the muck of the world stain your heart. We examine ourselves to find where the stench of sin lingers, but then to bring it to the cross so we can once again be cleansed by His grace. The muck is washed off and we're once again spotless as we sit down with Him at the table.

Jesus, thank You for dying on the cross to pay the price for my sins: the sins of yesterday, the sins of today, and the sins of tomorrow. Thank You for cleansing me once again and for leading me into the paths of righteousness so I may learn to walk in Your grace unspotted by the world. Amen.

For further study: Psalm 23:1–6, 51:1–17; John 14:1–4; James 1:19–27; Revelation 3:5.

OCTOBER 2
Who He Is

Therefore by their fruits you will know them. (Matthew 7:20)

I HAVE A barn filled with retired horses. Most of them are on long-term medications, and many don't really like being forced to take medication. My goal is for their final years to be as happy as possible, so I don't want to force them to take things either. The solution is apples! The horses love them, and the flesh is soft enough to push pills into. They're like big pill pockets for the equines in my life. I said all that to say I go through a lot of apples. I try to find them on sale when I can. The nice thing about the fall is that my friends sometimes become my supplier of free, soft, tasty apples that fall from backyard trees. Some years there are more apples than others from the trees, but they're always the exact same type of apple.

Jesus told us we could judge people by their fruit. He said you wouldn't gather grapes from thornbushes, or figs from thistles. A good tree produces good fruit. The fruit forms naturally according to the tree it arises from.

Sometimes we get a bit too focused on the things Jesus does—the fruit He's produced in our lives. In fact, we may demand His fruit. If we or our loved ones are sick, we want nothing more than the fruit of healing. Maybe we're in need of His guidance in an area. We can get pretty frustrated if for some reason He seems far away, like there's no fruit low enough for us to grab from the tree.

As much as we want the fruit, however, the fruit just points to the type of tree providing the fruit. The fruit is good because the tree is good. He heals us because He's a healer. He redeems us because He's a redeemer. He saves because He's a Savior. He loves us because He's a lover. The important thing isn't the fruit, even though that's really important to us personally. The true importance is that the fruit demonstrates who God is. He's not a vindictive, demanding, spiteful God. He's the God who loves us so much He gave His only Son to save us. He's the one willing to give up everything and die to redeem us. He's the God willing to touch our hearts and change us forever, the one who prepares a place for us so we can be with Him for all eternity. We enjoy the wonderful fruit produced by the greatest tree that ever was or ever will be.

> *Jesus, You chose to die on the tree to save us, and in saving us You showed us who You are: our Savior, lover, and friend. You're willing to give Your all, and You give us all things that are good, because You are goodness personified. We're so thankful for Your fruit, but even more so, we're amazed and thankful for who You are. We thank You for saving us and for being our Savior. Amen.*

For further study: Psalm 77:11–15; Matthew 7:7–11, 15–20, 12:33–35; James 1:17; 1 John 4:14.

OCTOBER 3
Don't Look Down

> Why are you cast down, O my soul? And why are you disquieted within me? Hope in God; for I shall yet praise Him, the help of my countenance and my God. (Psalm 43:5)

I WAS SCROLLING through Facebook and came upon a video of people trying to cross elevated glass walkways or swinging bridges. Many were terrified and having trouble as they looked down to the ground, oh so far away. They were safe, but they didn't feel safe. Sometimes they resisted other people's attempts to help them up. They were often trapped by their fear, unable to move forward or backwards.

Psalm 43 is a continuation of Psalm 42. In both psalms, the sons of Korah wrote about being trapped in grief. Disappointment filled the writers' hearts. Their enemies were oppressive and reproached them, yet each verse is followed by a chorus call to set their hope in God, their source of joy and salvation. God alone would make things right.

We also sometimes get stuck looking down, focused on our shame. Our enemy, the devil, reproaches us, oppressing our soul, reminding us of our sin, and paralyzing us in our grief and failure. As long as our gaze is cast down, we can't progress. We're stuck. We can't see that the Lord has us safely held in His everlasting grace. He sends people to encourage us, but sometimes our fear and shame prevent us from responding to their loving care. We have to shift our eyes from the depth of our shame to the sure and loving support afforded by the cross. When we feel overcome by past failure, when the enemy whispers to our soul that there's no hope, we can lift our eyes to the cross. Like the sons of Korah, we can tell ourselves, "Why are you cast down? Hope in God, praise Him! He is your Savior, the help of your countenance, and your God."

Father, how many times have we messed up in the past! How many times will we continue to mess up and sin! Yet You are still our God. As long as we stare at our failure, we're stuck, but when we gaze upon the cross, we remember that You have set us free. We're safe because You have made it so. Restore our joy as we praise You and thank You. Amen.

For further study: Psalms 42, 43, 51; Romans 10:8–11.

OCTOBER 4
A Tale of Three Gardens

And he showed me a pure river of water of life, clear as crystal, proceeding from the throne of God and of the Lamb. In the middle of its street, and on either side of the river, was the tree of life, which bore twelve fruits, each tree yielding its fruit every month. The leaves of the tree were for the healing of the nations. (Revelation 22:1–2)

WHEN I MOVED out to the country, I decided to try my hand at gardening. I dug up a patch of ground, added some nicely aged horse manure, and planted seeds. I'm not a great gardener. I still struggle to tell the good plants from the weeds, but I've had some moderate success. That first year, the harvest of lettuce, carrots, potatoes, and onions amazed me. The food had so much flavor! Over the years, I've managed to grow the easy things like cucumbers and zucchini, and my table has also been enhanced by tomatoes, squash, and pumpkins. There's something rewarding about serving a hot pumpkin pie made with fruit fresh from your own garden.

Gardens also figure importantly in the Bible. Our very first ancestors were given the Garden of Eden, with the tree of life as well as the tree of the knowledge of good and evil. They were tasked with protecting and caring for the garden, but sadly, they fell short. The first Adam gave it up to the devil's hands, allowing thorns and toil, murder and jealousy to enter the world. Death and the fear of death would now reign in the world that was once very good. But God had a plan.

Two thousand years ago, Jesus went to the Garden of Gethsemane to pray. His betrayal was at hand, the temptation to pack it in and give up assaulting His soul. Unlike the scene in the first garden, this second Adam in this garden would succeed where the first Adam failed. Jesus would crush the serpent's head and redeem us from the power of death. He would wear a crown of thorns. Thorns only arose in the first garden because of the fallen state of the world, cursing even the very ground. Jesus would wear this crown as His body died, redeeming all from the curse.

Of course, the world is still in a fallen state. Until Jesus comes to take us to our true home, disease and death remain. There is still betrayal and brokenness, but not without hope. God has prepared a third garden in a New Heaven and New Earth. The tree of life will once again bloom and reveal her fruits. Instead of thorns that wound us, there will be healing among the leaves. The glory of God will be restored in the garden we will enjoy for eternity.

Jesus, we're so grateful You are a God who doesn't fail, and You didn't fail us. You redeemed us from the curse of the fall. We still mess up at times, but we come to You, recognizing that You restore our hope. The garden to come will display Your glory. We set our hearts on the life to come, knowing all will be fully redeemed. Amen.

For further study: Genesis 2:7–3:19; Matthew 26:36–46; Revelation 22:1–7.

OCTOBER 5
True Colors

And we know that the Son of God has come and has given us an understanding, that we may know Him who is true; and we are in Him who is true; in His Son Jesus Christ. This is the true God and eternal life. (1 John 5:20)

I LOVE THE fall. I love the cool temperatures that make it nice to walk. There are no pesky insects biting my skin. The sound of the leaves crunching under my feet and the earthy aroma that arises stimulate my senses. Best of all are the beautiful colors of the fall leaves—bright reds, golden yellows, and brilliant oranges all replacing what was once only green.

In science classes, one learns that the brilliant colors of the fall leaves are actually the leaves' true colors. During the warm days of summer, so much chlorophyll is produced it overshadows the natural hues. Once the colder, darker days begin the taste of winter's trial, the tree can no longer pump sap and produce the overpowering chlorophyll, so the underlying color can now show through. Adversity brings out the tree's true colors.

When you put a sausage in a frying pan and turn up the heat, the sausage splits open and what's inside bubbles out. In times of trial or adversity, what's inside of us tends to spill out. Our true colors show. Do we really walk in faith? We know when it's put to the test!

God is truth, and there is no falsehood in Him. When He was put to the test, His true colors shone through in great glory. Falsely accused, He didn't strive to defend Himself but continued on the path needed to pay the price for our sin. He didn't just give lip service, saying He loved us. He proved it by laying His life down to redeem us, even when the heat was turned up high through beatings and abuse. Even when His blood ran cold in death, He stayed true. His true colors were manifested in all His glory when He was nailed to the tree of Calvary. There is no greater love than this.

I struggle sometimes with walking in a Christ-like fashion. This week a lot of things went wrong. They were minor trials and disappointments, and I struggled to hold my tongue. I wanted to complain, to be rude and demanding with people and generally be miserable. Pausing to take communion is my reminder that He loves me and there is no trial in my life that will take that truth away. He is in me and will help me to walk like He walked. Communion is my time to ask for forgiveness for my failures and to remember that I have received grace and can give grace.

Jesus, there is no unrighteousness or falsehood in You. You set Your heart to walk the painful road to the cross to save us from our sins. We are blessed by eternal life forever with You, and we are so very grateful. Forgive us for the times we walk in our complaints instead of Your grace. Help us to be more like You. Amen.

For further study: Isaiah 53:1–12; John 15:13; Romans 5:5–8; 1 John 1:1–7, 2:1–2, 4:7–8, 5:18–20.

OCTOBER 6
Thirst Quenching

Jesus answered and said to her, "If you knew the gift of God, and who it is who says to you, 'Give Me a drink,' you would have asked Him, and He would have given you living water." (John 4:10)

I OFTEN DRIVE long distances with only my dogs for company. We like to stop often and stretch our legs, maybe walking on a beach or doing a short hike. One year I decided to stop and walk the Nokomis Trail north of Lake Superior. I was planning on checking for the board at the trailhead saying how long the trail was, but I expected it to be short.

I parked and crossed the highway to the trail, but there was no sign. It was late in the season, so likely the sign had been damaged and not replaced. I thought, *Really, how long can it be?* And then I headed out without that important information. After an hour or two of walking, I was trying to decide if I should turn around, but I was hopeful it would come back out near the highway soon, so I pressed on.

Another hour and I found myself at the top of a mountain, regretting not having brought water with me. I was hot, sweaty, and very thirsty. A beautiful stream ran down the mountainside, but I had no water purifier with me. I felt the chance of it being contaminated was low, and I still had to walk the rest of the trail, so I knelt down and drank the water. It was the best water I'd ever had—clear, cold, and refreshing. It gave me the strength and energy to finish the trail in joy.

Pure, clear water tastes so much better when one is thirsty. In the Psalms, the sons of Korah write about panting for God like a deer pants for water. Jesus tells us there is a river of living water prepared for us in heaven. A woman in Samaria heard Jesus say that if she knew who He was, she could ask Him to give her living water so she would never thirst again. He was talking about our spiritual thirst for God. When we come to Him, He satisfies our soul and cleanses our spirit with the living water of His love. The peace and love He gives us bubbles out of us like a fountain of water spilling out on all who are around us.

Sometimes, life has a way of being like a mountainous trail that's hard to climb and takes longer than we expected. The way can be hot and fatiguing. At these times, we need to pause and drink deeply of the clear, living water given by our Savior. He restores our soul and energizes us in His love so that we can once again spill out His love to those around us. May we be so refreshed that we leave puddles of His love everywhere we go!

Jesus, You died and paid the price for our sins so we could drink of Your living water. We come to You dry and thirsty, knowing that You will refresh our souls. Thank You for loving us. Amen.

For further study: Psalm 42:1–4; John 4:1–42; Revelation 22:1–5.

OCTOBER 7
Leading or Seeking Followers?

Most assuredly, I say to you, a servant is not greater than his master; nor is he who is sent greater than he who sent him. (John 13:16)

I'VE NOTICED A lot of people these days who think they're a leader, but to me, they're just seeking followers. They seem to say or do whatever is needed to keep others following, rather than focusing on doing the things necessary to be a good leader. This is quite a contrast with Jesus.

Jesus is the ultimate leader. His followers span centuries and continents, yet He never catered to the desires of His followers. Jesus spoke of Himself as the bread of life that His followers would need to eat. This offended His followers, and many at that time left Jesus and followed Him no longer. Jesus also said that to be His follower, we should be like Him. He said this to His disciples when He took off His robes and donned the attire of a servant, stooping to wash their feet. Jesus said the real leaders in the kingdom of God would be servants of all.

When people said they wanted to follow Him, He didn't necessarily say the things they wanted to hear. Jesus was concerned with being the leader He was called to be. He would be the firstborn from the dead, the one to save us from our sins. His desire was for the whole world to receive that grace and become His followers, but He wasn't going to alter His words or His mission to gain those followers. In fact, He told them that the way would be hard. He was going to lay down His life, and we would have to lay ours down for others in order to truly follow Him. The world has a way of stomping on those who lay their lives down, but that shouldn't be a surprise, considering how the world crucified our Lord and Savior when He laid down His life for us.

During the Last Supper, Jesus taught His disciples about pausing to take communion by breaking the bread and drinking the wine in remembrance of Him. He demonstrated what it is to be a leader by being a servant. Sometimes we get so busy trying to amass followers, we forget what it really means to be a leader. Jesus never forgot who He was or His purpose. As we pause to take communion today, let's remind ourselves of what it means to be His follower.

> *Jesus, it can be difficult to follow You. We don't want to lay our lives down and be trod upon by the world. You remind us, though, that there is a high call to being a servant. To be called great in Your kingdom is worth more than any number of followers. We pause to remember Your call for us to serve others. Amen.*

For further study: Matthew 18:1–5; Mark 9:33–35; Luke 9:57–62; John 6:43–66, 13:1–16; 1 John 3:16.

OCTOBER 8
Misplaced Faith

Now faith is the substance of things hoped for, the evidence of things not seen. (Hebrews 11:1)

THE WORD "CREDIT" comes from the word meaning to trust and believe. The bank issues a credit card, extending credit to you because they trust and believe you'll pay it back with interest. I had a dear friend once who on occasion would run short of funds and would ask if I could loan her some cash. Usually when I did, I would just tell her to pay it forward. One time, though, she offered to work it off, and I took her up on the offer. She got the cash, and we tried to set a date for her to do what she'd promised. Something always happened to thwart that promise, and she ended up never doing the work we'd agreed on. This unfulfilled promise came between our friendship. In the end, we drifted apart. My faith in her ability to return the credit I had extended had been misplaced, and it damaged our relationship.

At times, my spiritual faith gets misplaced. I might place my faith in my ability to say the right prayer in order to get the answer I want from God. Maybe I place my faith in a fellow Christian to do the right thing, forgetting they are a fallible human being. When things don't go as I expect, my misplaced faith can damage my relationship with God. I may take it out on Him, believing He is the cause of the failure. I might start to doubt His love for me. But the problem doesn't lie with God. It lies with me putting faith in things other than Him.

We can have perfect faith in God's love for us because He's already proven it at the cross. We can trust in His promise to save us from our sins. We can be sure of our eternal home with Him in heaven. We can have total faith in the resurrection to new life. When we start to doubt His love or His power to save, we need to examine ourselves to see if we have placed our faith in something other than the omnipotent God full of mercy and grace. If we've misplaced our faith, we can find it again in Him.

> *Father, we trust and believe that You loved us enough to send Your only Son to save us. We have beheld His glory and received His grace given to us at the cross. Forgive us for times we have felt You failed us when we misplaced our faith. Help us keep our eyes on You. Amen.*

For further study: Psalm 118:5–9; John 1:14; Revelation 19:5–6.

OCTOBER 9
Hope

Now may the God of hope fill you with all joy and peace in believing, that you may abound in hope by the power of the Holy Spirit. (Romans 15:13)

HOPE IS EXPECTATION mixed with desire. It's a powerful emotion. Viktor Frankl makes a good argument that man cannot live without hope. Viktor endured incredible abuse and trauma in a Nazi concentration camp. He wrote in his book, *Man's Search for Meaning,* that the difference in many cases between those who survived the atrocities and those who died was in having meaning for their life, in having hope. Some hoped to be reunited with loved ones. Viktor hung on, determined to rewrite the manuscript that later became that very book. The original had been destroyed by the Nazis. He desired and expected to live to see the manuscript finished.

Paul told the Christians in Rome that he wished the God of hope would give them joy, peace, and hope. Don't overlook the first part of that verse—God is a God of hope. He's the foundation of our hope because He fully embraces hope. Have you ever wondered what God could possibly hope for? He is omnipotent. Can't He just have anything He desires? The Word of God proclaims that there's at least one thing He definitely hopes for. God won't make us receive His grace. We have to choose it. He desires and hopes that everyone will choose eternal life with Him.

With this hope, Jesus held on to His joy and peace. He was able to take the abuse and the beating without complaining about the injustice of it all. He submitted to the cross, laying His life down for us because of the joy He had in knowing we would be saved from our sins. If anyone fully understands the power of hope, it's Jesus.

God is indeed a God of hope. He's also able to give us hope. By His grace, we desire the life with Him that's yet to come. We expect it will come to pass, since He has demonstrated His great love for us. He has proven to be honest and true. We can trust Him, and so we can hope.

Jesus, You are indeed the God of hope, and we can put our hope and trust in You. We are blessed by Your love and await the everlasting life yet to come with You. Amen.

For further study: John 3:13–21; 1 Timothy 2:3–6; Hebrews 12:1–3.

OCTOBER 10
Faith, Hope, and Love

> And now abide faith, hope, love, these three; but the greatest of these is love. (1 Corinthians 13:13)

FIRST CORINTHIANS 13 is widely known as the love chapter. It's often quoted at weddings, as many of the verses describe what love is and what it's not. The last verse of the chapter says that faith, hope, and love abide, but the greatest of the three is love. People often talk about men and women of faith and how important faith is. The Bible even says that without faith, it's impossible to please God. That sounds pretty important. Of course, hope is important in our lives too. It's like an anchor for our soul. So why is love greater?

Paul was arrested for preaching the gospel. He ended up giving his testimony to the rulers of the nation before being sent to Rome for further trial. While they traveled by ship, Paul had a premonition that disaster was ahead, so they should overwinter on an island. The ship's captain, however, wanted to make a different harbor, so they pushed on. On the way, they got caught in a terrible storm. For fourteen days they were tossed by waves and unable even to cook food or eat. The sailors lost all hope.

Paul, however, was encouraged by God. He had faith their lives would be saved, as God wanted him to be a witness to the people of Rome. He restored hope to the sailors, and even broke bread and ate in their presence, encouraging them also to eat. Because Paul knew the depth of God's love for him, and Paul also loved the people he was traveling with and whom he would yet witness to, he could hold on to faith and hope. He had enough of both to encourage not only himself, but also the more than two hundred people who were in peril on the stormy seas with him.

In life we can find ourselves in the midst of stormy seas of doubt or trial. We run aground on the rocks of pain or struggle, sometimes by no fault of our own. If we're assured of the depth of God's love for us, and if our love for others flows deep, then faith and hope will splash up on the waves. That faith and hope will be enough not only for us but also for those around us. We can break the bread of communion with peace in our souls no matter how violently the storm rages.

> *Father, You so loved us that You gave Your only Son to save us. We're so grateful, and we take a moment now to remember just how deep Your love is. It's enough to carry us through all that life brings our way. Amen.*

For further study: Acts 26:1–27:44; 1 Corinthians 13:1–13; Hebrews 11:6.

OCTOBER 11
Each One's Reality

The heart knows its own bitterness, and a stranger does not share its joy. (Proverbs 14:10)

I ONCE HAD a case of a cat that suddenly became blind. The blindness didn't arise from a problem at all with her eyes. The eyes were perfect, as was the nerve that took signals from the eyes to the brain. The problem was in the brain. The brain wasn't functioning properly, and since it couldn't interpret the signals arriving from the nerves, the cat couldn't see anything at all.

The things we see and hear, and how things feel, depend not just on what's present in the environment but on how our brain sorts out the electrical signals coming to it. You could say that everyone has their own reality. The color I see may not be the same as the color you see! Likewise, the grief or joy I experience won't be the same as what you experience in a similar situation. We truly can't understand what another person experiences. Only one person besides ourselves can truly know what we feel.

God is the only one who really knows what we're going through, because He designed us. He knows because He took on human form and lived with us, and He lives within us. He's not a stranger to our struggles, and He rejoices with us in our triumphs. He can bring healing to our soul and also humility to our pride. He's able to lead us in the paths of righteousness like no one else can because He knows us intimately. He understands and can truly sympathize with our weaknesses.

Since He lives in us, He's also able to bring some of His reality to us. He makes real in us the mystery of His glory and great love for us. He reveals Himself in a way in which people who haven't invited Christ into their lives can't understand or perceive. He opens our eyes to those around us, both within the body of Christ and without, filling us with the compassion He feels for the broken and lost. He changes us from the inside out. He knows our reality, and He brings to our hearts a bit of His reality.

> *Jesus, sometimes our life is a struggle, and sometimes it's a joy. We're so grateful You understand us fully. You also open our eyes to Your reality, helping us to see You and walk with You. Thank You for bringing us into communion with You and Your body on earth. Amen.*

For further study: Psalm 139:1–18; Isaiah 53:3; John 14:23; 1 Corinthians 2:9–16; Galatians 2:20; Ephesians 2:11–22, 3:14–21; Colossians 1:24–29; Hebrews 4:15.

OCTOBER 12
Made in His Image

> Then God said, "Let Us make man in Our image, according to Our likeness; let them have dominion over the fish of the sea, over the birds of the air, and over the cattle, over all the earth and over every creeping thing that creeps on the earth." (Genesis 1:26)

WHEN GOD SAYS in Genesis that He's making man in His image, He uses the plural form: "*Let Us make man in Our image*" (emphasis added). People try to explain the Trinity in many different ways, but the easiest way for me to think about it is found in that same verse. Man is made in the image of God. God is a three-part being, and so are we. We have a body, soul, and spirit—three parts yet one person. If something were to happen to my body, I'd still be fully me.

I read a novel once about a lady with dementia who was losing her mind. The book was called *Still Alice*. The author wanted to highlight that even though this lady's soul wasn't operating like it used to, she was still a whole person—still Alice. If our spirit leaves our body and heads to heaven, it's still fully us. We are not diminished. If my body hurts, my soul and spirit feel the pain. If my soul is elated, my body and spirit also jump for joy. If my spirit is renewed, all of me has become something altogether new.

The Father, Son, and Holy Spirit rejoice in the presence of the angels when a person is saved. They all know firsthand what it's like to experience death and also what it's like to be resurrected to new life. Jesus may have walked the via dolorosa—the way of pain—but it resonated with each member of the Trinity because they are one. When the stone was rolled from the tomb, all rejoiced, and now they dance for joy over each sinner who repents.

Sometimes people think of Jesus as being the one who is kind and full of mercy, but God the Father is harsh and judgmental. After all, isn't the Old Testament filled with stories of judgment? We abhor the sacrifice of animals on the Old Testament altar.

Since the Trinity is one, if Jesus is full of mercy, so is the Father. Why then were all the innocent animals killed? you might ask. It comes down to the depth of God's great love. He loved us so much He would do whatever it took to save us. Innocent animals would pay the price for the guilty, until the fullness of time would come and the ultimate innocent man could pay the price once and for all for the guilty. The Old Testament is full of stories of God's great mercy. He is just, certainly, but He's also merciful. The two aspects are united perfectly in the fullness of the Godhead. The more we partake of communion, dwelling on the mercy of God, the more we see His mercy throughout the entire Bible.

> *Oh Lord, how awesome is Your mercy. You are just, but You have paid the price so we could become the righteousness of God. You were always willing to pay the price. The innocent in exchange for the guilty, because of the depth of Your love. We are forever blessed because Jesus, the perfect Lamb, died in our place. Amen.*

For further study: Deuteronomy 6:4; Zephaniah 3:17; Luke 15:10; 2 Corinthians 5:17; Hebrews 9:11–28; 1 John 5:6–8.

OCTOBER 13
Spiritual Famine

A satisfied soul loathes the honeycomb, but to a hungry soul every bitter thing is sweet.
(Proverbs 27:7)

LATELY, I'VE HEARD many reports of famines throughout the world. People are starving and dying of malnutrition due to war, social unrest, drought, and flood. People who are starving will do anything to fill their bellies. They'll eat things that are barely edible, regardless of how bitter it tastes. They'll sell whatever they have. They'll steal if need be. The hunger drives them to extremes. Some of us who are healthy and well fed try to help by sending food to the needy, but the food doesn't always get to where it needs to go. Enemies may intercept it to sell on the black market, yet all we can do is keep trying. Their lives are at stake.

There's also a spiritual famine in the land. A war rages for our souls, and spiritual drought parches the land. Those starving will do anything to try to fill the void in their spirits. They'll partake of things that are bad for them. They'll sell their soul, steal, or wound others. The most difficult people to work with in our communities are those with the greatest spiritual need and hunger. Some of the spiritually healthy and well fed try to help the starved get the spiritual food they truly need, but our enemy may intercept it. All we can do is keep trying. Their lives are at stake.

There are others among the well fed who, instead of sending their food to the needy, hoard and consume it for themselves; some sell food on the black market to enrich their own pockets. They're so well fed that they start to loathe the honeycomb. The spiritually fat may disdain the broken and needy and care not a wit for their salvation. They'll spend time decrying the broken for interfering with their own personal comfort.

Jesus said, *"Blessed are those who hunger and thirst for righteousness, for they shall be filled"* (Matthew 5:6). We maintain some spiritual hunger by giving of our spiritual food to those who are starving. It keeps us on our knees, seeking His grace. We recall our own spiritual hunger that was sated by the body and blood of Christ. We come to the communion table to remember from whence we came. We come to be restored when we've fallen and forgotten to give of our food to the needy. We're reminded to love as we ourselves have been loved, and that it's good to retain a bit of spiritual hunger even as we pause to help the starving.

> *Jesus, You have filled us with grace and all that is good. Keep us hungry for You and willing to give of Your grace to the spiritually starved. We recognize it can be difficult, as the starving will do anything and eat anything because of their deep hunger. Help us to act with compassion, knowing their very soul is at stake. Amen.*

For further study: Proverbs 28:27; Isaiah 58:6–12; Matthew 25:35–40.

OCTOBER 14
You and What Army?

> So he answered, "Do not fear, for those who are with us are more than those who are with them." (2 Kings 6:16)

IN THE MOVIE *Shrek*, the army is sent to arrest Shrek, just because he's an ogre. When they approach Shrek, the captain says he is arresting him, but Shrek just laughs and says, "You and what army?" The captain turns around to find the entire army has fled in fear.

There's an incident recorded in the Bible in which the Syrians send an entire army to capture one man—Elisha. Elisha's servant looks out and sees the army surrounding the house and is afraid, but Elisha remains calm. He tells his servant that there are more with them than with their enemy, and then he prays that the servant's eyes would be opened. The servant then sees a multitude of horses and chariots of fire all around. Heaven's army was on Elisha's side.

Gladys Aylward was a missionary to China. One day there was a prison riot, and the leader of the region called Gladys to deal with it, as his own guards were too afraid. He said if her God was true like she said, then He would defend her. Gladys was scared, but knowing it was God's reputation on trial, she marched into the prison, took an axe away from a murderer, and then ordered the men around like she was their teacher and they were naughty schoolchildren. They all complied and the riot ended. Later she learned that the standards in the prison were horrible, and she worked to ameliorate their conditions.

When an army of people came to arrest Jesus, Jesus spoke the words, "I am," and the entire group fell down backwards. Jesus said He could call an army of angels to defend Him, but He did not. He would willingly follow His destiny all the way to the cross. The guards surrounding Jesus's tomb after His burial couldn't hold Him back either. They too fell down as dead in fear when the tomb was opened.

Sometimes we can feel alone and overwhelmed. We pause to take communion to remember that Jesus lives in us. The man greater than a whole army makes His home with us. When the enemy comes against us with thoughts of insecurity or anxiety, we can boldly say, "Oh yeah, you think you can defeat me! You and what army?" The Greater One is with us and defends us.

> *Jesus, You are a mighty warrior, able to defeat a host of enemies with just the Word. We sometimes are afraid and feel alone, but we remember today that You are with us. You have chosen to make Your home with us. No matter what happens, we will ultimately never be defeated, because You are victorious. Amen.*

For further study: 2 Kings 6:8–23; Matthew 26:47–56, 28:1–4; John 18:1–9.

OCTOBER 15
The Grace of God

> But we were hoping that it was He who was going to redeem Israel. Indeed, besides all this, today is the third day since these things happened. (Luke 24:21)

IT'S HARD TO believe I've been in my current house twelve years already. The time has flown by. When I first decided to look for a farm, I had trouble finding one within a reasonable drive to where I work. I visited place after place over more than a year. Then I found a place. It was three hundred acres of beautiful property, although the house was in need of a lot of repairs. I put in an offer with conditions that had to be satisfied in order for me to get a mortgage.

The offer was accepted but the conditions weren't fulfilled. I was so sure this would be the place, my new home. It went right to the last day as the bank, my realtor, and I tried to get this deal completed. Sadly, at the very last moment, it completely fell apart. I was wanting to still try, but my banker and realtor weren't willing to work anymore with the seller. We'd worked so hard. I was so sure we could make it happen, but alas, we could not.

Oddly enough, within a few short days a new property came up. It was 160 acres and a twenty-minute drive to work. The house was in much better condition, with no need for the seller to make any immediate improvements for the bank to be happy. And it was the same price! Negotiations were quick and smooth because we'd done all the hard work and jumped through all the hoops on the place that didn't go through. Before the week was up, I had my farm, and in a much better location. The failure of the first sale at the last minute ended up being the grace of God.

We don't always recognize things that will in the end turn out to be the grace of God. Life throws us curveballs, and things don't always go as we expect. We're so sure of things sometimes, and then we end up disappointed.

When the disciples were with Jesus, they were positive He would deliver Israel from oppression. They were so disappointed and lost when their hero was led away by Roman soldiers to be crucified. They'd been so sure things were going to be different, and now here they were uncertain of what to do next. They were trying to process the tales the women told about Jesus being risen from the dead, but it didn't make sense.

Jesus appeared to them to make it clear He hadn't come to save Israel from Roman rule; He'd come to save the world from sin. What originally looked like a failure turned out to be the grace of God. Spending time in communion with God helps us to remember that life's disappointments may truly be the grace of God.

> Jesus, we're so amazed and thankful for Your amazing grace. Your death and resurrection were the victory over our sin and death. We may not recognize that when things didn't go as we expected, it was really an act of Your grace. Help us to remain patient, knowing it will all work out in the end because of Your grace. Amen.

For further study: Luke 24:1–32; Romans 8:18–28.

OCTOBER 16
Kissing It Better

Who Himself bore our sins in His own body on the tree, that we, having died to sins, might live for righteousness—by whose stripes you were healed. (1 Peter 2:24)

WHEN YOU WERE a young child and you fell off your bike and skinned your knee, did your mom ever come and kiss it better? You see parents do that from time to time. Their child runs up crying, having hurt himself, and his mom gives him a hug and then kisses the wound to make it better. Then the child stops crying and runs back to play, happy once more. Of course, the kiss didn't make the marks of the wound disappear, but the love that was expressed took away the painful effects of the fall and restored the joy. It was the love manifested in the kiss that brought the healing to the heart.

We've all fallen and sinned, wounding our soul. We run to our heavenly Parent, tears streaming down our faces. He embraces us in our brokenness, and His love takes away the painful effects of our fall and restores our joy. His love, manifested in the wounds that Christ bore, is the kiss that heals our soul and renews our spirit to a new life in Him.

Love is a powerful force. It was the force that gave Jesus the strength to pray in the Garden of Gethsemane "... *not My will, but Yours, be done*" (Luke 22:42b). Love was the force strong enough to enable Jesus not to revile in return when He was reviled. It was love that enabled Him to endure the brutal whipping and the crown of thorns. His love carried Him to Golgotha, where He was pierced in His hands and feet. It was love that poured out with the blood and water when the spear was thrust into His side. His love caused the wounds that brought our healing, and our love for Him enables us to run to Him with our falls and failures, that we might receive His touch to make it better.

Communion is a time when we can pause and remember where we have fallen and scraped our soul. With bitter tears of repentance, we can run to Him and let His love kiss it better.

> *Jesus, we've been healed by Your wounds, which were the manifestation of Your great love. We come to You again with our failures, knowing Your love is enough to make it better. Help us to run our race without falling. Thank You. Amen.*

For further study: Matthew 26:36–46; John 3:16, 19:1–37; 1 Peter 2:21–25.

OCTOBER 17
Courage through Obedience

And when Gideon had come, there was a man telling a dream to his companion. He said, "I have just had a dream: To my surprise, a loaf of barley bread tumbled into the camp of Midian; it came to a tent and struck it so that it fell and overturned, and the tent collapsed." (Judges 7:13)

MARIE ENS IS a missionary to Cambodia. She's established orphanages and done much good in the country. She was quoted in *Faith Today* as saying, "There is no way I could ever have envisioned what we have. I never had the nerve or the faith. All I had was obedience."[4] What a powerful statement. Her courage came through her obedience.

Gideon also was afraid to do what God had called him to do. The Israelites were being terrorized by the Midianites, and God had called Gideon to be their deliverer. He was to face the massive Midianite army with only a small number of faithful soldiers. God told Gideon if he was afraid, he should sneak into the enemy camp, and he would find courage.

When Gideon did that, he heard an enemy soldier recounting a dream of a loaf of barley bread overturning a tent. The interpretation of that dream was that Gideon would be victorious over them. Gideon took courage and stationed his men around the Midian camp. They had no weapons in their hands, but each one held a torch hidden inside a pitcher in one hand and a trumpet in the other. When Gideon gave the signal, they broke the pitchers, throwing up a great light, and blew the trumpets. This put the Midianite army into great confusion, and they ended up killing their own countrymen or running away.

Jesus, our bread of life, was obedient to the call to lay down His life for us. When He rolled away the stone in front of the tomb on the third day after His death, He toppled and overturned our sin nature. His light shone brightly, and we heard the trumpet call of salvation. He totally defeated the enemy of our soul and sent him running. We also walk in this world, and all we really have is obedience. We have no weapon in our hands but the light of the gospel and the trumpet call for others to come to the saving knowledge of Jesus Christ, and this is enough to defeat the enemy of souls and send him running.

> *Jesus, You are the bread of life who gave Your life for us. We're grateful that Your light shines in the darkness and You have set us on the road to righteousness. Help us let Your light shine through us to all who are around us. Amen.*

For further study: Judges 6:1–7:25; Jeremiah 6:16,17; John 6:51.

---

[4] "Canadian Woman Spends Lifetime in Missionary Service," *Faith Today*, January/February 2024, 10.

OCTOBER 18
Make Me Small

He must increase, but I must decrease. (John 3:30)

MY MOM KNOWS all the neighbors who live on her block, and even those on nearby streets. She knows their kids, their pets, and even their grandkids and grandpets. She's not nosey. She just cares about people. Me, on the other hand … I live on a quiet country road. There are only three houses on my street, so I only have two neighbors—and I only know one of them. I'm a victim of my time.

People these days rarely venture out to meet strangers or take the time to get to know people. In my mom's era, neighbors took the time to reach out to each other. Today we reach out through our phones but not always in reality. I'm too busy with my own life to take the time to reach out to people face to face. Even when I'm talking to someone in person, I may not give them my full attention. I might be drawn by the pinging of my phone, or distracted with thoughts of things I have yet to do. I may even be too busy thinking about what I want to say next so that I'm not really listening to what my friend is saying now. My personal self is too big in my mind, so it's taking up all the space there.

God is really big. He made the universe! The entire world cannot contain Him. Yet He made Himself small. He became small enough to fit into a tiny baby, born helpless in a barn. He made Himself subject to the world's laws, constrained by gravity, having to grow one cell at a time from the baby to the man. He made Himself small enough to walk the dusty streets and to wash the feet of His disciples. He became small enough to take a brutal whipping and to die a criminal's death, even though He was innocent of any crime. He who is big, made Himself small, so that He could live big in us.

Jesus crossed the universe He'd created and walked the road to the cross in love for me, yet I won't even cross the street in love for my neighbor. In my own self, I'll never be able to lay my life down for others. Only when He's big in me does it become possible. Let our prayer today be for the Lord to make us small in ourselves so that He might be big. Just as John the Baptist said about Jesus *"He must increase, but I must decrease,"* so Jesus must increase in us, and we must decrease.

In partaking of communion today, let's examine ourselves. Is there an area where we're putting our selfish desires ahead of giving attention and love to those around us? Let's bring it to Him, knowing that only by laying our pride at the foot of the cross and letting Him be big will we be able to be like Him and become small.

Jesus, make us smaller. Let us be just like You. You laid it all down in order to lift us up. Help us to lay down our lives for others, giving them the attention they deserve as a fellow child of God. Amen.

For further study: John 1:1–28; Philippians 2:1–11; 1 John 3:16.

OCTOBER 19
Free Will

> I call heaven and earth as witnesses today against you, that I have set before you life and death, blessing and cursing; therefore choose life, that both you and your descendants may live. (Deuteronomy 30:19)

ON SEVERAL OCCASIONS now, I've heard about people who believe there's no such thing as free will. Their argument is that we are products of our genetics and environment. These will dictate how our brain tends to function, so our responses follow naturally from that and not from our own choices. If you asked these people what that would mean for the justice system, I think they'd find it rather uncomfortable. How can someone be tried for murder if they had no choice in their actions?

How far away we have moved as a society from knowledge of the God who created us, a God of justice and of mercy! He is the God who gave us free will. He told Adam and Eve that they could choose to eat from any of the myriad of beautiful trees in the garden, including the tree of life, or they could choose to eat of the tree of the knowledge of good and evil, which would bring death. There would be a consequence to their choice. Nevertheless, He let them choose.

God doesn't want to be loved by programmable robots without free will. A robot's love or obedience means nothing. He wanted to be loved and to pour out His love on people who could choose to respond to that love or not. He wouldn't force us. Forced love isn't real love. Love must be freely given and received to have real meaning.

Likewise, God Himself, a God of love, has free will. Jesus chose to lay His life down for us. As He was being arrested in the Garden of Gethsemane, He said He could even at that moment call a legion of angels to deliver Him, but He wouldn't. A price needed to be paid for sin to bring justice, and He would willingly pay that price.

God has made the choice to love us even when we don't return that love. He makes the sun to rise on the just and the unjust. He loved us even while we were yet sinners. He loved us enough to walk the way to the cross. He asks us to choose to love Him and to love our neighbor. Every day we make a thousand small choices—some good, some bad. He chooses to never stop loving us regardless of our choices. He is the author of free will. He gave it, and He demonstrated it. He also chose to offer us mercy. We can accept it or reject it. To accept it is to choose life; to reject it leaves us to face judgment for our choices.

We pause to take communion to thank God for the choice He made to love us. We thank Him for paying the price of justice so we could receive His mercy. We choose to love Him because He first chose to love us. We choose life in Him and with Him.

> *Jesus, thank You for dying in our place. You have chosen us, and we choose You. Thank You for the life You have given for us and to us. Amen.*

For further study: Genesis 2:15–17; Deuteronomy 30:14–20; Matthew 5:44–45, 26:53; John 10:18; 1 John 4:19.

OCTOBER 20
Deep Roots

As you have therefore received Christ Jesus the Lord, so walk in Him, rooted and built up in Him and established in the faith, as you have been taught, abounding in it with thanksgiving.
(Colossians 2:6–7)

I LOVE MY farm. I have quite a large acreage, with several trails cutting through the bush. My favorite trail is just over three kilometers long, and it runs through hills and valleys, rocks and swamps. One particularly swampy area was a bit hard to traverse in the spring, so one year, I decided to move that part of the trail to higher ground. I was glad I did, because the next year we had a windstorm that brought down a group of five huge trees right across the old trail. Because those trees were in wet, swampy ground, they never bothered to sink roots deep into the soil. Their roots were all intertwined, so when one tree started to fall, the whole group came down together.

When I first asked Jesus into my heart, faith seemed so easy. Life was rich with rains of joy and blessings from the Spirit of God. I thought it would go on like that forever. There was such an abundance of grace, but my roots were shallow. Time and circumstances, however, brought a spiritual drought. I started to question my faith, whether it was real or worthwhile. I had to send my roots deeper to look for the living water to nourish my soul.

Over the years, I've seen other Christians tumble and fall, and some of them were even quite big in the faith. Sadly, the bigger they were, the more others tumbled with them. Their roots were too shallow to withstand the winds of pride or adversity. All I can think to myself is *There but for the grace of God go I.*

As I walk my path today, I'm thankful for the dry times. As my roots of faith struggled through the hard ground, they gained strength and a solidity to keep me standing in stormy winds. My joy and praise can quietly stretch upwards toward the Son like the branches of a stately oak. Bigger storms may yet come. All I can do is pray that my roots stay wrapped around the solid bedrock on which I stand. By the grace of God, and the dry seasons, they shall.

> *God, we thank You for the dry seasons that force us to examine our foundation and send our roots deeper down to Jesus, the rock on which we stand. Today we remember Your goodness and grace, even when the ground seems dry and hard. All is a gift from You. Amen.*

For further study: Job 14:7–9; Ezekiel 31:1–18; Matthew 7:24–27.

OCTOBER 21
Interior Decorating

A good man out of the good treasure of his heart brings forth good; and an evil man out of the evil treasure of his heart brings forth evil. For out of the abundance of the heart his mouth speaks. (Luke 6:45)

I'M NOT MUCH of an interior decorator. I seem to always pick colors that clash, or I leave painting half done. I had a leak of water in my basement, and now the drywall bears discolored spots from moisture, mold, and mildew, but I find it easy to ignore, since I don't go downstairs very often. I probably will need to rip out the drywall and fix things up, but it doesn't look like I'm ever going to get around to it.

The vet clinic I work at recently moved. The boss hired an interior designer, and I have to say that the place looks stunning. The building was gutted and completely redesigned. They did a much better job than I could have imagined. If I'd been in charge, it wouldn't have been fixed up so well. What a difference a professional touch makes.

One day, the Pharisees approached Jesus and told Him that it was wrong for His disciples to eat with unwashed hands. Jesus rebuked the Pharisees. He said His disciples were not defiled by this, but rather what comes out of a man defiles him. Jesus went on to explain that the heart of man controls what he says. If a man's heart is filled with things like murder, adultery, fornication, or theft, those kinds of things will be manifest out of his mouth. The person who hasn't leaned on Jesus has a heart that leans toward sin, like mold in the drywall. They need some interior decorating done!

Once we ask Jesus into our hearts, He not only plans some redecorating, but He completely guts the space. He takes away the sin growing like mildew, puts some nice fresh walls in place, and spruces the place up with the color of joy. Like any major reconstruction, the deconstruction of the old and placing of the new can take a bit of time. The process sometimes can be a bit frustrating. We want it to be perfect right away, but we have to look to the future and trust the designer. Our God is a master and a professional. He knows exactly how to work within our space. He's the best there is. We need not fear the process. The end result will be stunning. Our job is to give Him access to all the spaces of our heart, even the deep, dark corners we rarely go to.

Pausing to take communion is to pause and ask the Holy Spirit to reveal those secret areas of our hearts where the world has leaked in and caused some sin to remain. We give Jesus access to even those deep, dark corners. This master designer will be more than happy to clean up those hidden spots and make us new.

Jesus, we open our hearts fully to You, knowing that what's in our hearts is sure to come out of our mouths at some point. Holy Spirit, reveal the dark secrets hidden in our hearts so that we can turn them over to Jesus, confessing our sins and being cleansed of unrighteousness. Amen.

For further study: Ezekiel 36:25–27; Matthew 15:1–20; Luke 6:40–45; 1 Corinthians 4:5; 1 John 1:8–10.

OCTOBER 22
Home Safe and Sound

> For if we believe that Jesus died and rose again, even so God will bring with Him those who sleep in Jesus. (1 Thessalonians 4:14)

I RECENTLY TRAVELED to visit a sick relative. After my visit, I returned to my home and my church. While sitting with fellow members of the church around the table in prayer, one of the ladies prayed, "I thank You, Lord, that my sister is home safe and sound."

That phrase really struck me. I was at my earthly home safe and sound, but this earth is not our real home. Many people in this world are not in safe places, and many more aren't sound in body or mind, like the ailing relative I went to visit. But then, we're not really home yet.

There will come a day when we gather around the Lord's table. He'll pick up the bread to break it and pass it around, but first He'll bow His head and pray. "Father, I thank You that these dear children are all home, safe and sound."

One of the great promises of God is that He has prepared a place for us. We don't grieve the loss of a loved one like those who have no hope. We know a better place awaits. Jesus went before us, laying His life down and taking it up again, the firstborn from the dead, that where He is, we would be able to go. We have a place eternally at His communion table. For this we can be grateful, even in the midst of loss.

> *Jesus, You are the firstborn from the dead, paving the way for us to have a home with You in eternity. At times we grieve the loss of those we love, but we thank You that they're now home, safe and sound. Amen.*

For further study: John 14:1–4; 2 Corinthians 5:1–8; Colossians 1:15–18; 1 Thessalonians 4:13–18; Hebrews 13:14–15.

OCTOBER 23
Exceedingly Great Reward

After these things the word of the Lord came to Abram in a vision, saying, "Do not be afraid, Abram. I am your shield, your exceedingly great reward." (Genesis 15:1)

THERE'S A SAYING that goes, "The pain of change has to become less than the pain of staying the same." I understand that statement. I need to get out and walk more, getting some fresh air and exercise to improve my health and stay strong. On cool days like today, I'd rather sit at home in my comfy chair with a good book and a hot cup of tea. In order to get out of my chair, I had to make things a little uncomfortable.

A friend and I signed up for an online app that enables you to walk virtual trails. You have to sign up to complete it in a specified amount of time. We walk as a team, so she knows if I'm not pulling my weight. The embarrassment of her knowing I slacked off gets me up and out the door. I know as I become more fit, I'll no longer need the push of embarrassment. Walking will be its own reward. When that happens, the reward of change will be greater than the reward of staying the same.

Ultimately, we're more motivated by reward than by punishment. Maybe that's why becoming a Christian changes us so much. We know we'll have an eternal reward of heaven, but there are also all of the temporal rewards of joy and peace in the Holy Ghost. We're strengthened with might in our inner being. His love dwells in us and fills us. We receive a peace that passes all understanding. The rewards are endless and amazing.

Sometimes the wind blows cold and we forget all the great things we have in Christ. We long to slip back into the comfort of the old, familiar ways. This is why we pause to partake of communion. We remind ourselves that Christ is indeed our exceedingly great reward. There's nothing better than His love. It's also a marvelous thing to let His great love within us flow out to those around us. The reward of change is so much better than the reward of slipping back into our old life without Him. Sometimes we just need a little reminder, so we break the bread and sip the cup, basking in His abundant glory and grace once again.

Jesus, You've done so much for us. We're so blessed and abundantly rewarded by Your great love. Thank You for the grace bestowed upon us and the blessings You've given us. Amen.

For further study: Matthew 5:11–12; Romans 14:17; Ephesians 3:16–21; Philippians 4:6–7.

OCTOBER 24
He Knows My Name

> He who overcomes shall be clothed in white garments, and I will not blot out his name from the Book of Life; but I will confess his name before My Father and before His angels. (Revelation 3:5)

I RECENTLY WROTE a novel that was published. I'm new to this whole adventure, so I was taken aback by people asking for their copy to be signed. One lady from my church approached me to get her book signed. I knew I should know her name, but I couldn't think of it at all. I'm really terrible at remembering names. I didn't want to admit I couldn't remember her name, so I asked her if she'd like it addressed to anyone in particular. I was hoping the book was going to be a gift for a relative. She answered that I could address it to herself. I was busted! Embarrassing!

God, however, never has that problem. He always knows our name. He knows the name of every star in heaven. Remembering the names of the billions of people on the earth is nothing to Him. He knows the very hairs on our head, never mind just knowing our name. He says He will also confess our name before the Father and the angels. Our name is written in the Book of Life! He told the church at Pergamos that when we overcome, He'll give us a white stone with a new name written on it that only He and the person receiving it knows. He knows our current name, but He also knows the special name we'll receive from Him. Amazing!

He says He will give us that stone along with the hidden manna. Manna was angels' food provided to Israel when they fled from Egypt. We flee from our old life of sin and receive the true manna that came from heaven—Jesus, the bread of life. He is the bread that came down from heaven to redeem us. He knows us and is thinking about us. He loves us and laid His life down for us. He doesn't struggle to remember our name, for it's always in His heart and on His breath. His love for us runs deeper than life itself.

> *Jesus, You know our name, and You said You will confess it before the Father and the angels. We are awestruck by Your majesty and Your thoughts toward us. We pause to remember that You know us, and You also died for us, raising us to new life with You. Thank You! Amen.*

For further study: Psalm 139:14–18, 147:4; Isaiah 43:1–7; Jeremiah 1:5; Luke 12:6–8; John 6:22–58; Revelation 2:12–17.

OCTOBER 25
Roller Coaster Ride

This is the day the Lord has made; we will rejoice and be glad in it. (Psalm 118:24)

I USED TO like taking a group of kids on a trip to the amusement park. We'd rent a bus or pile into a couple of vans, leaving early in the morning to travel four hours. Then we'd spend the day lining up for the various rides and eating cotton candy and BeaverTails. We'd stay all day, only heading home as the sun dropped low in the sky and the park was closing. The kids could talk me into going on any ride or roller coaster—once. I wouldn't promise to ever ride it again. As I get older, I find that I don't handle all the twists and turns as well as I used to when I was a child myself. Sometimes those big padded shoulder restraints box my ears or cause pain. Even though I may enjoy the thrill of the loops and spins, I'm not a big fan of pain.

Life can be a bit like amusement parks and roller coaster rides. We travel at great speed from one day to the next. Sometimes we're climbing high heights of joy and anticipation, while other times we plummet to depths of despair. Sometimes we fly forward in faith, and other times our journey seems to go backwards. Sometimes life is scary; sometimes it's a thrilling adventure. Sometimes our stomach turns and we can't handle it, and at other times we enjoy a delicious feast of tasty treats. Photos capture our expressions in a snapshot of time before we're on to the next adventure. We may make a choice that results in pain, but we can choose to not do that same ride again, learning from our mistakes.

The wonderful thing is that no matter what we face, Jesus faces it with us. He's beside us on the ride. We may grip the bar in front of us with white knuckles, a scream catching in our throat, but He raises His hands in joy, telling us to enjoy the moment! He knows the roller coaster will grind to a stop and the ride will be over all too soon. The sun will start to set, and it will be time for Him to take us home. In the meantime, as we queue up for the various rides, we can chat with those around us, sharing His love and joy of life with our fellow adventurers.

Jesus, thank You for being beside us on this adventure. Every twist and turn is known to You. Help us face it all with joy, knowing You are with us through it all. Let us show that joy to everyone around us. Amen.

For further study: Psalm 118:14–29; Romans 8:18–39.

OCTOBER 26
Kite Flying

And they overcame him by the blood of the Lamb and by the word of their testimony, and they did not love their lives to the death. (Revelation 12:11)

MY DOG GINGER absolutely hated kites. If she got a hold of a kite, she instantly destroyed it, tearing it to shreds. One day as I sat reading, I noticed her staring at something in the park. I followed her gaze to a bright red kite with a long pretty tail being flown high in the sky. Both Ginger and I glanced toward the front door at the same time. Did I mention Ginger could open almost any door? The screen door was no barrier to her. We both leapt up to run for the door at the same moment. She was faster. She ran out of the house, the screen door banging against the wall as it flew open. I was right behind her as she headed up over the dike, her eyes glued to the kite. She was so intent on the murder of the kite that she didn't see the parked car. This was the same car that belonged to the nice family picnicking on the grass while their young son flew his kite. She hit the car with such force that she tumbled up and over the hood, rolling down on the other side. As I crested the dike, I saw the father jump up in shock. He had just seen a dog get hit by a car! Wait, that was his car. Someone must be stealing his car! No, wait, the car wasn't moving. Did the car get hit by the dog? All those thoughts could be seen on his face.

Meanwhile, Ginger had jumped up, shaken the cobwebs from her head, and recommenced her pursuit of the evil kite. The boy, distracted, started to let the kite fall while I yelled, "No, keep the kite in the air, or it will be gone forever!" The boy managed to refocus while I chased Ginger in big loops below the offensive kite until I managed to hook her collar, dragging her home still barking and growling, digging her toes in to resist. As soon as I got her safely in the house, I noted that the young family had packed up and left, the neighborhood obviously a little too strange for their liking.

We're a bit like that kite. We are firmly attached to Jesus. He helps us rise up on the wind of the Spirit, flying high on faith and grace. Our enemy, the devil, however, seeks to tear us to shreds. He runs at us, focused, with murder the only thing in his heart. If the connection between us and Jesus falters or is broken, we'll tumble and spin down, landing in some ditch or getting tangled in trees. We become easy prey for our enemy. Luckily, unlike the boy in the park, Jesus has no trouble keeping His concentration on the job. He knows the enemy will run into a barrier and hurt only himself in his attempt to reach us.

We pause to take communion to remind us of His shed blood. We pause to remember what He has saved us from. He laid His life down for us, so we can lay ours down for others. In remembering what He's done, we stay rooted and grounded in His love. Our connection to Him stays strong and we soar on the wind of His Spirit.

Jesus, You have saved us, and we will overcome all the enemy throws our way because of Your precious blood and our knowledge of Your love. Your precious love enables us to lay down our lives that we might live forever with You. Thank You. Amen.

For further study: Luke 22:20; Galatians 2:20; Ephesians 2:14–21; 1 John 3:16.

OCTOBER 27
Our Father

In this manner, therefore, pray: Our Father in heaven, hallowed be Your name. (Matthew 6:9)

JESUS'S DISCIPLES ASKED Him to teach them how to pray. Jesus gave them a prayer we commonly call the Lord's Prayer. Many of us know this prayer by heart. We've even repeated it together in church services. We think we fully understand it, yet we can always learn something new. The Holy Spirit can reveal new insights even in this well-known and beloved prayer.

Recently I had just such an experience. I was reading a book called *Rediscovering the Lord's Prayer* by Art Simon. He mentions that the prayer is to *our* father, collectively. Not just me, not just you, but all of us. I don't know why I never really noticed that before. God is certainly my dad. He's my protector and provider, my salvation and righteousness, my peace and shepherd, but He's also all that to you. He's all that to the most annoying person we know. He's Dad to the guy sitting in his car at the gas station, with a skull tattooed all over his face. He's Dad to the girl who always wears long sleeves because her arms are covered in scars from cutting. He's Dad to the family whose mom just died from a drug overdose. He's Dad to the construction worker outside, working in the rain and sleet. He is *our* Father in heaven. We who know Jesus are united by the cross in one body with Christ, and all humans are united by blood, going back to Adam and Eve, in one human family.

When we pray the Lord's Prayer, asking God's name to be holy, we're praying for the Lord of our salvation to be reverenced by all, for His righteousness to be manifested in *us*. Not just me, not just you, but all of us. I love my nieces and nephews and my great nieces and great nephews. They don't always make good choices, but I still love them because they're the children of the ones I love. God's children don't always make good choices, but I can love them simply because they're the children of the one I love.

Sometimes our brothers and sisters in this big human family can be prickly. Sometimes they can even be unsafe, and we must set up boundaries with them. Yet we can still love them as someone who can call God "Daddy." We can pray for them as someone who calls my dad their dad. When we lift up our voices in the Lord's Prayer, we can be cognizant that we pray not just for ourselves, but for all of humanity—Our Father in heaven, may Your name be holy in us all.

> *Father in heaven, Daddy, we come to You recognizing that we haven't always thought kindly of Your other children. We recognize we are all united as one family, and we pray today for Your salvation and righteousness to reach to all. Jesus, thank You also for uniting us by Your body and blood into one Christian family, being our shepherd, our redeemer, and our hope. Amen.*

For further study: Psalm 23:1; Matthew 6:9–13; Luke 11:1–13; Acts 17:24–30; Romans 8:15.

OCTOBER 28
Thy Kingdom Come

Your kingdom come. Your will be done on earth as it is in heaven. (Matthew 6:10)

IN THE SECOND line of the Lord's Prayer, we're told to pray for His kingdom to come on earth like it is in heaven. I always thought of this as praying for God's will to be done in my life, like marrying the right person, moving to the right city, accepting the right job, those kinds of things. I now think it's really about so much more than that.

In Matthew 13, Jesus sits down to teach the multitudes. He speaks about the Word of God being sown in people's hearts, like a seed sown on the ground. Some of it takes root and thrives, but some doesn't. He speaks of the kingdom of heaven being like good seed sown in the field, but an enemy sows weeds in the same field.

He also describes the kingdom as being like a mustard seed; even though it's tiny, it grows into a tree that shelters the birds. The kingdom is like leaven that has flour thoroughly mixed with it, or like treasure hidden in a field that a man goes and sells all he has to buy. It's like a pearl of great price for which a merchant goes and sells all he has to buy. He also told us that anyone who understands the kingdom of heaven is like someone who brings out treasures both new and old.

It's really quite the chapter. Nowhere in that chapter do I see the kingdom being about Christians finding the right spouse or job or house. Instead, it's about having His Word rooted in our hearts so we can go about our day with grace. I see it as being about Christians in a field, surrounded by the lost. His kingdom is about the smallest part of the living Word growing in our hearts to something great that shelters others. It's about Him permeating every aspect of our lives. I see it being about a man who sees a treasure in the dirt of the ground and sells all he has to buy the field and redeem the treasure. It means being willing to give all we have to gain the treasure of Christ. The kingdom of heaven is like treasures both new and old that we can showcase to the lost and dying world, hoping they also will come to the joy we have found.

When we pray for God's kingdom to come and His will to be done, we pray like Jesus prayed in the garden. He wanted God's will for the salvation of humanity to be done, so He was willing to go to the cross and lay down His life, even though it was going to be difficult and painful.

We're being reminded that the kingdom is about the Word of God being established in our hearts so we also can lay our lives down for others. This is why we pause to take communion as well. We partake of the bread and wine to remember what He's done for us and the call for us to let Him live in us and through us. May God's kingdom come and His will be done in us and in the world around us.

> *Jesus, just as You prayed for God's will to be done, so we also pray for God's kingdom to come and His will be done, in our hearts and in the lives of those around us. Amen.*

For further study: Matthew 12:38–13:1–53; Luke 22:19–20, 39–46; Romans 14:17; 1 John 3:16.

OCTOBER 29
Our Daily Bread

Give us this day our daily bread. (Matthew 6:11)

I'M SURE WHEN Jesus told us to pray for our daily bread, He knew that many people would be on gluten-free diets in the future. Bread, of course, was such a staple of daily life that it became synonymous with provision. We talk about money as bread or dough.

We need more than money, of course, to get through the day. Jesus, the bread of life, is our true provider. We need grace to cover our sins. We need joy to face our challenges. We need His mercy. We need His Word to come alive in our hearts. There have never been as many people on anti-anxiety and antidepressant medications as there are right now. If there was ever a time we needed a daily dose of Jesus, it's in this day and age.

In Proverbs, the writer prays for just the right amount of food for the day (Proverbs 30:8–9). Not so much that he's puffed up in pride, and not so little that he steals from others. We also can pray for enough grace for the day. We can ask for enough grace to cover the sins of the day but not so much we think we're somebody special. Paul said the thorn that bothered him was given to him so he wouldn't be puffed up in pride and would rely on God's grace. It was the right amount of Jesus for the day.

As always, there's more to be found in the Scripture from the Lord's Prayer regarding our daily bread. There's that little word *us*. Give *us* this day our daily bread. It's not just a prayer for me to have all my needs met but for all of us to receive grace for today. It's a prayer for all of us to have enough Jesus in us to change ourselves, our families, our cities, our countries, and our world. It's a prayer to have enough Jesus to face all our challenges with grace and to have enough to give away. It's a prayer for us to have that encouraging word to help someone else stand strong in the faith, and to have enough to bless each other. It's a prayer for us to have enough grace so that we won't hide, shyly pretending we don't see, but instead we speak to the lost and broken with grace and faith so they receive their daily bread.

Jesus is enough for my daily needs, but also for yours. He's enough for my neighbor and for yours. There's just the right amount of grace waiting for us each day if we only remember it's there for us.

Jesus, You are the bread of life. You are our provider, our source for all we need and all that is good. Thank You for bestowing enough grace for the day to each one of us. Help us to not hoard up Your grace, stealing it from others, but may we instead share Your grace and glory with all. Amen.

For further study: John 6:51; 2 Corinthians 9:6–15, 12:7–10; 2 Peter 1:2–3.

OCTOBER 30
Forgive Us Our Trespasses

And forgive us our debts, as we forgive our debtors. (Matthew 6:12)

IN THE LORD'S Prayer, when Jesus speaks of forgiveness of debts, some translations will use the word "trespasses" instead. This is referring to sin. Sin comprises all our mistakes and all the times we fall short of living up to the call of God for our lives. The Ten Commandments are like a short summary list of the ways we sin. Since they can be summed up further into loving God with all our heart and soul and strength, and loving our neighbor as ourselves, sin is reflected by all the times we fail to love.

This really challenges me. I greet God in the morning, spending time in communion with Him, but then on my drive to work, I signal my intention to change lanes, and the fellow in my blind spot speeds up instead of slowing a little to let me in. I find at that moment the most unloving thoughts in my heart. Throughout the day things happen: people impose upon me, or someone acts unkindly, and the thoughts of my heart reflect my lack of love. I may not act on those thoughts. I won't yell at the other driver or gesture rudely. I likely won't respond with cursing to the unkind people in my life, but my thoughts reflect my true sinful nature.

This is why we spend time once again in communion. As we break the bread and sip the wine, we're reminded that God has redeemed us from our sinful nature. We have a chance to examine ourselves and remember our own sins, but then we bring them to the foot of the cross. In confessing those sins, once again we're washed clean. There is such a freedom in the forgiveness received. Even if we sin seventy times seven in a day, He reaches out with grace and forgiveness. The quicker we come to the cross with our failures, the less of a hold the sin nature has on us. We become less likely to think those unloving thoughts and more likely to think thoughts of grace and blessing. His grace fills up those places where sin once resided. In receiving His forgiveness, we learn to forgive. In receiving His love, we learn to love.

> *Jesus, thank You so much for redeeming us from our sinful nature. We still mess up, but You are faithful to forgive us. As You fill us with Your love, we learn to love others. There is such a blessing for us and for others as we walk in Your ways. Let Your glory be manifested in us. Amen.*

For further study: Exodus 20:2–17; Proverbs 23:7a; Matthew 18:21–35, 22:34–40; Mark 12:28–34; Romans 13:8–14; 1 John 1:9.

OCTOBER 31
Lead Us Not into Temptation

And do not lead us into temptation, but deliver us from the evil one. Matthew 6:13a

WHEN A CARTOON character faces a dilemma, often a little angel appears on one shoulder, pushing him to make the right choice, while a little devil rests on the other shoulder, encouraging him to take the more selfish option. Usually, the little devil defeats the little angel, and the cartoon character ends up in all sorts of trouble. Even Pinocchio silenced little Jiminy Cricket, his voice of conscience, as he and his friends fell to temptation, only to find themselves turned into donkeys to be sold as labor for the salt mines.

One of the greatest Christians ever, the apostle Paul, spoke of the inner battle of will to do what is right over temptation. He spoke of wanting to do good but ending up doing what he didn't want to do (Romans 7:19). The devil indeed will tempt us with sin, but it appears we have a greater tempter living within us. We're drawn away from the good we wish to do by our own lust and pride.

Jesus also faced all the same temptations that are in the world: the lust of the flesh, the lust of the eyes, and the pride of life. I wonder if He was already wondering where to get food when the devil suggested He turn the rocks to bread. Was Jesus already thinking about redeeming the entire world when the devil said he would give the world to Jesus? Did Jesus wonder about how best to prove He was really the Son of God when the devil approached to say He should throw Himself down for the angels to rescue? Jesus defeated the tempter by quoting the Word of God.

When Paul was pondering his inability to resist the temptation to sin, he cried out "Oh wretched man that I am! who will help me?" (Romans 7:24, paraphrased). He then answered this question. Jesus Christ, the *Word* of God, would help him. Jesus defeated the tempter once and for all when He rose victorious from the tomb. That same Spirit who raised Him from the dead lives in us, redeeming us from sin. So herein lies the answer. God doesn't lead us to temptation, but He leads us to Himself, the one who overcomes the evil without and within.

We pause to receive communion and to remember that the same Spirit who raised Christ from the dead dwells in us. Jesus paid the price of our redemption and gives us victory over sin and death. The Word of God enables us to resist every temptation, whether from our spiritual enemy or our own lust and pride.

> *Jesus, You overcame the evil one and enable us to overcome the temptations common to humans. In ourselves we were helpless, but because of You, victory is always within our grasp. You are the Word of God, and by the Word we too can defeat our enemies without and within. Amen.*

For further study: Luke 4:1–13; Romans 7:7–8:15; James 1:12–18; 1 John 2:16.

NOVEMBER 1
Praise Went First

For Yours is the kingdom and the power and the glory forever. Amen. (Matthew 6:13b)

THE LORD'S PRAYER ends with a line of praise for our God. Often in the Bible, praise comes first and not just at the end of the psalm or after the victory is won. Jehoshaphat was the king of Judah when a great army came against him. He sought God in prayer and reminded God that they had no way to fight this huge enemy army. God told him that they wouldn't have to fight but that God Himself would bring the victory. The people rejoiced and praised God. They even went out to face the enemy with the singers and worshipers leading the way. The Lord fought for them, and the enemy was completely defeated. They could rejoice even more as they collected the spoils of the enemy, which took them three whole days to haul away.

Paul and Silas also sang praises to God, even in the midst of the inner prison in Philippi. As they sang hymns, the ground shook and the prison doors were opened. Paul was able to use this miracle to lead the guard and his family to salvation in Christ Jesus. The praise went before this victory of the saving of souls.

When Jesus and His disciples sat down at the Passover table, on the same night He would be betrayed, He gave thanks. When they finished supper, just before they headed to the Mount of Olives, they sang hymns. Praise went first before the greatest battle that ever would be. Praise went first before the greatest victory of all eternity. We have received His grace, so we rejoice. We sing praise now, even as praise went ahead of His great sacrifice. The Greek word for "grace" is rooted in the word for "a gift received," which is rooted in the verb "to rejoice." To say grace is to give thanks for the gift received. We can rejoice in the gift of grace, the forgiveness of sins, because Jesus also said grace. Even though He was headed for a great trial, He could praise God and give thanks. In receiving His gift, we also now praise God and give thanks. This is the essence of communion.

Jesus, on the night You were betrayed, You gave thanks. You were about to be beaten and pierced through, yet You sang hymns. Nothing will come to us today that You can't overcome, as You have already won the greatest victory of all—the victory over sin and death. We remember this today and praise You. No matter what trials we face, our praise for the God of heaven and earth will go before us and follow after us. Amen.

For further study: 2 Chronicles 20:1–30; Mark 14:26; Acts 16:25–34; 1 Corinthians 11:23–25.

NOVEMBER 2
Once and for All

By that will we have been sanctified through the offering of the body of Jesus Christ once for all. (Hebrews 10:10)

WHEN YOU WERE growing up, perhaps your parents would put their foot down with a statement like, "Once and for all, I'm telling you to do this." It's a sentence that says, "This is it." There's a finality about it. There will be no second or third or fourth chance. Act now or face the consequences.

The author of Hebrews tells us that before Jesus came, there had to be sacrifices year after year to try to cover the sins of humanity. It was a constant reminder of our shortcomings. When Jesus came, however, His blood was the final sacrifice. He died once and for all. There's a finality to it. No further sacrifices would be made. No further sacrifices need to be made. His sacrifice was also *for all*. It's God's will that all come to a saving knowledge of Jesus Christ. Jesus's blood was enough to purchase all of humanity. His blood was enough for all our sins, those of yesterday, today, and tomorrow. His mercies are new every morning because the one sacrifice was enough.

He died for all, but not all will receive it. We must act on His sacrifice, believing in Him, receiving His gift, or face the consequences. Jesus is the cornerstone of our faith. If we fall on Him with a broken heart, He receives us gladly, but the unrighteous will be crushed by that stone.

As we pause in our day to partake of communion, we're reminded He died once for all. We who have received this grace are also reminded that He has called us to demonstrate His love to others, that they too may recognize His sacrifice and receive His saving grace. We are His ambassadors to all, for He died once for all.

Jesus, Your blood is more than enough to pay the price for our sins. We thank You for loving the world and being obedient to the call to be the perfect sacrifice, once for all. Amen.

For further study: Psalm 118:22–24; Lamentations 3:22–23; Matthew 21:42–44; John 1:12; 2 Corinthians 5:18–6:2; 1 Timothy 2:3–6; Hebrews 9:27–10:18.

NOVEMBER 3
Put on the Armor

> The night is far spent, the day is at hand. Therefore let us cast off the works of darkness, and let us put on the armor of light. (Romans 13:12)

WHEN I RIDE horses, I wear a special type of padded jacket as well as a helmet. It's a bit like wearing armor against a fall. The jacket and helmet protect my chest and head from serious injury. A fall may still hurt, but not nearly as much as it would have if I weren't wearing protective clothing.

Different activities may call for different protective gear. A police officer on routine patrol may wear one type of armor, but someone in full riot gear may wear much more body armor. They may still get injured, depending on what they're facing, but the injury is less likely to be fatal.

Paul wrote to the Romans and told them to put on the armor of light. He writes about it in the context of fulfilling the commandments by loving your neighbor as well as by putting away old patterns of behaving, such as walking in strife and envy. Paul also wrote to the Ephesians and said to put on armor to be able to stand against the enemy of our souls. The context here is in praying for each other.

John also writes about God being light and having no darkness in Him. In 1 John, he writes that if we walk in darkness, we're not walking in truth, but if we walk in the light like He is in the light, we have fellowship with one another (1 John 1:5–7). The context is once again about how we relate to others in the body of Christ. The darkness of sin in ourselves, sin in others, the brokenness of this fallen world, and the spiritual attacks from the devil are always pushing in on us, but the armor of light repels them like the sunlight breaking over the horizon.

We put on body armor that protects our vital organs by staying in communion with the Lord and with each other. By putting away our old sinful nature through confessing and forsaking our sins, we peel off the thin rags that offer no protection from the wiles of our enemy. By walking in communion with our Lord, we put on His light and repel the darkness that would wound our hearts and minds.

> *God, You are light and in You there is no darkness. We spend time today in communion with You, putting off works of darkness so we might walk with You in the light. Forgive our sins and lead us in Your glorious light. Amen.*

For further study: Romans 13:8–14; Ephesians 6:10–20; 1 John 1:5–7.

NOVEMBER 4
The Belt of Truth

Stand therefore, having girded your waist with truth … (Ephesians 6:14a)

I'VE HEARD THE saying that we don't become a liar because we told a lie, but we tell a lie because we're a liar. When I mentioned that to someone, they were offended at first. I told them about a friend of mine who's the most honest person I know. If you tried to force her to tell a lie, she wouldn't. If anyone is honest to a fault, it's her. Sometimes people get frustrated with her because if there's even the faintest doubt about something, she won't say she knows the answer for sure. Sometimes people want to just be told an answer even if it's not 100 percent sure. My friend is so honest, she won't cave to that person's need for a sure answer if there isn't one. Just about everyone else lies to others from time to time. When fear grabs hold of us, that sin nature comes to the surface. I have caved to the pressure to tell a lie more often than I care to admit.

My honest friend won't tell lies to other people, but she's still plagued by the effects of fear. Her sin nature manifests in that she'll tell lies to herself. She's smart, witty, generous, and kind, but in her mind, she's a failure. She thinks she's stupid and that no one likes her. She's prone to depression and can walk under a dark cloud. She needs to put on the belt of truth. Truth is part of the armor that holds everything together.

The sword of the Spirit, which is the Word of God, hangs from the belt of truth so that it's readily available when needed. It's the truth of the gospel on which our faith is founded. It's the truth of our value in God's eyes that lifts us out of the darkness. It's the truth of His sacrifice for our sins that redeems us, which is the foundation of faith. It's the truth of the resurrection power that raised Jesus from the dead and also enables us to live according to a new nature, as a new person, no longer liars but righteous in the eyes of God. It's a foundational part of our armor to protect us from the enemy's lies.

Today as we partake of communion, confess the lies you've told others and yourself. Grab hold of the truth of the gospel and stand against those lies. Stand tall and strong. You are worth everything to God, enough for Jesus to come and redeem you from your fallen nature and to seat you in heavenly places with Him.

Heavenly Father, we're so thankful that You love us enough to send Jesus to redeem us. We have infinite value, and You have redeemed us from our old life of sin, establishing us in the truth. We are so blessed and loved. Thank You. Amen.

For further study: Psalm 116:5–13; John 8:44; Romans 3:4; Ephesians 2:1–10, 6:10–20; Colossians 3:8–10.

NOVEMBER 5

The Breastplate of Righteousness

… having put on the breastplate of righteousness (Ephesians 6:14b)

WHEN I WAS sixteen and a brand-new driver, I took my friends downtown to see a movie. I was inexperienced and ended up cutting a corner in the parking lot too short, causing the car to hit a post. This resulted in a considerable dent in the door. The movie was also more expensive than expected, and I ended up short on cash and gas when it came to drive everyone home. I told my friends I'd just stop at my house to get twenty dollars from my dad to put gas in the car before I took them home. As I ran to the house, I jokingly said I'd be right back if my dad didn't kill me about the dent in the car.

When I got back to the car, I noted that my friends had these stricken looks on their faces. They said they didn't think I was coming back. I found it all quite humorous. My dad responded as I'd expected. As he handed me the twenty dollars, he said, "Make sure you call the insurance adjuster in the morning." He wasn't at all put out. He knew kids mess up and stuff gets broken, but that was why he paid the insurance premiums. It would be my job to run the car in for assessment and repairs, so there were consequences to my actions, but this wasn't going to affect our relationship. We'd still sit together at the supper table, our relationship unstrained.

The armor of God that Paul tells us about in Ephesians includes the breastplate of righteousness. This is the part that protects our heart. It means we're in right standing with God even though we make mistakes. This doesn't mean there aren't consequences to our actions, or that God doesn't expect us to mature and become more skilled at doing the right things. What it does mean is that when our world batters and dents us even from our own screwups, our relationship with God stays intact. We can sit together at the table, our hearts united, because Jesus has paid the premium price.

> *Jesus, thank You for paying the price to save us from our sins. We come to the table knowing we are welcomed, accepted, loved. There's no uneasiness, and we need not walk on eggshells around You, because our hearts are united in love and righteousness all because of what You have done. Amen.*

For further study: Romans 3:21–28; Ephesians 6:10–20; Colossians 1:9–14; 1 John 2:1–2.

NOVEMBER 6
Shoes of Peace

And having shod your feet with the preparation of the gospel of peace (Ephesians 6:15)

A GOOD PAIR of rubber boots is pretty essential on a farm. The muck can get quite thick. They protect your feet from all the mess you have to walk through, but they're not good when we get freezing rain and the ground is covered in ice. Rubber boots have next to no traction on ice. My feet slide out from under me and I have to walk like I'm a penguin to try to stay upright. Luckily the stores sell these handy strap-on cleats. These are wonderful. I can pull them on over the rubber boots and instantly have nice little spikes on the bottom of my boots that dig into the ice, keeping me from slips and falls.

Roman soldiers had cleats on the bottom of their shoes as well. It helped them grip into the dirt so they could hold their ground even when being pushed on by enemy soldiers. I imagine Paul had something like that in mind when he spoke of the armor of God in Ephesians. He said we should put on the shoes of the preparation of the gospel of peace so we can stand against our enemy. The word for peace in the Greek refers to tranquility, safety, and health, and it emphasizes a lack of strife or, in other words, the reconciliation of God with man, and man with man.

Many things in this world can cause us to slip and fall in our faith. Anxiety and fear can beset us, keeping us up late through the night with worry. We worry about what people will think of us. We're anxious about personal failures and mistakes. The Bible, however, tells us not to be anxious but to bring everything to God in prayer, giving thanks. We're thankful for who He is and all He has done. These prayers are a preparation for the coming of the peace that passes all understanding. God fills our hearts with peace as we remind ourselves that we're in a good relationship with Him, and He guides us in good relationships with others. We're at peace knowing our sins are forgiven and that we're in right standing with Him. The enemy pushes us, accusing us day and night of all our mistakes, but we can stand strong and push back, saying, yes, what you say is true, but God has paid my debt and I am forgiven.

> *Jesus, we come to You with thanksgiving in our hearts, so grateful for what You've done and who You are. You set our feet firmly on the solid ground of Your love and grace. We have Your peace that passes all understanding because of You. Amen.*

For further study: Ephesians 6:10–20; Philippians 4:6–9; Revelation 12:10.

NOVEMBER 7
The Shield of Faith

Above all, taking the shield of faith with which you will be able to quench all the fiery darts of the wicked one. (Ephesians 6:16)

PAUL WRITES ABOUT putting on the armor of God and then, above all, taking the shield of faith to quench the enemy's fiery darts. The Roman soldier carried a shield made of thick leather that had been soaked in water. The fiery dart shot at him was an arrow filled with flammable liquid that, when it hit the soldier, would spill all over him. It was ignited by a small lit wick that was knocked loose upon impact. If the soldier wasn't protected by his shield, he could be badly burnt, even though he was wearing armor.

We learn in the book of Proverbs that firebrands and arrows symbolize deception. Satan is the father of lies and is always trying to deceive us. One of his greatest deceptions is that we are unworthy or unlovable. If that deception isn't blocked by the shield of faith, we'll burn within our armor, all our hopes turning to ash.

In Ephesians 5, Paul writes that husbands should love their wives like Christ loves the Church. Jesus laid His life down for us, sanctified us, and cleansed us by the washing of water by the Word. We need to lift up our shield of faith, soaked in the water of the Word, to quench those deceptive darts that tell us we're unloved. Our faith is our confident trust that God loves us completely. It's the assurance that we are loved and that He has made us worthy of that love by cleansing us with His blood. It's the hope and trust of a day coming when Jesus will present His bride, His Church, to the Father. This bride will be perfect, without spot or wrinkle, beloved and able to love in return.

We pause to take communion to remind ourselves of His love. We are soaking our shield in the water of His Word by remembering that He loved us enough to lay His life down on the cross. We also remember He enables our love for each other, which lifts the shield up to cover the body of Christ, preventing the enemy's deceptions from reaching His bride. Our faith is empowered by love.

Jesus, we're so blessed by Your love for us. You have cleansed us and perfected us. You call us Your bride and laid Your life down for us. Your Word of truth protects us from the lies of our enemy. Help us to manifest Your love one for another. Amen.

For further study: Proverbs 26:18; Galatians 5:6; Ephesians 5:25–29, 6:10–20.

NOVEMBER 8
The Helmet of Salvation

And take the helmet of salvation … (Ephesians 6:17a)

I USED TO have a card game in which you had to solve a mystery by asking yes/no questions. One of the cards explained that when helmets were first used in wars, the head injury statistics went up and not down. It asked why that was. The solution to the puzzle was that before the helmets were in common use, people with head wounds weren't recorded as injured because they usually died. They were recorded as fatalities.

The Bible tells us that the wages of sin is death, but Jesus paid the price to buy our salvation. The helmet of salvation saves us from the law of sin and death. I wish that meant we never got injured, but the battle rages on. This fallen world is always delivering blows, attacking our mind. We may still get a concussion even with a perfectly-fitting helmet. Things can shake us, blur our vision, and cause us pain. We may be assailed by doubts and fears. Our thoughts may stray back to sinful patterns.

This is why we pause to partake of communion. As we partake of the bread and wine, we're reminded that we are saved. The helmet is intact even if the world shakes us up a little. There will come a day when there will be no more tears or pain, but for now, we can come and sit at the foot of the cross to receive healing for our soul.

Thank You, Jesus, for saving us from our sins. You paid the penalty of death so we might live. One day, You'll wipe away every tear from our eyes. Until then, we come to sit with You, knowing You are the one who comforts and heals us. Amen.

For further study: Romans 6:23, 7:7–8:11; Revelation 21:1–4.

NOVEMBER 9
The Sword of the Spirit

And the sword of the Spirit, which is the word of God (Ephesians 6:17b)

MOST OF THE armor of God is designed to defend us from attacks, except for one piece—the sword of the Spirit. This is our weapon and the only piece of the armor used for offense more than for defense. Certainly, the entire set of armor is important. If you only have the sword while you try to fight, your feet slip and slide. As you try to fend off one enemy, another lunges at your unprotected chest and pierces your heart. Nevertheless, if our armor was only defensive, we'd make no headway into the enemy's territory. He'd keep us trapped, our backs up against the wall, unable to move forward. God has provided us with a weapon, however—the same weapon Jesus used to defeat Satan.

When Jesus was in the wilderness for forty days, Satan came to tempt Him. Jesus didn't fall for the devil's tricks but replied to each temptation with the Word of God. He pushed the enemy back so He could go forth among the people, doing the miracles to show the world He was the Son of God. He pushed the enemy back so He could fulfill His mission to lead those held captive by the devil to freedom. He gained ground on the enemy, taking back that which had been stolen.

Likewise, we gain ground when we defeat the enemy with the Word of God. When our backs are to the wall and we're crippled with anxiety, we can pray, bringing our cares to Him, giving thanks and rejoicing. In the process of praying and quoting His Word, we can start to move forward, not just to a land without anxiety but to the land of joy and rejoicing. I won't say the battle will be won overnight. Some hills are a struggle to conquer. We know, however, that the war is won, so we fight on, knowing ultimately there will be victory for the side of righteousness.

As we partake of communion, we pause to remember that God has given us His Word, and it's enough to gain back what the enemy has stolen.

> *Jesus, Your Word is true, and You have promised life to us. We stand up to resist the enemy that tries so hard to deceive and defeat us. We fight with Your Word and are victorious. Amen.*

For further study: Psalm 118:15–25; Joel 2:21–32; Luke 4:1–13; John 10:10; Ephesians 4:8–10, 6:10–20; Philippians 4:4–8.

NOVEMBER 10
The First Snowfall

"Come now, and let us reason together," says the Lord, "though your sins are like scarlet, they shall be as white as snow; though they are red like crimson, they shall be as wool." (Isaiah 1:18)

IT SNOWED ALL night—great big, soft, fluffy flakes of pure white, beautiful snow covering everything with its glory. My yard had been dirty brown with mud, but now it has been transformed. The first snowfall of the season always seems extra beautiful to me. Everything is so pure and clean. The world's traffic has not yet stirred it up and mixed it with dirt, making it a dingy gray. The snow is so bright that it's blinding as it reflects the light of the sun. If you took a brand-new white T-shirt out of its package and put it next to the pure white snow, it would look dull and gray. You can't bleach clothing white enough to compare to the glory of the freshly fallen snow.

In several places in the Bible, people saw Jesus dressed in white clothing—as white as snow, whiter than a launderer could possibly make them. They were seeing Him in His glory. When we come to Him, confessing our sins and receiving Him into our hearts, His blood cleanses us. Our sins are washed away, and we're clothed in His glory, as white and pure as snow. We are justified, redeemed, and made right in the sight of God.

I've heard preachers make a play on the word "justified," saying that it means "just as if I'd never sinned." I have to disagree. If I'd never sinned, my own righteousness would look like that dingy gray shirt. It may look white compared to other shirts in the store, but there's no comparison next to the pure light of God's glory. When we come to the foot of the cross and receive His grace, we are transformed, reflecting the pureness of His glory by His grace. It's something so much greater than if there was no sin.

There's nothing quite like that first time we come to the foot of the cross and feel His grace fill our souls. Our spirits light up with the brightness of His glory, and it shines out for all to see. As we walk around on the earth, however, the world stirs up the mud and dirt, staining our garments with bad attitudes and hurtful words. For this reason, we come to the communion table. At the table, we once again approach the cross and remember His body broken for us, His blood shed for the remission of sins. We confess the faults of this miry clay and receive the cleansing grace like a fresh fall of snow, reflecting the glory of the Son.

Jesus, thank You for being obedient to the sacrifice of Your body and blood so that we would be justified and made right in the sight of God. Cleanse us from the dirt of the world that has once again crept into our soul, and cover us in Your grace so that Your glory may be manifest for all to see. Amen.

For further study: Psalm 51:1–17, 69:13–14; Isaiah 64:6; Daniel 7:9; Mark 9:2–3, 1 John 1:8–9; Revelation 1:12–18.

NOVEMBER 11
Remembrance

> And He took bread, gave thanks and broke it, and gave it to them, saying, "This is My body which is given for you; do this in remembrance of Me." Likewise He also took the cup after supper, saying, "This cup is the new covenant in My blood, which is shed for you." (Luke 22:19–20)

NOVEMBER 11 IS the day we set aside as Remembrance Day in Canada and Veterans Day in the United States, when we pause to honor our fallen soldiers. Over the years and throughout the many world conflicts, many of our country's young men and women have paid the ultimate price for our freedom. Their blood was shed as they fought enemy forces on behalf of their fellow countrymen—those alive at the time and those not yet born. We would live a very different life if those heroic individuals hadn't laid down their lives to save us from tyranny.

At many of the ceremonies to honor the fallen held around the country, "The Last Post," a military bugle call played at day's end, is played to signify the death of the soldier. This is followed by a moment of silence, and then "Reveille" is played. This is the bugle call used at the start of the day, and in this case represents the soldier's resurrection to a heavenly life.

Our veterans certainly deserve to be remembered. We are forever grateful for their service and sacrifice, even as we pray for the day when wars cease forever. Jesus has promised that the day will come when there will be no more war or destruction. We have an ultimate enemy who has sought to destroy our very soul. He has raged, waging war against heaven, and he holds the earth in his demonic grip. This larger war has triggered and caused all others, and this is the war Jesus fought. The sacrifice of His innocent blood paid the ultimate price for our freedom from sin and death. He shed His blood on the cross for all alive at the time and those yet to be born. The heavenly trumpets might have sounded the mournful tune of His death on the cross. The heavens were silent, and darkness reigned, but only for a moment until "Reveille" would sound. The stone in front of Jesus's tomb was rolled away at His resurrection, and He obtained the victory for our souls. Battles still rage on, but Jesus calls us to remember that the victory has been won. The devil is defeated, and we are born again to everlasting life.

Jesus knew that at times the battles we face would make it look like He hadn't already been victorious. Conversely, He knew that life may be so good that we forget the sacrifice that enabled that blessed life. He knew we'd need a reminder, so He instituted the practice of communion. By taking of the bread and the wine, we remember He was willing to pay the price to redeem us from the enemy of our soul. Battles may still rage on, but this won't affect our freedom. This freedom from sin and death is for all eternity.

> *Jesus, we pause today to remember our veterans and countrymen who have sacrificed so much to buy our freedom, but we also pause to remember that You paid the ultimate price to buy our freedom from sin and death. You laid Your life down and You took it up again to lead us into everlasting life. We remember and give You thanks.*

For further study: Deuteronomy 6:4–12; Mark 14:22–24; 1 Corinthians 15:51–58; 2 Peter 1:3–14.

NOVEMBER 12
Ropes and Chains

> Now behold, an angel of the Lord stood by him, and a light shone in the prison; and he struck Peter on the side and raised him up, saying, "Arise quickly!" And his chains fell off his hands.
> (Acts 12:7)

ACTS 12 RECOUNTS how Peter was miraculously delivered from prison. He'd been captured during the days of a Passover celebration and was chained between two soldiers behind bolted doors and gates. Peter's execution was to occur the following morning. The situation looked hopeless. Suddenly, light shone in the darkness and an angel struck him, causing the chains to fall off. He commanded Peter to get dressed and follow as he led Peter through the locked gates that had opened on their own accord. Until he found himself in the open air, walking down the street, Peter had thought he was having a vision.

When we came to the foot of the cross, we were bound in chains and ropes of sin and defeat. The situation was hopeless—bound in sin, headed for death with no chance of freeing ourselves. Jesus, our Passover lamb, gave His body and poured out His blood. He was struck in His side by a soldier's spear, and our chains fell off! The doors that lead out of this world and into heaven opened of their own accord, and we are free.

Sometimes we can be deceived by the hopeless appearance of our situation, and we think receiving Jesus was merely a vision and not reality. We're accustomed to wearing our chains, as it's the reality we know best. The doors are open, but we stay put, holding the links in our hands. The rope that was placed around our neck is loose and untied, but we continue to wear it, feeling its fibers rub on our skin. We're free, but we hold on to the thoughts of our condemnation.

The hardest chains to put down are the ones that are familiar and easy to carry. Some of those chains we've carried most of our lives. It's all we know. Then there are the fibers of the rope that have embedded deep in our skin. Those ones hurt to pull out, so we prefer to leave them alone to fester. We may want to hold on to our resentments or pain. We're familiar with self-loathing and condemnation and comfortable carrying our self-righteousness and pride.

We come to the communion table to be reminded that He has died for us to set us free. We come to ask the Holy Spirit to reveal the links of the chain we hang on to so we can drop them on the ground. We come to ask where the fibers of sin are deeply embedded so we can let the Surgeon Jesus remove them, allowing our sores to completely heal. He is ever merciful. Our enemy is always trying to recapture us and bring us back into bondage, but daily the Lord's mercies restore us to a life of freedom. This is the essence of communion.

> *Jesus, You died once and for all, so we can now choose to die to the works of the flesh and to live in Your righteousness. This world still traps us at times, but we come to You, knowing You once again restore us to freedom. Thank You for Your everlasting grace and mercy. Amen.*

For further study: Lamentations 3:22–23; Acts 12:1–19; Romans 6:1–23; Galatians 2:20.

NOVEMBER 13
Imposter Syndrome

Jesus, knowing that the Father had given all things into His hands, and that He had come from God and was going to God (John 13:3)

IMPOSTER SYNDROME OCCURS when a highly trained and intelligent person feels they don't really know what they're doing. When people have a tiny bit of knowledge on a topic, they often think they know everything there is to know about it, and they feel smarter than the experts. When they're really well educated, however, they feel like they know only a tiny little bit on the topic, as they can see there is still so much more to learn. It's the really skilled person who will sometimes feel unqualified. They don't recognize their value.

Although Jesus was perfect, He didn't suffer from imposter syndrome because He also knew His value. When Jesus was with His disciples on the night before His betrayal, He put on the robes of the servant and washed their feet. John tells us Jesus could do this because He knew who He was. He knew He'd been given everything, that He had come from God and was going to God. He didn't feel unworthy but knew He was worth everything. Because He knew who He was, it didn't bother Him to stoop down, humbling Himself to do the actions of a lowly servant.

He would humble Himself further to be obedient to the call to the cross. By washing their feet, He was teaching the disciples that their Master was willing to serve them, and that they should be like Him. They should walk humbly and not be ashamed of being a servant to others. When Peter didn't want Jesus to stoop to wash his feet, Jesus said He had to wash Peter's feet if Peter wanted to be a part of Jesus. Peter then asked Jesus to wash all of him. Jesus said Peter was clean and only needed his feet washed. In this Jesus was telling us that the work on the cross would cleanse us completely. He was also telling us that as we walk in this fallen world, we'll still get its dirt on us. We'll sin and make mistakes, despite being Christians. We need to come to Jesus to get the dirt of sin washed off.

The key to not succumbing to imposter syndrome is in knowing who we really are and that we receive everything from Him; we come from Him and are going to Him. We know that we're saved from our sins and cleansed. And it's in knowing that we still sin and must come to Him regularly to have the dirt of the world washed off us again.

We won't succumb to imposter syndrome when we know we are valuable with precious gifts given by God, but also that we're sinners, cleansed by grace, in desperate need of our Savior. It's healthy pride and true humility in perfect balance because of the work Jesus did on the cross.

Jesus, You came to save us, and we are a part of Your body. Nothing is better than that. Wash our feet. We still fail at times as we navigate this fallen world, but You cleanse us. Help us to remain humble, servants of all, just as You came to serve humanity. Amen.

For further study: John 13:1–17; Romans 12:1–16.

NOVEMBER 14
Blurred Vision

> Where there is no revelation, the people cast off restraint; but happy is he who keeps the law. (Proverbs 29:18)

I FOUND OUT I was extremely nearsighted in grade 5. The day I got my first pair of glasses, it was quite an eye-opener! Suddenly grass was individual blades of bright green and not just a hazy green smudge. I could read the words on the blackboard from the back of the room. I'd always thought it was normal to not see the blackboard clearly from anything other than the front row. The world was so much brighter and clearer.

It might have been nice had that first pair of glasses been sufficient my whole life to correct my vision, but as I age, I repeatedly need to get new lenses to adapt to my aging eyes. Adjustments need to be made to bring back the clarity that has slipped away so subtly that I barely noticed its loss.

When I asked Jesus into my heart, I experienced a similar sensation. The world suddenly seemed clearer and brighter. Trees were greener; the sky was bluer. It was amazing. Now that I've been a Christian for some time, I can forget what it was like. My world slowly and almost imperceptibly blurs. Familiar sins can creep in, and I fail to recognize them as being abnormal. I need to go to the Eye Doctor Jesus and get some adjustments made so I can see clearly once more.

The Bible says that without a vision, the people perish (Proverbs 29:18). In other words, without a clear vision or revelation of Christ's atoning work on the cross, we tend to a life of sin and death. When we come to the cross, understanding what He has done, we're delivered from the sin that ensnares us. It would be nice, I suppose, if that revelation carried us the rest of our lives, and in some respects it does. In other respects, the disappointments and trials of the world sometimes blur that revelation, and we need to head back to the cross to get our vision restored to perfection. Thankfully, He's always faithful to restore us fully. These minor adjustments are easily made when we spend a bit of time in communion with Him.

> *Lord, sometimes our remembrance of the atoning work done on the cross gets blurred out by the cares, sins, and trials of today. We come to You now to remind ourselves of Your grace, to confess our sins, and to have You once again restore clarity to our vision. You are faithful, willing, and able to restore us fully in You. Thank You. Amen.*

For further study: Proverbs 3:5–6; 2 Peter 1:2–11; 1 John 1:9.

NOVEMBER 15
The Hiding Place

> You are my hiding place; You shall preserve me from trouble; You shall surround me with songs of deliverance. Selah. (Psalm 32:7)

CORRIE TEN BOOM was a Christian sent to the Ravensbrück concentration camp in the Second World War for hiding Jews from the Nazis. She wrote a number of books about this and about her tours around the world preaching the message of forgiveness of one's enemies. One of her first books was titled *The Hiding Place*. It was about the hidden room where she hid the Jews, but it was about more than that. It was also about her finding her hiding place in Christ. She describes how in her cell one day she saw an ant scurry between the blocks. The ant had a hiding place. Why didn't she have a place to hide from the tortures she was enduring? In that moment, she heard Jesus say to her, "Let Me be your hiding place."

She also wrote about seeing one of the guards after the war. This man who had been so cruel came up to shake her hand. She struggled. She didn't want to forgive him. She had to pray for God to help her. She reached out her hand purely in obedience to Christ. She felt no forgiveness in her heart, despite preaching on forgiveness that very night. As soon as their hands clasped together, God flooded her heart with true and honest forgiveness for her enemy. She had found her hiding place in Christ yet again, this time from Satan's poison arrow of unforgiveness.

In Psalm 32, David writes about being forgiven by God. He also writes that when he tried to hide his sin, he was slowly being destroyed by the poison in his soul. When he confessed his sin to God, he was delivered and restored. God became David's hiding place, bringing David freedom and joy.

We come to the communion table to be like David, to confess our sins, to have nothing hidden in our hearts, so that we might be hidden in Christ. We come to remember that Jesus's heart was pierced through so that ours could be hidden from Satan's poisonous arrows. We come to forgive others as we have been forgiven.

> *Jesus, You are our hiding place. You protect us from the true enemy of our soul, guarding our hearts. We confess our sins and failures. Reveal to us where we have tried to hide sin or unforgiveness, so that it might be revealed and cleansed. Thank You.*

For further study: Psalm 32:1–11; Colossians 3:12–17.

NOVEMBER 16
Supper Invitation

Now when one of those who sat at the table with Him heard these things, he said to Him, "Blessed is he who shall eat bread in the kingdom of God!" (Luke 14:15)

A FRIEND RECENTLY invited me out to dinner—her treat! She asked what restaurant I'd like to go to. I answered that since she was paying, she should pick. She ended up picking one of the most expensive restaurants in town. The meal was superb; the service, excellent. It was a real pleasure to sit at the table with my friend.

Our heavenly Father has also sent out invitations to a great feast. He's called all humanity to accept the invitation to the wedding of His Son. The feast is going to be better than any we have ever had. It will take place in the most expensive place in the universe, since the cover charge to this meal was the blood of Jesus Christ. We'll sit at the table with our friends from this earth but also our dearest friend who sticks closer than a brother—Jesus Himself. It is Jesus who will pass the bread and the wine.

God has sent the invitation to all. It's free. He paid the full cost. Sadly, some people will refuse the invitation. They're just too busy earning money in this world to bother looking at the invitation. Others have married someone who doesn't want to go, so they choose to reject the invitation. Some are too interested in enjoying the pleasures of this world to care about an invitation to the next one. Many people, however, are more than willing to hear the call and accept the invitation. One day we'll join them at the table set in eternity. For now, we come to the communion table, reminding us of all Jesus has done and for all that is yet to come.

Thank You, Jesus, for paying the price so we can come to Your table. You've prepared a place for us, and we are welcome to freely partake of Your grace. Amen.

For further study: Proverbs 18:24; Luke 14:15–23; John 14:1–4.

NOVEMBER 17
Road Maintenance

Keep your heart with all diligence, for out of it spring the issues of life. (Proverbs 4:23)

I LIVE AT the end of a country gravel road. The road can get a little rough at times. Large potholes form, it becomes corrugated from rain runoff, sinkholes can develop, and even culverts collapse, causing the road to cave in. This road is not a high priority with the city, since there are only a few houses on it. They do get around to doing some maintenance, scraping it level from time to time. They're also quick to fix more urgent problems, like broken culverts. Still, one needs to drive carefully, and a four-wheel-drive vehicle is a definite bonus. There's no road around here like a Roman road, which would last for centuries. Even on the paved roads, we barely get a season before new potholes develop. Our climate is too changeable and the frost heaves up the pavement. The city is forever having to do maintenance in the region. It's a never-ending job.

Hopefully, we all have four-wheel-drive faith. We want a faith that can get us places no matter what the terrain is like, but on a paved road we can travel more quickly and easily. In today's rapidly changing society, we need to regularly maintain our path to keep us going forward smoothly. We have to constantly guard our hearts from lies or secret sins. We need to watch for the sinkholes of jealousy and resentment. We need to lay down fresh pavement of prayers for all people, including those in government and authority.

Then as we speed along the road, we have to keep our eyes looking forward to Jesus. We can't let them wander into the ditches of worldly cares or desires lining the right and left side of our path. We can easily spin into one of those ditches should our eyes leave the road.

Sometimes the way is hard going. We may have to slow down to a crawl, but as long as we keep moving toward Jesus, we'll get to where we really want to go. If we can do some maintenance on the path, the journey will be a bit easier. We do maintenance by coming to the foot of the cross. We pause to confess where we are drawn to the ditch, or have sunk into a pothole. We come to lift up our prayers for others. We come to remind ourselves of His love for us, our love for Him, and the love He's put within us for others. That love will fill in the holes and smooth the road. This is the essence of communion. We remember the bread of life broken for us, and His blood poured out to redeem us. Once again, we find the way smooth before us as we look to Him.

Jesus, thank You for making our way smooth. You direct our steps and guide us in the way we should go. Thank You for Your love, Your forgiveness, Your grace. Fill our hearts even more with Your love, so that we might bring Your love to all we meet. Amen.

For further study: Proverbs 3:1–8, 4:23–27; 1 Timothy 2:1–8.

NOVEMBER 18
Been There, Done That, Got the T-shirt

I will remember the works of the Lord; surely I will remember Your wonders of old. (Psalm 77:11)

I PREFER TO travel in the fall compared to any other time of year. There are no bugs; the weather is cool but not usually freezing yet, and there's generally less traffic. Last fall I traveled through Halifax, Prince Edward Island, and Cape Breton. I toured chip factories and lighthouses, walked along the beach, and collected stones. I also bought T-shirts—a bunch of them. There are two from the Cows store, one of the Bluenose II, and another from Halifax. Don't get me wrong, I love the T-shirts, but I already own a lot of T-shirts. These new ones barely fit in my dresser. It seems when we travel, we like to pick up T-shirts as souvenirs. It reminds me of the saying we used a lot when I was a kid. If someone discussed some crazy thing they did, another might say, "Been there, done that, and got the T-shirt."

When I think of the crazy things I've done, when my faith was lacking and my fear was leading the way, I see that I've picked up a whole wardrobe of virtual T-shirts. You'd think I would have learned that there was no room for those in my mind's dresser, yet I persist. Interestingly, I find as I spend more time in communion with the Lord, He helps me do a bit of decluttering. He reminds me that I don't need to keep the souvenirs of the sins He's cast away into the sea of forgetfulness. There's no reason to remember those particular times in my life's travels, at least not with the guilt and shame they brought.

I may have bought that shirt, but I can toss it in the garbage can. I don't need to wear it anymore. It no longer represents who I am. Instead, He has purchased for me the covering of grace, which I can wear without guilt or shame. This is the only souvenir I really need. By pausing to remember what He has done and who He has made me to become, I slowly move away from being motivated to repeat the stupid things I've done out of fear. Sure, I still mess up, but the quicker I turn to the remembrance of His grace, the quicker I get rid of the stain, and the easier it is to move away from the old patterns of behaving.

In the Old Testament, the children of Israel set up memorial stones to remember what the Lord had done for them. Today communion serves as a memorial of the works of the Lord. It's our souvenir of His grace.

> *Jesus, thank You for giving us this way to remember all You have done for us. We take the bread, remembering Your body broken for us, and drink the cup, remembering Your blood shed for the remission of our sins. You have taken away the sin from us and clothed us in grace and righteousness. We are forever grateful. Amen.*

For further study: Joshua 4:1–8; Isaiah 61:10; Micah 7:18–19; Luke 22:19–20.

NOVEMBER 19
Written in Stone

> And when He had made an end of speaking with him on Mount Sinai, He gave Moses two tablets of the Testimony, tablets of stone, written with the finger of God. (Exodus 31:18)

I WAS GETTING work done that involved redoing some cement in the basement floor. One of my dogs decided to walk through it, leaving his footprints firmly established forever in the concrete floor. His steps have become written in stone. It's not like when I walk with my dogs on the beach, and their footprints quickly wash away with each passing wave. The footprints in my basement will be there as long as the house remains.

God Himself wrote upon stone when He gave the Ten Commandments to Moses to take to the people. Moses didn't even make it down the mountain before he found the people breaking the very first of the commandments. In his anger, Moses cast down the stones, breaking them. I'm sure God knew the commandments would quickly be broken, both figuratively in the broken stones and literally in the hearts and actions of humanity. Jesus summed up the Ten Commandments in two: loving God with all your heart, and loving others as yourself. He knew the only way the Ten Commandments could be fulfilled was if perfect love filled the hearts of humanity. The commandments had to be written in hearts of flesh if there was to be any hope of obeying them.

When Jesus walked the earth as a man, the Pharisees brought to Him a woman caught in adultery. In their hand were stones, like the pieces of the broken stone on which the commandments had been written. She had broken a commandment, and they were ready to throw the stones at her to crush her. Jesus, however, stooped and wrote on the sand, saying that whoever was without sin could throw the first stone. I believe Jesus was writing the sins of the Pharisees in the sand. One by one, from oldest to youngest, the accusers dropped their stones and left.

Jesus demonstrated His love for us by taking our punishment as sinners, even though He Himself had never sinned. He was the only one who could have thrown the first stone, yet it's as if He traded places with the woman and let the Pharisees rain down stones upon His head instead. He does that for us too, taking our place while the accuser hurls the stones of the broken commandments that were meant for us. We stand there and watch Him die in our place, knowing He has written our sins only in the sand, where they can be washed away by the waves of His grace. In so doing, He has written His love in our hearts.

We come to the communion table to remember that He took our place. We confess our sins, watching them being written in the sand and then once again washed away by His grace.

> *Jesus, we're so grateful that You took our place. We stand by and see You taking the stones of accusation meant for us, dying in our stead. We see You erasing our sins and clothing us with Your grace and love. We can never express our thanks enough for all You have done. Amen.*

For further study: Exodus 31:18–32:19; John 8:1–11; 2 Corinthians 3:2–11.

NOVEMBER 20
All's Well That Ends Well

Declaring the end from the beginning, and from ancient times things that are not yet done, saying, "My counsel shall stand, and I will do all My pleasure" (Isaiah 46:10)

THE HYMN "IT Is Well with My Soul" was written by Horatio Spafford after he experienced great tragedy. He had lost finances in the great Chicago fire, and zoning problems afterward prevented him from joining his wife and four daughters as they sailed to England. His family's ship was hit by another and sunk. All four of his daughters died. His wife sent Horatio a telegram that said "Saved alone." As Horatio sailed across the Atlantic to be with his wife, he asked the captain to point out the place where their ship had sunk. As his grief welled up, so did the words of the hymn:

> When peace like a river, attendeth my way
> When sorrows like sea billows roll;
> Whatever my lot Thou hast taught me to say
> It is well, it is well with my soul.[5]

Horatio was awash in sorrows, but he knew the beginning of his sorrow was not the end of his rejoicing. God had established a better end from the very beginning of creation. There would come a day when Horatio would once again be reunited with his girls for all eternity. All would be well one day, so it could be well with his soul today.

When Jesus was being led to the cross, the disciples were awash in sorrow. They didn't yet know the end that had been established from the beginning and that all would be well. The beginning of their sorrows was not the end of their rejoicing.

Likewise, this world doesn't always go as we hope or expect. Sorrows come at the loss of loved ones, or even the loss of hopes or dreams that once filled our hearts. Yet we can know the end from the beginning. Because we know the work done on the cross, we know the eternal home that awaits. All is well with our soul because we know that in the end, all is well.

> *Jesus, thank You for establishing our salvation and that all is well. The beginning of sorrows as You died was not the end of rejoicing, because You rose. You've gone before us to prepare a place for us. Amen.*

For further study: John 14:1–10, 16:16–22.

---

[5] Horatio Spafford, "It Is Well," hymnal.net, accessed April 1, 2025.

NOVEMBER 21
The Voice Behind

> Your ears shall hear a word behind you, saying, "This is the way, walk in it," whenever you turn to the right hand or whenever you turn to the left. (Isaiah 30:21)

I HAD THE good fortune of traveling to Europe and spending some time in Madrid with my sister. Our hotel wasn't far from the soccer stadium. While we were there, a game was played between Madrid and Barcelona. We didn't have tickets, but we went out into the street while people were streaming to the stadium. Police on stallions were doing crowd control, and the crush of people was incredible. It was like an ocean wave. We fought our way through it, struggling against the flow of people. I was very uncomfortable with the crowd, but my sister thought it was great. In the end, I convinced her to turn around and head back to our hotel. It was definitely easier going when we were moving in the same direction as the bulk of the crowd.

Isaiah talks about hearing a voice behind us when we turn to the right or left hand. I always pictured this like we are on a very narrow sidewalk, heading toward a deeper relationship with God. On either side of this sidewalk are great crowds of people pushing their way in the opposite direction. If we turn to either the left or right, we end up off the sidewalk and swept away by the crowd flowing away from God. Because we're being carried along by the mob, we find ourselves moving such that the voice of our Companion, still on the sidewalk, is now behind us, saying, "This is the way, walk in it."

It's easy to get caught up in the flow of the crowd. The crowd would have us hold on to resentments and hurt, whereas the voice behind us says, "Forgiveness is the way, walk in it." The crowd says I should look out for myself and not care about my neighbor, but the voice behind says, "Love your neighbor. This is the way, walk in it." The crowd says to love the world, but the voice behind us says, "Love God and not the things of the world. This is the way. Walk in it." The crowd says to store up treasures on earth, but the voice behind us says, "Store up treasures in heaven. This is the way, walk in it." The crowd would have us seek to fulfill our own needs or pleasures, but the voice behind us says, "Lay your life down for others as Jesus laid His down for you. This is the true way, walk in it."

As we partake of communion, pause to ask if there's any area where you're following the world's crowds instead of staying on the narrow road leading to a deeper relationship with Him. Let the Holy Spirit speak to your heart. Hear when He would say, "This is the way, walk in it." If we've turned aside, let's step back onto the right way and run to catch up!

> *Holy Spirit, You call to us and direct us in the way we should go. Speak to our hearts and reveal where we have turned aside, and bring us back on the narrow way that we should walk. Amen.*

For further study: Matthew 6:19–21; Mark 12:28–34; Ephesians 4:30–32; 1 John 2:15–17, 3:16.

NOVEMBER 22
The Tower of Babel

Therefore its name is called Babel, because there the Lord confused the language of all the earth; and from there the Lord scattered them abroad over the face of all the earth. (Genesis 11:9)

AFTER THE END of Noah's flood, God told the people to spread out over the earth. It was the same command He gave to Adam and Eve before they sinned. This was going to be a fresh start. The people, however, were united in language and purpose, and sadly, they purposed to use that unity to exalt themselves instead of fulfilling God's command. God didn't get angry and wipe out everyone, nor did He yell at them or punish them. Instead, He did something beautiful. He gave groups of people different languages. Since they no longer could communicate easily with each other, they spread out over the earth to establish their own cultures. He solved the problem by making our world a richer and more beautiful place.

We had a problem with sin abiding in our hearts. The sin caused us endless problems, and it hurt us and others. God, in His infinite wisdom, dealt with it by sending Jesus to take our punishment and set us free from the law of sin and death. When we ask Jesus into our hearts, love and grace take the place of that sin. He took the problem and made our lives and hearts richer and more beautiful. As we let His love lead us in our dealings with others, we also have an opportunity to make their lives richer and more beautiful. I won't say it's always easy to do. That's why we spend time in communion. It's our reminder of His wonderful grace that abides in us and that we can share with others. Our lives are enriched when we pause to remember all He has done for us, and all He is within us.

Jesus, thank You for enriching our souls. You abide in us and live through us. We are so grateful for You and ask that You help us to reflect Your grace to all we meet and in all we do. Amen.

For further study: Genesis 1:28, 11:1–9.

NOVEMBER 23
And There Was Light

Then God said, "Let there be light"; and there was light. (Genesis 1:3)

ONE NOVEMBER, I was visiting a northern city overseas. The sun rose late in the morning, and it set long before the afternoon was over. The skies were also cloudy and overcast every day. It was gloomy and depressing.

One afternoon, our group stepped outside during a brief time when the clouds parted and brilliant sunshine streamed toward us. It was at that moment, upon seeing the sun, that I realized just how much I had missed it. It was so amazing how much that brief window of sunlight cheered us all up. It was like a breath from heaven. Of course, the sun had always been shining. It had never stopped, but it was just hidden from our point of view until that moment.

When the Lord God created the heavens and the earth, the earth was without form and void, and darkness was on the face of the deep. It was a situation of chaos and emptiness at the same time, but God spoke into the darkness and created light. This was even before He made the sun to control the light. All it took to bring order and light was a word from God.

Occasionally, we go through spiritual times like those overcast days during a dark fall season. We can feel depressed. The world seems dark and dreary. Maybe we feel overwhelmed with the tasks to do and the responsibilities put upon us. Our world is in chaos, and our hearts are void of positive emotion. We need a word from God.

All it will take to bring order and lightness to our hearts is the Word of God that says we are loved, that He cares enough for us to send His only begotten Son to save us. His Son shone in our spiritual darkness and brought forth light. It happened on the day we were saved. We pause to take communion to remind ourselves that when our world seems dark, He is the light. He is always there, always shining for us. He never stops. Sometimes He's hidden from our point of view, but He will break forth upon us. It's a sure thing, proven by His obedience to walk the way to the cross and by the empty tomb. His love is clear. The darkness will give way to the light. The season will change. The clouds will blow away. It may not be today, but it will happen, because the Son has never stopped shining despite our current situation.

Jesus, thank You for being light to our darkness. You have saved us from our sins, and now You continue, always shining into our lives no matter what our circumstances. Amen.

For further study: Genesis 1:1–19; John 1:5–13, 3:16; 1 John 1:5.

NOVEMBER 24
Drain the Infection

Indeed it was for my own peace that I had great bitterness; but You have lovingly delivered my soul from the pit of corruption, for You have cast all my sins behind Your back. (Isaiah 38:17)

AN INFECTION CAN become quite serious. Pus can build up in an abscess that can threaten a person's very life. A surgeon may have to lance and drain the infection so antibiotics or other therapies have a chance of clearing things enough to save the life. Some older therapies can also be very effective. For example, after draining, a serious abscess in an animal may be treated using poultices of honey. The high sugar content can help control the bacteria and keep fluid moving into the region to help flush out the infection. The lancing or flushing of a wound can be painful, but the infection is much more painful, and much more dangerous.

Hezekiah was a king in the Old Testament who had a boil serious enough that his life was in danger. The prophet Isaiah told Hezekiah to put his affairs in order because he was going to die. Hezekiah, in bitterness of soul, prayed to the Lord to save him. The Lord then told Isaiah to return and tell Hezekiah that the Lord had heard his prayer, and he would live for another fifteen years. The Lord also instructed Isaiah to have a poultice of figs placed on the boil. This drew out the infection, and Hezekiah lived.

Sin can be like a serious infection in our lives. Left untreated, it's life-threatening. If we bring it to Jesus and let Him lance that sin-boil with the spear that pierced His heart, and then pack the hole with the sweetness of His grace, our lives are saved.

As we walk in this fallen world, occasionally we get small wounds and pustules of sin. If we go to Him, sometimes it's painful to confess our sin, but it's much more painful if we neglect it and let it fester. It's better to let Him pack in His grace and bring healing to our soul. The quicker we take it to Him, the easier it is to deal with. Part of communion is examining ourselves to see where we've let some dirt of the world get in and cause a sin-boil that needs to be lanced. Thankfully, in confessing it and letting His blood wash us, we're once again completely clean, with conscience clear.

> *Jesus, we pause to remember that You died for us and rose again, delivering us from the consequences of our sin. We don't want to sin, but sometimes we slip up. You are still there for us, freeing us from shame and guilt. You love us and bring us Your healing grace. Thank You. Amen.*

For further study: 2 Kings 20:1–11; Isaiah 38:1–22.

NOVEMBER 25
Abuse Prevention

> Therefore when Jesus perceived that they were going to come and take Him by force to make Him king, He departed again to a mountain by Himself alone. (John 6:15)

AS I WRITE this, there's a lot of talk about non-disclosure agreements. These bans on disclosing terms of a settlement are often put in place to protect an abuser by preventing the victim from talking about the abuse they suffered. Sadly, the human race is rather prone to abusing each other. Even in the church, which is made up of people who have experienced God's grace, abuse can happen, whether financial, physical, or even emotional.

Once at a Christian conference during the offering, the speaker said that God had told him ten people would give one thousand dollars. He then told the ushers to lock the doors and not allow anyone to leave until those ten people volunteered their donation. We all sat there, silent and shocked. No one really knew what to do. The situation became very uncomfortable. Eventually ten people volunteered their donation just to make it all stop. Funny, I don't remember who that fellow was or what he spoke about. I only remember the abuse he perpetrated upon us. He was certainly not representing our Lord and Savior.

Abuse involves manipulation and coercion, and Jesus never manipulated or coerced people. Nor did He allow Himself to be manipulated or coerced. He never forces us to follow Him. He just gives us the choice to follow Him or not. He never forces us to lay down our lives for others, but He gives us the ability to choose to do so. Love does no harm to the one who is loved. Jesus is perfect love, so He never abuses us into serving Him or others.

When the devil tried to trick and manipulate Jesus into becoming a king on earth instead of fulfilling His call to establish the kingdom of heaven, Jesus resisted Him with the Word of God. When the people tried to force Jesus to be their king on earth, He slipped away by Himself to spend time in prayer. He loved us enough not to be manipulated or coerced into an earthly reign that would be of no eternal benefit to us. He resisted manipulation and coercion with prayer and knowledge of the Word of God. Because of His love for us, He gives us the free choice to accept His love. No manipulation. No coercion. Just simple faith in who He is and what He's done. No one forced Jesus to lay down His life for us. He did so willingly, out of love. We pause to remember that and to let His love fill us so we do the right thing for our friends, neighbors, and enemies.

> *Jesus, thank You for the great love with which You love us. You willingly laid Your life down for us so we may live. We are forever grateful. Help us to follow You in obedience, laying our lives down one for another. Amen.*

For further study: Matthew 4:1–11; John 6:15, 10:18; Romans 13:10; 2 Corinthians 9:7.

NOVEMBER 26
Full Tanks

> Having faith and a good conscience, which some having rejected, concerning the faith have suffered shipwreck. (1 Timothy 1:19)

I'VE GOT A nice new car. I really like it, but the gas gauge, for some reason unknown to me, seems really hard to notice. I often only notice it's low when the dash computer starts flashing me low fuel notices.

The other day I was driving home, and there were no nearby fill-up stations. I suddenly got a notice on the dash that I could only drive for twenty-five more kilometers before I'd be out of gas. That was just about the distance to the next gas station. I ended up rolling into the station on fumes. I really have to pay more attention. It wouldn't do at all to run out of gas in the middle of nowhere. It would be like being shipwrecked. Unable to proceed, I'd be unable to get the work done I wanted to do, stuck somewhere with a loss of time and money as I try to get fuel for the tank.

Paul warned Timothy about people who were shipwrecked in their faith. They weren't paying attention and their faith ran out of gas. They no longer had a clear conscience, having slipped away into sin. Paul had written earlier that the whole purpose of the commandment of God was to love with a pure heart that flowed from a good conscience and sincere faith. Paul also told the Ephesians to stay filled with the Spirit, being joyful and giving thanks, encouraging one another and submitting to one another. This comes readily when our faith tank is full and our conscience clear. His love fills us and flows out of us.

One of the ways we keep our faith tank full and our conscience clear is by coming to the communion table. Here we remind ourselves of the amazing grace that saved us, and we bring our failures and have our consciences cleared. At the table we give thanks, and our joy is renewed. We may come to the table with a tank that's nearly full and only needing a little top-up, but we also may roll slowly to the table, drifting in on fumes, our tank reading empty. In either case, we can be refilled and move forward to where we're being called to go.

By coming to the table regularly, we avoid running out of gas at a time we need it most. We'll have a full tank when the emergency call comes at two in the morning. We'll have the full tank to transport others to the place of grace. Our tank will be full when we go to visit that relative who tries our patience. Keeping our tank full can save us a lot of heartache and loss. Let's come to the communion table today and fill up on His grace.

> *Jesus, thank You for filling our tanks with Your love and grace. We confess our sins and You forgive us, giving us a clear conscience and a heart of pure love. Holy Spirit, fill us completely that we may encourage and bless each other with the joy of Your presence. Amen.*

For further study: Ephesians 5:15–21; 1 Timothy 1:5.

NOVEMBER 27

Jonah

> So he prayed to the Lord, and said, "Ah, Lord, was not this what I said when I was still in my country? Therefore I fled previously to Tarshish; for I know that You are a gracious and merciful God, slow to anger and abundant in lovingkindness, One who relents from doing harm." (Jonah 4:2)

MANY PEOPLE ARE familiar with the story of Jonah in the belly of the whale, but they may not know all the details. Jonah, a prophet of the Lord, is told to go to Nineveh and preach that God's judgment is coming upon them for their many sins. Now it so happens that Jonah hates the Ninevites. He has no desire to obey this commandment of God, so he hops on a ship going in the opposite direction to try to run away from God.

A great storm arises and the sailors find out it is God chasing Jonah. They're at a loss of what to do, since they will perish in the storm if nothing changes. Jonah tells them to throw him overboard. Really, Jonah would rather die than do what God has told him to do. God sends a big fish to swallow Jonah, and Jonah spends three days in it before he repents and agrees to do what God asked. The preaching of Jonah causes all of Nineveh to turn to God.

Now here is where the story becomes really interesting. Jonah goes up on a hill to see what God will do. He's angry and miserable, sitting under the hot sun. God causes a plant to grow up and shade Jonah. Jonah is thankful for the plant, but then God sends a worm to eat the plant and it dies. Jonah is miserable again and pleads with God to kill him. God then rebukes Jonah for having pity for the plant but not for the many people, including young children and all the livestock, that were in Nineveh.

Have you ever wondered why God sent Jonah to preach to the Ninevites? He could have chosen someone who felt more tenderness for the people, or someone more willing and obedient. Why did He choose Jonah? In my opinion, He chose Jonah because of His great mercy. You see, Jonah was filled with hatred and bitterness against the Ninevites. It was like the worm that ate the plant; it was destroying him from the inside and withering his soul. God wanted the Ninevites to repent of their sin and be saved, but He also wanted Jonah to be free from the hatred that was destroying him. Jonah was a follower of God, and he knew God was a God of mercy, but Jonah didn't want God to have mercy on his enemies, only on himself. Jonah needed a reminder that there was a lot more to God's saving grace than he realized. Jonah was in just as much need to repent and find mercy as the people he hated.

Years later, Jesus would come to earth as a man. He'd proclaim that He would suffer the judgment of sin for three days and nights, just like Jonah suffered in the belly of the whale. Jesus would do so to bring God's mercy and salvation to everyone who would receive it. He would destroy the worms of sin and hatred that would eat us from the inside, and restore us to flourishing health. What an amazing, glorious God who loved us so much that He would extend His everlasting mercy freely to us all.

> *Jesus, thank You for saving us. Thank You for taking our place in judgment and setting our spirits free. Your mercy is truly everlasting and amazing. Amen.*

For further study: Jonah 1:1–4:11; Matthew 12:38–41.

NOVEMBER 28
Enlighten My Darkness

Your word is a lamp to my feet and a light to my path. (Psalm 119:105)

I'M REALLY BLESSED to have a large property. It's mainly rocks and trees and swamp, but it allows for some nice hiking trails. I will say it's quite the job to maintain the trails. Trees blow over, branches hang low weighed down by snow, and stumps and rocks heave out of the ground. There are always things to trip on or to walk into if you're not paying attention. I don't often walk the trails in the dark, even if I wear a headlight. It can be a challenge to light the path ahead to spot the trail markers and low-hanging branches while also watching where I put my feet to avoid tripping.

John wrote that God is light, and if we walk in the light, we have fellowship with one another, and Jesus's blood cleanses us from sin. In other words, He lights our path, showing us where we're headed and how to follow the twists and turns of relationships, but He's also light to our feet. He shows us the areas where we could trip and fall into sin. At one time we walked in darkness, weak and powerless against sin, but the entrance of Jesus to our hearts brought light to that darkness. He gave us the strength and ability to battle the enemy within by the strength of His grace.

Here again is the essence of communion. It's our relationship with God through the sacrifice of Jesus and His cleansing grace lighting up the things that would trip us. Communion is also about our relationship with others, or the path we're walking in this world as we head toward our eternal rest in the next. It's about our love for God and for each other. Thankfully, His love lights the way. His Word gives us the ability to see our path and follow it.

> *God, You are light, and in You there is no darkness. You've brought us out of darkness and into the light. We see where we messed up in the past, and we receive Your saving grace. You also show us the way we should walk, and You keep us from falling. Help us to stay on Your path, walking in fellowship with You and with others. Amen.*

For further study: Psalm 18:28–30; 1 John 1:5–7; Jude 1:24–25.

NOVEMBER 29
Spiritual Food

> Beloved, I pray that you may prosper in all things and be in health, just as your soul prospers.
> (3 John 1:2)

AS A VETERINARIAN that treats exotic animals, I know the value of good nutrition. Despite decades of vets trying to get the word out there about the importance of the right food for the animal, many of the diseases we see in exotic pets still come from poor diets. They may come in with bone disease from poor calcium, thyroid disease from lack of iodine, obesity, liver disease, or a myriad of other conditions directly related to a poor diet. We also see other diseases indirectly related to the diet. Poor immune systems allow infections to be established, obesity strains joints, muscle weakness contributes to injuries, and the list goes on. The animals need to be fed the right variety of ingredients in the right proportions to help maintain a healthy body.

The other day, my friend told me that I read books like they're food. I thought that was a pretty good analogy. I read all kinds of books. Some may be like breakfast and just get my day off on the right foot, while others are very nutritional and stimulate my brain. Others are like an energy bar during a marathon. They stimulate me to love and good works when my strength is starting to fail. Some books are more like dessert—light, fluffy reading with no real value other than a bit of entertainment. To have a healthy soul, I need to ingest the right mix of ingredients in the right proportions. If I try to just live off the dessert, I'm going to become weak and unhealthy.

Our spirit needs good food too. Many things are food to our spirit. The word of God is our main meal, but there are also walks in nature, where we revel in the glory of God's creation. We're fed when we spend time in prayer. Praise and worship with the body of Christ nourishes us. A friend may speak a word to us that's like a power bar when we're weak from running the race.

Spending time in communion with our Lord also feeds us. I like to partake of communion right after I get up in the morning. It's like a good breakfast to start my day. You may prefer to spend time in communion at a different time of day, but it will still nourish you. As we take time to let the Holy Spirit reveal hidden flaws so they can be brought to the cross, our spiritual immune system keeps working perfectly to bring health and cleanse the body of sin. As we partake of the bread and wine, we fill up on His grace. Our faith is strengthened and we grow spiritually. Let's come to the table and partake of some good food!

> *Jesus, thank You for the nourishment of Your love. Your grace and glory fill us and satisfy us. You feed us with Your body and blood so we may grow in all things, being strong in the faith so that we can walk in Your love with strength and ability. Amen.*

For further study: Isaiah 55:1–3; Hebrews 5:13–14; 1 Peter 2:1–3.

NOVEMBER 30
Old Clothes

Not pilfering, but showing all good fidelity, that they may adorn the doctrine of God our Savior in all things. (Titus 2:10)

I WAS GOING through a closet a while back and found my old college jacket. It was still in good shape, and I wondered why I never wore it. I really liked that jacket. I brought it downstairs and hung it on the hook by the door. When I went to put it on, I realized why it had gone untouched in my closet. I could barely do up the zipper. The back rode up high on my waist, and the sleeves constrained my movements. As much as I wanted to use it, that jacket just didn't fit me anymore. I wondered if I could somehow make the jacket fit. I really wanted to wear it. Eventually I had to be honest with myself. That jacket was never going to fit me. It needed to go in the bin to be sent away. At one time, it was fine for me to wear it, but that time was over.

There are "clothes" we used to wear that seemed to fit us just fine at the time. We'd put on wrath, self-righteous indignation, lying, swearing, cheating, bitterness, or pride. If we take these attitudes out of the closet and try them on again, they don't really seem to fit anymore. Occasionally, however, we try to force them on. We'll try to justify our wrath or tell ourselves it's just a white lie. No one will know this clothing doesn't fit, so I'll just pull those sleeves down a little harder and suck in my gut.

When we come and sit at the communion table, we hear the ripping of those too tight clothes. If we're honest with ourselves, we have to acknowledge that those behaviors just don't fit us anymore. They need to be tossed into the garbage can. Instead, as we come to the table, we find new clothes that fit quite well. Maybe we still have to grow and fill out in a few areas for the fit to be perfect, but it's still pretty good. The clothing is comfortable and allows freedom of movement.

This covering of grace is also beautiful. It shines different colors depending on how the light of the Son shines upon it. As we kneel, it reflects the bright red of His blood shed for our sins. We rise and the sky-blue color of heaven's salvation reflects off the material. As we lift our eyes to heaven, the dazzling white of His righteous purity shines out, and as we twirl toward our neighbor, the brilliant gold of His glory shimmers like satin. This clothing of grace fits and can be worn to all functions and in all situations. There's nothing like it. We come to the cross to be unclothed from the old and clothed with the new. Sometimes we just need a reminder that those old clothes don't fit anymore. It's time to throw all those old ways into the bin as we reach only for our new covering of grace.

Jesus, thank You for clothing us with Your grace. Keep us from picking up our old ways and lead us to reflect Your glory everywhere we go. Amen.

For further study: Galatians 5:16–26; Ephesians 4:17–32; Titus 2:9–15.

DECEMBER 1
Nearing the End

And do this, knowing the time, that now it is high time to awake out of sleep; for now our salvation is nearer than when we first believed. (Romans 13:11)

WRITING A YEAR-LONG devotional is a huge task. I have to admit, I really don't feel capable. There are only a few more weeks to write, but in my mind, I tend to think it's impossible to finish. How could I come up with any more ideas for the end of the project? It's too hard. I wonder why God would ask me to take on such a project. It's simply too big for me.

Sometimes I wish that Christianity wasn't so logical, that His grace in my life wasn't so obvious, and that His love wasn't so real. Then I could be like other people I know, who just live for their own pleasures. But Christianity is logical. It makes sense and fits what we see in the world around us. His grace is obvious in my life and heart, bringing me peace where there should be no peace. His love has changed me in ways I could never have changed myself. There's no denying it. So when I'm overwhelmed, I need to turn to the rock of my salvation and ask Him why this task is so important.

I hear the Spirit whisper in my ear. The task is important, because we're nearing the end. And then I see why, like Paul, I need to press on. We all need to be reminded of His love for us. We all need to move deeper in our relationship with Christ, because the end of the age is coming. Soon Christ will return to gather up all the saints and bring us home, and there will be no more time to show His love to the lost and broken. The time is short. If we continue in what He calls us to do, He can use it to reach others, to encourage them and lead them into the best of all relationships. At the same time, we acknowledge that the job is too big for us. That's why the Holy Spirit steps in. It's not because we're good or talented that this gets done but because God is good, and He is able. Our job is to press into our relationship with Him and let Him fill our hearts with His love.

Jesus pressed on to fulfill all He came to earth to do. He persevered. He continued to the cross so that we could enter into the best of all relationships. Our salvation was impossible for us to accomplish through our own works. It was too big for us. That was why God stepped in to do it for us. We receive the love He so freely bestowed upon us. As His love fills us, He asks that we spread that love around to others, because the time is short and the end draws near.

Jesus, You are coming soon. We can forget the end of the age approaches, but with each day that passes, we're another day closer to the trumpet call. Help us to press into a deeper relationship with You so that we might freely give Your love to those around us, friend or foe. Amen.

For further study: Psalm 61:1–8; Matthew 10:7–8; Philippians 3:8–16; 1 Thessalonians 4:16–18; 1 Peter 4:7–11.

DECEMBER 2
Beauty for Ashes

> To console those who mourn in Zion, to give them beauty for ashes, the oil of joy for mourning, the garment of praise for the spirit of heaviness; that they may be called trees of righteousness, the planting of the Lord, that He may be glorified. (Isaiah 61:3)

WHEN A VOLCANO erupts, it can cause great devastation. The hot lava can destroy things in its path, but also a thick layer of ash can settle on the ground over a large area. I remember when Mount St. Helens erupted in 1980 and the amount of ash in the air affected the atmosphere across Canada, darkening the skies. One of the surprising things was how quickly the vegetation could recover afterward. Life sprouted from the ground where the ash had lain thickly. Fireweed, lupins, even trees worked their way back into the region, growing strong, as the ash acted like fertilizer. What had once looked like a dark, dead, and hopeless situation was once again green and vibrant with life.

When Jesus was obedient to lay His life down on the cross, it looked hopeless. The sky was darkened, and death seemed victorious. His disciples mourned, collecting His body and burying it in the tomb. All was lost; all was hopeless. The disciples feared that the soldiers would soon be coming for them as they sat behind locked doors, heavy with grief and fear.

But out of the ashes of defeat, beauty was rising. Jesus took off the grave clothes and stepped from the tomb. He appeared to the women who had followed Him, and He also showed up behind locked doors to speak to His disciples. They could rejoice in His presence, their heaviness replaced by praise. His resurrection fertilized the burgeoning faith and helped the disciples to grow vibrant and strong. They would be trees of righteousness, the planting of the Lord, and He would be glorified. They would boldly carry the gospel to the lost across the known world and spanning the generations, reaching even to you and me.

When it seems as if a volcano has erupted in our lives—maybe a friend has died, we've lost a job, or a home has been destroyed by fire—the world can seem dark and all can seem lost. A day is coming, however, when beauty will arise from the ashes, joy will return, and we will wear His praise like a garment. Life will return. He has paid the price for our eternal victory. We can trust in Him because He has already done it.

> *Jesus, we bless You and thank You. We praise Your holy name. You are the beauty in the ashes, the oil of joy for our mourning, and You clothe us in praise. We trust You to work all things out in time as You restore what the enemy tried to destroy. Amen.*

For further study: Isaiah 61:1–7; John 20:1–31.

DECEMBER 3
Restoration and Maintenance

But also for this very reason, giving all diligence, add to your faith virtue, to virtue knowledge, to knowledge self-control, to self-control perseverance, to perseverance godliness, to godliness brotherly kindness, and to brotherly kindness love. (2 Peter 1:5–7)

IF YOU OWN a house, a car, or a bike, you know you have to maintain these things. Some maintenance is pretty routine and minor, like oil changes and topping up tire pressure, but other things can be more involved. Sometimes things break down and need to be completely restored.

I needed foundation repairs done on the house, as water and mice were getting in. The restoration was quite involved and quite a mess for a time. It was nice when it was all done and everything was cleaned up. Even if you don't own a house or car, living life requires things to be maintained. There's always dirty laundry that needs washing, dishes that need doing, dust that needs to be dusted. Things get moved around that need to be put away. There always seems to be something that needs our attention. It's easy to neglect these things, but we regret it when we do. The mess builds up around us. Things get in that shouldn't. Our lives become more disordered.

Our spiritual life is similar. It's easy to neglect routine maintenance. After all, things seem to be going along fine. Eventually, however, our lives become more disordered. Thoughts or behaviors creep in that don't belong, and if we neglect it long enough, the foundation of our faith will crack. Restoration will become a big job that makes more of a mess before things are cleaned up and repaired. If we keep on top of routine maintenance, things go a lot better.

Partaking of communion is like an oil change for the car. As we examine our hearts, we flush out the behaviors that have crept in, like the times we've lost our self-control, or didn't act kindly to others. We get rid of those old behaviors and are refilled with the new, fresh, clean oil of the Spirit. We bring all our dirty laundry to the cross and let His blood wash us clean. He creates order out of our disorder and leads us in the path of love. Coming to the table often and frequently is better than waiting until things break down and we need a major restoration. But should things break down, at the foot of the cross we find the one who can repair the damage. There may be a cost in the consequences of the break, but He will bear the brunt of it. It may be a bit messy to set things in order again, but He's able to do it.

Jesus, thank You for restoring our souls. We come to You, exposing our dirty laundry so that You can wash us clean. Thank You for Your saving grace that cleanses us from all sin. Amen.

For further study: Proverbs 4:23–27; Colossians 1:19–23; 2 Peter 1:3–14.

DECEMBER 4
Sweet Fragrance

And walk in love, as Christ has also loved us and given Himself for us, an offering and a sacrifice to God for a sweet-smelling aroma. (Ephesians 5:2)

I GOT HOME from a trip one time and found an overwhelming perfume fragrance in my house. It turned out my pet-sitters sprayed their perfume as a room freshener. To be honest, I wasn't overly happy about it, as I have a sensitivity to perfumes. I washed walls and furniture and for the most part got the smell down to a reasonable level, but with one exception. One of my Bibles had absorbed the perfume into its pages. I don't know what it is about that book that it picked up so much of the scent. Maybe it's the thinness of the pages. In any case, with every turn of the page, the fragrance wafts up. It's been five months and the odor is in no way diminished.

The Bible speaks of Jesus's sacrifice for us being as a sweet-smelling aroma to God. This fragrance of His sacrifice should cling to us like my pet-sitters' perfume has clung to the pages of my Bible. We are His body on earth and are commanded to walk in love just like He did. We're called to give of ourselves so others will notice the scent of heaven as they read our behavior like we read the pages of our Bible. Every day we have choices to make that will determine what others experience when they interact with us. They'll either encounter the fragrance of God or the stench of death. Communion is our time to remind ourselves of the wonderful grace we've received and the grace we have within us to give.

Jesus, Your sacrifice was a sweet-smelling aroma to God. Help us to love like You loved so people will be aware of Your presence within us. Amen.

For further study: 2 Corinthians 2:14–3:6; 1 John 3:16.

DECEMBER 5
Dual Citizenship

Concerning His Son Jesus Christ our Lord, who was born of the seed of David according to the flesh, and declared to be the Son of God with power according to the Spirit of holiness, by the resurrection from the dead. (Romans 1:3–4)

BEFORE A PLANNED trip to Spain, I spent a bit of time on a language learning app. Once in Spain, I could often find someone to speak English and help translate my desires or needs, but when I couldn't find someone to translate, the few words I learned were able to roughly communicate my needs. The learning app was helpful, but definitely not like learning by total immersion in a culture and language.

Gladys Aylward was a woman born to a working-class family in London, England at the turn of the twentieth century. She struggled to learn, and she dropped out of school to become a parlor maid. Her heart longed to be a missionary in China, but she was turned down by mission boards. They felt she would never learn the complex Chinese language. Gladys persevered and eventually made it to China on her own. There, totally immersed in the culture, she learned the language fluently within a few years. She picked up the culture and became so completely Chinese in her nature that when she traveled back to Britain in 1949, her own parents didn't recognize her. She was born a citizen of Great Britain yet became a citizen of China. God used her mightily and she led many, including a Mandarin official, to faith in Jesus and citizenship in heaven.

Jesus also was totally immersed in humanity. He didn't just try to speak into our lives as a foreigner. He became one with us. He didn't just play on an app trying to understand what it was like to live as a man. He became a man. He walked the dirt roads. He felt His stomach rumble with hunger. He knew what it was to be thirsty. He dealt with the same struggles. He had hopes and desires and felt our emotions. He experienced the pain of the sinful and fallen world while retaining the purity and citizenship of heaven. He was totally immersed in the world without losing the glory of heaven. He had dual citizenship and paved the way for us to become citizens of heaven with Him.

When we partake of communion, we recognize He came as a man, giving His body to be broken for our sin. Jesus, however, was without sin, so the pouring out of His blood was the sacrifice to bring cleansing to our souls and renewal of our spirits. He made it possible for us to become new creations and citizens of a better place. We live on earth for the moment, but He purchased for us the right to become citizens of the kingdom of heaven.

> *Thank You, Jesus. You came as a citizen of earth that we might become citizens of heaven. You made the way for us to be set free of our sins and to become something entirely new. Holy Spirit, reveal to us areas of our hearts that still cling to the world's citizenship, and renew us again to the righteousness of the place we truly belong. Amen.*

For further study: John 1:14; Philippians 3:20–21; Hebrews 2:14–18, 4:14–16.

DECEMBER 6
Don't Be a Litterbug

Let no corrupt communication proceed out of your mouth, but what is good for necessary edification, that it may impart grace to the hearers. (Ephesians 4:29)

I PASSED A couple of signs the other day. One said "Don't Litter," and the other was a French translation of that, which in a word-for-word translation said "Keep your garbage with you." The sign made me smile because I recalled road trips in my childhood home province of Manitoba. Manitoba didn't just tell people to keep their garbage with them. Instead, they provided a place for the garbage. Dotted along the highway were large, round white receptacles the province called Orbits. Just before each of these objects was a sign that said "Put Your Trash into Orbit." It was a great play on words, and we kids loved it. We always wanted to stop so we could toss our trash into Orbit. Manitoba knew we'd have trash; we just needed a bit of encouragement to put that trash in a place designed for it instead of strewing it along the roadway, corrupting the land.

I find as I go about my day-to-day life that I seem to accumulate garbage: anger, frustrations, discouragements, bad thoughts or habits, feelings of insufficiency, or a poor self-image. As it builds up and life gets messier, I sometimes end up flinging that garbage where it doesn't belong. I might toss an angry word at family, or fling frustrations at co-workers. If I was a better Christian, maybe I'd learn to keep my garbage with me instead of flinging it around to corrupt others. If I'm a great Christian, I'll take that garbage and deliver it to the place designed to deal with it. I could send it into the orbit of God's grace for it to be properly incinerated.

This is the whole purpose of spending a few moments every day in communion. We pause to examine ourselves and note where we've let some garbage pile up. By remembering Jesus's sacrifice for our sins, we bring that trash to the foot of the cross, where it can be properly dealt with. We receive His cleansing grace and the knowledge that we are supremely valued in the eyes of God. With this knowledge, we have no garbage left to fling at others. Our vessel is clean inside and out.

Jesus, thank You for cleansing us. You've taken away our sin, and we've received Your grace. Garbage will accumulate as long as we travel this fallen world, and we thank You that You are ever able and willing to take that garbage and send it away from us forever. Amen.

For further study: Matthew 23:25–26; Ephesians 4:23–32; Titus 3:1–7; James 3:2–18.

DECEMBER 7
Against You Only

Against You, You only, have I sinned, and done this evil in Your sight—that You may be found just when You speak, and blameless when You judge. (Psalm 51:4)

OFTEN WHEN I curl up in my rocking chair with my tea and communion wafer, I pause to ask God if there's something in my life that needs attention. There usually is. For example, the other day the Holy Spirit reminded me how my frustrations were very evident during a challenging day at work. It wasn't my co-workers' fault that the cases were difficult and the emergency phone line was ringing non-stop, yet I let them take the brunt of my frustration.

As I dwelt on this, I thought of David. He had committed a much worse sin against his co-worker. Uriah was one of David's faithful and mighty men who served in the army. David stole Uriah's wife and even had Uriah murdered to cover up the deed. Imagine that—David! A man after God's own heart did such a thing. Nathan the prophet confronted David about this, and, thankfully, David received the rebuke and correction with grace. He repented of his sin and wrote Psalm 51, where he says to God, *"Against You, You only, have I sinned."*

This line gives me pause. Against God only? Really? After all, Uriah's wife, Bathsheba, was seduced by David, and Uriah himself was murdered. I would say David sinned against them. He also sinned against the Israelites. They trusted David to serve God and do what was right. He also sinned by breaking trust with all his mighty men of valor. How could they know they wouldn't be next to be set up for murder? And what about the captain David ordered to put Uriah in the front line of death? David's sin was against them all, was it not?

These were my thoughts as I contemplated my own sin in allowing my flesh to rule over me and wound my co-workers. As I lifted up the communion wafer, I was reminded that Jesus said that whatever we do to others, we do to Him. I bow my head in shame and say, "Forgive me, for I have sinned against You."

As David wrote in Psalm 51, in our broken and contrite hearts before God, we find mercy. We can come to the communion table and partake of the bread and the wine and be cleansed again. He has extended the hand of forgiveness and lifts us up once again to our feet. Tomorrow is another day, and may we walk through it reminded always to treat others as we would treat Christ Himself.

Jesus, we receive Your grace and forgiveness. Only You can enable us to walk in grace toward others. We get there by knowing we have been forgiven and changed by You. We're not able on our own to walk in grace, but with You and for You, it is possible. Amen.

For further study: Psalm 51:1–17; Matthew 25:31–46.

DECEMBER 8
The Difference

For God so loved the world that He gave His only begotten Son, that whoever believes in Him should not perish but have everlasting life. (John 3:16)

I DON'T KNOW if people still do this, but there was a time when at televised sports events, a few people would lift up a sign that said "John 3:16." One day a few of my employees came to me and asked if I knew what the sign meant, since they thought it looked like it might be a Bible reference. At the time I don't think I explained it very well. Sure, I quoted the Scripture. What Christian hasn't memorized John 3:16? It's one of the first memory verses given to children in church. I'm just not sure I explained the amazing significance of this verse.

In other religions in the world, many of the devotees love their god. They may do sacrifices or behave in certain ways to worship their god. They may adore their god. They may reverence and fear their god and do things to appease their god. In some religions, the devotees try to be the right kind of follower so that they may even become a god. John 3:16, however, shows just how different Christianity is from all the others.

Christianity isn't so much about us loving our God as it is about our God loving us. It's not about us making sacrifices to our God but our God becoming the sacrifice for us. It's not about us doing things to appease the god we fear but about holding a deep reverence for a God who would do what was needed to appease the guilt of sin. It's about Him taking the penalty of that sin on Himself, dying in our place so we could live. Christianity isn't about us trying to be good to become a god; it is about our God becoming one of us so we could take on His goodness. All that is summed up in John 3:16. The rest of the Bible sets the background and expands on this main thing. It truly is amazing.

Pausing to take communion is pausing to remember all that's entailed in that one verse. It reminds us that God became man, lived a sinless life, but died for our sins and imparted His life to us. No other religion can compare to the glory we receive in Him.

Father, we're so grateful that You so loved the world You gave Your only Son, that we who believe on Him would not perish. Thank You for the everlasting life bestowed on us. We were unable to save ourselves, but You have saved us. There is nothing like it, and we are eternally blessed. Amen.

For further study: John 3:1–18.

DECEMBER 9
See My Son!

> And suddenly a voice came from heaven, saying, "This is My beloved Son, in whom I am well pleased." (Matthew 3:17)

IN A COUPLE of places in Scripture, God the Father speaks from heaven and calls out that Jesus is His beloved Son. When the voice came from heaven, not all heard it as a clearly spoken voice; some just heard unintelligible noise. Not everyone was paying attention or understood.

In my imagination, I see a father's beaming face. Maybe his child has just wobbled off on a two-wheeler bike with the training wheels removed. The father points at him and says, "See that boy? He's my son. I love him so much!" Some of the neighbors maybe look on and don't see anything special. Or maybe his brand-new baby daughter has just taken her first breath and been placed in his arms. He looks down tenderly and then looks at his family all around. "Do you see my baby? I love her so much." Meanwhile, the nurse in the corridor sighs at everyone just standing in her way.

Of course, we're all God's children, made in His image. What if we opened our ears to hear our Father's voice as we looked at everyone we see? As we pass the man begging on the street corner, we listen to hear the Father say, "Do you see My son? He's had a really rough go of things and made some bad choices, but I love him so much." Or maybe as we pass our money to the tired and cranky cashier, we listen to hear, "Do you see My daughter? She's under so much strain. She doesn't have enough money to buy her own groceries even as she's busy scanning yours. The irony of it wounds her deeply. I love her so much."

Perhaps we sit on the sidelines watching a race. One wins, others pass the finish line far behind, and someone comes in last. The Father thunders over all, "Do you see My beloved children? I love them all so much!" Or maybe as we sit here struggling with our own trials, thinking even of our own wounded heart, if we listen, we hear the Father saying, "Do you see yourself as I see you? You are My beloved child. I love you so very much."

God indeed loves the world. He loves us enough to send Jesus to die for us. He loves us enough to give His all to us. His love is without end. His love doesn't depend on our choices, our abilities, or our circumstances. It depends only on Him, and He is faithful and true.

Father, we listen and hear Your voice saying, "See My son? I love him so much. Do you see My beloved daughter? I love her so much. Do you see what I see, My children whom I love? Do You see how much I love you?" As we go about our day, may we hear Your voice always speaking of Your love to all people, ourselves included. Amen.

For further study: Mark 9:7; Luke 9:35; John 3:16; 1 Corinthians 1:9; 2 Peter 1:15–19.

DECEMBER 10
The 2 Degree Difference

But as for you, brethren, do not grow weary in doing good. (2 Thessalonians 3:13)

ON THE FIRST day of grade 10 Phys Ed, we had to run five minutes. It almost killed me! Some of the kids were throwing up. Every week, the teachers added a minute to the run. It was so hard at first, but at the end of the year, the entire class was running steadily for over thirty minutes, and we were keeping up conversation with each other while we did it. Just being consistent and adding small changes at a time made a huge difference in the end.

John Trent wrote a book called *The 2 Degree Difference*. He explains that if a rocket is aiming for the moon and is off by two degrees, it's going to miss the moon by thousands of miles. Likewise, if the rocket is going to miss the moon by thousands of miles, the rocket scientists only have to make a two-degree adjustment to get it back on track. Small changes, with consistency, will do more than trying to make a huge change all at once.

Over the course of the year, as I spent a few minutes every morning in communion, I added another few minutes of praying for my closest friends and family members. After contemplating the grace I've received from the Lord, it's easy to pray for His grace to abound to those I love. This small two-degree change has been easy to do.

I don't know if you just picked up today's devotion by chance or if you've followed along with me since the beginning of January. In either case, it hasn't been a big deal to take time or energy to pause in your day and partake of communion. Five minutes is all it's taken. But the change in your heart attitude may be massive. If you're like me, you've found that by consistently coming to the Lord's table, your gratitude to Him has grown. You've likely felt more free and cleaner in your soul. Loving people becomes easier. When you hear a story of someone doing bad things, sympathy for their lost and broken state comes to mind more than disgust. It's easier to pray for people than judge them. Forgiveness comes a bit easier. Love grows in our hearts more freely, less tangled by the weeds of sin and self-righteousness.

Maybe today we only run in faith for five minutes, and even that's a struggle, but later, we may run more steadily and not even be out of breath because of the small and consistent change in our time with our Savior. We're approaching the end of this devotional, but let us hold fast to our faith, building on it, knowing our Lord is guiding us to the final heavenly goal.

> *Jesus, thank You for loving us. You've forgiven us, and You lead us in forgiveness for Your children. You have loved us and cause love to abound in us for others. You have changed us. Sometimes we've forgotten, but we pause today to remember and to rejoice in You. Amen.*

For further study: Galatians 6:9; 2 Thessalonians 2:13–17; 2 Peter 1:1–8.

DECEMBER 11
Jumanji: The Next Level

> And as it is appointed for men to die once, but after this the judgment, so Christ was offered once to bear the sins of many. To those who eagerly wait for Him He will appear a second time, apart from sin, for salvation. (Hebrews 9:27–28)

JUMANJI: THE NEXT LEVEL is about kids being sucked into a video game and having to play it to the end successfully in order to get out. They find the old video controllers when they're sent by the principal to clean a storeroom as a means of punishment. The principal had admonished them, saying they only had one life and they were messing it up.

Once they get sucked into the video game, they start the game with three "lives." Over the course of the game, they all end up down to their last life. They're afraid of what might happen if they lose that last life, so they're unsure how to proceed to complete the game. One of the kids suddenly comments that the principal was right—all they ever had was one life. It's their choice what they do with it. This gives them courage to face their fears and complete the game.

The Bible has always been clear that we only have one life to live on earth before entering eternity. It's our choice what we do with it. God has given us free will, and He won't force us to make good choices. He encourages us and helps us, but He never forces us. The good news is that as long as we're breathing, it's never too late to choose to do what's right. It's never too late to move closer to Jesus.

Jesus also only had one life to give as a sacrifice on earth. He laid that life down for us so we could inherit eternal life with Him. He knew the purpose of His life, and He was willing to pay the price to fulfill that purpose. Unlike us, He wasn't easily distracted from that purpose. He knew the choice He had to make—the one that led to the cross—and He finished what He came to do with courage and grace.

> *Jesus, we're grateful You made the choice to walk the way of the cross in order to save us and give us eternal life with You after our life on earth is through. Help us to remember that we only have one life on earth to impact others with Your love, and strengthen us to make good choices so that when we stand before You, we hear the words "Well done!"*

For further study: Matthew 25:14–30; Galatians 2:20; Hebrews 9:25–28; 1 John 5:6–13.

DECEMBER 12
Self-Esteem

And the Angel of the Lord appeared to him, and said to him, "The Lord is with you, you mighty man of valor!" (Judges 6:12)

IN THE BOOK *Le Courage, Comment L'activer*, the author, Isabelle Fontaine, says that we don't improve a child's self-esteem by giving everyone a prize but by giving them challenges that will grow their self-esteem as they overcome them. She's on to something, I think, although she's missing the Christian principle that our value comes first from God.

Gideon didn't have much self-esteem when he was first approached by the Angel of God. He was threshing wheat in a wine press because he was trying to hide the harvest from being stolen by the Midianites. The Angel said the Lord was with Gideon, and He called Gideon a mighty man of valor! Gideon didn't feel like a mighty man of valor. He felt that he and his family were unimportant in Israel. God felt otherwise.

God had called Gideon to raise up Israel to stand against their enemies. He saw the might that was hidden in Gideon, even as Gideon was hiding in the wine press. The Lord first gave Gideon the task of pulling down the idols. Gideon was afraid, so he did it under the cover of night. After the successful completion of that task, Gideon was a bit more courageous. He still asked for proof that God was speaking, and he still felt fear, but he was able to do greater and greater things as his trust in God grew. God had seen the mighty man of valor within Gideon first, until Gideon was able to see it as well. God knew the might within Gideon, because God knew He was with Gideon.

On occasions when we look at ourselves, or the people around us, the value and might within seems hidden from our view. Circumstances beat us down and increase our fear and anxiety. As we pause to partake of communion, we're reminded that we are the body of Christ on earth. We have tremendous value because He is in us. He has called us and is with us. We are well able to do all He asks us to do. We can look in the mirror and know God says, "God is with you, mighty man of valor! God is with you, mighty woman of valor!" We can also look at others, who maybe cause trouble as they act out of their fear, and say, "There is a mighty person of valor." They may not know it yet. Their might is hidden right now, but God is well able to bring it to fruition. His blood is sufficient and more than able to help them overcome.

Thank You, Lord, that You see in us the value we sometimes can't see ourselves. You have called us to receive Your love and pass Your love on to others. We're able to do this because our might and strength are in You. Help us to see in each other the value You see, even when it's hidden from our view. Amen.

For further study: Judges 6:11–8:32; 1 Samuel 16:7.

DECEMBER 13
Where Is God?

> "Behold, the virgin shall be with child, and bear a Son, and they shall call His name Immanuel," which is translated, "God with us." (Matthew 1:23)

I'VE HAD THE great privilege to travel on several occasions to Europe. There are many magnificent churches everywhere one goes. Great artwork fills these huge stone cathedrals: beautiful stained glass, brilliant sculptures covered in gold, and stunning paintings. Some of these buildings took centuries to build, with people working on the structure not for their own use but for future generations. You can tell the craftsmen longed to bring glory to God, even though it was the people yet to come who would enter the building to worship.

On one of these trips, I walked into one of the churches to admire the beauty, but I was struck more by the smell of mold. Tourists mingled, looking at the stained glass, but there appeared to be no one who came to worship. I found myself asking God where He was in this great structure. Was His glory to be found in the gold-covered sculptures of the saints? Was His glory in the craft of the stone cutter who laid the foundations? Could it be found in the faded paintings or the stained glass depicting the life of Christ? Or was His glory to be found in the old beggar sitting on the cold stone outside of the massive wooden church doors, petting the dog asleep at her side? Or was His glory in the child in the courtyard leaping up to catch the bubbles blown by a street performer?

God told Joseph to take Mary as his wife because she was a virgin who conceived the Son of God. Jesus was Immanuel—God with us. He would come to make His home with the descendants of Adam. God chose to put His glory in vessels of clay, not in those of silver and gold. He chose a stable for His birth instead of a palace. He is Immanuel. His temple is in us and not in a building of stone. Sure, the cathedrals are magnificent. You know the craftsmen were dedicated to the Lord, but we can't lose sight that God has chosen to dwell in people—the leader and the beggar, the rich and the poor, the happy and the sad. He's as at home in someone who walks among the golden sculptures as He is in someone who sleeps in a cardboard box on skid row. We can ask God where He is in this fallen world, and we'll hear Him say, "I am here. I am in you." He is in me. Jesus paid the price so He could dwell with us in all His glory.

> *Immanuel, God with us, we are so blessed and amazed the Lord of the heavens and earth would choose to dwell with His fallen creatures. You transform us and make us new by Your presence. May we always reflect Your glory. Amen.*

For further study: Matthew 1:18–25; 1 Corinthians 6:19–20; 2 Corinthians 4:6–7.

DECEMBER 14
Pray Your Bills

Now may He who supplies seed to the sower, and bread for food, supply and multiply the seed you have sown and increase the fruits of your righteousness, while you are enriched in everything for all liberality, which causes thanksgiving through us to God. (2 Corinthians 9:10–11)

CORRIE TEN BOOM in her book *No Good if Detached* wrote of trouble and anxieties being like a debt, bills that need to be paid. She then talked about taking all these things to God in prayer to let Him pay those bills out of the abundance of His grace toward us.

Interestingly, just after I read this, an unsaved friend said to me that the trouble with Christians is that they believe they can do whatever they want, since all is forgiven. I countered that the Bible talks about this. Paul asked, *"Shall we continue in sin that grace may abound?"* (Romans 6:1b). And then he answered, *"Certainly not!"* (Romans 6:2a). The person I was speaking with countered with, "Christians believe all is forgiven, so their behavior shouldn't matter." I was at a bit of a loss as to how to explain that even though we believe we are forgiven, having received such a marvelous grace in the forgiveness of our sins, we really have turned our backs on sin. Then I thought of Corrie and her analogy of heaven's bank account to pay our bills.

If people are unable to extend grace, I would question whether they ever truly believed that Christ has paid their tremendous sin debt. They're still overdrawn with an empty bank account. They can't truly extend grace if they've never received it. But when we understand the extent of our debt, we're overcome by love, realizing the price Jesus paid for us. Love is able to flow out when the bank account of our hearts has been filled with it.

Of course, as Corrie noted, there are still times in this life when trials and troubles come our way. We make mistakes and run up some fresh debt in sin or anxiety. We know, however, what to do with our sin and anxieties. We take them to the foot of the cross and confess them to our Lord and Savior. The abundance of the richness of His grace is able to pay those bills and refill our empty account. When we pause to partake of communion, we're doing just that. We remember all He has done and the abundance of His love for us so that we can rest in His grace.

> *Jesus, we're so grateful You paid the debt we could not. It was a tremendous debt that cost Your precious blood in order to be paid. Our love account is now filled to overflowing because of all You have done. Thank You for Your amazing grace. Amen.*

For further study: Romans 5:9–6:23; Colossians 1:9–14.

DECEMBER 15
What Would Love Do?

> Love suffers long and is kind; love does not envy; love does not parade itself, is not puffed up; does not behave rudely, does not seek its own, is not provoked, thinks no evil; does not rejoice in iniquity, but rejoices in the truth; bears all things, believes all things, hopes all things, endures all things. Love never fails. (1 Corinthians 13:4–8a)

A FEW YEARS ago, it was popular for Christians to wear a bracelet with WWJD written on it. This stood for "What would Jesus do?" It was a helpful reminder that we are to act like Christ. Sometimes it's hard to know what to do, so asking ourselves what Jesus would do could bring clarity to our decisions.

Unfortunately, in this fallen world where so much has changed from the first century when Jesus walked on the earth, it may be hard to imagine just what He would do. We have no Scriptures dealing with social media or even driving your car. Naturally we can still draw on the wealth of Scripture to decide our path, but in the heat of the moment, it may be hard to think clearly.

Maybe the best way to think of what to do would be to think of the question, "What would love do?" After all, God is love. If we want to know what Jesus would do, we really have to think of what love would do. In 1 Corinthians we're given a clear description of exactly what love would do, or not do. Love is patient and kind. It thinks of others and their needs. It's truthful. Love will make the hard choices, and love will not fail.

Of course, I have failed to love well in many cases, especially with friends and family. You'd think it would be easier to behave with love to those we love the most, but somehow, it's often easier to be kind to a stranger than to a member of our own household.

And so we come to the communion table. We remember we were bought with love and born again to give love. We bring our failure to the foot of the cross and pick up the banner of love to start afresh. If we haven't failed in our love for others, that's wonderful, yet we still come to the table to have our love strengthened further. At the communion table, we find forgiveness for our lack of love, and we can fill up on love so we can give love.

> *Jesus, thank You for the great love You have toward us. You are love personified. Help us to be more like You in every way. Amen.*

For further study: 1 Corinthians 13:1–13; 1 Peter 2:21–24; 1 John 4:7–21.

DECEMBER 16
There You Are

> Let nothing be done through selfish ambition or conceit, but in lowliness of mind let each esteem others better than himself. (Philippians 2:3)

IN MY JOB as a veterinarian, I often go to conferences to learn new things. Often we have a chance to eat and interact with our colleagues. I happen to be quite shy, and these times can be really stressful. If I sit at an empty table, will anyone else sit there? If others sit there, will they talk to me or ignore me? If I ask to join a table that already has people, they still may not talk to me and I'll feel out of place and alone. I don't know what to say if the others don't initiate the conversation. If I meet some nice people and have a great time, it's because of their efforts, not mine. My failure may be based on fear, but I think it has its root in pride. Pride wants others to see my need and fill it. Pride wants people to elevate me. Humility would seek to raise others instead.

I came across this quote by Frederick L. Collins: "There are two types of people—those who come into a room and say, 'Well, here I am!' and those who come in and say, 'Ah, there you are.'"[6] The point is, we can walk into a room thinking only of ourselves and wanting other people to make us comfortable, or we can walk in thinking there are great, kind, and interesting people out there whom we want to meet. We can walk into a party expecting others to entertain us, or we can look for people who seem shy or uncomfortable, reaching out to make them feel welcome. When we go with the attitude that others should make us feel comfortable, we often have a miserable time. But when we go with the attitude of making others feel comfortable, they have a great time, and so do we. We also make new friends and build relationships. It's a win-win.

It makes perfect sense when you think about it. After all, Jesus came to earth as a man to interact with us and reach out to us. He didn't just sit on His mat and wait for people to recognize who He was and make Him feel special. He walked around and called out to people to come to Him. Ultimately, He thought about what He needed to do to build a relationship with us—to save us. He didn't think of His own comfort—quite the opposite, in fact, as He gave up His own comfort completely at the cross. Because Jesus was thinking of our needs and reaching out to us, we were greatly enriched, but so also was the kingdom of God.

Paul tells us we should be like Jesus and think of others over ourselves. We should put away our pride and conceit. We need to look out for the interests of others. In doing that, it turns out we are often looking out for our own interests as well. Win-win.

> *Jesus, You set the example of putting the needs of others over our own. Just as You enriched heaven by putting our needs ahead of Yours, we also are enriched when we follow You and live by Your example. Help us to put away our fear and pride and look to see who we can reach out to with Your love. Amen.*

For further study: Matthew 4:19; Philippians 2:1–9.

---

[6] "Frederick L. Collins Quotes," Goodreads, accessed May 21, 2025, https://www.quotes.net/authors/Frederick+L+Collins+Quotes.

December 17
Heliographs

> Beloved, now we are children of God; and it has not yet been revealed what we shall be, but we know that when He is revealed, we shall be like Him, for we shall see Him as He is. (1 John 3:2)

NICÉPHORE NIÉPCE AND his brother Claude are credited with the birth of photography. Niépce was able to use long exposure to sunlight to produce the image from outside of his window onto metal plates covered in asphalt. He called his images heliographs, or sun drawings.

I like that word "heliograph," and it makes me think of another kind of *Son* drawing. When we open our hearts to exposure of the Son of God, He produces an image of heaven's grace on our hearts. It's a birth of something new and amazing. Others look at the image and are in awe, amazed with the image. When we first receive Him, the image is a bit spotty, but with ongoing and prolonged exposure to the Son, the image starts to become clearer and more distinct. The developing is never completely finished this side of the grave, yet it can only improve with time. There will come a day when we join Him in eternity, and the reflection of His image will be perfectly clear. But until then, it can always be improved by exposure to His presence.

If we were to walk away and hide ourselves from Him, the image would begin to weather and fade by the trials of the soul. If we keep our hearts open to His light, the image will sharpen in greater detail. His love becomes easier to see, as it overshadows our old nature. When the disciples were arrested, the religious leaders could tell that these men had been with Jesus, as His effect on them overpowered the fading image of their old lives.

As I sit today with the bread and wine of communion, I am reminded of His love being burned into my heart and soul. I ask Him to make me His heliograph—an image for others to look on and be awed by. He is responsible for creating the image. I only must keep my heart open to His exposure.

> *Jesus, we look to You and ask for the image of Your grace and love to grow in clarity and vivacity in us. May others look on us and see You. Amen.*

For further study: Acts 3:1–4:22; Romans 8:18–19.

DECEMBER 18
A Christmas Carol

> Therefore, if anyone is in Christ, he is a new creation; old things have passed away; behold, all things have become new. (2 Corinthians 5:17)

I LIKE DICKENS. His writing is filled with great descriptions of interesting characters. I particularly enjoy reading his short story "A Christmas Carol." There have been well over one hundred adaptations of this book as a play, in public readings, cinema movies, DVDs, and even various TV shows. This story is about Ebenezer Scrooge, a greedy miser who, after encountering the ghosts of Christmas, changes his ways.

Someone who holds tight to his money, or doesn't enjoy the Christmas season, is regularly referred to as a Scrooge. Unfortunately, by focusing on Scrooge the miser, they miss the whole point of the book. As Scrooge is forced to face the choices of his past and the mistakes he's made, he sees that he is headed for death and judgment. He can only turn his life around by recognizing the meaning of Christmas, the grace of Jesus Christ, who came as a man to take away his punishment. This grace working in Scrooge makes him no longer the greedy miser but a generous and beloved man, one who spends the rest of his life doing good to his fellow man, lifting others out of the pit of despair.

Dickens writes, "Scrooge was better than his word. He did it all, and infinitely more; and to Tiny Tim, who did NOT die, he was a second father. He became as good a friend, as good a master, and as good a man, as the good old city knew, or any other good old city, town, or borough, in the good old world … and it was always said of him, that he knew how to keep Christmas well, if any man alive possessed the knowledge. May that be truly said of us, and all of us! And so, as Tiny Tim observed, God bless Us, Every One!"[7]

It's funny how Scrooge, by the grace of God, became a totally different man, yet what we remember are his sins. When people refer to someone as a Scrooge, he's identified by his failures. Shouldn't we identify Scrooge with who he became because of the love of God? In our own lives, sometimes it's easier to focus on people's failures. Past hurts are remembered so easily. We so often see even our shortcomings and mistakes. The failures loom large in our memory, while we forget the grace of God at work within us all. God has blessed us and called us into His body. Our old self has been crucified with Him, and we are created new. We partake of communion to be reminded that we are not defined by the sins of our past, and we extend the hand of grace to ourselves and others.

> *Jesus, thank You for changing us. Others may define us by our past sins, but we are defined by Your grace. Help us to live true to that grace so others see You in us. Amen.*

For further study: Romans 6:6–23; 2 Corinthians 5:11–21.

---

[7] Charles Dickens, *The Charles Dickens Library: Christmas Stories* (New York: Gramercy Books, 1996), 76–77.

DECEMBER 19
Holding Fast

Let us hold fast the confession of our hope without wavering, for He who promised is faithful.
(Hebrews 10:23)

A CHARLIE BROWN CHRISTMAS is an animated Christmas special that has played on TV for over fifty years. It's become a staple of the holiday for many people across North America. We feel encouraged when Linus recites the announcement of the birth of Christ to the shepherds from the book of Luke, proclaiming this is what Christmas is all about.

This TV special almost never happened. It was written quickly and made on a small budget with simple animation. It included jazz music, didn't use a laugh track, used child voices, had a slow pace, and quoted the Bible. Executives were convinced it would be a complete flop, and one of the producers, Lee Mendelson, said the executives would have canceled it if it hadn't been completed just a week before it was due to broadcast. They had no choice but to run it, having nothing to replace it. Over the years it has continued to enjoy extremely high ratings, and it has not lost its popularity.

Charles Schulz, the creator of the *Peanuts* cartoon strip, was adamant the TV special contain the true meaning of Christmas. The producers felt religion shouldn't be a part of it, but Schulz held fast to his convictions. If it didn't contain the true meaning of Christmas—Jesus Christ being born as a man to take away the sins of the world—there would be no point. Jesus coming to us brings hope when all seems lost. Jesus takes our mistakes and converts them to something with meaning. He takes our weak, broken lives and decorates them to make us like strong trees showing His glory. He steps into the mess of our daily lives and makes it something beautiful. Charles Schulz knew that and made sure that was portrayed.

We like this special because we also know that Christmas is really all about Jesus. It's not about the presents, the decorations, or the plays. It's about God, who would become man and live a sinless life yet pay the penalty for our failures so we might receive His glory. Just like this Christmas special reminds us of the true meaning of Christmas, so also partaking of communion reminds us of all Jesus has done. It's a reminder of His grace and glory dwelling in us and that He takes all of the failures and messes of our lives and turns them into something with meaning and beauty.

Jesus, thank You for taking our weakness and giving us Your strength. Thank You for taking our failures and giving us Your victory. Thank You for taking our disappointments and giving us hope. We pause to remember all You have done and do for us. Amen.

For further study: Isaiah 61:3; Luke 2:8–20; Romans 8:28, 15:13; Hebrews 10:19–24.

DECEMBER 20
Silly Hats

I will greatly rejoice in the Lord, my soul shall be joyful in my God; for He has clothed me with the garments of salvation, He has covered me with the robe of righteousness, as a bridegroom decks himself with ornaments, and as a bride adorns herself with her jewels. (Isaiah 61:10)

I LOVE WANDERING the mall this time of year. I don't really purchase a lot of presents, since most of the gifts I buy are donations to ministries as opposed to sending something people will have to dust. I do like window shopping, however, and seeing all the smiling faces on people around me. Now I can hear some of you groan. "Smiling faces! Ha! This time of year people are stressed and anxious, rushing around to buy presents, over-extended and angry." True. However, I have discovered something that always makes people smile.

I like to wear silly winter hats. I have a Santa hat of course, but also one with ears like a bear, one that dangles long with a shiny pom-pom on it, a cookie monster hat, and my favorite—one that is the head, complete with horns, of a Scottish highland cow. When people look at me and see the silly hat, they always smile. I, of course, have completely forgotten I'm wearing it, so when they smile, I just think everyone is happy, and that makes me smile. The joy is multiplied over and over again. I can't help but smile even as I write this. Hopefully you're smiling as you read it.

It really doesn't take much to bring joy to people's lives. There are other situations where joy is more elusive. That was why Jesus went to the cross to pay the debt for our sin. He covers us in His grace, and we can now rejoice that we are free from the power of sin and death. Our circumstances may not be the best at the moment, but our hearts can still rejoice. Happiness is fleeting, but joy is eternal. It was purchased for us at great cost. Sometimes we can get our eyes on our circumstances and forget to walk in joy. Partaking of communion is a little reminder of the grace that has been so freely given to redeem us and bring us joy.

> *Jesus, we rejoice in You and all You've done for us. You paved the way for our freedom and gave us the gift of everlasting life. Your joy fills us even when our circumstances are unhappy. We are reminded of this today, and ask You to help us to walk in the joy You have so freely provided. Amen.*

For further study: Luke 2:8–14, 10:20; Philippians 4:4; 1 Thessalonians 5:16.

DECEMBER 21
Puzzle Pieces

If it is possible, as much as it depends on you, live peaceably with all men. (Romans 12:18)

I LOVE TRADITIONS that spring up around the holidays. One of the traditions I grew up with was that at the start of the Christmas holidays, my dad would open up a large puzzle on a big table in the dining room. As we got older, the puzzles grew larger and more challenging. We'd work as a family setting in the pieces—some bright and colorful, some dark, but all necessary. I remember one of the puzzles, when completed, was missing a piece. If you do puzzles, you know how unsatisfying it is to be missing a piece of a jigsaw puzzle.

On the box it said if you were missing a piece to take a piece adjacent to the missing area and mail it in to the company. We assumed they would send us the pieces adjacent to the one we sent in. Imagine our surprise when a whole new copy of the puzzle arrived a short time later in the mail. A little while later, when cleaning up after the holidays, wouldn't you know it, but we found the original missing piece under the piano. *That's great*, I thought, *now we have two copies of the puzzle and can give one away*. Until I realized the first one was still missing a piece—the one we had to mail in.

I think the people in my life are a bit like the pieces of a jigsaw puzzle. Some are darker, while others shine with brightness. Sometimes I've tried to fit myself where I didn't fit, trying to connect with the wrong people. Some people fit near my spot, but I'd rather not have them in that place in my life. I think God would say that all were necessary for the picture He is creating. Some we need to connect with closely, but others will take places more distant in our lives, yet all are critical. He has an end picture in mind, and it won't be as satisfying if anyone is missing.

I think this makes me a little more philosophical about the people I struggled with. They had a role to play in developing my character and keeping me close to my Lord, who at the end of the age will make sense of all the puzzling things. For now, He calls me to remember what He has done, letting Him be my example. He calls me to bless those who persecute me, to be kind, to overcome evil with good, just as He did. Pilate had just as much of a part to play as did Peter and John. The dark and the light both are needed to complete the picture. We can give thanks in the knowledge that the puzzle of our life will fit perfectly within the larger picture of the glory of His sacrifice on the cross.

> *Father, You are the ultimate one who can put together all the pieces of our lives and make them something beautiful. Your glory shines upon the picture You have created. At times we struggle, fighting You as You place us gently where we need to be for all to be completed. We trust You, knowing one day we will see the final glory You had in mind. Thank You. Amen.*

For further study: Jeremiah 29:11; Romans 12:1–21; 1 Corinthians 12:1–31.

DECEMBER 22

Signposts

And this will be the sign to you: You will find a Babe wrapped in swaddling cloths, lying in a manger. (Luke 2:12)

I GREW UP in Winnipeg, Manitoba, but went to university in Saskatoon, Saskatchewan. Many times over those years, I made the long drive between the two cities. The first time I drove to Saskatoon, I noted there were often signs marking an upcoming curve in the road. I was mystified by these signs. This flat prairie highway was easy enough to see and follow. Then I drove the same highway in the winter! When the snow would blow across the fields, the highway was near impossible to see. You could see a faint gray trail ahead of you, and as long as the road was straight, it was easy enough to stay on it, but when there was a curve, it was extremely difficult. The sign was critical to help you guess when you should start turning to avoid driving off into a farmer's field. Sometimes in the winter the snow would even cover the signs. The shape of the sign was a good clue, but you never really knew how far away the next town was, or if you'd just passed the last gas station for one hundred kilometers.

When Jesus was born, the angels said a sign that He was the Messiah would be that He would be found in a stable, wrapped in swaddling clothes and lying in a manger. There were many other signs, of course, that Jesus was the Messiah, not the least of which were all the miracles He did. When He rose from the dead, that was the sign that clinched it, but it wasn't always easy for people to read these signs.

Even though Mary had seen the open tomb, and the angels proclaimed Jesus had risen, when she met Him, she thought He was the gardener and asked where He had taken Jesus's dead body. The disciples on the road to Emmaus heard the news Jesus had risen, but as Jesus met them and walked with them, they didn't recognize Him, even though their hearts burned within them, telling them this wasn't just an ordinary traveler. They recognized Jesus when they sat at the table and Jesus gave thanks and broke bread. Jesus had given this common everyday practice in the breaking of bread as a sign for people to remember His purpose. He would die for our sins and raise us to new life with Him.

Sometimes the signs of His love for us are hard to see. Circumstances can obscure them, and we travel not truly understanding where we are or where we're headed. Pausing to partake of communion is like pausing on the road to wipe the snow off the signs and make the path a little clearer.

> *Jesus, thank You for all You've done. Sometimes we forget. The signs of Your love are obscured by the world's fog, yet we look to You to make all things clear in their time. Amen.*

For further study: Luke 2:8–20, 24:13–35; John 20:1–18, 30–31.

DECEMBER 23
No Room at the Inn

And she brought forth her firstborn Son, and wrapped Him in swaddling cloths, and laid Him in a manger, because there was no room for them in the inn. (Luke 2:7)

LUKE TELLS US that Caesar Augustus called for a census requiring everyone to be registered in their hometown. Joseph and Mary, who were both of the lineage of David, traveled to the city of Bethlehem to be registered. When they arrived, there was no room for them. Now think about this: they've traveled to their hometown and there's no room for them anywhere, not even at the inn. Don't you find this odd? They must be surrounded by friends and relatives, yet no one is willing to put them up—with Mary pregnant and about to give birth! This is rather shocking, if you ask me. My own relatives would be offended if I didn't want to stay with them. The thought occurs to me that maybe there were wagging tongues and scornful looks.

"Look at Mary, about to give birth! Yet we all know it hasn't been nine months that they've been together. We can do the math! She's played the harlot! And look at Joseph. He didn't divorce her. He must be the guilty one! And we thought they were both such upstanding people."

Was the inn really full? No room even for a woman about to give birth? Or was it the innkeeper saying, "Hey, look, I'm really sorry, but I live and work in this town all the time. Having you here could ruin my reputation and my business. Tell you what, I'll look the other way if you head to the stable. At least there will be a roof over your heads and she won't give birth in the street."

Maybe the problem wasn't that there was no room in Bethlehem, but rather there was no room in the hearts of their friends and relatives. Have you ever felt like that? Either rightly or wrongly, that people had no room in their hearts for you? That you didn't fit in? Jesus gets it. He knows what it feels like. Even before He was born, He felt the sting of rejection—rejection that would conclude with a brutal death on the cross. But the miracle of His sacrifice for us is that even while we were yet sinners, Christ died for the ungodly. He made room for us in His family and in heaven. His heart is big enough for us.

He gave us the practice of communion for us to pause and remember that He has made room for us. Others may reject us, but He has accepted us in the beloved. It's also a moment for us to pause and examine ourselves. Have we closed our hearts to others? Communion is about turning back to the love of God and allowing that love to enlarge our hearts and make room for us to love others.

> *Heavenly Father, we thank You for Your eternal and beautiful love. Your love was so great that Jesus paid the price for our sins. We remember His body broken so we could be accepted into His family. Forgive us for our own scornful judgments of people. Enlarge our hearts to love You and others. Amen.*

For further study: Isaiah 53:1–12; Luke 2:1–7; Romans 5:6–8; Ephesians 1:3–6.

DECEMBER 24
A Gift Freely Given

Therefore, as through one man's offense judgment came to all men, resulting in condemnation, even so through one Man's righteous act the free gift came to all men, resulting in justification of life. (Romans 5:18)

THERE ARE OCCASIONS like Christmas and birthdays when it's customary for people to give gifts to one another. Sometimes, this season of gift giving can cause problems. You know the situations where this occurs. Maybe someone gives you a gift but they expect you to treasure it and use it and will be offended if you don't. Perhaps you're given a gift, but you groan inwardly, thinking that you're obligated to reciprocate. Maybe your pride insists it also be a better gift than the one you were given, and you don't have the will or the means to do that. Perhaps the gift giver has gone to great sacrifice to give the gift, but they find their gift is underappreciated or not even wanted by the receiver. Maybe the intended receiver politely accepts it but then throws it away. They might make sport of it and trample on it. Maybe they refuse to accept it, or even slam the door in the face of the courier trying to deliver the gift.

A gift freely given is given with no strings attached. It can be accepted or refused, trampled or treasured, and the giver won't be offended. The gift giver may be sad that the sacrifice they made wasn't appreciated, but they're not offended, nor do they retaliate against the intended receiver.

When Adam ate of the tree of the knowledge of good and evil, sin entered the world. We inherited sin and remain under the shadow of death. Jesus came by His own free will to buy us back. He laid His life down as a free offering to pay the price for our sin. He gave us Himself as a free gift. We could do nothing to earn it. We can't pay Him back for it. We can only receive it.

Some choose to refuse it. Some disdain the gift and trample it. Others are polite but put it aside and don't really accept it. Some are rude and slam the door in the face of those who would deliver the gift. Some receive it but feel obligated to live up to a certain standard to reciprocate. They soon find the sense of obligation and lack of willingness or means to pay it back causes them to resent the gift. Other people, however, receive the gift with joy. They treasure it and know there is no obligation to reciprocate. The amazing thing is, those who freely and truly receive His love find themselves able to freely and truly give His love with no strings attached. Jesus is able to abide in them and work through them.

As we take communion, let's acknowledge the free gift of His sacrifice for our sins. And as we examine ourselves, let's discern if there's an area where we've served God out of obligation. Now is the time for us to repent, knowing He loves us freely. We can't pay Him back; we can only receive His gift with joy.

> *Jesus, we acknowledge we were sinners, but Your free gift has saved us from our sins and given us eternal life. Forgive us for when we have given resentfully or under obligation. Help us to also give freely as You have given to us. Amen.*

For further study: Matthew 10:8; Luke 6:27–38; Romans 6:23; 2 Corinthians 9:6–15.

DECEMBER 25
Gold, Frankincense, and Myrrh

> And when they had come into the house, they saw the young Child with Mary His mother, and fell down and worshiped Him. And when they had opened their treasures, they presented gifts to Him: gold, frankincense, and myrrh. (Matthew 2:11)

WE'VE HEARD THE tale and even sung the songs of the kings (wise men) who came from Persia to worship the Christ Child. They followed the star that led to Jesus, worshiped Him, and gave Him gifts. These gifts would be very important for the family. We know at that time they weren't rich. When Mary and Joseph presented Jesus at the temple to dedicate Him, they brought a gift of two doves. This was the gift the poor were to give when a son was the firstborn. Someone who was wealthier was to give a lamb and a dove.

Herod would soon try to kill Jesus, reaching out to murder all the children of Bethlehem. The gifts of those wise men would finance the holy family's flight to Egypt and safety. Those gifts indeed were very precious and carried great value. All of the needs of this young family living in a foreign country would be met. But these gifts also carried even greater significance.

The first king knelt before Jesus in worship, and opening his bag, presented Him with gold. Gold, of course, is associated with royalty and kingship. Palaces are adorned with gold. The foundation of a king's crown is gold. As this first wise man bows down, he's saying, "Here is my gift of gold, for You are the King of all kings. You are my King."

The next king comes and opens his bag. Out of it comes a jar of frankincense. Frankincense was used in the censers of the priest. A coal from the altar would be used to light the incense and make a sweet-smelling aroma. The priests also would anoint the regular offerings coming to the altar with frankincense before burning them. Frankincense speaks of the priesthood. This king, as he bows before the child, is saying, "Here is my gift of frankincense, for You, Jesus, are the High Priest of all priests. You are my Priest."

The third kneels down and, with a great depth of sadness reflected in his eyes, pulls out his gift of myrrh. Myrrh was a valuable spice used in perfumes and embalming. It's a bitter, red-colored compound that was also used to deaden pain. Myrrh was used to purify, but it was used in pain and death. In a few decades, Jesus would be offered myrrh on the cross, and Nicodemus would bring one hundred pounds of myrrh to anoint Jesus's body for burial. This wise man bows before the child and holds back his tears as he says, "Here is my gift of myrrh, for You will die for the sins of the world. You are my Savior."

Jesus is the Savior of the world. He becomes our Savior when we receive Him personally as the sacrifice for our sins. If you haven't recognized Jesus as your Savior, now is a great time to do so! If you have, ask the Holy Spirit to reveal any areas where you haven't allowed Him to reign in your life as king, priest, and Savior, that you might repent and once again be cleansed.

> *Jesus, we recognize You as king, priest, and Savior. Though You were without sin, You laid down Your life as a sin offering for us so we could be saved. We bow before You and worship You. Amen.*

For further study: Leviticus 12:1–8; Matthew 2:1–12; Luke 2:21–24; 1 Timothy 6:14–16; Hebrews 4:14–16; 1 John 4:14.

DECEMBER 26
Boxing Day

A word fitly spoken is like apples of gold in settings of silver. (Proverbs 25:11)

DECEMBER 26 IS Boxing Day in Commonwealth countries. It's a holiday that originated in Britain in which gifts and sometimes even leftover food would be boxed up and given to the servants to take home to their families as they celebrated a day off after having served the master's household on Christmas Day. Nowadays it's become more a time to celebrate shopping and sales, plus those ever-present returns of unwanted gifts. It's a far cry from its origin of giving a bonus to others. It's become more about "me and my wants."

Years ago, I read a book called *Silver Boxes* by Florence Littauer, about how our words can be gifts to others, like a present wrapped in a pretty silver box. It's based on the Scripture in Ephesians that says our words should be used to build people up. Sometimes our words to others, especially those in our circle of close family or friends, aren't at all like a gift presented in a pretty box. They can wound and tear down instead of edify and build up. Our words become nothing like what God originally intended for our relationships, just like Boxing Day has become nothing like its origins.

What would happen if we considered every day in the spirit of the original Boxing Day? What if we presented our words to each other as gifts meant to encourage people to become all that God intended them to be? Our relationships could be forever changed. After all, our relationship with God was forever changed when He "boxed" up Jesus, the Word of God, in a lowly manger to present Him to us. Jesus let Himself be put in a box for a time to live as a man, experiencing the limitations of human flesh. Yet this was a precious gift sent to us to build us up into the body of Christ. It was the gift of eternal life and endless encouragement to be all we can be in the kingdom of heaven. Sometimes religious practices lose sight of their origin, which is the love poured out for us with the spilled blood of Jesus. It becomes more about me and what I want. Communion is about reminding us of our roots and encouraging us to share that love with those around us.

> *Jesus, You are the Word of God, given to us as a precious gift. Help us grow in Your love so our words are gifts to those around us, made to edify and not destroy, to heal instead of wound, just like You are to us. Amen.*

For further study: Proverbs 25:11–13; Ephesians 4:29–32.

DECEMBER 27
Comfort in Quiet

For thus says the Lord God, the Holy One of Israel: "In returning and rest you shall be saved; in quietness and confidence shall be your strength." (Isaiah 30:15a)

I WAS AMAZED by the relationship my dad had with his best friend. They were so comfortable with silence. They would golf together in the morning then come back to our house for the afternoon. Both would walk in the door, help themselves to a coffee, and sit down with the paper. By some unperceived signal, they'd both rise from their chair at the same time and head to the dining room table, pulling out the game of Scrabble. Once the game was done, my dad's friend, Sam, would stand up, speak a few words to my mom or whoever else was in the house, and then head home. The entire afternoon, those final words would be the only ones spoken, other than the odd laugh or comment on a word well played during the game of Scrabble. They were so comfortable in each other's presence, and they knew each other so intimately, there was no need for words. There was just a calm presence. I struggle with being silent. I feel like I have to fill the space with my words because I lack confidence in the strength of the relationship to withstand the quiet without embarrassment.

When the Israelites were fleeing from the Egyptians, they still lacked confidence in God's power and love for them. They shouted their complaints, but God said they should hold their peace. He was fighting for them. When the disciples asked Jesus how to pray, He told them they didn't have to fill the space with their words, thinking they would be heard because of their much speaking. He knows our heart intimately, and as we grow in knowledge of His heart and presence, we can draw strength in quietness and confidence in Him. Similarly, when God seems silent, we start to recognize that His presence is still strong and sure. The depth of His love means there is no need to fill the space with vain babbling, trying to convince us of His love and friendship. We can grow in relationship so that we're just as comfortable with the silence as with the speaking.

In this space between Christmas and New Year's, we hopefully have a chance to relax a bit between the busyness and preparations brought on by the holidays. We can draw strength from a quiet time, pondering God's love for us. We can revel in the intimacy that needs no words to express its heart because it's felt in the spirit and the soul. Take a moment to enjoy His presence. Remember His great love so beautifully demonstrated for us when God became a man and dwelt among us. He is always with us, because the price was paid to bring us into such a close relationship.

Lord, we rest in Your presence. We're confident in Your love for us because You have demonstrated it so clearly. You live in us and with us. We need not be embarrassed by Your silence, since it reflects the depth of intimacy, the knowledge of the security of the relationship. We are ever grateful for Your love. Amen.

For further study: Exodus 14:10–31; Psalm 46:10; Matthew 6:7–15.

DECEMBER 28
Heart Desires

Delight yourself also in the Lord, and He shall give you the desires of your heart. (Psalm 37:4)

I ADOPTED A new cat recently. The poor fellow is terrified being in a new environment. He's hiding and won't let me approach him. He doesn't realize I only want good things for him. I love him just because of who he is. He doesn't have to do anything to earn my love and care. He doesn't have to look differently or be anything other than the beautiful creature he is. I long to let him discover the comfort and peace that await him just by sitting on my lap. I want to meet all his needs and give him joy. I know he wants those things too, but he's too caught up in the emotion of the moment to realize I can fulfill the true desires of his heart. Right now, he can only see the false desire of wanting to be somewhere else, and not the good I have prepared for him.

I think I get that way with God at times. I think my desire is for a new job, better home, nicer car, more money, or any number of wishes. I close my eyes to the good God has prepared for me, since I'm caught up in the emotion of the moment. I think if God loved me, He'd give me things to make me happy in this life. I refuse to see that His ultimate goal isn't to answer my false desires but to give me the true desires of my heart. He wants to meet my real needs. He has given Himself to me, longing for a relationship where I can lean upon Him and find peace and comfort in the beating of His heart. If I would just trust Him, I would find that His desires for me are my true desires.

John understood the power of God's love. It was John who lay his head on Jesus's breast as they sat at the table and shared the bread and the wine. Even when banished to the Isle of Patmos, John had intimate times with the Lord as he experienced the revelation of Jesus Christ shared with us in the last book of the Bible. Such was the power of love. John had reached out and received the love of God. He understood God's provision for him and accepted it. In this he received the desires of his heart, despite the trials in his physical life. John knew God's goal was not to give him things to make him happy in this life, but to give Jesus, Himself, to John and make him supremely happy in the life to come. May we also trust God to fulfill our deepest and truest desires.

Jesus, thank You for coming to earth to save us. You gave Your all to us, even giving us Your very life, that we might find the fulfillment of our hearts' desires. Help us trust You even when things seem scary or difficult. Help us to recognize Your hand reaching out to us in love and friendship. Amen.

For further study: Psalm 37:3–6, 145:14–19; John 13:23; Revelation 1:1–10.

DECEMBER 29
The Elevator Pitch

For God so loved the world that He gave His only begotten Son, that whoever believes in Him should not perish but have everlasting life. (John 3:16)

PEOPLE IN MARKETING talk about an elevator pitch. This is a quick summary of your idea that you could express to someone if you met them in an elevator and they'd get the gist of your idea before they arrived at their floor. Imagine if you got in an elevator and someone stepped in and said, "You're a Christian, aren't you? So what's Christianity really all about?" Could you give them a clear answer in the short time you have?

I heard of a young man in seminary who was in that position. He was ashamed that he couldn't provide an answer in the short time he had to reach the hurting person who had asked. It made me wonder how I would fare in a similar situation. What is Christianity's elevator pitch? It occurs to me Christianity is summed up by love. It's about the God of all creation, who loves us enough to free us from bondage and brokenness, a God who wants to see us become all we can be, to fulfill all our dreams. He was willing to come to earth as a man and give His all and die because He loves us. It's about recognizing we're not worthy of a love like that, but He gives it anyway. Christianity is about receiving that love and letting that love transform us in our spirit and soul. It's about growing in that love so that we start to pour out love to others. This love is expressed completely by the cross: as we receive the vertical love from heaven, we can pass it horizontally to all humanity.

This is why we pause to take communion. Jesus celebrated communion with His disciples just before He walked to the cross at Golgotha. It's our reminder of His life given to give us life. He is the bread and the wine, our sustenance and our Savior. As we enter into the depth of the love that allowed Him to be broken and spilled out for us, He enables us to be broken and spilled out for others. It's a miraculous work of grace. Communion leads us to the foot of the cross, to remember He has poured out His love on us. It reminds us that He has forgiven all our sins. We have received His love and can give His love. It reminds us of His grace. We give thanks as He gave thanks. We rejoice as He rejoices. We are transformed by the power of His love. Partaking in communion is like God giving us His elevator pitch to remind us of the heart of the gospel.

Jesus, we thank You for giving Your all so we could have life and life more abundantly. We recognize it really is all about love. Help us to feel, know, and recognize the depth of Your love. Fill us with Your love so we can spread it to everyone we meet. Amen.

For Further study: Matthew 10:8, 22:35–40; Ephesians 3:14–21, 5:1–2; 1 John 3:16.

DECEMBER 30
Flying Home

Love does no harm to a neighbor; therefore love is the fulfillment of the law. And do this knowing the time, that now it is high time to awake out of sleep; for now our salvation is nearer than when we first believed. (Romans 13:10–11)

HAVE YOU EVER traveled anywhere and been away from home for a time? As you head home, the way isn't always easy. There are storms and delays, and other passengers may be grumpy or angry. Things get lost or stolen. You're tired and weary, anxious to get home. As you struggle to find your place, being jostled and pushed by others, you have a choice. You can give in to the fatigue and struggle, snapping at others and pushing back, or you can put all that anger and frustration aside. You can choose to recognize that you'll be home soon and none of the struggles will have mattered. You'll be able to relax. In a short time, you can rejoice in the trip you had and forget the difficulties.

So here we are, Christians on this earth, knowing that this place is not really our home. As we get older, time flies faster and faster. We truly are "flying home." We don't know how long the journey will be. We have no idea of the setbacks and roadblocks we'll run into. We may struggle with loss. The thief will try to steal our joy and peace. People will push us. There are plenty of opportunities for fatigue, anger, and frustration. The only thing that really matters is loving God with all our heart and loving our neighbor as ourselves.

When we get home, none of the other struggles will have mattered. We'll be able to relax, sitting at the table that Jesus has prepared for us. He will pass us the bread and the wine. We will all rejoice as we recount our trip during our brief time on the earth. Until then, every day we have a choice. We can give in to fatigue and frustration, or we can remember that we walk in communion with the God of all creation, the one who loves us and lives in us. When we get home, the only important thing will be the love and joy we shared with others during the journey; all the struggles will no longer matter.

As we partake of the elements of communion, we pause to remember that our time on earth is short, but His love is for all eternity. His love is amazing. It's enough that He gave His all so we could have life and life more abundantly. We often need a reminder to keep it all in perspective. That's what communion is all about.

> *Heavenly Father, we thank You for the gift of Your Son, for the amazing love You have given. We thank You that a place is prepared for us. One day we'll head home to You, forgetting the pain of the world and rejoicing in Your presence. Help us to remember we are headed home and that the struggles of today are temporary. They will be quickly forgotten as we rejoice in You. Help us to choose to love, walking with You on this journey, spreading Your love to all we meet. Amen.*

For further study: Psalm 90:12; John 10:10, 14:1–4; 1 Corinthians 15:51–58; 2 Corinthians 5:1–10; Hebrews 11:8–16.

DECEMBER 31
Crowning the Year

You crown the year with Your goodness, and Your paths drip with abundance. (Psalm 65:11)

ON THE LAST day of the year, it's customary to reflect back on the past twelve months. News outlets will give a summary of all that occurred, the good and the bad. Radios will list and play the songs that hit the top of the charts over the course of the year. Magazines will proclaim who were the greatest people, or what were humanity's greatest achievements for the year. People will speculate on what might occur in the year to come. Predictions will be made or goals set for the new year.

A magazine may choose their "person of the year," but as Christians, we know Jesus is always the Man of the Year. He's also the Man of the decade, century, all time. There is no one like Him, who is God and equal to God, yet for a time gave up His heavenly place to become a man. No one else was able to pay the price for our sins and failures. No one else loves us so much that even when we were His enemy, He was willing to give His life for us and to us. The song of His love that plays in our hearts is always the best song of the year. The greatest news is always that God so loved the world that He gave His only Son, so the world through Him would be saved. No matter what the weather, no matter what our circumstances and experiences, He was there through it all, crowning it with His goodness.

With all that happened over the last year, or what will happen tomorrow, He was with us and will continue to be with us through it all. We can wake up knowing He will crown the day with His goodness. We can lay our head down to sleep at night, secure in the depth of His love for us. He proved it on the cross. He has made us a new creation and given us eternal life. And if one day in heaven's realm we find ourselves literally crowned with His goodness, like the Christian elders who went before us, we will cast that crown before Him, knowing it was all His doing. He is the one who is worthy of all praise.

> *Jesus, we have been and are continually so blessed by Your presence. You have given us the gift of eternal life. You have freed us from sin and filled our hearts with Your song. You crown our year with Your goodness. You crown our day with Your goodness. You are always with us, and we treasure You. Thank You always for all You have done and for who You are. Amen.*

For further study: Deuteronomy 31:6; Psalm 40:1–5, 65:1–13, 136:1–26; John 3:16; Revelation 4:1–11.

www.ingramcontent.com/pod-product-compliance
Lightning Source LLC
Chambersburg PA
CBHW081143230426
43664CB00018B/2790